Databases and Information Systems II

T0191851

Databases and Information Systems II

Fifth International Baltic Conference, Baltic DB&IS'2002
Tallinn, Estonia, June 3–6, 2002
Selected Papers

Edited by

HELE-MAI HAAV

Institute of Cybernetics at Tallinn Technical University,
Tallinn, Estonia

and

AHTO KALJA

Department of Computer Engineering of Tallinn Technical University,
Tallinn, Estonia

KLUWER ACADEMIC PUBLISHERS
DORDRECHT / BOSTON / LONDON

A C.I.P. Catalogue record for this book is available from the Library of Congress.

ISBN 978-90-481-6182-9

Published by Kluwer Academic Publishers,
P.O. Box 17, 3300 AA Dordrecht, The Netherlands.

Sold and distributed in North, Central and South America
by Kluwer Academic Publishers,
101 Philip Drive, Norwell, MA 02061, U.S.A.

In all other countries, sold and distributed
by Kluwer Academic Publishers,
P.O. Box 322, 3300 AH Dordrecht, The Netherlands.

Printed on acid-free paper

Table of Contents

Information Systems Development

Information Systems and Software Engineering

Mobile Computing, Databases, and Agents

Data Mining

Conference Committee

Honorary General Chair

Andres Keevallik, Tallinn Technical University (TTU), Estonia

Organising Co-Chairs:

Margus Kruus, Department of Computer Engineering of TTU, Estonia
Sulev Kuiv, Institute of Cybernetics at TTU, Estonia

Co-ordinators

Saulius Maskeliunas, Institute of Mathematics and Informatics, Lithuania
Juris Borzovs, Riga Institute of Information Technology, Latvia
Janis Barzdins, University of Latvia, Latvia
Hannu Jaakkola, Pori School of Technology and Economics, Tampere UT, Finland

Doctoral Consortium Co-Chairs:

Jaan Penjam, Institute of Cybernetics at TTU, Estonia
Mait Harf, Institute of Cybernetics at TTU, Estonia

Publicity Chair:

Monika Perkmann, Institute of Cybernetics at TTU, Estonia

Publishing Chair:

Rein Lõugas, Institute of Cybernetics at TTU, Estonia

Registration Chair:

Marje Tamm, Institute of Cybernetics at TTU, Estonia

Programme Co-Chairs:

Hele-Mai Haav, Institute of Cybernetics at TTU, Estonia
Ahto Kalja, Department of Computer Engineering of TTU, Estonia

Programme Committee:

Witold Abramowicz, Poland
Janis Barzdins, Latvia
Juris Borzovs, Latvia
Albertas Caplinskas, Lithuania
Johann Eder, Austria
Hans-Dieter Ehrich, Germany
Jorgen Fischer Nilsson, Denmark
Janis Grundspenkis, Latvia
Remigijus Gustas, Sweden
Leonid Kalinichenko, Russia
Hannu Kangassalo, Finland
Patrick Lambrix, Sweden
Jozef M. Zurada, USA
Saulius Maskeliunas, Lithuania
Mihhail Matskin, Norway
Boris Novikov, Russia
Monika Oit, Estonia
Algirdas Pakstas, UK
Jaan Penjam, Estonia
Jaroslav Pokorny, Czech Republic
Gunter Saake, Germany
Klaus-Dieter Schewe, New Zealand
Jaak Tepandi, Estonia
Bernhard Thalheim, Germany
Do van Thanh, Norway
Enn Tyugu, Estonia
Olegas Vasilecas, Lithuania

Benkt Wangler, Sweden
Tatjana Welzer, Slovenia
Naoki Yonezaki, Japan
Arkady Zaslavsky, Australia

Additional Referees

Peter Ahlbrecht, Germany
Per Backlund, Sweden
Ahto Buldas, Estonia
Marjan Druzovec, Sweden
Silke Eckstein, Germany
Janis Eiduks, Latvia
Åsa G. Dahlstedt, Sweden
Ingolf Geist, Germany
Hele-Mai Haav, Estonia
Thomas Herstel, Germany
Marko Kääramees, Estonia
Roland Kaschek, New Zealand
Susanne Kjernald, Sweden
Vahur Kotkas, Estonia
Marek Kowalkiewicz, Poland
Margot, Lepasaar, Estonia
Karl Neumann, Germany
Oksana Nikiforovs, Latvia
Ralf Pinger, Germany
Robert Redpath, Australia
Pavel Rusakovs, Latvia
Lena Strömbäck, Sweden
Juha Takkinen, Sweden
Tarmo Uustalu, Estonia
Juris Viksna, Latvia
Jørgen Villadsen, Denmark
Jan Villemson, Estonia
Krzysztof Wecel, Poland

Advisory Committee:

Janis Bubenko, Royal Institute of Technology, Sweden
Arne Solvberg, Norwegian University of Science and Technology, Norway

Preface

Databases and database systems in particular, are considered as kernels of any Information System (IS). The rapid growth of the web on the Internet has dramatically increased the use of semi-structured data and the need to store and retrieve such data in a database. The database community quickly reacted to these new requirements by providing models for semi-structured data and by integrating database research to XML web services and mobile computing.

On the other hand, IS community who never than before faces problems of IS development is seeking for new approaches to IS design. Ontology-based approaches are gaining popularity, because of a need for shared conceptualisation by different stakeholders of IS development teams. Many web-based IS would fail without domain ontologies to capture meaning of terms in their web interfaces.

This volume contains revised versions of 24 best papers presented at the 5th International Baltic Conference on Databases and Information Systems (BalticDB&IS'2002). The conference papers present original research results in the novel fields of IS and databases such as web IS, XML and databases, data mining and knowledge management, mobile agents and databases, and UML based IS development methodologies. The book's intended readers are researchers and practitioners who are interested in advanced topics on databases and IS.

The BalticDB&IS series of conferences aim at providing to relevant academics and practitioners a wide international forum for exchanging their achievements in the field of databases and IS. The objective of the conference was to bring together researchers as well as practitioners and PhD students to present their work and to exchange their ideas, and trigger co-operation.

The 5th International Baltic Conference on Databases and Information Systems (BalticDB&IS'2002) took place on June 3-6, 2002, in Tallinn,

Estonia. This conference continued the series of successful bi-annual Baltic workshops held in Trakai (1994), Tallinn (1996), Riga (1998), and Vilnius (2000).

The conference was organised by the Institute of Cybernetics and the Department of Computer Engineering of Tallinn Technical University (TTU). The conference was approved by IEEE Communication Society for Technical Co-Sponsorship.

The International Programme Committee representing 18 countries received 60 submissions from 23 countries. Each paper was reviewed by 3 referees from different countries. As a result, 41 papers were accepted for presentation at the conference and included into the local conference proceedings. After the conference, the Programme Committee selected 24 best papers to be published in this book.

Many people contributed to the success of the BalticDB&IS'2002. We appriciate the authors for their contributions and the invited speakers for sharing their views with us. We are very grateful to members of the Programme Committee and the additional referees for carefully reviewing the submissions. We thank all the organising team led by Sulev Kuiv, the Institute of Cybernetics at TTU, and Margus Kruus, the Department of Computer Engineering of TTU. We extend our gratitude to the Baltic co-ordinators Juris Borzovs, Riga Institute of Information Technology, Janis Barzdins, University of Latvia, and Saulius Maskeliunas, Institute of Mathematics and Informatics, Lithuania. We are obliged to all the supporting institutions, namely, Baltic Fund of VLDB Endowment, IEEE Communication Society, Microsoft Research Ltd., IBM, and the Department of State Information Systems of Estonian Ministry of Transport and Communication. We are grateful to Kristiina Kindel and Monika Perkmann for development of web-based IS for the conference management. We thank Marje Tamm for conducting most of the correspondence with the participants and the authors.

We express our special thanks to Rein Lõugas for preparation of camera-ready copy of manuscripts. Finally, we would like also to express our sincere thanks to F. Robbert van Berckelaer, Kluwer Academic Publishers, for his help throughout the entire project.

July 2002

Hele-Mai Haav

Ahto Kalja

FRAGMENTATION OF OBJECT ORIENTED AND SEMI-STRUCTURED DATA

Klaus-Dieter Schewe

Massey University, Department of Information Systems
Private Bag 11 222, Palmerston North, New Zealand
k.d.schewe@massey.ac.nz

Abstract   Due to the increasing demand to provide data from databases for servicing web-based applications and the de facto distribution of data on the
web the problem arises to generalize database distribution techniques
from relational to object oriented and semi-structured data. The major
difference between these two is that object orientation refers to a predefined schema, whereas semi-structured data is meant to be schema-less.
The paper generalizes horizontal and vertical fragmentation first to an
object oriented datamodel, then to semi-structured data and XML. In
this context, the paper discusses the problem of preservation of unique
object identifiability with respect to fragmentation. Furthermore, splitting will be introduced as a a third kind of fragmentation.

Keywords: distributed databases, semi-structured data, object-oriented databases

1.   Introduction

The World Wide Web is considered to be the largest database that
ever has been created. However, for the time being, the web is a huge
collection of web-pages, which is largely unstructured and created in an
ad-hoc way focussing much more on fancy presentations than on clearly
structured content.

There is an emerging awareness that full benefit of data dissemination
via the web can only be obtained, if web-based system learn from the established database culture. The model of semi-structured data and the
very similar Extensible Markup Language (XML) [1] provide one approach to an integration of databases and web-based systems. A more
'traditional' approach is to base the integration on extended views, i.e.,
to have databases underlying web-based systems [3]. The major differ-

1

H.-M. Haav and A. Kalja (eds.), Databases and Information Systems II, 1–14.
© *2002 Kluwer Academic Publishers.*

ence between these two approaches is that the latter one aims at servicing web applications by the provision of data from databases, whereas the former one aims at enabling (large portions of) the web data itself to be considered as a database.

So let us assume that we want to provide data from databases to web-based applications, but allow these data to be determined by object oriented database schemata as they are used in [5] or that they are semi-structured data. The datamodel from [5] can cope with various underlying type systems, which allows the relational datamodel to be considered as a special case. This has already been exploited in [7] to define generic query algebras.

Then the obvious problem arises that data is collected at various locations, i.e., data is de facto distributed. This, however, requires that database schemata are distributed. Therefore, the first objective of this paper is to address the generalization of distribution techniques for the case of relational databases to object oriented databases. To be precise, we will only address the problem of schema fragmentation.

Fragmentation of relational database schemata is usually divided into two parts [4]. Horizontal fragmentation exploits the fact that relations are finite sets. So split a relation into a disjoint union. Each of the new relations could result from applying a selection operation to the original relation. Vertical fragmentation exploits relation schemata to be sets of attributes. So split a relation into new relations each resulting from a projection operation being applied to the original relation. The union or the join, respectively, of the new relations resulting from horizontal or vertical fragmentation, respectively, reconstruct the original relation.

Generalizing horizontal fragmentation to the object oriented case could again exploit databases to be defined by sets. This would result in new classes. However, the object oriented datamodel allow to use the set type constructor—as well as other bulk type constructors for multisets and lists—not only on the class level, but also in nested structures. Thus, we should discuss, how to generalize horizontal fragmentation to fragmentation on the type level. In both cases, the original database should be reconstructable by using a union operation, but we have to take special care for lists.

Generalizing vertical fragmentation means to exploit the tuple type constructor. Again, if the outermost constructor in a class definition is the record type constructor, we would obtain a fragmentation on the class level. Looking inside nested structures would result in a fragmentation on type level. Special care is needed to preserve the property of unique object identifiability [2]. In both cases, the original database should be reconstructable by using a generalized join operation [7].

With respect to object oriented data a third choice for fragmentation arises from splitting classes and introducing references. The splitting operation was introduced in [6] to support object oriented database design, but it is natural to exploit it for distribution as well, as the major result is to replace a class by two new ones without changing the information capacity of the schema.

Generalizing fragmentation techniques to the object oriented case also means to take care of references to classes that are fragmented. These references then have to be replaced by references to the fragments.

As to semi-structured data and XML the approach taken in this paper starts from the simple observation that a database for an object oriented schema can be easily considered as semi-structured data and vice versa. It is also no problem to define an object oriented database schema that would capture semi-structured data. The major problem, however, is that semi-structured data are meant to be schema-less, i.e., that changes to the data are not required to stay within the boundaries defined by a schema. We shall see that this is only a minor problem for fragmentation, if we allow schemata simply to evolve.

2. Object Oriented and Semi-Structured Data

We will briefly review a simple version of the object oriented datamodel (OODM) from [5] without going into details. In particular, we omit the behavioural part completely. Then we look at semi-structured data and XML. Finally, we give an overview on query algebra [7] as far as it is needed for distribution.

2.1 Fundamentals of the OODM

The OODM is based on an underlying type system. For our purposes here it is sufficient to consider a type system defined as follows (in abstract syntax):

$$t = b \mid x \mid (a_1 : t_1, \ldots, a_n : t_n) \mid \{t\} \mid [t] \mid \langle t \rangle \mid (a_1 : t_1) \cup \cdots \cup (a_n : t_n).$$

Here b represents base types, $(\cdot)$ a record type constructor, $\{\cdot\}$ a set type constructor, $[\cdot]$ a list type constructor, $\langle \cdot \rangle$ a multiset type constructor, and $\cup$ a union type constructor. x is used for type variables, here only for the purpose of defining classes. In order to have object identifiers, we require that among the base types there is at least one type ID, the values of which are the oid-s.

Now consider a type with variables $x_1, \ldots, x_n$, but with no occurrence of ID. Replacing all these variables x_i by pairs $r_i : C_i$ with some mutually distinct labels r_i (called *references*) and names C_i (called *class names*) results in a *structure expression*.

A *class* consists of a class name C, a structure expression exp_C, and a set $\{C_1, \ldots, C_n\}$ of class names (called the *superclasses*). If we replace all $r_i : C_i$ in exp_C by the base type *ID*, the resulting parameter-less type t_C is called the *representation type* of the class C.

A *schema* is a finite set of classes that is closed in the sense that all class names appearing in a structure expression or as a superclass must be names of classes defined in the schema.

EXAMPLE 1 Choose the following schema as an example:

Class REGION
    Struct (name: *STRING*, central : h: CITY, cities : { c : CITY })

Class CITY Struct (name: *STRING*, in : r: REGION)

A *database db* for a schema $\mathcal{S}$ assigns to each class $C \in \mathcal{S}$ a finite set $db(C)$ of pairs (i, v), where i is an oid and v is a value of type t_C, such that certain conditions are satisfied. Informally, these conditions are the uniqueness of identifiers, the inclusion of the set of oid-s in a class in the set of oid-s for each of its superclasses (inclusion integrity), the appearance of each oid occurring in a value v as an oid i in the referenced class (referential integrity), and (weak) value-identifiability.

EXAMPLE 2 The following is a database for the schema in Example 1 (abbreviating REGION to R and CITY to C):

$db(\text{R}) = \{(\&o_{11}, (\text{name} : \text{Taranaki}, \text{central} : \&o_{21}, \text{cities} : \{\&o_{21}, \&o_{22}\})),$
$\quad\quad (\&o_{12}, (\text{name} : \text{Manawatu}, \text{central} : \&o_{23}, \text{cities} : \{\&o_{23}\})))\}$
$db(\text{C}) = \{(\&o_{21}, (\text{name} : \text{New Plymouth}, \text{in} : \&o_{11})),$
$\quad\quad (\&o_{22}, (\text{name} : \text{Stratford}, \text{in} : \&o_{11})),$
$\quad\quad (\&o_{23}, (\text{name} : \text{Palmerston North}, \text{in} : \&o_{12})))\}$

We adopted the convention to start oid-s with an &.

2.2   Fundamentals of the SSDM and XML

The semi-structured datamodel tries to meet the requirements for data on the web. The major difference to object oriented data is that semi-structured data are defined without a schema. According to [1] we could use the following language for schema expressions:

$\langle$ ssd-expression $\rangle ::= \langle$ value $\rangle \mid$ oid : $\langle$ value $\rangle \mid$ oid
$\quad\quad \langle$ value $\rangle ::= $ base_value $\mid \langle$ complex_value $\rangle$
$\langle$ complex_value $\rangle ::= \{\ell_1 : \langle$ ssd-expression $\rangle_1 ,$
$\quad\quad\quad\quad\quad \ldots, \ell_n : \langle$ ssd-expression $\rangle_n\}$

The labels ℓ_i in complex values need not be distinct. For the oid-s similar rules apply as for databases. Each oid may appear at most once in the form "oid $\langle$ value $\rangle$", in which case the oid is said to be *defined* in the ssd-expression. Each oid that appears in the form "oid" in an ssd-expression, in which case the oid is said to be *used* in the ssd-expression, must also be defined. There is no typing, though we could of course add base types for the base values and the type *ID* for oid-s. The following example shows the similarity between ssd-expressions and object oriented databases.

EXAMPLE 3   Consider the following ssd-expression:

$$db = \{ \text{R} : \&o_{11} : \{ \text{name} : \text{Taranaki}, \text{central} : \&o_{21},$$
$$\text{cities} : \{ \text{c} : \&o_{21}, \text{c} : \&o_{22} \} \},$$
$$\text{R} : \&o_{12} : \{ \text{name} : \text{Manawatu}, \text{central} : \&o_{23}, \text{cities} : \{ \text{c} : \&o_{23} \} \},$$
$$\text{C} : \&o_{21} : \{ \text{name} : \text{New Plymouth}, \text{in} : \&o_{11} \},$$
$$\text{C} : \&o_{22} : \{ \text{name} : \text{Stratford}, \text{in} : \&o_{11} \},$$
$$\text{C} : \&o_{23} : \{ \text{name} : \text{Palmerston North}, \text{in} : \&o_{12} \} \}$$

Indeed, it contains the same information as the database in Example 2. The major difference is that complex values represent a mix of record and set values, and oid-s are not bound to predefined classes.

Semi-structured data can be easily rewritten in XML. The major differences—apart from other differences that are discussed in [1]—are that

- labels in complex values are written with an opening and a closing tag, i.e., $\langle \ell_1 \rangle \; ssd_1 \; \langle /\ell_1 \rangle \; \ldots \; \langle \ell_n \rangle \; ssd_n \; \langle /\ell_n \rangle$ instead of $ell_1 : ssd_1, \ldots, \ell_n : ssd_n$,

- complex values do no longer represent sets, but ordered lists,

- oid-s and references to oid-s must occur as *attributes* within the opening tag,

- each XML-expression must have an opening and a closing tag.

We leave it to the reader to rewrite the ssd-expression from Example 3 into an equivalent XML-expression.

2.3   Queries

Let us have a brief look at query algebras now. In [7] it has been shown that such algebras can be defined by operations defined on the type system plus a single generalized join operator. Then other operations including nesting and unnesting can be defined in terms of these operations.

As we are only interested in fragmentation, we may restrict our attention to a very limited subset of such an algebra.

- For record types $t = (a_1 : t_1, \ldots, a_n : t_n)$ we need the *projection* π_X with X being any sequence of the labels a_i. By abuse of notation we may also use this projection, if the type t occurs within another type t', as we can always 'lift' the projection operation on t to an operation on t'. Formally, this requires to apply a map$(\cdot)$ operation, if t occurs within a bulk type, i.e., set-, list- or multiset-type. map(π_X) applies π_X to all elements of a set, list or multiset preserving the order and multiplicity, respectively, in the last two cases. Similarly, we have to apply π_X only to a component of a record, if t occurs within a record type.

- For bulk types, e.g., set types $\{t\}$, we need a *selection* operation $\sigma_\varphi = \texttt{filter}(\varphi)$ with a function φ that takes values of type t to a truth-value $\mathbf{T}$ (true) or $\mathbf{F}$ (false). Applying this operation to a set, list or multiset results in the subset, sublist or submultiset, respectively, containing just those elements that are mapped to $\mathbf{T}$ by φ. Same as for projection operations the selection can be 'lifted' from t to t', if the type $\{t\}$ occurs within the type t'.

- For the bulk types we also need a *union* operation $\sqcup$. For set types this is the usual union $\cup$ of sets. For multisets it is the operation that adds up multiplicities. For lists it is list concatenation.

- Finally, we need the generalized *join* operation, which is defined as $v_1 \bowtie_t v_2 =$

$$\{z : t_1 \bowtie_t t_2 \mid \exists z_1 \in v_1. \exists z_2 \in v_2. \pi_{t_1}(z) = z_1 \wedge \pi_{t_2}(z) = z_2\}.$$

The definition is based on the fact that for a common supertype t of t_1 and t_2 with functions $\pi_t^i : t_i \to t$ there exists a common subtype $t_1 \bowtie_t t_2$ together with functions $\pi_{t_i} : t_1 \bowtie_t t_2 \to t_i$ such that $\pi_t^1 \circ \pi_{t_1} = \pi_t^2 \circ \pi_{t_2}$ holds, and for any other common subtype t' with functions $\pi'_{t_i} : t' \to t_i$ with $\pi_t^1 \circ \pi'_{t_1} = \pi_t^2 \circ \pi'_{t_2}$ there is a unique function $\pi : t' \to t_1 \bowtie_t t_2$ with $\pi_{t_i} \circ \pi = \pi'_{t_i}$.

3. Split Fragmentation

The work in [6] introduced a splitting operation as a database design primitive. The operation replaces a class by two new classes, one referencing the other. This operation can be used for fragmentation, and it will be different from horizontal and vertical fragmentation, which both arise from generalising fragmentation techniques for the relational datamodel.

3.1 The Splitting Operation

The splitting operation for the OODM is quite simple. Suppose the schema contains a class C and the structure expression exp occurs within the structure expression exp_C. Then we simply add a new class C' with $exp_{C'} = exp$ to the schema and replace exp in exp_C by a new reference $r' : C'$.

EXAMPLE 4 For Example 1 we could split both classes REGION and CITY with $exp = STRING$, and introduce a new class VAL_NAME. The result would be the schema

Class REGION Struct (name: n : VAL_NAME, central : h: CITY, cities : { c : CITY })

Class CITY Struct (name: n : VAL_NAME, in : r: REGION)

Class VAL_NAME Struct $STRING$

Accordingly, the database in Example 2 would be replaced by the following one (using the additional abbreviation V for VAL_NAME), which contains five new oid-s for the valid names 'Taranaki', 'Manawatu', 'New Plymouth', 'Stratford' and 'Palmerston North'.

$$db(R) = \{(\&o_{11}, (\text{name} : \&o_{31}, \text{central} : \&o_{21}, \text{cities} : \{\&o_{21}, \&o_{22}\})),$$
$$(\&o_{12}, (\text{name} : \&o_{32}, \text{central} : \&o_{23}, \text{cities} : \{\&o_{23}\})))\}$$

$$db(C) = \{(\&o_{21}, (\text{name} : \&o_{33}, \text{in} : \&o_{11})),$$
$$(\&o_{22}, (\text{name} : \&o_{34}, \text{in} : \&o_{11})),$$
$$(\&o_{23}, (\text{name} : \&o_{35}, \text{in} : \&o_{12})))\}$$

$$db(V) = \{(\&o_{31}, \text{Taranaki}), (\&o_{32}, \text{Manawatu}), (\&o_{33}, \text{New Plymouth})$$
$$(\&o_{34}, \text{Stratford}), (\&o_{35}, \text{Palmerston North})\}$$

3.2 Splitting for Semi-Structured Data and XML

Basically, the splitting operation results in introducing new oid-s and a new class name. Transferring this to semi-structured data would mean to remove the content of some ssd-expressions and to replace them by oid-s. These ssd-expressions, however, would appear together with the new oid-s under a new label that is used directly within the outermost ssd-expression, which was assumed to be a complex value. The following example should make this clear.

EXAMPLE 5 Splitting the ssd-expression from Example 3 in analogy to Example 4 will result in the following new ssd-expression:

$$db = \{R : \&o_{11} : \{name : \&o_{31}, central : \&o_{21},$$
$$cities : \{c : \&o_{21}, c : \&o_{22}\}\},$$
$$R : \&o_{12} : \{name : \&o_{32}, central : \&o_{23}, cities : \{c : \&o_{23}\}\},$$
$$C : \&o_{21} : \{name : \&o_{33}, in : \&o_{11}\},$$
$$C : \&o_{22} : \{name : \&o_{34}, in : \&o_{11}\},$$
$$C : \&o_{23} : \{name : \&o_{35}, in : \&o_{12}\},$$
$$V : \&o_{31} : Taranaki, \text{VAL\_NAME} : \&o_{32} : Manawatu,$$
$$V : \&o_{33} : New\ Plymouth, \text{VAL\_NAME} : \&o_{34} : Stratford,$$
$$V : \&o_{35} : Palmerston\ North\}$$

Due to the close relationship between the SSDM and XML it is straightforward to apply the splitting operation to XML-expressions. We would turn elements into empty elements with reference to a new oid, and the new oid-s would be placed within new elements that contain the removed content of the emptied elements.

4. Horizontal Fragmentation

We now approach the generalisation of horizontal fragmentation techniques from the relational datamodel [4] to the OODM, the SSDM, and XML.

4.1 Horizontal Fragmentation on Class Level

According to the definition of databases for an OODM schema, each class will be associated with a set of pairs. Hence, we have the trivial generalisation of relational horizontal fragmentation.

For this let C be some class. Take boolean valued function φ_i such that for each database db we obtain $db(C) = \bigcup_{i=1}^{n} \sigma_{\varphi_i}(db(C))$ with disjoint sets $\sigma_{\varphi_i}(db(C))$.

We then replace C in the schema by n new class C_i, all with $exp_{C_i} = exp_C$. For classes D referencing C, i.e., $r : C$ occurs within exp_D, we have to replace this reference $r : C$ in exp_D by $(a_1 : r_1 : C_1, \ldots, a_n : r_n : C_n)$ with new pairwise distinct reference names $r_1, \ldots, r_n$.

EXAMPLE 6 Take the schema from Example 1 and fragment the class CITY using $\varphi_1 \equiv name \leq Paraparaumu$ and $\varphi_2 \equiv name > Paraparaumu$.
Then the new schema will be

Class REGION **Struct** (name: $STRING$, central : (ltp : h_1: CITY$_1$) $\cup$ (gtp : h_2: CITY$_2$), cities : { (ltp : c_1: CITY$_1$) $\cup$ (gtp : c_2: CITY$_2$)})

Class CITY$_1$ **Struct** (name: $STRING$, in : r: REGION)

Class CITY$_2$ **Struct** (name: $STRING$, in : r: REGION)

The database from Example 2 then fragments into

$$db(\text{R}) = \{(\&o_{11}, (\text{name} : \text{Taranaki}, \text{central} : (\text{ltp} : \&o_{21}),$$
$$\text{cities} : \{(\text{ltp} : \&o_{21}), (\text{gtp} : \&o_{22})\})),$$
$$(\&o_{12}, (\text{name} : \text{Manawatu}, \text{central} : (\text{ltp} : \&o_{23}),$$
$$\text{cities} : \{(\text{ltp} : \&o_{23})\})))\}$$
$$db(\text{C}_1) = \{(\&o_{21}, (\text{name} : \text{New Plymouth}, \text{in} : \&o_{11})),$$
$$(\&o_{23}, (\text{name} : \text{Palmerston North}, \text{in} : \&o_{12}))\}$$
$$db(\text{C}_2) = \{(\&o_{22}, (\text{name} : \text{Stratford}, \text{in} : \&o_{11}))\}$$

4.2 Horizontal Fragmentation on Type Level

The chosen underlying type system allows arbitrary nesting of type constructors. So the set type constructor may appear within a structure expression, say exp_C. This suggests to apply fragmentation here as well.

Assume $\{exp\}$ appears in exp_C. Then we could first apply the splitting operation which results in exp in T_C being changed to $r' : C'$ with new reference name r' and new class name C', and $T_{C'} = exp$. Then we could apply horizontal fragmentation to C' using selection operations $\sigma_{\varphi_1}, \ldots, \sigma_{\varphi_n}$, i.e., for each database db we would obtain $db(C') = \bigcup_{i=1}^{n} \sigma_{\varphi_i}(db(C'))$ with disjoint $\sigma_{\varphi_i}(db(C'))$.

This would lead to n new classes $C_1, \ldots, C_n$, all with $T_{C_i} = exp$. Since in this case there is exactly one reference to C', we would replace $\{exp\}$ in T_C by $\{(\ell_1 : r_1 : C_1) \cup \cdots \cup (\ell_n : r_n : C_n)\}$, or equivalently by $(\ell_1 : \{r_1 : C_1\}, \ldots, \ell_n : \{r_n : C_n\})$.

Finally, we could undo the splitting, which has the same effect, as if $\{exp\}$ in T_C would just have been replaced by $(\ell_1 : \{exp\}, \ldots, \ell_n : \{exp\})$. Note, however, that such an undo of the previous splitting would mean that the fragmentation does not really lead to new classes. However, it enables a subsequent vertical fragmentation.

Instead of considering just a set type constructor we could also look at multisets or lists. In this case, however, the detour via splitting is excluded. The case of multisets, i.e., $\langle exp \rangle$ occurring in T_C is easy, as we know that a selection σ_{φ_i} does not affect multiplicities. So in this case we would replace $\langle exp \rangle$ in T_C by $\langle (\ell_1 : exp) \cup \cdots \cup (\ell_n : exp) \rangle$, or equivalently by $(\ell_1 : \langle exp \rangle, \ldots, \ell_n : \langle exp \rangle)$.

In the case of lists, we could also replace $[exp]$ in T_C by $[(\ell_1 : exp) \cup \cdots \cup (\ell_n : exp)]$, but this is only equivalent to $(\ell_1 : [exp], \ldots, \ell_n : [exp])$, if the list is ordered, say by some partial order $\leq$, and the selection preserves the order, i.e., $\varphi_i(x) = \varphi_j(y) = \mathbf{T} \Rightarrow (x \leq y \Leftrightarrow i \leq j)$ holds.

It may of course be the the case that the order in the list is just arbitrary—in fact, a good design would have chosen a multiset in this case—so that we can simply ignore the ordering condition.

4.3 Horizontal Fragmentation of Semi-Structures Data and XML

The horizontal fragmentation of an ssd-expression representing a database corresponds to the fragmentation in the OODM with respect to a set type. Within in an ssd-expression this appears in the form of a complex value $\{\ell : exp_1, \ldots, \ell : exp_n\}$ using the same value. At least we could always achieve this form by bundling the expressions under one label ℓ into a single complex value, which uses just this label.

Using the core query language from [1, Sect. 4.2] with the path expression $\_^*.\ell$, and the creation of new oid-s using $\&\mathrm{new}(\cdot)$, we could write

> **select** $\mathrm{new}_1 : \&\mathrm{new}(X_1) : X_1 , \ldots , \mathrm{new}_n \ \&\mathrm{new}(X_n) : X_n$
> **from** old$.\_^* Z,\ Z.\ell\, X_1\ ,\ldots,\ Z.\ell\, X_n$
> **where** $\varphi_1(X_1)$ **and** $\ldots$ **and** $\varphi_n(X_n)$

to obtain the new fragments with the labels $\mathrm{new}_1 , \ldots \mathrm{new}_n$. However, replacing $\ell : X_i$ in old$.\_^* Z$ by $\ell_i : \&\mathrm{new}(X_i)$ requires an update rather than a query.

EXAMPLE 7 Take the ssd-expression from Example 3. Consider old $=$ CITY and ℓ=name. Let $\varphi_1(x)$ be $x < \mathrm{Q}$ and $\varphi_2(x)$ be $x \geq \mathrm{Q}$. The above query simplifies to

> **select** $\mathrm{NAME}_1 : \&\mathrm{new}(X_1) : X_1 , \mathrm{NAME}_2 \ \&\mathrm{new}(X_2) : X_2$
> **from** CITY Z, Z.name X_1, Z.name X_2
> **where** $X_1 < \mathrm{Q}$ and $X_2 \geq \mathrm{Q}$

and the result of the fragmentation will be the ssd-expression (using the abbreviation N for NAME)

$\{\mathrm{R} : \&o_{11} : \{\mathrm{name} : \mathrm{Taranaki}, \mathrm{central} : \&o_{21},$

$\mathrm{cities} : \{\mathrm{c} : \&o_{21}, \mathrm{c} : \&o_{22}\}\},$

$\mathrm{R} : \&o_{12} : \{\mathrm{name} : \mathrm{Manawatu}, \mathrm{central} : \&o_{23}, \mathrm{cities} : \{\mathrm{c} : \&o_{23}\}\},$

$\mathrm{C} : \&o_{21} : \{\mathrm{name}_1 : \&o_{31}, \mathrm{in} : \&o_{11}\}, \mathrm{N}_1 : \&o_{31} : \mathrm{New\ Plymouth},$

$\mathrm{C} : \&o_{22} : \{\mathrm{name}_2 : \&o_{32}, \mathrm{in} : \&o_{11}\}, \mathrm{N}_2 : \&o_{32} : \mathrm{Stratford},$

$\mathrm{C} : \&o_{23} : \{\mathrm{name}_1 : \&o_{33}, \mathrm{in} : \&o_{12}\}, \mathrm{N}_1 : \&o_{33} : \mathrm{Palmerston\ North}\}$

5. Vertical Fragmentation

Now let us approach the generalisation of vertical fragmentation from the relational datamodel to the OODM and the SSDM (and similarly for XML).

5.1 Vertical Fragmentation on Class Level

According to the definition of OODM schemata each class C in a schema has a structure expression exp_C derived from a type. For vertical fragmentation we must assume that the outermost constructor in the structure expression was the record type constructor, say $exp_C = (a_1 : exp_1, \ldots, a_n : exp_n)$. As for the relational datamodel, we would like to replace C by new classes $C_1, \ldots, C_k$ with $exp_{C_i} = (a_1^i : exp_{i_1}, \ldots, a_{n_i}^i : exp_{i_{n_i}})$ such that $\{a_1, \ldots, a_n\} = \bigcup_{i=1}^{k} \{a_1^i, \ldots, a_{n_i}^i\}$ holds, and for any database db we can reconstruct $db(C)$ by joining all the projections $\pi_{X_i}(db(C))$ (with $X_i = \{a_1^i, \ldots, a_{n_i}^i\}$) giving $db(C) =$

$$(\ldots(\pi_{X_1}(db(C)) \bowtie_{t_{1,2}} \pi_{X_2}(db(C))) \bowtie_{t_{1,2,3}} \cdots \bowtie_{t_{1,\ldots,k}} \pi_{X_k}(db(C))).$$

Here $t_{1,\ldots,i} = (a_{x_1^i} : t_{x_1^i}, \ldots, a_{x_{t_i}^i} : t_{x_{t_i}^i})$ with $\{a_{x_1^i}, \ldots, a_{x_{t_i}^i}\} = (X_1 \cup \cdots \cup X_{i-1}) \cap X_i$, and t_x is the representation type for the structure expression exp_x.

References to the class C, say $r : C$ in some exp_D are handled by replacing $r : C$ in each exp_D by a new structure expression with an outermost record constructor and new references $r_1, \ldots, r_k$, i.e., replace $r : C$ by $(b_1 : r_1 : C_1, \ldots, b_k : r_k : C_k)$.

The preservation of (weak) value identifiability is a bit more tricky. Recall from [5] that value-identifiability for a class C means that for each database db and each $(i, v) \in db(C)$ there must be a query that would result in $\{(i, v)\}$ and nothing else. Weak value-identifiability would allow to reach (i, v) by following a sequence of references and subclass links starting from a value-identiable class.

Therefore, in order to preserve value-identifiability, we must require that at least one of the new classes C_i is value-identifiable; the others may just be weakly value-identifiable. As the new classes will use all the same object identifiers, i.e., we always have $(i, v_1) \in db(C_1), \ldots, (i, v_k) \in db(C_k)$, we could replace $r : C$ simply by $r : C_i$ choosing one of the new classes that is value-identiable. In this case, however, the selected class C_i must be a superclass for all the other new classes.

As the new classes use exactly the same oid-s, we could enforce this by requiring that there is a cycle of IsA-references involving all the new classes C_i, and only some of them (including the (weakly) value-identiable one) would be referenced from classes D that previously referenced C. Note that other object oriented datamodels would exclude such cycles.

EXAMPLE 8 Consider the schema from Example 1. The class REGION has a record-structure with the labels name, central and cities. We could choose $X_1 = \{$name, central$\}$ and $X_2 = \{$cities$\}$. Thus, REGION would be replaced by

Class REGION Struct (name: $STRING$, central : { h: CITY })
CIT_IN_REG IsA REGION Struct (cities : { c : CITY })

Assuming that REGION was value-identifiable with identification type (name: $STRING$, the new class REGION would again be value-identifiable, whereas CIT_IN_REG would only be weakly value-identifiable.

The class CITY references the class REGION in the original schema. As we preserved the name of the class, there is no need to change the structure expression of this class.

Now take a look at the database from Example 2. The vertical fragmentation of Region leads to the following new database for the fragmented schema (using the shortcut CR for CIT_IN_REG):

$$db(\mathrm{R}) = \{(\&o_{11}, (\text{name} : \text{Taranaki}, \text{central} : \&o_{21})),$$
$$(\&o_{12}, (\text{name} : \text{Manawatu}, \text{central} : \&o_{23}))\}$$
$$db(\mathrm{CR}) = \{(\&o_{11}, (\text{cities} : \{\&o_{21}, \&o_{22}\})), (\&o_{12}, (\text{cities} : \{\&o_{23}\}))\}$$
$$db(\mathrm{C}) = \{(\&o_{21}, (\text{name} : \text{New Plymouth}, \text{in} : \&o_{11})),$$
$$(\&o_{22}, (\text{name} : \text{Stratford}, \text{in} : \&o_{11})),$$
$$(\&o_{23}, (\text{name} : \text{Palmerston North}, \text{in} : \&o_{12}))\}$$

This database does not provide a reference from CITY to CIT_IN_REG.

5.2 Vertical Fragmentation on Type Level

We can also discuss vertical fragmentation for the case that a tuple type constructor is used inside a structure expression, say $(a_1 : exp_1, \ldots, a_n : exp_n)$ occurs within exp_C. Then we can proceed in a similar way as for horizontal fragmentation. First introduce a new class C' with $exp_{C'} = (a_1 : exp_1, \ldots, a_n : exp_n)$, and replace $(a_1 : exp_1, \ldots, a_n : exp_n)$ in exp_C by a new reference $r' : C'$. Then vertically fragment the new class C' into $C_1, \ldots, C_k$, and replace the reference $r' : C'$ in exp_C by a new structure expression $(b_1 : r_1 : C_1, \ldots, b_k : r_k : C_k)$ with new references r_i.

We could finally undo the splitting with a result that would also have resulted, if we replaced directly $(a_1 : exp_1, \ldots, a_n : exp_n)$ in exp_C by a new structure expression $(b_1 : exp'_1, \ldots, b_k : exp'_k)$, where exp'_i is the structure expression of C_i, i.e., it has the form $(a_{j_1^i} : exp_{j_1^i}, \ldots, a_{j_{m_i}^i} : exp_{j_{m_i}^i})$.

5.3 Vertical Fragmentation of Semi-Structures Data and XML

Record types correspond to complex values in ssd-expressions with different labels. We can assume that labels appearing more than once have been collected in a new complex value with an additional value. So we can concentrate on ssd-expressions that have the form $\{\ell_1 : exp_1, \ldots, \ell_n : exp_n\}$. Let $\{\ell_1, \ldots, \ell_n\} = X_1 \cup \cdots \cup X_k$. Then we would replace all such ssd-expressions by a new ones that have the form $\{r_1 : \&o_1, \ldots, r_k : \&o_k\}$ with new oid-s $\&o_1, \ldots, \&o_k$. In addition, we would create k new top-level label, say $new_1, \ldots, new_k$, and obtain new ssd-expressions $new_i : \&o_i : \{\ell_{j_1^i} : exp_{j_1^i}, \ldots, \ell_{j_{m_i}^i} : exp_{j_{m_i}^i}\}$ with $X_i = \{\ell_{j_1^i}, \ldots, \ell_{j_{m_i}^i}\}$ collecting all the oid-s $\&o_i$ under the label r_i.

EXAMPLE 9   Let us take a look at the ssd-expression in Example 3. Applying a vertical fragmentation of REGION, i.e., $\{name : ssd_1, central : ssd_2, cities : ssd_3\}$ using $X_1 = \{name, central\}$ and $X_2 = \{name, cities\}$ will result in the following ssd-expression:

$db = \{$R $: \&o_{11} : \{name : Taranaki, central : \&o_{21}\},$

      R $: \&o_{12} : \{name : Manawatu, central : \&o_{23}\},$

      CR $: \&o_{31} : \{name : Taranaki, cities : \{c : \&o_{21}, c : \&o_{22}\}\},$

      CR $: \&o_{32} : \{name : Manawatu, cities : \{c : \&o_{23}\}\},$

      C $: \&o_{21} : \{name : New Plymouth, in : \&o_{11}, one\_of : \&o_{31}\},$

      C $: \&o_{22} : \{name : Stratford, in : \&o_{11}, one\_of : \&o_{31}\},$

      C $: \&o_{23} : \{name : Palmerston North, in : \&o_{12}, one\_of : \&o_{32}\}\}$

Note that the requirement that an oid can only be defined once in an ssd-expressions forces us to use different oid-s for CIT_IN_REG.

From here it is obvious how to transform vertical fragmentation from the SSDM to XML.

6.   Summary and Conclusion

In this paper we introduced three techniques for fragmenting object oriented database schemata: splitting, horizontal fragmentation and vertical fragmentation. Horizontal and vertical fragmentation arise from generalising the relational theory of fragmentation, and exploit the fact that generalised query algebras can be easily defined. We discussed how to handle the unique identifiability of objects and the adaptation of references in this context. We observed that semi-structured data can be regarded as object oriented data as well provided that the notion of schema is relaxed and 'evolving schemata' are allowed. This allows the fragmentation techniques to be adapted to semi-structured data and XML as well.

These fragmentation techniques can be used to set up distributed databases relying on object oriented or semi-structured data and to provide the data for services on the web.

Of course, the next natural step is to address the allocation of fragments to computer nodes in a network. As in the relational case this is a non-trivial optimisation problem with respect to the load on the network. Detailed analysis on which data is requested with which frequency will be necessary for this task, and will also have an impact on the suitability of the fragmentation. The theory can then be incorporated into approaches to design and develop web-based applications.

References

[1] Abiteboul, S., Buneman, P., Suciu, D. Data on the Web: From Relations to Semistructured Data and XML. Morgan Kaufmann Publishers 2000.

[2] Beeri, C., Thalheim, B. Identification as a Primitive of Data Models. In T. Polle, T. Ripke, K.-D. Schewe (Eds.). Fundamentals of Information Systems. Kluwer Publishing 1999, pp. 19-36.

[3] Feyer, T., Schewe, K.-D., Thalheim, B. Conceptual Modelling and Development of Information Services. In T. W. Ling, S. Ram (Eds.). Conceptual Modeling – ER '98. Springer LNCS 1507, pp. 7-20.

[4] Ozsu, M. T., Valduriez, P. Principles of Distributed Database Systems. Prentice-Hall 1999.

[5] Schewe, K.-D., Thalheim, B. Fundamental Concepts of Object Oriented Databases. Acta Cybernetica, vol. 11 (4), 1993, pp. 49-84.

[6] Schewe, K.-D., Thalheim, B. Principles of Object Oriented Database Design. In H. Jaakkola, H. Kangassalo, T. Kitahashi, A. Márkus, (Eds.). Information Modelling and Knowledge Bases V. IOS Press 1994, pp. 227 - 242.

[7] Schewe, K.-D. On the Unification of Query Algebras and their Extension to Rational Tree Structures. In M. Orlowska, J. Roddick (Eds.). Proc. Australasian Database Conference 2001.

VALUE RECONCILIATION IN MEDIATORS OF HETEROGENEOUS INFORMATION COLLECTIONS APPLYING WELL-STRUCTURED CONTEXT SPECIFICATIONS

Dmitry O. Briukhov, Leonid A. Kalinichenko, Nikolay A. Skvortsov, Sergey A. Stupnikov
Institute for Problems of Informatics RAS

Abstract   Method for value reconciliation in Local as Views (LAV) mediators of heterogeneous information collections applying well-structured specifications is presented. This approach extends a procedure for heterogeneous information sources registration at subject mediators with LAV organization. Conflicts in value semantics and representation in contexts of the mediator and a collection should be recognized and explicitly specified. According to the proposed method, value semantics contexts should be defined for the mediator and for a collection. In such context for each value kind a type is to be specified that includes a generic function converting values from a collection context into the mediator context (and/or back). Each type attribute having the respective value semantics is to be typed with such type definition. Such structuring of type attribute semantics definition gives significant economy in development of value conversion functions needed to reconcile values between the mediator and collection contexts.

Keywords: distributed databases, heterogeneous databases, middleware

1.   Introduction

Mediation architecture introduced in [14] defines an idea of a middleware positioned between information collections (information providers) and information consumers. Mediators support modelling facilities and methods for conversion of unorganized, non-systematic population of autonomous

H.-M. Haav and A. Kalja (eds.), Databases and Information Systems II, 15–28.

information collections kept by different information providers into a well-structured information source defined by the integrated uniform specifications. Mediators provide a uniform query interface to multiple data collections, thereby freeing the user from having to locate the relevant collections, query each one in isolation, and combine manually the information from them. In an approach to the mediator architecture known as Local as Views (LAV) [4] schemas exported by collections are considered as materialized views over virtual classes of the mediator schema. Queries are expressed in terms of the mediator schema. Query evaluation is done by query planning making its rewriting in terms of the source schemas [11, 3]. The LAV architecture is designed to cope with a dynamic, possibly incomplete set of collections. Collections may change their exported schemas, become unavailable from time to time. LAV is potentially scalable with respect to a number of collections involved.

According to another approach, called Global as View (GAV) [5, 13], the global schema is constructed by several layers of views above the schemas exported by pre-selected sources. Queries are expressed in terms of the global schemas and are evaluated similarly to the conventional federated database approaches [12].

The work reported in this paper has been done in frame of a research project (supported by the grant of the Russian Foundations for Basic Research N 01-07-90084) devoted to investigation of the LAV mediator architecture, models and algorithms intended for the subject mediation approach. This approach is applicable to various subject domains in science, cultural heritage, mass media, e-commerce, etc. A mediator schema (including terminological, ontological, structural and behavioral specifications) defines a context specific for concrete subject domains. Various information collections can be registered at the mediator at any time. Users may not know anything about the registration process and about the collections that have been registered. To query information in the subject, users should know only the subject domain definition – the mediator schema. In this project for the canonical model of a mediator the SYNTHESIS language [8] that is a hybrid semi-structured/object model [9] has been chosen.

In [2] methods and tools required to support information collections registration at the mediator were presented. For the LAV mediation strategy it was proposed to apply the information source registration similarly to the process of compositional information systems development [1]. Local source metainformation definitions are treated as specifications of requirements and classes of the mediator level with the related metainformation - as specifications of pre-existing components. To get local classes definitions as materialized views above the mediated level, complete type specifications are assumed. Ontological specifications are used for identification of the mediator classes semantically relevant to a source class. Maximal subset of source information relevant to the mediator classes is identified (due to use of the most common reducts to identify maximal commonality between a source and federated level class specifications). Concretizing types are defined so that the mediator classes instance types could be refined by the source instance types. This is a natural direction supporting a plan rewriting a mediator query in terms of registered sources. Such refining direction (bottom-up) is in contrast to conventional compositional development [1] where specification of requirements is to be refined by specifications of components (top-down). Such inversion is natural for registration process in the LAV mediator architecture: a materialized view (requirements) is constructed over virtual specifications (components).

Heterogeneous information collections are autonomous units created in different information contexts. The contexts depend on a subject domain of a collection, concepts definitions and real world models applied, value representation used. Heterogeneity of contexts manifests in different understanding of concepts of subject domains, different types definitions, different value appearance. The method [2] considered contextualization of collections in the mediator's context. Ontologies, structural and behavioral type and class specification were emphasized in this method.

After ontological and structural specifications of collections are contextualized in the mediator, the value semantics and representation in collections and the mediator may remain different. It means that during registration, various *features* of values should be taken into consideration. Different scales, measurement units, formats of data representation are just a few of the examples of such features. Heterogeneity of object values may be resolved with the help of value transformation rules applied on moving data from one context to another.

A systematic approach for resolving of the value heterogeneity is needed. In every case where values of object attributes in the mediator and collection contexts are not compatible it is required to develop a respective reconciliation function. In this paper an approach is introduced for providing systematic specifications during registration of information collections at subject mediators intended for reconciliation of value semantics and representation conflicts in different contexts.

A specifically structured description of type attribute semantics is proposed. For this purpose in the mediator context classes of values having specific semantics should be identified. For each of such classes a concept defining value semantics in terms of characterizing the value features should be specified. Features may have different values for concepts in different contexts. For proper features evaluation in a concrete context a specific function is to be included as a part of the value semantic concept. Finally, for each such class of values a type is to be specified that includes a generic function converting values between contexts. This function is controlled by the respective value features in the contexts involved. Each type attribute having the respective value semantics is to be typed with such type definition. Similarly a value context is to be defined for each collection during collection registration. In such local contexts the concepts defining values semantics are defined as sub-concepts of the respective mediator concepts. Generally, a redefinition of feature evaluation function for a local context may be required. The proposed structuring of type attribute semantics definition gives significant economy in development of value conversion functions reconciling different contexts.

The paper is structured as follows. After brief characterization of the related work, a short introduction into the technique of metatype specification in SYNTHESIS is given. The intention of this introduction is to make further examples in the text better readable. Main contribution of the paper is contained in sections presenting an approach for well-structured context definitions in mediators and collections and their application to value conflicts reconciliation between the mediator and a collection contexts. The conclusion summarizes the results of the paper.

2. Related Work

Similar issues of value conflicts reconciliation were treated in the COIN project [6] that addressed problems of logical connectivity (the ability to exchange meaningful information) among disparate data sources. A multiplicity of both sources and receivers was considered. Data semantics in different contexts need to be defined applying specific structuring of specifications separating schema and context definitions.

In essence, each information source in the architecture is tagged with a context; a context being a set of axioms which describe certain assumptions about the data. For instance, if A is a database containing information on a company's finances and the dates in which those finances were recorded, then the context associated with database A would contain any underlying information needed to properly interpret those financial figures and dates, such as the scale factor, the currency, and the format of the date. Using this context information, the COIN architecture is able to resolve semantic conflicts.

Besides schema definition, the context axioms for the source and conversion functions are defined. Type definitions in a schema include signatures for the modifiers in the system. A relationship between type instances and modifiers that characterize representation of the type instances is established. Modifiers have varying interpretations depending on the context.

Context axioms are a set of definitions for the modifiers of each type given in the schema. The values returned by a modifier depend on a given context in which they are created. Modifiers can also be defined intentionally. Conversion functions define how the value of a given semantic object can be derived in the current context, given that its value is known with respect to a different context. Query mediation within the COIN framework is accomplished using a top-down logic evaluation strategy resulting in a query plan which describes what sources and conversion operations are needed to mediate data exchanges at each step.

An approach presented in this paper differs in its orientation on the LAV mediators and object paradigm.

In [7] object attributes were treated as type definitions. Association metatypes establishing properties of association types were introduced. By means of an instance section of an association metatype meta-attributes of an association type may be defined. Similar approach to interpret meta-attributes in the object model is used in this paper.

3. Technique of Metatype Specifications in SYNTHESIS

The fundamental concept of the SYNTHESIS object model [8] is an abstract value. All data components in SYNTHESIS are abstract values. Abstract values are instances of abstract data types (ADT). Objects specialize abstract values with new properties -an ability to have a unique identifier and a potential ability to belong to some class (classes).

A type in the language is treated as a first-class value. Such values may be defined in specifications, on typing of variables, may be produced by type functions and type expressions. A class in SYNTHESIS is treated as a subtype of the set type. Class and type specifications are abstract and completely separated of their implementations. A number of various correct implementations (concretizations) may correspond to such specifications.

All operations over typed data in the SYNTHESIS language are represented by functions. Functions are given by predicative specifications that are given by mixed pre- and post -conditions. To express conditions related to changing of the information resource states, an ability is needed to denote variables expressing a resource state before and after function execution. For that a reference to a value of a variable after execution of a function is denoted by primed variables.

Predicative specifications are expressed using formulae of the SYNTHESIS object calculus. To specify formulae a variant of a typed (multisorted) first order predicate logic language is used. Every predicate, function, constant and variable in formulae is typed. Predicates in formulae correspond to classes, collections and functions. Variables, constants and function designators are used as terms. Each term has a well-defined type.

In the SYNTHESIS language the type specifications are syntactically represented by frames, their attributes - by slots of the frames. Additional information related to attributes can be included into metaslots. Syntactically frames are included into figure brackets { and }, slots are represented as pairs *<slot name>* : *<slot value>* (a frame can be used as a slot value), slots in a frame are separated by semicolons. Metaslots (that are represented by frames) are written immediately after the slots to which they are related.

The multilevel type system of the SYNTHESIS language is organized as follows. On the level of types the type objects are located providing for definition of concrete and generic types. On the second level (the level of "types of types") the metatype objects are located that include as their instances the types of the first level. On the third level the metatypes objects are located that include the metatypes of the second level as their instances, and so forth.

Thus the multilevel type system sets a classification relationship on types that is orthogonal to the subtype relationship. Metatypes behave like (meta)classes that in their turn are organized as follows. A class specification combines information about two kinds of objects: about a class as an object itself and about objects - instances of the class.

Generally metaclasses provide for introducing of generic concepts and of common attributes (or of their categories) for similar classes, for introducing of common consistency constraints and deductive rules for such classes and their attributes. Metaclasses provide for proper grouping of application domain information and for proper differentiation of various application domains.

In the language the attribute specifications of objects may be treated in their turn also as types of association objects establishing a correspondence between a set of objects in an association domain and a set of objects in an association range. Thus a specification of a type attribute may be considered as a specification of an association type.

Treating of an object attribute as an association type motivates an introduction of association metatypes establishing properties of association types. It is said that an object attribute (as an association type) belongs to a particular attribute category that is explicitly introduced by an association metatype.

By means of an instance section of an association metatype additional attributes of an association type may be defined as it was explained above, thus "attributes of attributes" can be defined (e.g., for an attribute price attributes of this type can be introduced, such as price status (e.g., season price), currency). If for a particular type attribute a metaslot is declared and it is defined that the attribute belongs to a certain attribute category, (categories) then a merge of the specifications given in the metaslot and in an instance sections of the respective association metatypes is formed.

4.   Definition of Contexts

The proposed approach to value reconciliation between local collection and mediator contexts consists in applying well-structured type attribute specifications. Conflicts in data representation in different contexts are frequently met due to the simplifications of attribute type schemas. Type *string* or *integer* may be used to represent values having different meaning (e.g., salary, budget, date, currency may have different semantics and formats in different application contexts). A certain context may impose specific assumptions about data that may not be explicitly defined in a schema.

To provide attribute specifications in each context with more value semantics a concept defining value semantics in terms of *features* characterizing the value should be defined. This concept is defined as an association metatype with an instance type containing value features specifications.

For example, for attributes meaning *money amount* an association metatype can be defined to specify that such attribute values will be characterized by *currency* and *scale factor* features. The instance type may contain also a function that makes possible to assign to these features values specific for a concrete context.

Further, for such class of values (*money amount*) a type is to be specified having an attribute that is declared as an instance of the association metatype introduced. This type includes also a generic function converting values between different contexts. This function is controlled by the respective features values in the contexts involved. Each type attribute having the respective value semantics is to be typed with such type definition.

The specification example in SYNTHESIS follows. We start with specifying of the mediator context.

```
{Rate;
    in: type;
    fromCurrency: string;
```

```
        toCurrency: string;
        exchangeRate: float
}
{rate;
    in: class;
    instance_section: Rate
}


{Currencies;
    in: type;
    country: string;
    currency: string
}
{currencies;
    in: class;
    instance_section: Currencies
}


{MoneyFeatures;
    in: metatype, association;

    instance_section: {MF;
      in: type;
      currency: string;
      scaleFactor: float;

      context_curr: {in: function;
        params: {+country/string};
        {{currencies(z/Currencies) & z.country = country &
          this.currency' = z.currency &
          ((z.currency = 'JPY' & this.scaleFactor' = 1000)|
          (z.currency <> 'JPY' & this.scaleFactor' = 1))}}
      }
    }
}


{MoneyAmount;
    in: type;
    sum: float;
      metaslot
        in: MoneyFeatures
      end;
    currency_convert: {in: function;
      params: {+T/type, +newMA/T, -returns/T};
      {{(meet(MoneyAmount,T) = MoneyAmount) &
```

```
        ex x/Rate (rate(x) &
        x.fromCurrency = this.sum.currency &
        x.toCurrency = newMA.sum.currency &
        returns.sum'= this.sum * x.exchangeRate *
        newMA.sum.scaleFactor / this.sum.scaleFactor)}}
    }
}

{Company;
    in: type;
    name: string;
    revenue: MoneyAmount;
    country: string
}
{company;
    in: class;
    instance_section: Company
}
```

Association metatype *MoneyFeatures* defines the concept of money amount notion for the mediator attributes. In this specification the instance type is defined containing attributes (features) *currency* and *scaleFactor* and the *context_curr* function. This function is intended for the *currency* and *scaleFactor* value assignment in the mediator context. *MoneyAmount* type attribute *sum* is defined as an instance of metatype *MoneyFeatures* acquiring thus its semantics. Method *currency_convert* specifies generic function converting values between contexts

Mediator type *Company* has three attributes: *name*, *country* and *revenue*. The attribute *revenue* is typed with the *MoneyAmount* type. The type *Rate* and class *rate* are auxiliary data specifications used in *currency_convert* function for conversion of currencies.

Specification of local collection is formed during collection registration at the mediator. Process of registration is defined in [2]. Here we consider additional actions required for value semantics definition and reconciliation. Association metatype *LocalMoneyFeatures* is defined to represent semantics of money amount similarly to that of the respective mediator metatype. Instance type of local metatype is defined as a subtype of the instance type of the mediator metatype *MoneyFeature*. Note that in the local context the *context_curr* function is redefined to reflect specificity of the local context.

```
{LocalMoneyFeatures;
    in: metatype, association;
    instance_section: {LMF;
        in: type;
```

```
         supertype: MF;

      context_curr: {in: function;
         params: {+country/string};
         {{currencies(z/Currencies) & z.country = country &
           this.currency' = z.currency &
           ((z.currency = 'JPY' & this.scaleFactor' = 100) |
           (z.currency = 'RUR' & this.scaleFactor' = 30) |
           (z.currency <> 'JPY' & z.currency <> 'RUR' &
           this.scaleFactor' = 1))}}
         }
      }
}


{MoneyAmt;
    in: type;
    supertype: moneyAmount;
    sum: float;
      metaslot
        in: LocalMoneyFeatures
        end
}


{Organization;
    in: type;
    name: string;
    revenue: MoneyAmt;
    state: string
}
{organization;
    in: class;
    instance_section: Organization
}
```

Local collection specifications in the example include type *Organization* that is ontologically relevant to type *Company* of the mediator. Semantic meaning of a schema specification element is provided by linking this element to ontological concept defined for a given context (of a collection or a mediator). If an element of specification is semantically related to a concept then it becomes an instance of the ontological class corresponding to this concept. It is used for finding of ontologically relevant elements of specifications. Ontological relevance of specification elements in different contexts is identified during collection registration.

Attributes *name, revenue* and *state* of type *Organization* are semantically relevant to the respective attributes of *Company*. *MoneyAmt* type is registered as a subtype of *MoneyAmount*. Its attribute *sum* is redefined so that it acquires semantics from *LocalMoneyFeature* concept that is valid in the collection context. The attribute *revenue* of type *Organization* is defined with *MoneyAmt* type.

Conversion function *currency_convert* is constructed so that its parameter is an instance of *T* type. *T* also is passed as a parameter and should satisfy the precondition: *meet(MoneyAmount,T)* = *MoneyAmount*. According to this type expression [10], *MoneyAmount* and its subtypes are admissible input types. The value of this type contains also meta-attributes values that have been evaluated for the respective context. The function returns reconciled value of the *T* type. Another instance involved is *this* instance that is of type *MoneyAmount* if the function is called from the mediator context or of type *MoneyAmt* if the function is called from a collection context. The function converts *this.sum* from the respective context into the *returns.sum* in the opposite context. Using auxiliary class *rate* the function finds exchange rate for the source and target currencies. Then the function calculates *returns.sum* from *this.sum* modifying it with the exchange rate found applying different scale factors of attribute in different contexts.

5. Application of Context Definitions to Attribute Value Reconciliation

We consider both way of value reconciliation – from a collection context to the mediator context and in a reverse order.

During registration of the local type *Organization*, this type becomes ontologically related to the mediator type *Company* and the common reduct for these types *R_Company_Organization* is specified. This reduct is such subspecification of *Company* type that there exists a reduct of *Organization* type that refines this reduct of *Company*. In our example the common reduct looks simply as follows:

```
{R_Company_Organization;
    in: reduct;
      metaslot
        of: Company;
        reduct: CR_Company_Organization;
        taking: {name, revenue, country}
      end
}
```

A slot *of* refers to the reduced mediator type *Company*. A list of attributes of the reduced type in the slot *taking* contains names of its attributes that are to be included into the reduct. In our case the reduct includes all attributes of *Company*. Concretizing reduct *CR_Company_Organization* is intended to specify how *R_Company_Organization* instance should be interpreted by an instance of the *Organization* type:

```
{CR_Company_Organization;
    in: c_reduct;
      metaslot
        of: Organization;
        reduct: R_Company_Organization;
        taking: {name, revenue, state}
      end
    simulating: {
      R_Company_Organization.name ~
          CR_Company_Organization.name;
      R_Company_Organization.country ~
          CR_Company_Organization.state;
      R_Company_Organization.revenue ~ cvt_revenue
    };
    cvt_revenue:{in: function;
      params: {+ext/CR_Company_Organization,
              -returns/MoneyAmount};
      {{ex o/Organization (o/CR_Company_Organization = ext &
        new(m/MoneyAmount) & m.sum.context_curr(o.state) &
        returns'=o.revenue.currency_convert(MoneyAmount,m)}}
    }
}
```

Slot *reduct* refers to the respective common reduct. Predicate *simulating* shows how the common reduct state is interpreted by an instance of the collection. E.g., it defines that attribute *name* of reduct *R_Company_Organization* is refined by attribute *name* of concretizing reduct *CR_Company_Organization* and value of this common reduct attribute is to be taken from the concretizing reduct attribute value. It also defines that attribute *revenue* of the common reduct *R_Company_Organization* is modeled by the function *cvt_revenue* resolving the value conflict. This function creates an instance of *MoneyAmount* type, contextualizes this instance in the mediator context and calls *currency_convert* function as a method of *revenue* attribute in *organization* class object identified by the concretizing reduct value. Note that the attribute *o.revenue* is of type *MoneyAmt* and exists in the collection context.

Now we consider a reverse way of attribute value reconciliation – starting with a value in the mediator context and delivering a value in a collection context. Assume that as a part of the mediator query we get

```
country = 'Japan' & revenue = 10000 & company(comp)
```

The problem is how to rewrite the constant *10000* that has the mediator context semantics to a collection context applying the same *currency_convert* function. To do that two money amount value instances need to be created – the first one (*m*) is in the mediator context that actually is *10000* extended with the mediator context money amount features and the second one is in the local context (*ml*) having the respective collection semantics. The following is the call of *currency_convert* together with the money amount instances creation and their semantics evaluation in the proper contexts.

```
new(m/MoneyAmount) & m.sum.context_curr('Japan')
& m.sum == 10000 & new(ml/MoneyAmt) &
ml.sum.context_curr('Japan') &
returns' = m.sum.currency_convert(MoneyAmt, ml)
```

6.   Conclusion

The paper presents a method for value reconciliation in mediators of heterogeneous information collections applying well-structured specifications. Such value reconciliation specifications are formed during registration of information collection at a LAV mediator. According to the proposed approach, value semantics contexts should be defined in the mediator and in a collection. The contexts are formed by concepts defining value semantics of each kind of specific value in terms of characterizing the value features. For proper features evaluation in a concrete context a specific function is to be included as a part of the value semantic concept. Technically such concept definitions are specified as association metatypes and extend the ontological specifications of the mediator and a collection. In such context for each value kind a type is to be specified that includes a generic function converting values from a collection context into the mediator context (and/or back). Each type attribute having the respective value semantics is to be typed with such type definition. Such structuring of type attribute semantics definition gives significant economy in development of value conversion functions needed to reconcile values between the mediator and collection contexts.

References

[1] Briukhov, D.O., Kalinichenko, L.A. Component-based information systems development tool supporting the SYNTHESIS design method. In Proceedings of the East European Symposium on Advances in Databases and Information Systems (ADBIS'98), Springer, LNCS No. 1475, 1998.

[2] Briukhov, D.O., Kalinichenko, L.A., Skvortsov, N.A. Information sources registration at a subject mediator as compositional development. In Proceedings of the Fifth East European Symposium on Advances in Databases and Information Systems (ADBIS'01), Springer-Verlag, 2001, pp. 70-83.

[3] Duschka, O., and Genesereth, M. Answering Queries Using Recursive Views. In Principles Of Database Systems (PODS), 1997.

[4] Friedman, M., Levy, A. and Millstein, T. Navigational Plans for Data Integration, In Sixteenth National Conference on Artificial Intelligence (AAAI-99), Orlando, Florida, 1999.

[5] Garcia-Molina, H., Hammer, J., Ireland, K., Papakostantinou, Y., Ullman, J. and Widom J. The Tsimmis Approach to Mediation: Data Models and Languages. Journal of Intelligent Information Systems, 1997.

[6] Goh, C., Bressan, S., Lee, T., Madnick, S., Siegel, M. A Procedure for the Context Mediation of Queries to Disparate Sources. International Logic Programming Symposium, 1997.

[7] Kalinichenko, L.A. Rule-based concept definitions intended for reconciliation of semantic conflicts in the interoperable information systems. In Proceedings of the Second International Baltic Workshop on DB and IS, Tallinn, June 1996.

[8] Kalinichenko, L.A. SYNTHESIS: the language for description, design and programming of the heterogeneous interoperable information resource environment. Institute for Problems of informatics, Russian Academy of Sciences, Moscow, 1995.

[9] Kalinichenko, L.A. Integration of Heterogeneous Semistructured Data Models in the Canonical One. In Proceedings of the First All-Russian Conference on Digital Libraries, St. Petersburg, 1999.

[10] Kalinichenko, L.A. Compositional Specification Calculus for Information Systems Development. In Proceedings of the East-European Symposium on Advances in Databases and Information Systems (ADBIS'99), Springer-Verlag, LNCS, 1999.

[11] Levy, A., Rajaraman, A. and Ordille, J. Querying Heterogeneous Information Sources using Source Descriptions. In Proceedings of the 22nd Conference on Very Large Databases, 1996, pp. 251-262.

[12] Sheth, A. and Larson, J. Federated Database Systems for Managing Distributed, Heterogeneous, and Autonomous Database. ACM Computing Surveys, 1990.

[13] Subrahmanian, V. S. Hermes: a Heterogeneous Reasoning and Mediator System. http://www.cs.umd.edu/projects/hermes/publications/postscripts/tois.ps

[14] Wiederhold, G. Mediators in the Architecture of Future Information Systems. IEEE Computer, 1992.

REACTIVE LOAD BALANCING IN DISTRIBUTED DATABASE MANAGEMENT SYSTEMS

Josep M. Muixi
GFT Consulting, Spain
IT Architecture Department
josep-m.muixi@gft.com

August Climent
Ramon Llull University, Spain
Computer Science Department
augc@salleURL.edu

Silvia Canals
Universitat Politecnica de Catalunya, Spain
Computer Science Department
scanals@upc.edu

Abstract   Distributed Database Management Systems (DDBMS) offer advantages and new possibilities to traditionally centralized database environments; but decisions taken at deployment or initial configuration time, affect the final behavior of the hole system directly. So, distribution does not imply immediate improvements necessarily: some new concepts and issues need to be considered, as availability, distributed security, distributed concurrency, or load balancing. Focus in this article will be on load balancing DDBMS environments; some techniques have been presented in the past and a new mechanism is to be introduced in this article. Particularities of this new load balancing mechanism, as no centralized component need or dependency, and its probabilistic nature form the basis of a new set of load balancing technologies. Performance results are reported based on public standards for OLTP performance measurement.

Keywords: distributed databases, load-balancing, performance, OLTP, reactive distributed query execution, just in time, probability theory.

H.-M. Haav and A. Kalja (eds.), Databases and Information Systems II, 29–41.

1.   Introduction.

DDBMS architectures can become complex to be defined, managed and maintained. They have been studied and categorized in previous literature [14]. These architectures allow more independent and local control of data and provide easy alternatives in designing and upgrading the distributed system.

Data availability is increased by *Replication* methods [9] applied to distributed architectures. Globally improved performance is obtained at the expense of some extra handling logic; *replication* is very common in currently available systems, representing a significant benefit on most of cases.

Query planning —including *optimization* and *scheduling*— for Database Management System (**DBMS**) operations and their application to **DDBMS**s has been discussed extensively in literature. *Optimization* and *scheduling* act as key pieces of load balancing strategies, as from their direct application, load is finally distributed in the system.

Parallelism adoption in Database Management Systems (**DBMS**s) helps to increase performance in a high degree under normal circumstances and its use is a must [1]. Once at this point, further research was dedicated to studying the application of *pipelining* techniques to these *parallel* systems.

The general concept of *workload balance* for distributed systems has been traditionally focused on the idea of obtaining a scheduling plan of tasks over a set of CPUs given a generic operation to be executed over this architecture [4], but *workload balance* for **DBMS**s is an issue which has been addressed in fewer cases in the past [10], when attention has been centered mostly on query processing optimization.

[14] present an introduction to *workload balancing problem* in the Distributed Database Management System context. Several solutions have been proposed for multiprocessor machines and distributed systems [10].

The problem addressed is the distribution of relational operations among nodes of a **DDBMS**, in a way that the load is balanced from a global view of the system, improving performance of the **DDBMS** and getting a normalized and efficient use of the **DDBMS** resources as described in [1]. A representative set of centralized *workload balancing* policies were abstracted and simulated in our *DDBSim*Tool[1], and finally contrasted with the results obtained simulating the distributed Just-in-Time strategy introduced here.

---

[1] *DDBSim* is a simulator for Distributed Database Management System architectures, developed with the main objective to get experimental performance results.

The method presented here introduces a real distributed *load balancing* method integrated with *query planning* and *query execution* phases of distributed query order executions.

2. Basic Workload Balance Strategies.

Basic workload balance strategies applied to **DDBMS**s can be classified in these five categories [1]:

- No load-balancing (No) This is current standard adopted in many commercial systems. Normally the queries are processed under a predefined plan and assigned for execution in a static form.

- Round Robin (RR) Load is assigned to the next node listed in a circular list. Easy to implement, it is probably the most used strategy because of its high revenues compared to the minimum effort required in its implementation.

- Join-the-Shortest-Queue (SQ) Incoming load is assigned to those nodes with shortest queues of tasks to process.

- Join-the-Fastest: Processor Utilization (Pr) Processors showing the lowest utilization will be the next candidates to get incoming load.

- Join-the-Fastest: Response Time (Rt) Incoming load is assigned to nodes which recently showed the fastest response times servicing previous requests.

An initial classification of these mechanisms, based on data dependency, classifies **No** and **RR** as *no-centralized* strategies, and **SQ**, **Pr**, and **Rt** as *centralized* ones.

Having been discussed and detailed in past literature, all of the centralized strategies are really difficult to be applied in real world **DDBMS**s; anyway they form a good basis on which to consider future work on load balancing strategies for these environments.

3. Just-in-Time Workload Balancing.

In this section our new concept of workload balancing policy is introduced.

3.1 Context and Motivations

From previous work [10], we can conclude that a balanced system is one which delivers high performance under all load conditions; the less balanced a system is, the less performance we could expect from it. The main objective of this study will be, therefore, trying to find new methods to optimize, or at least improve, system load balance for **DDBMS** environments.

The method shown here employs a new philosophy in scheduling operations in a **DDBMS**. This method is based on previous studies for multiprocessor environments where database query executions are modelled as hierarchical trees of operations [5]; applying the same model for distributed query executions, and using new mechanisms defined in this article based on reactive actions, an effective and improved load balancing policy can be achieved.

The proposed strategy for database operations scheduling is based on the fact that operation executions can be carried out in more than one node[2] of the distributed architecture; normally this is achieved with the help of data *replication*. If no *replication* exists in the database, probably no alternative nodes to execute query operations will be able to be targeted.

In general, scheduling for queries to be executed over any database is done in a near-static or fixed form, or based on some dynamic information about current status of the database, data location, resource availability, etc ... Problems with the first approach appear as no load distribution exists over replicated data and distributed resources. The second approach is closely related to final mechanisms and techniques used in the application of the method; anyway, using dynamicity has been tied historically to the figure of a global scheduler or manager module which centralizes some system status information; this approach is clearly better than the static one, but also has some disadvantages: the system overload generated by the need to have a centralized component updated with system resources statistics and status information, and the unpredictable evolution in time of system load, can turn the best scheduling approach at scheduling time t_{schd} in to the worst plan execution at execution time t_{exec}.

As we aim to show load balancing techniques and their contribution to system performance, we will rely our study on load metrics for distributed environments presented in 3.2. We present our results based on a standard performance metric, TPC Benchmark^{TM}-C (TPC-C)[3].

---

[2]Depending on the distributed architecture, nodes will be composed or understood differently; in this work, a node is assumed as the set of components able to execute an operation of a distributed query plan, sharing or not resources.

Performance metric reported by **TPC-C** is a throughput that measures the number of orders processed per minute or *tpmC*.

The main objective of this text is to introduce a way to get the best response time for database operations once a good *scheduling plan* of these operations has been prepared; methods to prepare *scheduling plans* are not studied here; anyway, this text is based on them to present our method theory; the method presented here only has impact at runtime, with no significant modification to the *optimization* or *scheduling* phases of query execution processes.

Where the method introduced here offers its superior ability to manage load balancing is in its characteristic to react to current or just in time system load, in a decentralized way; logic to take decisions to improve performance is distributed across the system.

3.2   Load Metrics

In [3] some load metrics and their interpretation are presented. *Imbalance* and *Dynamicity* are the two metrics used in our comparison section for distinct *workload balance* techniques versus our method.

Imbalance Standard deviation (σ) of the load of the N system nodes, normalized to the average system load (λ).

$$\sigma = \frac{1}{\lambda}\sqrt{\frac{\sum_{i=1}^{N}(L_i - \lambda)^2}{N}} \tag{1}$$

with

$$\lambda = \frac{1}{N}\sum_{i=1}^{N}(L_i)$$

being L_i the load of the ith system node

Dynamicity Normalized standard deviation of the load changes between time t and $t + \Delta t$.

$$\Delta\sigma(t, t + \Delta t) = \frac{1}{\lambda(t)}\sqrt{\sum_{i=1}^{N}\frac{(\Delta L_i(t, t + \Delta t))^2}{N}} \tag{2}$$

---

[3]TPC Benchmark^{TM}, TPC-C^{TM}, and tmpC^{TM} are trademarks of the Transaction Performance Council (*http://www.tpc.org*).

being $\lambda(t)$ the average system load at instant t.

Imbalance acts as a static photo of load distribution across all system nodes. A system tends to be balanced at a determined instant in time as its *imbalance* tends to zero; on the other hand, as greater is this value, so is the unbalancing of the system.

Dynamicity expresses the way in which *imbalance* varies through time. A static system will be such a system that its *imbalance* keeps static, so its *dynamicity* tends to zero; if the *imbalance* is changing through time, the system *dynamicity* will be non-zero. This metric will allow us to get an idea of how fast the load is moving through the system.

Please refer to [3] for further conclusions and details about these metrics.

3.3   *JitWob* Method

3.3.1   Method overview.   All the *Workload balancing* strategies introduced in section 2 form a basic range of mechanisms to provide load balancing; some other techniques have appeared with alternative strategies making use of ideas from other fields of knowledge unrelated to computer science such as economics [13].

SQ, **Pr** and **Rt** methods are based on the assumption of load information availability: current load information of the whole system should be accessible in order to take a decision to balance the overall system load. These possible centralized solutions tend to present problems and their effectiveness depends totally on relation: *system information collection rate versus system load variation rate.*

Load balancing has been dealt always with the assumption of nodes load information availability, and as a concept unrelated to *query planning*. Just-in-Time Workload Balancing (*JitWob*) evolves the query execution process and goes one step ahead, splitting *load balancing* logic into *scheduling* and *execution* phases. The concept of *execution* phase being considered typically a passive phase disappears with *JitWob*; now workload balancing logic is also applied at execution time: it is a *reactive load balancing* policy.

JitWob does not collect any information about real-time load of the system, as no centralized point exists for such a task; on the other hand, the system is able to react to balance its load once operations have been distributed among required nodes —at runtime—, providing Just-in-Time *load balancing.*

Just-in-Time Workload Balancing uses the best of existing load balancing approaches, and achieves a new way to balance operation execution. Under *JitWob*, each query-generating node acts independently as an *optimizing* and *scheduling* engine, allocating operations for the final execution of a query operation to all required nodes of the distributed architecture, in the same way it could be implemented following any of the existing scheduling strategies. If some statistical information is needed it can be collected from a statistics repository if the *scheduling* algorithm being used requires it, as is being done in existing *scheduling* algorithms. *JitWob* acts by balancing system load at runtime, when operations have been sent to nodes and 'just-in-time' load is found; at this point the *JitWob* algorithm can choose between accepting the execution of that operation in that node, wait for a lower load on that node, or re-schedule it to another node.

3.3.2   Method theory.   Under *JitWob*, the *optimizing* phase of any query is managed in the same way as usual: an optimization algorithm is responsible for creating the best operations map to execute the query; this map can be represented as a *bushy tree* $\mathbb{B}$ of operations.

The *scheduling* phase of the query execution is to create the allocation plan for each one of the operations O_i composing graph $\mathbb{B}$ among the different nodes composing the **DDBMS** architecture considering dependencies. All of these algorithms manage *execution dependency, system fragmentation* and *replication* as main parameters to define final nodes allocation, under the normal assumption of *synchronous execution time*; for further details, please refer to [4]. The final result of this process is an allocation table $\mathbf{A} = (A_i)$ with as many elements as nodes appear in the *bushy tree* $\mathbb{B}$ created in the previous phase; such a table assigns an operation O_i to a node in the distributed database $N_{opt(i)}$ where the execution should be optimal, so that:

$$\mathbf{A} = (A_1, A_2, \ldots A_n) \quad | \quad \forall \, A_i \;\; \exists \;\; (O_i \rightarrow N_{opt(i)})$$

n being the number of operations in the *bushy tree* obtained.

JitWob proposes only a subtle modification to these algorithms creating such a scheduling plan; at scheduling time, the final allocation table $\mathbf{A}'$ should include not only the best target node for its execution $N_{opt(i)}$, but also alternative node locations ordered by preference $N_{alt(1)}, N_{alt(2)}, \ldots N_{alt(k)}$, where execution of that operation is also feasible. The final relation created during scheduling phase could then be:

$$\mathbf{A}' = (A_1', \ldots A_n') \quad | \quad \forall \, A_i' \;\; \exists \;\; (O_i \rightarrow N_{opt(i)}, N_{alt(1)}, N_{alt(2)}, \ldots N_{alt(k)})$$

k being the *JitWob* depth with a maximum value of $N-1$, with N as the number of nodes in the **DDBMS**.

The intention of this modification is that if an overload is detected in any of the nodes $N_{opt(i)}$ participating in the query execution at runtime

—once each operation has been allocated or distributed to each node— *JitWob* will be able to choose a different node from relation A'_i, trying to find the best alternative in each case. This being the main idea behind new proposed *JitWob* methodology, some variants can be found depending on the way of selecting alternative nodes. Here is where *Probability Theory* starts its role, and let us apply different *JitWob* policies according to the different probabilistic distributions used in selecting an alternative node for allocation —this is applied at scheduling time as well as runtime if reallocation is needed due to local overload—. Results presented here are obtained under a *gaussian probabilistic distribution*; so this is the preferred strategy used in our simulations. *Gaussian probabilistic distribution* is applied to current set of alternate nodes where current operation can be alternatively executed, assigning more probability to nodes considered more appropriate by the scheduling mechanism; once probability laws have elected the new node based on this distribution, allocation of current operation is transferred there. *Probabilistic Theory* states that the operation is to be done at any time, being a guarantee of its execution. In order to avoid *starvation*, older operations are prioritized over newer ones.

4. *JitWob* Results.

4.1 Simulation Parameters.

Architecture basic characteristics of **DDBMS** and client composition used in simulations are summarized in table 1.

Table 1. *Main parameters describing simulated architecture.*

System Components	Clients (× 28,800)		Servers (× 128)	
	Quantity	Description	Quantity	Description
Processor	2	Pentium III @733MHz	8	Pentium III @900MHz
Cache	1	256KB	1	2MB
Memory	4	128MB	32	512MB
Disk Drives	1	9.1GB	25	12GB
Network speed		100Mbits		1Gbits

Database population simulation was based on standard **TPC-C**. Tables were replicated all over the server nodes accordingly to the needs: data relationships, sizes and dependencies. No table partitioning was used in tests. *Replication* is the key factor for *JitWob* to improve final system performance in the same way as to get fast data availability in current **DDBMS**s, so special care was taken in this point.

4.2 *JitWob* Compared

All policies studied implement the same algorithm for the *optimization* phase. Differentiation appears at the *scheduling* phase where each policy applies its strategy.

Simulation results are presented in two forms:

Graphical load results: Show system *imbalance* and *dynamicity* for a period of 10 minutes in a stable period of load, exactly in the timeframe compressed between 5 minutes after measurement interval starts and 5 minutes before measurement interval ends.

Performance summary: Table 2 shows performance results in *tpmC* units as defined in **TPC-C** standard for a variety of client configurations.

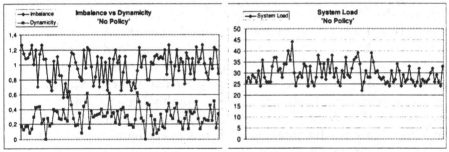

Figure 1. Simulation load results for *No Load Balance* Strategy.

No Load Balance policy is the easiest technic where destination nodes for operations of a query are predefined and have no variation over time: it is the simplest policy to implement and one of the most common found in the real world. The main reason for distributing operations (if distributed) is data availability, load balance having no significant weight on final decision of scheduling algorithm. Figure 1 shows related graphical results for *No Load Balance* policy. Despite its lack of controlling system load, this is a good solution for non high loaded systems and no critical ones. Clearly, the system always loads the same nodes for the same query executions; because of this, system *imbalance* is high showing that load is heterogeneous among the system nodes. *Dynamicity* remains low, indicating that *imbalance* does not vary, keeping the system unbalanced; but it varies abruptly to higher levels sporadically, showing how this imbalance is varying in time, creating the image of a totally unbalanced system. *Imbalance* is clearly higher than *dynamicity*. Performance results shown in table 2 offer the lowest performance results in any of the simulated cases.

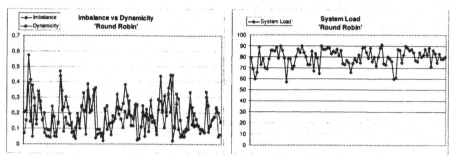

Figure 2.   Simulation load results for *Round Robin* Strategy.

The *Round Robin* policy works very well in real cases and is the most implemented load balancing strategy on the market. Its effectiveness depends on the homogeneity of operations and system nodes; another advantage of this policy is its independence of global system load information. Results of simulation using *Round Robin* appear in figure 2. *Imbalance* is kept low, as well as *dynamicity*, but this one suffers some high peaks; these peaks are mainly caused because load distribution is not based on system status and some localized overloads can appear. *Dynamicity* and *imbalance* indexes keep similar values. *System Load* under extreme query load is about 80%, notably higher than the previous results (30%) obtained under *No Load Balancing* policy; accordingly, the performance results obtained using this policy improve substantially the ones got with previous one.

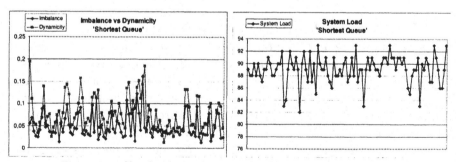

Figure 3.   Simulation load results for *Shortest Queue* Strategy.

Applying *Shortest Queue* policy an improvement over previous strategy is obtained: figure 3 shows how *imbalance* is reduced in this case and how *dynamicity* is sightly superior to it. Some peaks still exist in both graphics, but they are substantially inferior to previous cases.

System Load gets values of almost 90%; performance results are again outperforming previous strategy ones.

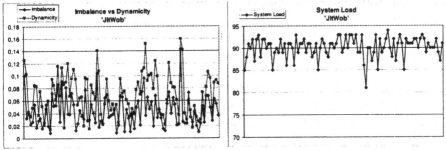

Figure 4.   Simulation load results for *JitWob* Strategy.

Simulation results for *JitWob* policy appear in figure 4. *Imbalance* and *dynamicity* get lower values than in previous cases —indicating a more balanced and stable system—; what is remarkable is the fact that no peak in its values is superior to peaks obtained in previous methods in percentage. *System Load* measure shows a system taking advantage of all its resources in a more stable form through time, which makes final performance results outperform other strategies (see table 2). *JitWob* strategy improves performance under extreme load conditions, and has less or no effect under normal load due to its innate 'react on the fly' philosophy without loading the system to do its work.

Table 2. Simulation performance results in tpmC *obtained for the different load balancing policies studied when applied to the simulated architecture under standard* **TPC-C** *load.*

Number of users	No Policy	Round Robin	Shortest Queue	JitWob
35,000	12,121.55	14,527.22	15,744.83	15,792.74
32,000	16,143.88	19,155.26	20,143.01	20,342.16
30,000	18,497.14	25,934.97	29,720.81	30,376.29
28,800	**19,312.93**	**28,353.02**	**34,221.01**	**36,312.93**
25,000	18,262.34	26,002.45	29,212.87	31,361.09
20,000	16,173.54	21,921.29	23,129.08	23,341.32
15,000	10,372.70	12,254.09	12,173.94	12,167.15

A priori, from the innate nature of *JitWob* algorithm, we could predict a better or at least equal performance of *JitWob* versus standard algorithms being used; performance results obtained and summarized in table 2 strengthen this. *JitWob* strategy improves performance under extreme load conditions, and has less or no effect under normal load.

5.   Conclusions

JitWob has been the most effective *load balancing* strategy and the one which, overall, has achieved the greatest improvement in performance. It is clear that overhead caused by *JitWob* policy is minimum, so no performance overload can be considered from its use. In case of no replicated or no overloaded databases, *JitWob* adds no exceptional value to execution of query operations. On the other hand, if replication and overloading of some nodes is probable, then *JitWob* acts as the most suitable and easy-to-implement solution. Its decentralized and probabilistic philosophy provide robustness and independence to distributed nodes, outperforming in load balance performance.

JitWob simplicity, compared to other *workload balancing* strategies, make it a true candidate for real systems.

References

[1] Abdelguerfi, M. and Wong, K.-F. "Parallel Database Techniques", IEEE Computer Society Press, 1998.

[2] Chen, M.-S., Yu, P.S., and Wu, K.-L. "Optimization of Parallel Execution for Multi-Join Queries", IEEE Transactions on Knowledge and Data Engineering, June 1996.

[3] Corradi, A., Leonardi, L. and Zambonelli, F. "Diffusive Load-Balancing Policies for Dynamic Applications", IEEE Concurrency, January-March 1999.

[4] Jonsson, J. and Vassell, J. "Evaluation and Comparison of Task Allocation and Scheduling Methods for Distributed Real-Time Systems", IEEE 0-8186-7614-0/96, 1996.

[5] Lee, C., Shih, C.-S., and Chen, Y.-H. "Optimizing Large Join Queries using a Graph-Based approach", IEEE Transactions on Knowledge and Data Engineering, Vol.13, No.2, March/April 2001.

[6] Li, K. and Cheng, K.H. "Complexity of Resource Allocation and Job Scheduling", 1st. IEEE Symp. Parallel and Distributed Processing, 1989, pp. 358-365.

[7] Lo, M.-L., Chen, M.-S., and Ravishankar, C.V. "On Optimal Processor Allocation to Support Pipelined Hash Joins", Proc. ACM SIGMOD, May 1993, pp. 67-78.

[8] March, S.T. and Rho, S. "Allocating Data and Operations to Nodes in Distributed Database Design", IEEE Transactions on Knowledge and Data Engineering, Vol.7, No.2, 1995.

[9] Nicola, M. and Jarke, M. "Performance Modeling of Distributed and Replicated Databases", IEEE Transactions on Knowledge and Data Engineering, Vol.12, No.4, July/August 2000.

[10] Rahm, E. "Dynamic Load Balancing in Parallel Database Systems", Proc. EURO-PAR 96 Conf. LNCS, Springer-Verlag, Lyon (Invited paper), Aug 1996.

[11] Scheuermann, P. and Inseck, E. "Adaptive Algorithms for Join Processing in Distributed Database Systems", Distributed and Parallel Databases Vol.5. Kluwer Academic Publishers, 1997, pp. 233-269.

[12] Spiliopoulou, M. and Hatzoopoulos, M. "Parallel Optimization of Large Join Queries with Set Operators and Aggregates in a Parallel Environment Supporting Pipeline", IEEE Transactions on Knowledge and Data Engineering, June 1996.

[13] Stonebraker, M., Devine, R., and Kornacker, M. "An economic paradigm for query processing and data migration in Mariposa", Proc. 3rd. Int'l Symp. on Parallel and Distributed Information Systems, Sept 1994, pp. 58-67.

[14] Özsu, M.T. and Valduriez, P. "Principles of Distributed Database Systems", 2nd Edition, Prentice Hall, 1999.

[15] Yu, M. J. and Shen, P.C. Y. "Adaptive Join algorithms in Dynamic Distributed Databases", Distributed and Parallel Databases Vol.5, Kluwer Academic Publishers, 1997, pp. 5-30.

UNDENIABLE DATABASE QUERIES

Ahto Buldas

Cybernetica AS

Akadeemia tee 21, 12618 Tallinn, Estonia

ahtbu@cyber.ee

Meelis Roos

Cybernetica AS

Lai 6, 51005 Tartu, Estonia

mroos@cyber.ee

Jan Willemson

Cybernetica AS

Lai 6, 51005 Tartu, Estonia

jan@cyber.ee

Abstract

Let D be a public on-line database that is maintained by a party who is possibly not completely trustworthy. We study cryptographic techniques preventing the party (1) from undetectably modifying the content of D, and (2) from giving contradictory answers to the same query q, after a relatively short cryptographic digest d of D is made public. Previous work by Buldas, Laud and Lipmaa gives efficient solution for queries that require the answer Yes or No. The goal of this paper is to widen the scope of their techniques and cover much more complex types of queries. We present efficient methods for the queries that return a list of consecutive records as the reply. We show that the amount of additional cryptographic code that must be included into the answer can still remain quite small.

Keywords: databases, authenticated database queries, authenticated search trees

H.-M. Haav and A. Kalja (eds.), Databases and Information Systems II, 43–54.

Introduction

In our everyday life, we will more and more rely on electronic data sources (web databases, public registries, logistics timetables, public key infrastructures etc). Mostly, these public sources are trusted blindly and the information obtained e.g. from some web database is rarely verified. There are many applications where this verification is not mission critical – if the movie theatre's timetable on the theatre's web page is out of date we will not be able to see the movie we wanted to, but we can take another one or even go to a pub instead.

On the other hand, the number of public services with higher security requirements is growing. As a motivating example we consider the case of distributing digital certificate validity information. Digital certificates were first proposed by Kohnfelder [5] as a way to overcome the problem of authentic and efficient binding of private keys to physical persons and thus make the use of public-key cryptography [4] practical for digital signatures. Distribution of authentic validity information of public key certificates is crucial to the security of public key infrastructures.

For X.509 public key infrastructure corresponding Online Certificate Status Protocol (OCSP) [9] has been proposed. In the original scheme, OCSP server is itself a trusted authority who is not obliged to prove its statements in any way. It was shown by Ansper, Buldas, Roos and Willemson [1] that these trust requirements can be decreased by rearranging the certificate validity information distribution infrastructure a bit. They proposed the idea about the Certification Authority committing himself to the state of his database and a special (non-trusted) authority (called Notary) distributing certificate validity information together with proofs.

The current paper discusses the process of forming the commitments and constructing the proofs in more detail. We also consider some more general cases than just getting "yes/no" answers as the replies from the online database: giving the value for a predefined function and outputting replies about intervals.

This paper continues the research started with [2] and expands the ideas towards securing general databases. We want to create an universal method to build authentic databases and to help design secure databases from the ground up. Similar attempts to build authenticated databases were made in [6, 3] but they have slightly different goals – they still leave the database holder fully trusted and only secure data distribution.

1. Statement of the Problem

Let us have a public registry with the corresponding database R and some authorized clients who can make queries about the current state of the database and obtain replies. We consider a situation where it is crucial for the clients to be able to verify the correctness of the replies, i.e. to make sure that to the given query q there is only one possible reply, namely the one that was presented by the registry.

In order to build such a framework, assume first that the data in the registry is updated (new records are added, old records are deleted, etc.) once a day at a certain time (e.g. 8 AM). After each updating procedure the registry *commits* himself to the current state by producing an imprint $d = D(R)$ of the database and sends it to a special Publication Authority (PA in Figure 1). PA will clearly identify d as the imprint of *that day* and distribute it authentically to all the clients.

When the user sends a query q to the registry's server the server responds by sending a reply $r = P(q, R)$ (Figure 1). There is a public verification algorithm V at client's disposal which if given triple (q, r, d) answers 1 or 0 depending on whether the response to the query is correct or not (see Figure 1). We always assume the **condition of correctness** – for any correct query (i.e. belonging to the query language L) the equality

$$V(q, P(q, R), D(R)) = 1$$

holds.

We also require the following **condition of security**: it is difficult for the registry or anyone to find a quadruple (q, r, r', d) so that $r \neq r'$ and

$$V(q, r, d) = V(q, r', d) = 1. \qquad (1)$$

The security condition actually says that the registry can not give different responses r and r' to the given query q if the database imprint has been distributed uniquely and authentically.

This condition was first defined for binary answers in [2]. The above specification generalizes the previous specification to general database queries.

Requirements for the Publication Authority. Public server accepts exactly one imprint a day from the registry and does that in an authentic way. Nobody else can put forward an imprint instead of the registry and the registry can not put forward several different imprints in one day.

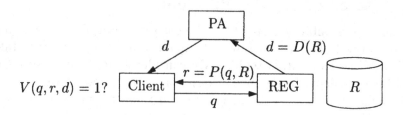

Figure 1. Diagram describing the work of the secure registry

Now we are to ready state the following problem which is going to be the subject of the current paper:

> Find efficient (in the sense of size of a response and storage size of the registry) algorithmic implementations for the triples of functions (P, D, V) which satisfy the condition of security (1).

Authentication trees. It is quite clear that the implementation and its efficiency depend a lot on the query language L and on its structure and complexity as well as the properties of the set of all possible answers.

In the trivial case (i.e. if the query language is $L = \{0, 1\}^k$ and the set of answers is $\{0, 1\}$) the solution was given by Buldas, Laud and Lipmaa [2]. They use an *authenticated search tree* similar to the Merkle's authentication tree [8] with each node labeled with one query argument (key) k and one hash value that is obtained as a message imprint $y = H(H_l, k, H_r)$. Here H_l and H_r are the imprints of the left and right descendant, respectively (see Figure 2). H is a *cryptographic hash function* (meaning it is computationally hard to find x and x' so that $H(x) = H(x')$ — see e.g. [7], chapter 9). Hence, in order to prove that the hash value y depends on, say, H_l it is sufficient to give the values k and H_r so that anyone can recompute the hash and compare it to y.

Such a reasoning can be generalized to more complicated data structures, for instance to trees. To prove that the top of the tree y depends on leaf x we need to provide the information to recompute the path from x to y. It takes $\log |R|$ steps where $|R|$ denotes the number of records in database R (so $\log |R|$ is the height of the tree). On each step we need to compute one hash value. We have one input to the hash function from the previous step and so we need 2 additional inputs. The length of the proofs in the trivial scheme is thus about $2 \log |R|$. The set of all these additional inputs is the proof of y depending on x. For instance, to prove that the top of tree in Figure 2 depends on the value 25 we first compute H_2 (two NIL's are the additional inputs), then compute

H_3 (30 and NIL are the additional inputs) and finally compute H_4 (H_1 and 20 are the additional inputs). Verification succeeds if computed and published values of H_4 match.

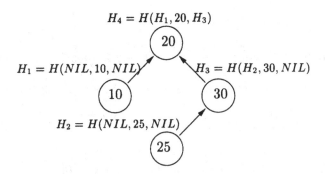

$$H_4 = H(H_1, 20, H_3)$$

$$H_1 = H(NIL, 10, NIL)$$ $$H_3 = H(H_2, 30, NIL)$$

$$H_2 = H(NIL, 25, NIL)$$

Figure 2. The authentication tree that satisfies the condition of undeniability for functions $\{0,1\}^k \rightarrow \{0,1\}$

2. Queries Resulting in One Record

The first solution for functions of type $f : \{0,1\}^k \rightarrow \{0,1\}^m$ was proposed by Arne Ansper in private communication. It uses an AVL-tree modified in the following way: in addition to the key (the variable q by which the search is performed) each node has also the result of the query (or its imprint) $f(q) = P(q, R)$. Each node is labeled with a hash value that is obtained as the imprint $H(H_l, q, f(q), H_r)$, where H_l and H_r are the imprints of the left and right descendants respectively. The size of the proofs in this scheme is about $3 \log |R|$ (we have 4 inputs to the hash function and to prove something about one argument we need 3 additional inputs).

The size of the proof can be decreased to $2 \log |R|$ if we assume that only leaves are added to the tree and the values $f(q)$ are present only in the leaves. In this case the verifier of the authentication path must check that the node containing the value of the function is really a leaf and that on every step of the verification (with key q in the node) the inequality $x < q$ holds if we use the left descendant (we can also say that the authentication path goes to the left of the node or that the value x is in the left subtree of current node) and the inequality $q \leq x$ holds if the right descendant is used. Note that in normal authentication tree both of these inequalities are strict.

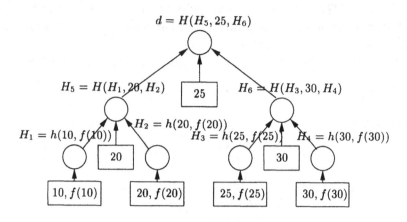

Figure 3. Authentication tree for functions $f : \{0,1\}^k \to \{0,1\}^m$

The described above authentication tree provides for example a partial solution to the problem of suspended certificates – the set of query results can be {Valid, Invalid, On Hold}.

The solution described above unfortunately suits only to "flat" databases that have been stored as a subset of Cartesian product $L \times f(L)$ where function f has been constructed for only a certain type of queries. The structure of real practical databases is much more complicated and each query may contain several independent searches by several indices. Although theoretically every database query can be formalized as a function $f : L \to \{0,1\}^m$, the set L would in general grow very large and it would be infeasible to build an authentication tree for all possible elements of L. Thus the question of undeniable replies in practical databases is still open and needs research.

In the rest of the paper, we first find a solution to the authentication of intervals instead of single values. The trivial solution is optimized for size by encoding the authentication tree efficiently. Canonical data structures are shown to give even more reduction in size but so far they only come with expensive database modifications.

3.   Intervals by one Index

We try to find a solution for ensuring undeniability for more complicated queries. We start with the queries that specify certain interval of one index instead of one certain value and can have several records instead of one as the answer:

$$I = [(x_1, f(x_1)), (x_2, f(x_2)), \ldots, (x_m, f(x_m))],$$

where $a \leq x_1 < x_2 < \cdots < x_m \leq b$.

3.1 Trivial Solution

It turns out that this problem can be solved quite easily if we add authentication paths (from the leaf to the top of database tree) separately for each response record as a proof. The proof must convince the verifier that the records really form an interval: (1) no records are missing and (2) no records outside this interval satisfy the criteria of the query. To accomplish this we must add two records to the proof:

1 Lower bound – a record $(x_L, f(x_L))$ that directly precedes the minimal element of the interval with respect to the attribute the query is made by;

2 Upper bound – a record $(x_R, f(x_R))$ that directly follows the maximal element of the interval

When verifying the proof we must check that

1 the sequence

$$[(x_L, f(x_L)), (x_1, f(x_1)), (x_2, f(x_2)), \ldots, (x_m, f(x_m)), (x_R, f(x_R))]$$

forms an interval (i.e. these elements are correctly ordered and are each other's neighbours in the database as shown by the authentication paths);

2 the digest of the subtree generated by the sequence (Figure 4, medium grey nodes) is equal to some given value d (the digest of the database);

3 $x_L < a \leq x_1$ and $x_m \leq b < x_R$.

Unfortunately this method is quite inefficient as the length of the proof would be proportional to the length on the interval. Indeed, for the proof we would need to present the whole subtree that is generated by the sequence itself, the bounds (light grey nodes) and the proofs of the bounds. Assuming that the attributes x_i and the search keys are k bits long and that the proofs themselves are thus $k \log_2 n$ bits in the worst case (n being the number of the records in the database) we get the length of the whole proof to be approximately

$$(m - 1)k + 4k \log_2 n = mk \left(1 + 4\frac{\log_2 n}{m} - \frac{1}{m}\right)$$

where m is the length of the interval.

In what follows, we explore the ways of decreasing this length as the obtained linear estimate would in practice mean that cryptographic codes could potentially from a significant percentage of the response size.

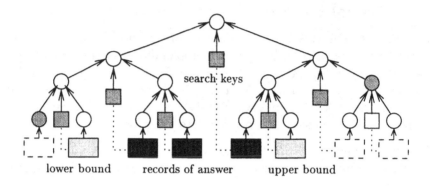

lower bound   records of answer   upper bound

Figure 4. Authentication of the interval. Medium grey nodes (elements of the proof) represent the information needed for authentication

3.2   Encoding the Structure of the Tree

The main idea behind saving the space is the observation that most of the search keys in the proof (the ones that fit into the interval $[a, b]$) can be computed from the records in the response. However, we must preserve the structure of the tree so we know which arguments to combine together. One of the simplest methods of representing a binary tree is to use the following encoding rules:

- The code of one-node tree is 0.

- If r is the root of tree T and T_0 and T_1 are corresponding left and right subtrees of the root r (with codes K_0 and K_1, respectively) then the code of tree T is $1K_0K_1$.

This encoding works if we do not have any nodes with one and only one descendant in the tree. Fortunately our current data structures conform to this condition: the data is in the leaves and there is no point of keeping a node with only one descendant in the tree.

A subtree along with the encoding corresponding to the proof is shown in Figure 5. Note that the number of zeroes in the code corresponds to the number of leaves l and the length of the code is equal to the number

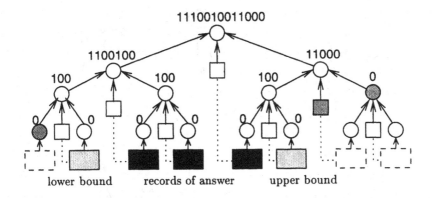

Figure 5. Proof based on encoding of subtree

of nodes in the subtree. Thus the length of the code is $2l - 1$. The length of the whole proof is approximately

$$2(m - 1) + 4k \log_2 n = 2m \left(1 + 2k \frac{\log_2 n}{m} - \frac{1}{m} \right)$$

which (for large values of m) is about $k/2$ times less than in case of the trivial solution but remains still linear in the length of the interval m.

Note that for example the balancing procedures of AVL trees preserve the search keys in the nodes, i.e. the search key in the node always shows the minimal element of the right subtree. To show this simple fact we present a figure with balancing procedures of AVL trees: rotation (Figure 6, left) and double rotation (Figure 6, right). Thus the encoding of tree structure is indeed sufficient for presenting the proof in AVL trees.

3.3   Canonical Data Structures

To get rid of linear dependence on the length of the interval we must leave out the description of the structure of the subtree from the proof. However we can not just throw the description away because in an l-variable groupoid expression there are exactly

$$C_l = l^{-1} \binom{2l - 2}{l - 1}$$

possible placements of parentheses (and corresponding binary tree structures). This is about $2^l/l$ and so a verification algorithm trying all the possibilities would have too high time complexity. This consideration

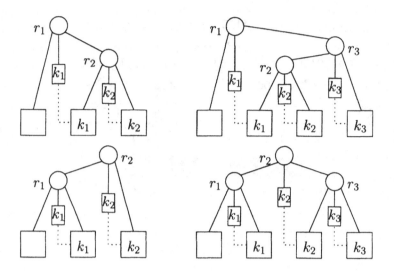

Figure 6.   Preservation of search keys while balancing the search tree

gives us the absolute minimum of the number of bits required to represent the structure of the tree. We get

$$\log_2 C_l = \log_2 \binom{2l-2}{l-1} - \log_2 l \approx l - \log_2 l.$$

So the only possibility to decrease the size of the proof seems to be the usage of so-called canonical data structures where the shape of the subtree is uniquely derivable from the records in the interval.

Consider some sequence $(x_1, f(x_1)), (x_2, f(x_2)), \ldots, (x_n, f(x_n))$ with n elements. Let $h = \lfloor \log_2(n) \rfloor$ and T_0 represent a full binary tree with 2^h leaves. Define a new node r_0 so that T_0 is the left subtree for the node r_0. Elements $(x_1, f(x_1)), \ldots, (x_{2^h}, f(x_{2^h}))$ are stored as the leaves of the subtree T_0 and the rest of $n - 2^h$ elements form a new sequence. Now we do the same procedure recursively with the new sequence.

Assume that the tree T_1 was constructed from the rest of the elements and r_1 was a new node above it. We make r_1 to be the right ancestor for the node r_0 and now we have a new tree T with the root r_0. The search key in root r_0 is defined as the least element of subtree T_1 (i.e. x_{2^h+1}). The resulting binary tree is an example of canonical search structure.

If now $(x_{l+1}, f(x_{l+1})), (x_{l+2}, f(x_{l+2})), \ldots, (x_{l+m}, f(x_{l+m}))$ is some interval of m records then the structure of the subtree generated by that interval depends only on:

- n – total number of records in the database;

- l – initial point of the interval;

- m – length of the interval.

The size of each of these numbers is $\log_2(n)$ and size of one authentication path is $k\log_2 n$ so the size of the whole proof is $ck\log_2(n)$ for some constant c.

3.4   Can a Canonical Search Tree be Efficiently Balanced?

The main shortcoming of the canonical search tree described above is the absence of efficient balancing procedures. Their complexity seems to be linear in the number of records (for example, consider adding a new element in front of all others — Figure 7) which means that it is unlikely that anyone would use this data structure in large databases. On the other hand, for large databases decreasing the proof's contribution is especially important.

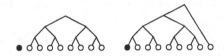

Figure 7.   Re-balancing of a canonical search tree

If we use just the sequence numbers of the records in the database to construct the search tree, either the insertion of a record in front of the others or appending a record after the others causes re-parenting of all (or a fixed percentage of) the records in the resulting sequence. Thus the complexity of re-balancing becomes linear to the number of records in the sequence (as in Figure 7). This can be proved if we assume that we don't have nodes with single descendant and each node has a fixed limit on the number of descendants.

So we cannot use just the sequence numbers of the records in database to construct efficiently balanced canonical search trees. It is still open whether different kinds of search trees exist that are efficiently balanced. In particular, it looks promising to build the trees not by using the sequence number but the contents of the records. The contents of existing records don't change when new records are added an so we can change the tree only locally and recompute the hashes to the top. This should give us logarithmic complexity. The construction of these search trees is a problem for future research and is not covered in this paper.

4. Open Problems

As mentioned above it would be very interesting and useful to explore the problem of the existence of efficiently balanced canonical search trees.

The concrete structures of authenticated search trees need to be more precise and the idea of using them needs to be worked trough in detail. The preliminary results allow us to affirm that this direction promises interesting and useful results the in theory of databases as well as in applied cryptography. Extending the concept to multidimensional search trees is also necessary.

So far we have only dealt with databases (data tables) with one relation. It would be interesting to investigate a possibility of creating authenticated search structures into any relation algebra which is going to be one of the next topics to investigate.

References

[1] Ansper, A., Buldas, A., Roos, M., and Willemson, J. Efficient long-term validation of digital signatures. In Advances in Cryptology - PKC 2001, Springer Verlag, February 2001, pp. 402–415.

[2] Buldas, A., Laud, P., and Lipmaa, H. Accountable Certificate Management using Undeniable Attestations. In Sushil Jajodia and Pierangela Samarati, editors, 7th ACM Conference on Computer and Communications Security, ACM Press, November 2000, pp. 9–18.

[3] Devanbu, P., Gertz, M., Kwong, A., Martel, C., Nuckolls, G., and Stubblebine, S. Flexible authentication of xml documents, 2001.

[4] Diffie, W. and Hellman, M. New directions in cryptography. IEEE Transactions on Information Theory, 1976, 22: 644–654.

[5] Kohnfelder, L. M. Toward a practical public-key cryptosystem. 1978.

[6] Martel, C., Nuckolls, G., Devanbu, P., Gertz, M., Kwong, A., and Stubblebine, S. General model for authentic data publication, 2000.

[7] Menezes, A. J., van Oorshot, P. C., and Vanstone, S. A. Handbook of Applied Cryptography. CRC Press, Boca Raton, New York, London, Tokyo, 1997.

[8] Merkle, R. C. Protocols for public key cryptosystems. In Proceedings of the 1980 IEEE Symposium on Security and Privacy, IEEE Computer Society Press, April 1980, pp. 122–134.

[9] Myers, M., Ankney, R., Malpani, A., Galperin, S., and Adams, C. RFC2560: X.509 Internet Public Key Infrastructure Online Certificate Status Protocol - OCSP. June 1999.

TOLAP

Temporal Online Analytical Processing

Olaf Herden

Oldenburg Research and Development Institute
for Computer Science Tools and Systems (OFFIS),
Escherweg 2, 26121 Oldenburg, Germany
olaf.herden@offis.de

Abstract   This paper deals with temporal aspects in data warehouses and their effects on Online Analytical Processing (OLAP) environments. After sketching the multidimensional data model and demonstrating a conventional OLAP architecture the term Temporal OLAP (TOLAP) is introduced. A TOLAP environment is an extended conventional OLAP environment being able to handle temporal data. We choose a metadata based approach where all temporal information are stored in a repository and no modifications to the data warehouse itself are necessary. Furthermore, we propose coloured tables for the presentation of results at the end user's client.

Keywords: data warehouse, OLAP, temporal database.

1.   Introduction

Data Warehouses (DWH) have been established as the core of decision support systems [17]. A DWH is characterised as 'a subject–oriented, integrated, time–variant and non–volatile collection of data in support of management's decision making processes' [10]. On top of a DWH different applications, particularly with regard to decision support, can be realised. Beside conventional reporting, OLAP (Online Analytical Processing) has reached maturity as an interactive and explorative way of accessing data [6, 9].

One important application domain for DWHs and OLAP is the analysis of an enterprise's sales [18]. Questions like 'How many times have products of a specific group been sold in the last few years?' have to be answered, for example. But today's DWHs are mostly organised as snapshot databases. For this reason some important tasks cannot be

H.-M. Haav and A. Kalja (eds.), Databases and Information Systems II, 55–66.
© *2002 Kluwer Academic Publishers.*

answered sufficiently — e. g. in order to control the success of a reorganisation of the product assortment it is necessary to compare the sales of old and new products.

On the other hand, there has been deep research (but not with regard to DWHs) on temporal databases so far [11, 15]. Amongst other things temporal databases allow to assign a valid time to data. Thereby a past state of data can be reconstructed during retrieval.

The combination of DWHs and OLAP on the one side and temporal aspects on the other side has not been handled in depth so far. Consequently, important questions like 'Show all sales considering the assortment structure of last year' cannot be answered sufficiently with today's systems.

We propose an extension of existing DWH/OLAP environments by temporal aspects. Therefore we need valid time information about dimensional data. These additional information is stored in a metadata repository, the schema of the DWH remains untouched. The OLAP server is extended to be able to execute temporal queries. When using this kind of queries some effects can occur — e. g. some elements are not valid at a special time. To treat this problem we propose to use coloured tables for the explicit presentation of these effects.

The remainder of the paper is organised as follows: Section 2 sketches the multidimensional data model, DWHs and OLAP. In section 3, we introduce TOLAP (Temporal OLAP) by extending a conventional OLAP environment. Section 4 shows the application of this architecture and demonstrates the feasibility by some examples. Moreover, the coloured tables are introduced in this section. The paper closes with a summary and an outlook on future work.

2. Multidimensional Data Model and OLAP

This section sketches the state of the art by introducing the fundamentals of the multidimensional data model, describing a conventional OLAP environment, and reflecting some related work in the area of temporal data in DWHs.

2.1 Multidimensional Data Model

Data in a DWH are integrated from different operational systems of an organisation, potentially supplemented by data from external systems. Modelling these data is typically done multidimensionally [13, 12, 2]. The main characteristic of the multidimensional model is the separation of data into facts and dimensions. While facts (also called measures or quantitative data) are numerical values describing an aspect being relevant for analysis, dimensions (also called qualifying data) are expressing the user's view of data.

Imagine an organisation's sales the number of sold articles is an important topic with respect to analysis and can be identified as fact. Time, space and product are qualifying dimensions. The combination of a fact and its dimensions is called (hyper)cube.

For providing information on a suitable level of granularity for analysis, data in dimensions may be grouped into hierarchies. In our example, branches might be aggregated to cities and these in turn are summarised to regions. Elements on the same level of granularity belong to one dimensional level. The hierarchy tree of a dimension is defined by the dimension's instances as nodes and their aggregation relationships as edges.

2.2   OLAP: Architecture, Query Language and Presentation

Besides conventional reporting the multidimensional view of data also enables explorative and interactive data analysis. This process is called OLAP (Online Analytical Processing) [7, 16, 3].

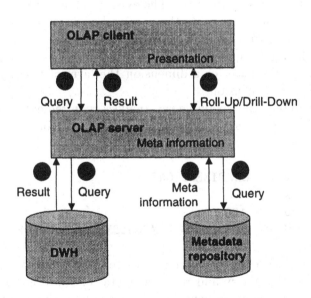

Figure 1.   Conventional OLAP architecture

During this process the user also has a multidimensional view of the data and may operate on the cube, e.g. by navigating along the hierarchies. Going down to a level of finer granularity is called *Drill–Down*, the inverse operation is referred to as *Roll–Up*. Typically OLAP environments are realised as three tier architectures [4, 8, 14] as depicted in figure 1. The client provides an user interface to receive the user's analysis instructions as well as a component for result presentation. The OLAP server handles the query processing, and the storage layer consists of the DWH and a metadata repository. This repository stores information about facts, dimensions and hierarchies as well as details about the implementation.

Typically, the user makes his requirements to the client via a graphical interface. The client translates these requirements into a SQL–like presentation having a syntax like this:

```
SELECT <Fact>,<Dimension>
   FROM <Cube>
   [WHERE <Expression>]
   {WITH GRANULARITY <Level> ON DIMENSION <Dimension>
      [WHERE <Expression>]};
```

The SELECT clause specifies the fact the user wants to analyse and the FROM clause names its cube. The expression in the WHERE clause allows a restriction to the facts that are to be retrieved. By specifying a level we can determine on which degree of granularity the data of this dimension should be queried. When leaving out the optional WITH GRANULARITY clause for a dimension the level of finest granularity is chosen for this dimension.

Referring to our sales example the analysis requirement 'Show me the numbers of all products sold more than one hundred times in city A' can be expressed as:

```
SELECT Number, ALL_DIMENSIONS
   FROM Sales
   WHERE Number > 100
   WITH GRANULARITY City ON DIMENSION Space WHERE City='A';
```

Defining such a query corresponds to step 1 in figure 1. The OLAP server receives this query and retrieves meta information about the selected cube and its implementation by executing the steps 2 and 3. Under consideration of this information the OLAP server queries the DWH (steps 4 and 5) and returns the result to the client (step 6). The client presents the data to the user. During the following analysis process (step 7) the OLAP Server can reuse the meta information determined in step 2 and 3. Navigation on the cube is specified by the statements ROLL-UP <Dimension>.<Level> and DRILL-DOWN <Dimension>.<Level>, respectively, whereby the corresponding dimension level is changed. For example DRILL-DOWN Space.Branch will show us the more detailed information of sold products in a branch.

In case of two dimensions, the result can be depicted in terms of a flat table. In case of more than two dimensions, nested tables are used [16]. Figure 2 gives an example of a nested result and its modification by applying the *ROLL-UP* operator[1].

ROLL-UP Product.Group

	2000		2001	
	North	South	North	South
VCR Type 1	100	150	150	100
VCR Type 2	200	250	250	200
VCR Type 3	150	100	150	150
Camcorder Type 1	400	400	400	450
Camcorder Type 2	500	600	550	600

	2000		2001	
	North	South	North	South
VCR	450	500	550	450
Camcorder	900	1000	950	1050

Figure 2. Nested table and the ROLL-UP operator

2.3 Temporal Data in DWHs

Within a cube the facts have an implicit valid time, assigned by their time dimension. In contrast, the dimensional elements have the character of a snapshot database. However, this kind of handling data and dimensional structures does not fulfill all requirements in practical use of OLAP. For example, the product assortment can change over time, e. g. a product can vanish or a new one can be added, or the hierarchical structure can be modified, e. g. a product moves from one product group into another one.

In this case, a typical analysis requirement is to compare the new grouping with the old one [1]. In order to solve this problem, [5] proposes to annotate the edges of a hierarchy tree with valid time intervals. Unit of these intervals' borders is the level of finest granularity of the time dimension. This meta information is defined for every hierarchy in the schema. The structure is named *valid time matrix*. In this matrix the parent nodes are the rows and the children nodes are the columns, every cell takes a set of valid time intervals. Figure 3 depicts the hierarchy tree of the product dimension for the years 2000 and 2001 and the corresponding valid time matrix. The VCRs type 1 and 2 and both camcorders are assigned to their product groups over all the time. VCR type 3 has been removed from the assortment at the end of 2000, and the types 4 and 5 belong to the assortment since 2001.

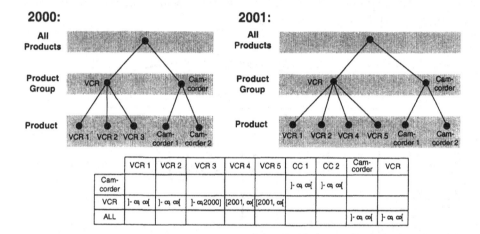

	VCR 1	VCR 2	VCR 3	VCR 4	VCR 5	CC 1	CC 2	Cam-corder	VCR
Cam-corder						]- ∞, ∞[	]- ∞, ∞[		
VCR	]- ∞, ∞[	]- ∞, ∞[	]- ∞,2000]	[2001, ∞[	[2001, ∞[				
ALL								]- ∞, ∞[	]- ∞, ∞[

Figure 3.   Hierarchy trees and corresponding valid time matrix

3.   Extensions for the Management of Temporal Data

In this section the concepts and architecture described before will be extended to enable Temporal OLAP (TOLAP). TOLAP environments allow the formulation of queries containing valid time. These queries can be processed by the TOLAP server and a TOLAP client is able to present the results. Accordingly the query language, the OLAP Server and the presentation at the user interface have to be extended.

3.1   Extension of the Query Language

When formulating a TOLAP query we have to fix a valid time for every dimension. Therefore the query language is extended by a WITH TIME <Date> ON DIMENSION <Dimension> clause. This clause specifies which dimensional elements are used by the subsequent OLAP process. For each dimension (except the time dimension) the user is required to select exactly one valid time. Again, the finest granularity of the time dimension is used as time unit.

Assuming that the product assortment as well as the space dimension have been changed from 2000 to 2001, we may formulate the following query in order to retrieve information on the sales of the products of 2000 in the regional structures of 2001.

```
SELECT Number, ALL_DIMENSIONS
   FROM Sales
   WITH GRANULARITY Group ON DIMENSION Product
   WITH GRANULARITY Branch ON DIMENSION Space
   WITH TIME 2000 ON DIMENSION Product
   WITH TIME 2001 ON DIMENSION Space;
```

3.2 Extension of the OLAP Architecture

The OLAP architecture from figure 1 has to be modified as follows: information about valid time has to be stored in the metadata repository, the OLAP server must be able to receive queries with valid time clauses and the communication between OLAP server and metadata repository has to be extended to store versioned meta information. Figure 4 shows the extended architecture in which the modified components are emphasised by a dark grey.

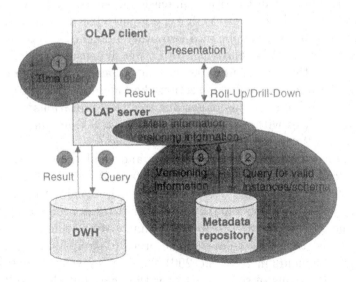

Figure 4.   TOLAP architecture

The TOLAP architecture works as follows: the client submits a query with valid time to the server (step 1), the server interprets this query and calculates which version should be used for which dimension. Then the server queries the metadata repository to retrieve the valid instances for the desired valid time (step 2 and 3). By using this information the OLAP server can query the DWH (step 4) in the acquainted way.

3.3 Extension of the Presentation Component

During the analysis phase (steps 6 and 7), the presentation component of the TOLAP environment should show the user which data are affected by the temporal query. The presentation should indicate whether data are (aggregated) fact data in the DWH or whether they have been transformed into another dimensional structure, for example. An appropriate choice for visualisation are coloured tables, supplemented by a legend which explains the colourings. These aspects will be treated more detailled in the next section.

4. TOLAP at Work: Updates at the Instance Level

To put the exposition from the last section into concrete terms we distinguish between updates at the instance level with and without dependencies. For example, the appearance of a new VCR or closing a branch can be classified as an instance change without dependency because both events are independent of the other dimensional elements. In contrast a dependency exists when a new VCR type is introduced as successor of an old type or a branch is split into two other branches — the new instances have some kind of relationship to other dimensional elements in this case. While the case of updates without dependencies is described in detail in the remainder of this section the handling of updates with dependencies is left out in this paper due to space limitations[2].

In case of updates without dependencies the valid time matrix introduced in section 2 can be used as metadata structure.

Under the assumption of the hierarchies and valid time matrix from figure 3, figure 5 depicts a possible analysis trace. As result of the initial query we get a coloured table with a legend which explains the meaning of the colourings: the grey colour indicates that these products did not belong to the assortment at the specified time. After rolling up we get another coloured table. By colouring the product group VCR that contains different elements in 2000 and 2001 the user is given a hint that he may compare the sums of sold VCRs over the years but the result is of limited expressiveness, e. g. the increasing sales of VCRs in the example is caused by the change of the product assortment and the hierarchy, respectively. Additional information for the user is not necessary at this point because the effect of different grouping can be compensated by drilling down again.

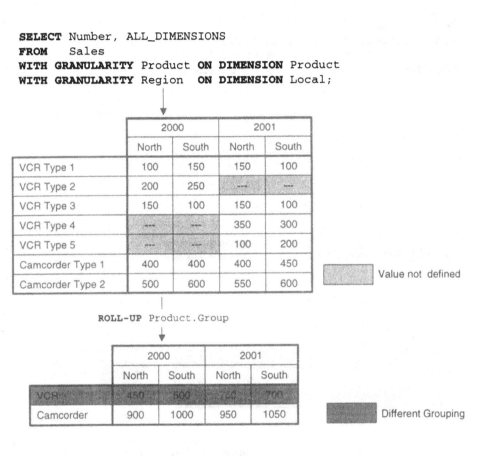

```
SELECT Number, ALL_DIMENSIONS
FROM    Sales
WITH GRANULARITY Product ON DIMENSION Product
WITH GRANULARITY Region  ON DIMENSION Local;
```

	2000		2001	
	North	South	North	South
VCR Type 1	100	150	150	100
VCR Type 2	200	250	---	---
VCR Type 3	150	100	150	100
VCR Type 4	---	---	350	300
VCR Type 5	---	---	100	200
Camcorder Type 1	400	400	400	450
Camcorder Type 2	500	600	550	600

Value not defined

ROLL-UP Product.Group

	2000		2001	
	North	South	North	South
VCR	450	500	750	700
Camcorder	900	1000	950	1050

Different Grouping

Figure 5. Simple TOLAP analysis

When using a valid time clause within a query another kind of time effect may appear. Instances being not valid at the selected time would be omitted but they should be grouped into the special pseudo group 'OTHER'. When executing the query at the top of figure 6 the OLAP server asks the metadata repository for products valid in 2000 and receives the set {VCR Type 1, VCR Type 2, VCR Type 3, Camcorder 1, Camcorder 2}. The VCR types 4 and 5 were not known in 2000 but the scope of the whole query also contains 2001. Therefore the sales values for unknown types are summarised in the row 'OTHER'. After executing a ROLL–UP the composition of the VCR group differs again and thus has to be marked.

```
SELECT Number, ALL_DIMENSIONS
FROM    Sales
WITH GRANULARITY Product ON DIMENSION Product
WITH GRANULARITY Region  ON DIMENSION Local
WITH TIME        2000     ON DIMENSION Product;
```

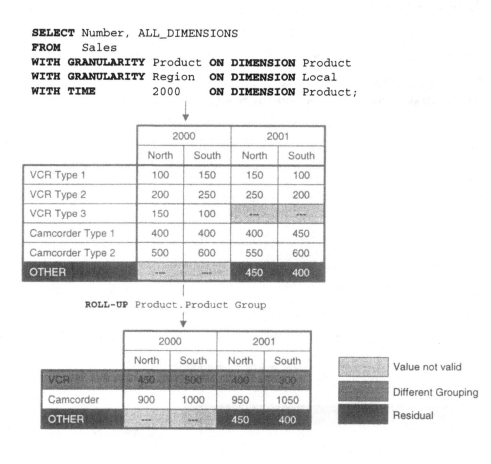

Figure 6. TOLAP analysis with valid time

The lower part of figure 6 shows three different colourings reflecting the effects which are occuring by the time query:

- one for instances not valid at this time (light grey),

- one for groupings with the same name but different elements (middle grey) and

- one for residual values excluded from the chosen valid time for the dimension (dark grey).

While the first one is a piece of information for the user and the second can be solved by drilling down, the last entry of the legend should be combined with an offer to the user for getting additional information. In the example depicted in figure 6 there should be given an explanation which instances are hidden behind 'OTHER' because the drill down operator cannot be applied to this pseudo group.

5.   Summary and Outlook

After an introduction we sketched the multidimensional data model and a conventional OLAP architecture that does not consider time aspects. Moreover, we have pointed out that a fact is time stamped implicitly by its time dimension. The management of valid time for dimensions requires additional meta structures. Then we proposed an extension of the conventional OLAP architecture in order to handle temporal data. We called this a TOLAP (Temporal OLAP) architecture. The extension concerns the OLAP server, the client and the metadata repository, while the DWH remains untouched. The approach allows the administration of modifications at the instance level. Finally, we demonstrated the operation of the TOLAP system by several examples of a sales cube. The results of querying the TOLAP server were presented to the user in terms of coloured tables.

To enforce the research topic TOLAP, we want to tackle the following tasks in the nearest future:

- The communication between the OLAP server and the metadata repository has to be refined.

- Efficient algorithms for recalculation need to be determined. Especially redundancy of recalculated and mapped values has to be considered.

- The OLAP language ought to be extended by a statement that allows to change a dimension's valid time during analysis.

- Besides updates at the instance level also schema evolutions may be considered.

66

Notes

1. For reasons of simplicity all examples in this paper use the SUM-operator.

2. Information about this topic can be requested by the author via email.

References

[1] Anahory, S. and Murray, D. Data Warehousing in the Real World: A Practical Guide for Building Decision Support Systems. Addison–Wesley, June 1997.

[2] Barquin, R. and Edelstein, H. Building, Using, and Managing the Data Warehouse. Prentice Hall, 1997.

[3] Berson, A. and Smith, S. Data Warehousing, Data Mining, and OLAP. McGraw-Hill, 1st ed., 1997.

[4] Business Objects Inc.. Homepage BusinessObjects.
http://www.businessobjects.com/, 2002.

[5] Chamoni, P. and Stock, S. Temporale Daten in Management Support Systemen (in German), Wirtschaftsinformatik, vol. 40, December 1998, pp. 513–519.

[6] Chaudhuri, S. and Dayal, U. An Overview of Data Warehousing and OLAP Technology, SIGMOD Record, vol. 26, March 1997.

[7] Codd, E., Codd, S., and Salley, C. Providing OLAP to User-Analysis: An IT-Mandate. Hyperion Solutions, 1993.

[8] Cognos Inc.. Homepage Cognos. http://www.cognos.com/, 2002.

[9] Colliat, G. OLAP, Relational, and Multidimensional Database Systems, SIGMOD Record, vol. 25, no. 3, 1996, pp. 64–69.

[10] Inmon, W. Building the Data Warehouse. John Wiley & Sons, Inc., 1st ed., 1992.

[11] Jensen, C., Clifford, J., Elmasri, R., Gadia, S., Hayes, P., and Jajodia, S.
A Consensus Glossary of Temporal Database, SIGMOD Record, vol. 23, January 1994.

[12] Kimball, R. Meta Meta Data Data. Making a List of Data About Metadata and Exploring Information Cataloging Tools, DBMS Online, March 1998. .

[13] Kimball, R. The Data Warehouse Toolkit. John Wiley & Sons, Inc., 1996.

[14] Oracle Inc.. Homepage Oracle. http://www.oracle.com/, 2002.

[15] Snodgrass, R., ed. The TSQL2 Temporal Query Language. Kluwer Academic Publishers, 1995.

[16] Thomsen, E. OLAP Solutions – Building Multidimensional Information Systems. John Wiley & Sons, Inc., 1st ed., 1997.

[17] Turban, E., Aronson, J., and Aronson, J. Decision Support Systems and Intelligent Systems. Prentice Hall, 6th ed., 2000.

[18] Westerman, P. Data Warehousing: Using the Wal–Mart Model. Morgan Kaufmann, 1st ed., 2000.

XML DATA WAREHOUSE: MODELLING AND QUERYING

Jaroslav Pokorny
Faculty of Mathematics and Physics, Charles University, Prague, Czech Republic

Abstract   A large amount of heterogeneous information is now available in enterprises. Some their data sources are repositories of XML data or they are viewed as XML data independently on their inner implementation. In this paper, we study the foundations of XML data warehouses. We adapt the traditional star schema with explicit dimension hierarchies for XML environment. We propose the notion of XML-referential integrity for handling XML-dimension hierarchies. For querying XML data warehouses, we introduce a semijoin operation based on approximate matching XML data and discuss its effective evaluation.

Keywords: XML, data warehouse, dimension, XML-star schema, XML-referential integrity, semijoin

1.   Introduction

A large amount of heterogeneous information is now available in enterprises. Such data stores may be classical formatted databases but also data collections coming from e-mail communication, e-business, or from inner digital documents that are produced by enterprise applications.

A data warehouse (DW) is an integrated repository of data generated from many sources and used by the entire enterprise. The dimensional model (DM) is a logical representation of a business process whose main features are user understandability, query performance and usefulness for reporting, issue resolution, and predictive modelling. As the viable technique in DW environment, DM is widely accepted. A usual approach to DM is based on dimension and fact tables grouped into a structure called a star schema.

In a real environment of the enterprise, it is not too hard to imagine that some its data sources are repositories of XML data or that they are viewed as

H.-M. Haav and A. Kalja (eds.), Databases and Information Systems II, 67–80.

XML data independently on their inner implementation. An increasing interest appears to conceive XML data as database data [1] or, particularly, as DW data. In [10] we tried to build a DW over XML data, i.e. we supposed that dimensional data is XML data. The notion of DM was modified and accommodated substantially and a star schema structure with explicit hierarchies [9] was used as a basic data structure in the new approach to XML-based DW. We assumed XML data equipped by Document Type Definitions (DTD). Then, on the schema level, a particular dimension is modelled as a sequence of DTDs that are logically associated by so called XML-referential integrity. Obviously, facts may be modelled as XML data as well.

XML data is traditionally divided into two categories: document centric and data centric. The former has only few, interspersed mark-ups, the latter is solely created and interpreted by some application logic. We suppose rather data centric XML data for our DW. However, the information in an XML DW is never complete. It follows from the possibilities of XML data specification via regular expressions allowed by DTDs. Consequently, only partial (or approximate) matching of XML data is appropriate for testing if the referential integrity is satisfied by two XML collections.

Having such a theoretical framework for XML-based DW, a natural question is arising: how to query such data in practice. In other words, usual approaches to querying stars should be reformulated. We design a basic algorithm for this purpose. It uses a semijoin operation accommodated for XML data.

The paper is organized as follows. Section 2 shortly introduces the main concepts. In Section 3 we give a brief overview over XML and present a tree model for XML data and DTDs. Section 4 defines notions needed for characterization of XML collections, for specifying XML-referential integrity, and for establishing dimensions over XML data. We define XML-star schemes with explicit dimension hierarchies and dimensional XML-databases. We also design an algorithm, which makes it possible to extract fact data from a dimensional XML-database. We conclude by a discussion of some decisions chosen in the approach, summarize results and point out further research issues.

2. Dimension Modelling and Tables

Informally a *DM-schema* is a description of *dimension* and *fact tables*. An associated diagram is called *DM-diagram*. A variant of this approach is called a *star schema*, i.e. the case with one fact table surrounded by dimension tables. Each dimension table has a single-part primary key that corresponds exactly to one of the components of the multi-part key in the fact table. Attributes of dimension tables (*dimension attributes*) are used as a source of constraints usable in DW queries. A *fact* is a focus of interest for the enterprise. It is modelled by values of non-key attributes in the fact table that functionally depend on the set of key attributes. Each fact is "measured" by values of a tuple of dimension values.

2.1 Dimension Hierarchies

On the conceptual level, particular members of each dimension hierarchy are sets of entities that can be described as entity types. Although more complex hierarchies are distinguished in literature, we keep to *simple hierarchies*, whose members compose a path in a directed graph. Consequently, we can model such hierarchies by a chain of tables connected by logical references (foreign keys).

The notions can be formalized following [9]. We consider *dimension table schemes* $D_i(\Omega_i)$, $i=1,\ldots,n$, $n\geq1$, and a *fact table schema* $F(\Omega)$, where Ω_i and Ω are sets of attributes. One attribute from Ω_i is called the *key* of D_i table and is denoted KD_i. The *key of F* is $\cup_{i=1..n} KD_i$.

Other (non-key) attributes of F are usually called *facts*. We call such fact table schema F *specified w.r.t.* dimension table schemes $D_i(\Omega_i)$, $i=1,\ldots,n$. Extensions of table schemes are sets of rows similarly as in relational databases. We call them *tables*. We use upper letters D, F, ... for table schemes and D^*, F^*, ... for tables.

Definition 1 (Dimension Hierarchy): Let D be a set of dimension table schemes. Then a *(simple) dimension hierarchy N* is a pair <H, CC>, where H is specified as

    (a) $H \subseteq D \times D$ or $\{D\}$, $D \in D$,

    (b) H is an acyclic path, and

    (c) $CC = \{CC_{ij} \mid (D_i, D_j) \in H\}$. Each CC_{ij} is defined syntactically as follows:

        if KD_j is the key of D_j, then KD_j is also an attribute of D_i.

Ds in H are called *members* of N. We write usually $N: D_1 \rightarrow \ldots \rightarrow D_k$. From the condition (c) we can observe that KD_j in D_i is a foreign key in the same sense as in the logical connection of F to a dimension table. Condition (b) implies the existence of a unique *root* member of H. Actually, facts in F table are usually directly dependent on data stored in root tables.

Let D_i^* and D_j^* be tables. The *cardinality constraint* CC_{ij} is *satisfied* by these tables when for each row u from D_i^* there is only one row v in D_j^*, such that $u.KD_j = v.KD_j$. The tables of a hierarchy N are *admissible for* N if they satisfy all cardinality constraints from CC.

2.2   Stars with Explicit Dimension Hierarchies

We will use explicit hierarchies in star schemes [9]. This approach, known also as snowflakes, is useful for querying a database equipped by such schema.

Definition 2 (Star Schema with Explicit Dimension Hierarchies): Let N be a non-empty set of dimension hierarchies, D_N the set of their hierarchy roots, and F a fact table schema specified w.r.t. D_N. A *star schema with explicit dimension hierarchies* is a pair <N, F>.

A fragment of a DM-diagram is depicted in Figure 1. It follows from definition F that the cardinality constraint is defined between F and each root table of N, for each $N \in N$.

A *dimensional database S^* over a star schema with explicit hierarchies S* is a set of dimension tables and a fact table. For each $N \in N$ the associated dimension tables must be admissible for N. Also F and the root table of N must satisfy the cardinality constraint.

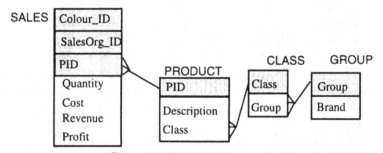

Figure 1. A fact table schema and a dimension hierarchy

Observe that rows of the fact table and of its any dimension table are in many-to-one relationship. CCs also imply that there is a referential integrity between F and each N root as well as between each two adjacent members of N.

3.   Basics for XML

The data in XML [13] is grouped into *elements* by *tags*. XML elements may contain attributes. Subelements' nesting is specified by regular expressions. An XML document *valid* w.r.t a DTD can be the root in any element specified in the DTD. An example of DTD is in Figure 3. The document in Figure 2 is valid w.r.t. this DTD.

```
<catalogue>
<product pid = "PA312">
    <name> Canon 246/V </name>
    <description>A thing...<description>
    <class> camera </class>
    <dealer did = "K2OP1">
        <d_name>J.Smith </d_name>
        <address >
            <locality> Edinburgh
            </locality>
            <ZIP> E12 8QQ </ZIP>
        </address>
    <dealer>
</product>
<product pid = "PA108">
    <name> Sony III </name>
    <description> A tool <description>
    <class> CD player </class>
</product>
</catalogue>
```

```
<!DOCTYPE catalogue[
<!ELEMENT catalogue(product)*>
<!ELEMENT product(name,
        description, class, dealer?)>
<!ATTLIST product pid ID #REQUIRED>
<!ELEMENT dealer (d_name, contact?,
                        address*)>
<!ATTLIST dealer did ID #REQUIRED>
<!ELEMENT name PCDATA>
<!ELEMENT d_name PCDATA>
<!ELEMENT description  PCDATA>
<!ELEMENT address(locality, ZIP)>
<!ELEMENT locality PCDATA >
<!ELEMENT ZIP PCDATA >
<!ELEMENT contact(fax |phone)
<!ELEMENT fax PCDATA >
<!ELEMENT phone PCDATA >
]>
```

Figure 2. XML document describing a
catalogue

Figure 3. DTD catalogue

Applications of XML require appropriate models both of XML data and DTDs. For example, XML-graphs are well-known as a tool for describing semantics of XML-based query languages (e.g. XML-QL [3]). Tree- and graph-oriented models are used also for DTDs (e.g. [7], [11]). For the sake of simplicity, most of the formal models neglect differences between attributes and elements and the ordering of elements.

In [10] we modified types of labelled ordered tree objects [11]. A *labelled ordered tree object* (*loto*) over a set of tags Σ is a finite tree such that each node has an associated tag from Σ and the set of children of a given node is totally ordered. For example, the loto corresponding to the XML document in Figure 2 is in Figure 4. A *loto type definition* (*ltd*) over Σ consists of a root type in Σ and a mapping associating a (regular) language L_m over Σ with each $m \in \Sigma$. For the root the mapping assigns the root element of the modelled DTD. Lotos can be associated with a ltd. Informally, a loto *satisfies* an ltd over Σ if its root has the type of ltd's root and for each of its nodes m the sequence of tags associated with children of m is a word of L_m. A set of lotos satisfying the ltd is denoted $T(\text{ltd})$. Observe that ltds do not contain PCDATA elements. In example of ltd in Figure 5 (without empty languages), e.g., the language L_{product} contains sequences (words) (name, description, class, dealer) and (name, description, class).

A key feature of our approach is the usage of XML views of XML data. They can be evaluated by standard view mechanisms, and used for integrity checking and query processing in XML DWs. Here, a *view V over a collection C* is given by a *view query* in a query language for XML data. By *materialization* of *V* in *C* we mean a set of XML data, denoted *V(C)*, which is obtainable by evaluating *V* on *C*. In particular, *V(C)* may be empty.

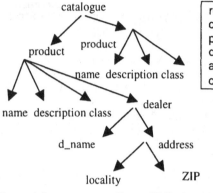

```
root: catalogue;
catalogue:product*;
product:(name, description, class, dealer?);
dealer:(d_name, contact?, address⁺);
address(locality, ZIP?);
contact(fax │phone);
```

Figure 5. Ltd for catalogue DTD

Figure 4. Loto corresponding to XML data in Figure 2

4. Re-building a Dimension Hierarchy from XML Data

We suppose XML collections $C_1, ..., C_n$, $n \geq 1$, and their respective DTDs $DTD_1 ... DTD_n$, $n \geq 1$. DTD_C denotes the DTD of *C*. A collection *C* contains valid XML data rooting in a DTD_C element. The collections may be independent in some sense, i.e. the same information can be represented in two documents with different DTDs in multiple ways, similarly as in distributed databases. Each collection can be a source for one or more dimension members of one or more dimensions. The overall architecture of XML-star schema is drawn in Figure 6.

The design of a dimension hierarchy means to explore dimension members and then logical associations among them (see Table 1).

4.1 How to Describe a Dimension Member

In task 1, we restrict the source DTD to a DTD_D that is more feasible for manipulation. We use a *subDTD* of the given DTD. By definition in [10], it is a DTD and describes XML data sufficient for the dimension member *D* specification. An extension D^* on *C* contains XML data valid w.r.t. DTD_D and having the same root element tag given in DOCTYPE clause of DTD_D. For example, DTD dealer in Figure 7 is a subDTD of DTD catalogue.

Observe, that e.g. the addresses that are not dealer addresses are not in Dealer*. Elements of subDTD **dealer** are also elements of **catalogue**.

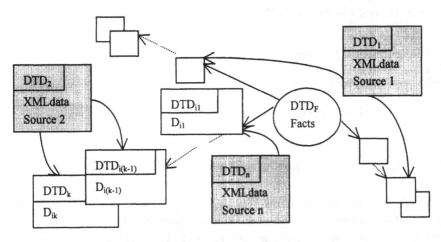

Figure 6. XML-star schema

Obviously, in a more general approach we could construct a structurally different DTD_D that is meaningful for defining a dimension member and is not a subDTD of DTD_C in our sense.

Table 1. From DTD to XML-referential integrity

	Task	Method	Result
1	finding the data in C which is essential for a dimension member D	design (informally from DTDs and/or with a conceptual schema)	DTD_D specification
2	choice of information (D-core) characterizing, perhaps uniquely, most of documents in D	design (informally from DTDs and/or with a conceptual schema)	D-core
		view specification of D-core by an XML query language	$V_{D\text{-core}}$
		finding DTD specification of D-core	$DTD_{D\text{-core}}$
3	forming the notion of the XML-referential integrity based on C-cores between C_1 and C_2	view specification of C_2-core in C_1 by an XML query language	$V_{(C1 \rightarrow C2)\text{-core}}$

```
<!DOCTYPE dealer[
<!ELEMENT dealer(d_name, contact?, address⁺)>
<!ELEMENT d_name PCDATA>
<!ELEMENT address(locality, ZIP?)>
<!ELEMENT locality PCDATA >
<!ELEMENT ZIP PCDATA >
<!ELEMENT contact(fax |phone)
<!ELEMENT fax PCDATA >
<!ELEMENT phone PCDATA >]
```

Figure 7. SubDTD for dealer

4.2   Characterisation of a Dimension Member

In task 2, we actually solve the problem of keys for XML data. In principle, the problem is associated with hierarchical keys [2]. First, we forget ID attributes as possible adepts for such keys. ID attributes are not scoped. Moreover, nobody can ensure their uniqueness in the environment of more XML collections. Similarly, attributes like SSN, InvoiceNo, etc. need not be also reliable. Also, XML data is usually repeating in *C*. Another problem concerns non-completeness of XML data. For example, the pair (name, address) of a dealer can serve as a key for dealers. But, due to the regular expressions used in DTD dealer, some dealer addresses contain ZIP data only optionally. Thus, our characterizations should meet weaker requirements than those for the keys in relational databases. They should

– distinguish any two XML documents in *D* as best as possible,
– be suitably simple,
– be XML data,
– be valid w.r.t. a DTD.

In [2], a key specification is a pair $(Q, \{P_1,...,P_n\})$, where Q is a path expression and $\{P_1,...,P_n\}$ is a set of simple path expressions[1]. The path expression Q identifies a set of nodes, which refer to the target set, on which the key constraint is to hold. Paths P_i specify sets of nodes. Consider the key specification (product, {name, description}). The target set is given by product element. If two products have the same name, then they must distinguish in their description.

Our approach is similar but not identical. We "cut of" paths Q via the subDTD concept, i.e. Q is empty (ε). We also do not use only simple paths. For example, for books such a key consists of ISBN, but probably (title, author*) is sufficient. In notation of [2] we would expressed the key as (ε, {title, author*}). Further, key specifications of [2] are directly on XML data

---

[1] Simple paths are merely sequences of elements tags.

level and not on the schema level, in the database terminology. There is also an approach to keys specified on the DTD level [4]. However, its authors consider keys based only on XML attributes.

We do not use the notion of key, because of vagueness of above requirements. The characterization of D in our approach is called *core* of D, shortly *D-core*. On the extension level we talk about *core elements*. Core elements satisfy the weak identifiability, i.e. each document from D generates one core element at most.

It is on the designer responsibility to ensure this integrity constraint. Unfortunately, it is not always possible to require this function to be total and injective. The rigidity of these properties inherited from the notion of primary key is here lost due to the incompleteness of XML data in D and its possible duplicates.

In [10] we have shown how
- to define the D-core data as a view V over D^*, and
- to find its $DTD_{D\text{-core}}$.

D-core should be expressible by a DTD. We use $DTD_{D\text{-core}}$ to denote such a DTD. XML data extracted from D^* and valid w.r.t. $DTD_{D\text{-core}}$ is called *D-core data*. We denote this data set by $T(DTD_{D\text{-core}})$. It is not always guaranteed that $T(DTD_{D\text{-core}})$ is exactly the data in materialization of the associated view [10].

For example, only one fax or one phone number is sufficient to identify a dealer. Then the associated view can be expressed in XML-QL language as in Figure 8. It provides "heterogeneous" core elements, with a fax or a phone for each dealer, who has the contact non-empty. The only user-defined tag used in queries is **dealer_core**. The associated DTD is in Figure 9

```
WHERE <dealer>
          <contact> $e </contact>
       </dealer> IN "http://kocour.cz/..."
CONSTRUCT <dealer_core>
            $e
          </dealer_core>
```

```
<!DOCTYPE dealer_core[
<!ELEMENT dealer_core (fax |phone)>
<!ELEMENT fax PCDATA >
<!ELEMENT phone PCDATA >]
```

Figure 8. A view query for Dealer-core   *Figure 9.* $DTD_{Dealer\text{-core}}$

4.3   XML-referential Integrity

The idea how to define the constraint XML-referential integrity for collections C_1 and C_2 is to connect logically those documents $d_1 \in C_1$ and $d_2 \in C_2$ that match on the core data described by $DTD_{C2\text{-core}}$. In other words, d_1

contains data, which is the same (in some sense), as the core data of d_2. C_2-core plays for DTD_{C1} the similar role as a foreign key in a relational database.

We specify a view, we denote it $V_{(C1 \rightarrow C2)\text{-core}}$, that generates XML data from C_1 of the same structure as the data valid w.r.t. $DTD_{C2\text{-Core}}$. We should also specify $DTD_{(C1 \rightarrow C2)\text{-core}}$. Note that since DTD_{C1} distinguishes from DTD_{C2}, and $V_{C2\text{-core}}$ and $V_{(C1 \rightarrow C2)\text{-core}}$ are different view queries, $DTD_{C2\text{-core}}$ and $DTD_{(C1 \rightarrow C2)\text{-core}}$ will be also different in general. On the other hand, we do not need to construct $DTD_{(C1 \rightarrow C2)\text{-core}}$ explicitly for specification of the XML-referential integrity. Any checking referential integrity is based on data from $V_{(C1 \rightarrow C2)\text{-core}}(C_1)$. Given $V_{(C1 \rightarrow C2)\text{-core}}$ and $DTD_{C2\text{-core}}$, it is decidable whether lotos associated with data from $V_{(C1 \rightarrow C2)\text{-core}}(C_1)$ are also lotos from $T(\text{ltd}_{C2\text{-core}})$ [11].

The problem of checking a referential integrity can be mapped to the problem of embedding a pattern tree in the tree determined by $V_{C2\text{-core}}(d_2)$. Obviously, unlike lotos the content of leaves must already be considered. We prefer partial matching of trees in which the mapping of the nodes of tree$_1$ to nodes of tree$_2$ preserves (1) labels, (2) types, and (3) parent-child relation. We denote the relation of partial matching by $\leq:$. Certainly, if $d_1 \leq: d_2$ and $d_2 \leq: d_1$, then $d_1 = d_2$. This equality is based on the fact that associated trees distinguish only in ordering of their elements. The partial (unordered) tree embedding problem, generally NP-complete, has an effective solution in practice [12]. The principle of the XML-referential integrity and its checking is shown in Figure 10.

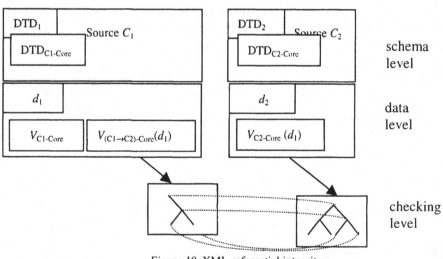

Figure 10. XML-referential integrity

There are more reasons why we do not prefer an exact matching. For example, different orders of elements in d_1 and d_2 can be supposed or $V_{C1 \rightarrow C2\text{-core}}(C_1)$ data occurs only partially in its pattern in C_2. A justification for the choice follows from the intuition that the dimension member D_i^* contains more information about an entity e than the linkage data of e in elements of D_{i-1}^*.

Definition 3 (XML-Referential Integrity): Let C_1 and C_2 be collections with DTD_{C1} and DTD_{C2}, respectively. Let $V_{C1\text{-core}}$ and $V_{C2\text{-core}}$ be views defining C_1- and C_2-core data, respectively. Then an *XML-referential integrity based on C-cores* is satisfied by C_1 and C_2 iff

$$\forall\ d_1 \in C_1 \exists\ d_2 \in C_2\ (V_{(C1\to C2)\text{-core}}(d_1) \leq: V_{C2\text{-core}}(d_2))$$

Observe, that the matching is automatically true if $V_{(C1\to C2)\text{-core}}(d_1)$ is empty. Thus, the definition behaves according to the notion of referential integrity given for relational databases in the SQL language [6]. For some d_1 there is no document d_2 having a link through C_2-core.

For collections C_1 and C_2, we denote the statement XML-referential integrity based on C-cores by $C_1 \subseteq: C_2$. Note that comparing the XML-referential integrity to the relational one, there may be more d_2 documents satisfying the condition from Definition 3.

5. XML-star Schema with Explicit Hierarchies

The notion of XML-star schema with explicit dimension hierarchies is formulated according to [10] as follows.

Definition 4 (XML-Dimension Hierarchy): Let $C_1,..., C_n, n \geq 1$, be a set of XML collections with their respective DTDs $DTD_1,..., DTD_n$. Let D be a set of DTDs whose each member is a subDTD of a DTD_i, $i \in <1,n>$, $DTD_{Di\text{-core}}$ describes its D_i-core. Then a *(simple) XML-dimension hierarchy N* is specified as

    (a) $N \subseteq D \times D$ or $\{D\}, D \in D$,

    (b) N is an acyclic path.

    (c) If $(D_i, D_{i+1}) \in H$, then $D_j \subseteq: D_{i+1}$.

Dimensional data for N: $D_1 \to ... \to D_k$, is given by the union of D_i^*, $i = 1,...,$ k, where for (D_i^*, D_{i+1}^*) the statement $D_i \subseteq: D_{i+1}$ is satisfied.

For the sake of simplicity, we represent fact data similarly to rows of a fact table, i.e. the resulted XML data is composed from homogenous elements each dimensional component of which will be in accordance with core data of the root of the associated dimension N. We say that DTD_F of such fact data *is specified* w.r.t. a set of hierarchy roots. Fact data is not discussed here.

Definition 5 (XML-Star Schema with Explicit Dimension Hierarchies): Let N be a non-empty set of XML-dimension hierarchies, D_N the set of their hierarchy roots, and F a DTD_F specified w.r.t. D_N. Then an *XML-star schema with explicit dimension hierarchies* is a pair $<N, F>$.

A *dimensional XML-database* S^* over an XML-star schema with explicit hierarchies S is a collection of dimensional data for N, for all $N \in N$, and XML fact data F^* valid w.r.t. DTD_F. F^* satisfies the constraint $F \subseteq: D$ for each $D \in D_F$.

5.1   Querying a Dimensional XML-database

We will suppose a simple query language whose queries are expressed by restrictions on members of dimension hierarchies. We denote such a restriction φ and write in relation algebra style $D(\varphi)$. In general, the restriction can be any predicate (possibly empty) on the element content according to the respective DTD_D. Besides equality expressions, range expressions are typical. Path expressions as they are used in XQuery language [14] are just enough to illustrate our approach. For example, the expression Dealer(dealer[contact/phone = '21914265']) restricts dealer elements in the Dealer dimension member to that ones that have the subelement <phone> 21914265</phone>.

The next operation we need is a semijoin. This operation, we call it *C-seminjoin*, applied to two collections of XML data C_1 and C_2 extracts XML data from C_1, which successfully matches data from C_2. The matching is done by matching the data from $T(DTD_{(C1 \rightarrow C2)\text{-core}})$ and $T(DTD_{C2\text{-core}})$. The matching condition is given by predicate $\leq:$. In a relational environment, we would do the semijoin over a foreign key and the associated primary key of two relations.

The basic idea how to evaluate a query over a dimensional XML-database is to navigate each dimension hierarchy N from its last member with non-empty φ to the root of N. For the sake of simplicity, we will suppose that the member is D_{ki}.

Algorithm: Evaluation of a query over a dimensional XML database
Input: XML-star schema with explicit dimension hierarchies S, S^*, q;
Output: a subcollection of F^* satisfying q;
1. **for** i:=1 **to** $|N|$ **do**
     restr$_2$:= $D_{ki}(\varphi_{ki})$;   //start with the last member of N and restrict it
     j:=k_i-1;
     while j $\neq$ 0 **do**
        restr$_1$:= $D_j^{\cdot}(\varphi_j)$;   //continue with its left neighbour and restrict it
        restr$_2$:= C-semijoin(restr$_1$, restr$_2$);   //restrict $D_j^{\cdot}$ by C-semijoin
        j:= j-1;
     end while
     root$_i$: = restr$_2$ //each root$_i$ contains data necessary for
     end for   //processing F^*

2. result:= (...(C-semijoin(F, root₁),...), root$_{|N|}$);
   //a subcollection of F obtained by subsequent applications of C-semijoin

We describe the semantics of C-semoijoin in a procedural manner. Let C_1 and C_2 be XML collections. Then the result of C-semoijoin(C_1, C_2) is obtainable by the following steps:

1. core₂:=$V_{C2\text{-core}}(C_2)$ //materialize $V_{C2\text{-core}}$ on C_2
2. C-semijoin := $\{d \mid d \in C_1 \wedge \exists\, d' \in \text{core}_2\,(V_{(C1 \to C2)\text{-core}}\,(d) <: d')\}$ //matching cores

Obviously, various optimization techniques can make a real query evaluation more feasible. The existence of an index on elements important for D-cores is a simple example of such strategy.

5.2   Discussion

We summarize briefly remarks to the choices of alternatives:

a) The definition of D-cores we have adopted here is quite weak. It mirrors the fact that we need not uniqueness of keys as in relational databases. Our choice is in accordance to the semistructured nature of XML data contained in our DWs. In some applications of data centric DWs we can design D-cores that are based on real foreign and primary keys. This situation occurs if XML data originates from relational databases.

b) Consider the principle of XML-referential integrity. In contrast to a), even the embedding a pattern tree in a tree can be too restrictive for some applications. Return, e.g., to (title, author*) for books. Suppose that it contributes to $\text{DTD}_{Di\text{-core}}$ and $\text{DTD}_{(D(i-1) \to Di)\text{-core}}$ of dimension members D_i and D_{i-1}, respectively. For two sets of authors A and A' of respective documents $d \in D_{i-1}$ and $d' \in D_i$, the non-empty $A \cap A'$ can be sufficient for a successful matching. We require $A \subseteq A'$.

c) The choice of the language we use to specify restrictions on Ns is important to the expressive power of the approach. Path expressions from XQuery fulfil reasonable minimal requirement for such a language.

6.   Conclusions

We have investigated the approach to DW based on XML data. Specifically, we have focused on the possibility to create XML DWs with the star architecture and explicit dimension hierarchies. We have shown that in contrast to the simple foreign key - primary key linkage of dimension members, a form of approximate matching must be used in an XML environment. Furthermore, we have shown that querying such DW in a usual way is possible. We can use partially features of recent XML query languages for this purpose and the new query operation C-semijoin, which is based on an approximate matching predicate. In future development, various possibilities of its choice should be studied. Certainly, the choice will depend on the application requirements.

An important question is how to design D-cores. Starting from XML data and DTDs, we develop, in fact, the DW from the bottom-up starting on the representation level. It is the same as to design dimensions from a set of relational schemes. A conceptual view on XML data seems to be useful at least for specifying referential integrities in XML collections. In future we would like to show how the dimensional design for DW could be carried out transforming XML metadata (DTDs, XML schemes) into equivalent conceptual schemes. First steps already exist to this goal (e.g. [5]).

References

[1] Bourret, R.: XML and Databases.
http://www.rpbourret.com/xml/XMLAndDatabases.htm.

[2] Buneman, P., Davidson, S., Fan ,W., Hara, C., Tan, W.-Ch.: Keys for XML. Proc. of WWW10, May 1-5, Hong-Kong, ACM Press, 2001, pp. 201-210.

[3] Deutsch, D., Fernandez M.F., Florescu D., Levy M. A., Suciu D.: A Query Language for XML. WWW8/Computer Networks 31, 1999, (11-16): 1155-1169.

[4] Fan, W., Libkin, L.: On XML Integrity Constraints in the Presence of DTDs. Proc. ACM SIGACT-SIGMOD-SIGART Symp. on Principles of Database Systems, 2001, pp. 114-125.

[5] Golfarelli, M., Rizzi S., Vrdoljak, B.: Data warehouse design from XML sources. Proc. of ACM Fourth International Workshop on Data Warehousing and OLAP (DOLAP 2001), J. Hammer Ed., ACM Press, 2001, Atlanta, pp. 40-47.

[6] ISO/IEC 9075:1999: Information Technology --- Database Languages --- SQL. Part 2: Foundations. 1999.

[7] Lee, D., Chu, W.W.: Constraint-preserving transformation from XML Document Type Definition to Relational Schema. Proc. of 20th E-R Conf., Salt Lake City, 2000, pp. 323-338.

[8] Mani, M., Lee, D., Munz, R.: Semantic Data Modelling using XML Schemes. In: Proc. of E-R Conf., Yokohama, 2001, pp. 149-163.

[9] Pokorny, J. "Data Warehouses: a Modelling Perspective." In Evolution and Challenges in System Development (Eds. W.G.Wojtkowski, S. Wrycza, J. Zupancic), Kluwer Academic/Plenum Press Publ., 1999, pp. 59-71.

[10] Pokorny, J.: Modelling Stars Using XML. Proc. of ACM Fourth International Workshop on Data Warehousing and OLAP (DOLAP 2001), J. Hammer Ed., ACM Press, 2001, Atlanta, pp. 24-31.

[11] Papakonstantinou, Y., Vianu, V.: DTD Inference for Views of XML Data. Proc. ACM SIGACT-SIGMOD-SIGART Symp. on Principles of Database Systems 2000, pp. 35-46.

[12] Schlieder, T.: Schema-Driven Evaluation of Approximate Tree-Pattern Queries. Proc. of EDBT 2002, C.S. Jensen et al. (Eds), LNCS 2287, Springer Verlag, 2002, pp. 514-532.

[13] XML: Extensible Markup Language 1.0. http://www.w3.org/TR/REC-xml, 1998.

[14] XQuery 1.0: An XML Query Language. W3C Working Draft 20 December 2001 http://www.w3.org/TR/2001/WD-xquery-20011220/.

THE XML QUERY EXECUTION ENGINE (XEE)

Dieter Scheffner

Humboldt-Universität zu Berlin, Dept of Computer Science, 10099 Berlin, Germany

scheffne@dbis.informatik.hu-berlin.de

Johann-Christoph Freytag

Humboldt-Universität zu Berlin, Dept of Computer Science, 10099 Berlin, Germany

freytag@dbis.informatik.hu-berlin.de

Abstract

The characteristics of XML documents require new ways of storing and querying such documents. In this paper, we introduce the concept of our XML Query Execution Engine (*XEE*), its components, and its current implementation. *XEE* provides a testbed for our Access Support Tree and TextArray data structure of which the basic idea is to separate the (logical) structure of a document from its "visible" text content. Based on this concept, we bring together database and information retrieval technology to improve storage, retrieval, and querying of large XML document collections, in particular with respect to updates. We further explain our current approach of efficiently implementing Access Support Trees for secondary storage and reveal issues that arise when implementing such a system.

Keywords: XML, data structures, database management system

1. Introduction

XML has become widely accepted for both data representation and exchange of information over the Internet. For this reason, the amount of data in XML format is rapidly growing, making appropriate systems for their handling necessary. Conventionally, the management of large numbers of data is sensibly left with database management systems (DBMSs), which are well-known for their efficiency in handling immense amounts of data. However, DBMSs are designed for structured rather

H.-M. Haav and A. Kalja (eds.), Databases and Information Systems II, 81–94.
© *2002 Kluwer Academic Publishers.*

than for semi-structured or unstructured data. XML documents or data are semi-structured beside other characteristics. For this reason, it is hard for conventional DBMSs to handle any kind of XML data efficiently. Thus, systems are required that integrate well established features of DBMSs with the ability to manage large numbers of data that greatly vary in structural and access-related requirements in an efficient and reliable way.

In this paper, we introduce our approach of a system capable of storing, retrieving, and querying XML documents, namely the *XML Query Execution Engine* (*XEE*). We describe concepts used and the current state of our implementation. In contrast to other similar systems, the design of *XEE* is based on an alternative approach for managing XML documents and data. That is, we build the *XEE* system on top of an appropriate *XML data type*—the *Access Support Tree* (*AST*) and *TextArray* (*TA*) data structure [10]. To the best of our knowledge, the storage concept, on which our data structure is based, has not been investigated yet in detail. Therefore, one important goal of our *XEE* system is to provide a testbed for the AST/TA data structure. We advocate two things with this approach. First, we integrate established database and information retrieval technology into such systems. Second, we support XML document management already on the physical system level to enable efficient implementations for storing, retrieving, and querying XML documents.

For the motivation of our approach in detail and a discussion of conventional approaches for managing XML documents, we refer, due to space limitations here, to our technical report (see [11]).

2. The AST/TA Approach for Managing XML Documents

In the following, we refer to *generic* XML documents only, i.e., documents having no constraints other than *well-formedness*, thus consisting of an *XML document element* only. We further consider XML documents to consist of both structure and content. The content of a document is the "visible" text as a human reader sees the document when using a browser. We illustrate this situation in Fig. 1, where the "visible" text content of the corresponding XML document is shown on the right hand side. We recognize that the entire "visible" text content of an XML document is "in document order" and is not interspersed with markups. The visible portion of the text is a user has in mind when formulating a query about the text content of documents.

XML document

```
<story>
  <header>
    <author from="1832" to="1908">Wilhelm Busch</author>
    <title><published year="1865"/>Max und Moritz</title>
  </header>
  <body>
    <section>
      <heading>Vorwort</heading>
      <verses>
        <verse>Ach, was muß man oft von bösen</verse>
        <verse>Kindern hören oder lesen!</verse>
        <verse>Wie zum Beispiel hier von diesen,</verse>
        <verse>Welche Max und Moritz hießen;</verse> ...
      </verses>
    </section> ...
  </body>
</story>
```

The text content of the document

```
Wilhelm Busch
Max und Moritz


    Vorwort

Ach, was muß man oft von bösen
  Kindern hören oder lesen!
Wie zum Beispiel hier von diesen,
Welche Max und Moritz hießen;
        ...
        ...
```

Figure 1.   A sample XML document and its "visible" text content

Based on this observation, we designed our AST/TA data structure [10]. We distinguish the Access Support Tree and the TextArray of a *document element*. The entire logical structure of the document element, including element attributes, comments etc., is incorporated and stored in an ordered tree—the Access Support Tree (AST). The TextArray (TA) stores the entire "visible" text content of an XML document as a single contiguous string maintaining the original order of text in the document, i.e., the text content is neither fragmented nor interspersed with markup. In our approach XML documents are represented by AST/TA pairs in physical storage.

The relationship between AST and TA is established by logical references called *text surrogate values*. A text surrogate value is a vector indicating the start position and the length of a text segment referenced to in a TA. Every vertex of the logical structure receives a text surrogate value, thus text segments might be reached from any vertex and ASTs become indexes. When we apply this linkage concept to documents that do not change their text content in length, text surrogate values alone are sufficient. We introduce *offsets* that adjust the text surrogate values after updates changing the length of the text in TAs. Hereby, the number of vertices to be modified is kept as small as possible. Otherwise, all values that span or follow the location of update in the logical structure would have to be modified, making such updates inefficient.

Figure 2 shows the concept of representing an XML document by an AST/TA pair. The AST vertices $(r, ..., x)$ represent their corresponding document components, i.e., elements, a comment, and text components. For example, vertex r labeled with **header** refers to the document element itself. Vertex t represents a comment. Text vertices such as v and x carry no labels. In addition to labels, element vertices may have an attribute set assigned to. Thus, vertex s (**author** element) comes with the refinements of **from="1832"** and **to="1908"**. Expressions in parenthesis, e.g., (**14,14**), depict text surrogate values; expressions in square brackets such as [**0**] denote offsets. That is, the vertices u and x both refer to the text segment that starts at position **14** in the TA and has a length of **14**. Arrows give a notion of text surrogate values in the figure pointing to the start of corresponding text segments in the TA. In our example, all offsets are equal to 0, since we assume the document not being updated yet. For conceptual details of our AST/TA data structure, we refer to [10]. The AST/TA data structure is especially designed for update functionality, a feature that is often neglected in other approaches.

The AST/TA may be characterized as a "hybrid approach", since we separate structure from content at the same time managing both parts as an atomic unit. However, our approach differs from the *hybrid approach* described earlier by Böhm et al. in [1]. The advantage of our "hybrid approach" is that the decomposition of documents remains always the same. There is no administration overhead.

3. System Overview

Efficient operations in databases require special support at the physical level. Therefore, we decided to design and to build a system based on an appropriate data structure, namely our AST/TA data structure, to overcome performance limitations as they appear in systems based on, e.g., relational, object-relational, or object-oriented approaches. The objective of the XML Query Execution Engine (*XEE*) is to provide a testbed for our AST/TA data structure whose the storage concept has not been investigated yet in all details. Since our focus is on such issues,

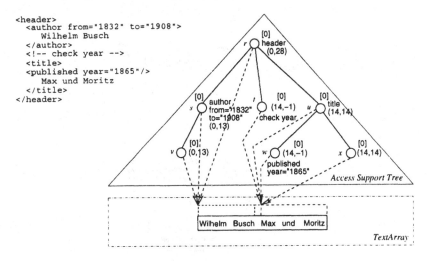

Figure 2. The simplified concept of AST/TA

we do not consider concurrency control, recovery, parallelism, distribution etc. at the current state of the system.

3.1   The Overall Architecture

The system architecture of our *XEE* system is based on the fundamental requirement for DBMSs to achieve both physical and logical data independence. For this reason, we implement suitable query languages for accessing the documents stored with the system. Additionally, we provide a comprehensive logical view of all documents by mapping the internal data representation (AST/TA data structures, indexes etc.) to appropriate data models. The latter is important, because query languages, such as *XQuery* [15], are based on their corresponding model. Hence, our *XEE* system integrates the principles of the *ANSI/X3/SPARC* architecture. That is, the system architecture consists of three layers: the internal, the conceptual, and the external layer (see Fig. 3).

3.2   Storage Management

The storage manager—the buffer manager in cooperation with the file manager—hides the underlying storage layout. It is responsible for retrieving, writing, and caching data blocks or pages on behalf of their client applications. In our *XEE* system, the storage manager maps requests for individual pages to the related data blocks in the corresponding files.

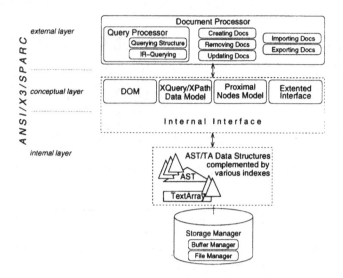

Figure 3.   Architectural Overview

3.3   The TextArray

As the Access Support Tree (AST) and TextArray (TA) are independent from each other, the text content of XML documents is managed by and stored in TAs only. We store the data of TAs as *large objects* on disk; TAs reside in separate files. For this purpose, it is necessary to fragment the byte sequences of TAs into disk pages. The storage manager is responsible for retrieving and writing those pages.

TAs are designed for retrieving and writing arbitrary sequences of characters or words from or to the "visible" text content of XML documents [10]. To facilitate text or information retrieval support appropriately, TAs must provide both sequential and random access to text segments of documents they manage. As TAs are designed for *non-normalized* text (sequences of characters) and *normalized* text (sequences of words)—see [10], we provide generic access to TAs by a suitable interface. Furthermore, TAs have no fixed length. Due to possible document updates, TAs may change their size during their lifetime. We must take into account this requirement when implementing TAs. Therefore, TAs are *large objects* based on *positional B+-tree* indexes, supporting both efficient sequential and random access and efficient updates. In particular, the AST/TA integrates specific needs with respect to the combination of XML and the different data models we support in our system.

3.4   The Access Support Tree

ASTs manage and store the logical structure—the "markup"—of XML documents in one file. In contrast, all text content (cmp. Fig. 1) is managed by TAs. Therefore, ASTs are qualified for accessing the structure or meta data of XML documents. Unlike the implementation of TAs, the implementation of ASTs is far more challenging.

We face the following main challenges when implementing an AST based on secondary storage:

1 AST vertices have *text surrogate values* adjusted by *offsets* assigned to. It is important to update these values efficiently.

2 ASTs must be serialized and fragmented into byte sequences having a maximum size of one disk page.

3 We must decide which parts or subtrees of an AST are stored on the same page.

4 ASTs consist of vertices that are different in size and may change their size in updates.

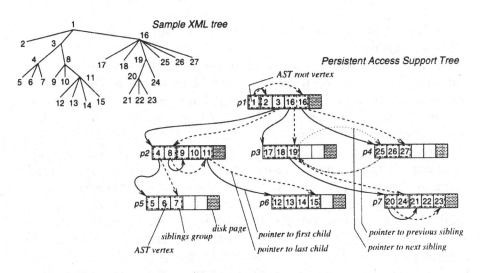

Figure 4.   Sample XML tree and its corresponding Persistent AST

We propose to follow the idea of Kha et al. to address the problems (1), (2), and (3). In [6] the authors describe a data structure for indexing XML documents based on *Relative Region Coordinates* (*RRC*s). Region coordinates describe the location of content data in XML documents;

they refer to start and end positions of text sequences in XML documents. RRCs are region coordinates being adjusted by offsets relative to the corresponding region coordinate of the parent node in the index structure. In our AST data structure, we use *text surrogate values* combined with *offsets* in analogy to RRCs. When updating the text content of an XML document that is stored as AST/TA pair, we must update a number of text surrogate values and offsets in the AST (see [10]). This problem is analogous to the *RRC-update problem* described in [6].

Kha et al. designed their index structure to perform RRC updates efficiently. Their idea is to store index nodes whose coordinates are likely to be changed at the same time on the same disk page [6]. Hereby, the number of disk I/Os is kept as small as possible when updates occur. Such a group of nodes, which must fit on a disk page, is called *Block Subtree (BST)*. The nodes in a BST are organized as a tree representing a fragment of an *XML tree*. The individual BSTs are linked together, such that they represent the complete tree. Thus, every BST has (exactly) one root node, which is linked to a leaf node of the parent BST—if a parent BST exists. For details, we refer to [6].

We adopt the approach of mapping BST index structures to secondary storage, because of both (a) enabling efficient updates of text surrogate values and their offsets and (b) having disk pages arranged into trees, i.e., every disk page is linked to at most one parent page. The latter feature is the key to our approach for implementing efficient offset handling, which we explain later.

Figure 4 illustrates our approach of mapping the sample XML tree (introduced earlier in [6]) to our *Persistent Access Support Tree* ($AST^{\mathcal{P}}$). We store all children of a vertex as a siblings group on a disk page. Consider, e.g., the siblings group 5, 6, 7, which is stored on page *p5* and represents the children of vertex 4 (page *p2*). Parent and child vertices are connected by pointers. A parent vertex has a pointer to its first and a pointer to its last child. Vice versa, a siblings group has a pointer its parent vertex. (For clarity reasons, we left such references out in Fig. 4.) A disk page can store more than one siblings group, e.g., see page *p2*. Here, we find two groups, 4, 8 and 9, 10, 11, which make up a tree of siblings groups. Group 4, 8 is the root group for this page. In general, every page has exactly one siblings group representing the root for this page. If a parent vertex for such a root group exists, it is stored on a different page—the parent page. Hence, our $AST^{\mathcal{P}}$ incorporates the BST index concept. Following the BST index concept further, we divide groups of siblings, in case they do not fit on a single page. For example, the siblings 17, 18, 19, 25, 26, 27 are split up in two pages (*p3* and *p4*). According to [6], we provide a copy of the parent vertex (16) in the parent page for each child page. We may establish additional links between siblings fragments for only performance reasons on different pages as shown in Fig. 4 between *p3* and *p4*. We neglect such links in our further considerations, since they are not urgent and would violate the tree concept here.

Kha et al. also describe in [6] how to create and manipulate such tree structures. We may easily transfer these algorithms to our AST^P. However, there are still open issues we must consider. For example, we must take a look at algorithms for splitting and for merging pages when overflows or underflows occur, respectively. This contemplation is especially important, because we must use a page layout different from that used for BST indexes—ASTs consists of vertices of variable and changing size. We present ideas on our page layout later.

AST^Ps build trees based on links between parent and child pages. We require text surrogate values being immediately recalculated rather than just aligned by offsets, assuming that pages loaded into main memory can be processed fast. We note, such recalculations take place when offset updates happen; thus, the corresponding pages must be written anyway. For this reason, the only offsets we still need are offsets for disk pages (*page offsets*).

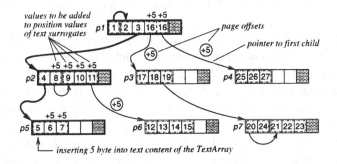

Figure 5. The page offset concept of AST^P

Figure 5 shows the principle of page offsets. Suppose, we insert 5 byte of text into the text segment that the text vertex 5 spans over. Therefore, we must update the *length values* of the text surrogates along the path of vertices 1, 3, 4, and 5 on the pages *p1*, *p2*, and *p5*. All *position values* in text surrogates of sibling vertices that are to the right of this path, must be increased by +5. In our example this is valid for both vertices 16 and for the vertices 8, 6, and 7. As page *p2* must be written anyway, we additionally increase the *position values* of surrogates of the vertices 9, 10, and 11. Note, that we change values on three pages only (*p1*, *p2*, *p5*)—the update path. Three offsets for the pages *p3*, *p4*, and *p6* still must be recorded. We record page offsets in the *Offset Dictionary*, which may occupy one or more pages attached to the AST$^{\mathcal{P}}$ file. The Offset Dictionary only needs as much entries as pages are in use in an AST$^{\mathcal{P}}$. The advantage of using only page offsets instead of vertex offsets is twofold. First, we save space on AST pages, because vertices do not need offset data anymore. Second, much less offsets must be updated on behalf of the whole tree. Furthermore, we may easily check the dictionary whether there is an entry different from 0, making unnecessary access to the Offset Dictionary superfluous.

We briefly explain the page layout. A page starts with an array of entries in which each entry has a fixed length and represents the entry point to the data of the vertex it manages. This array section is followed by additional management structures. The data of vertices such as element and attribute names etc. constitute the tail of all sections. Thus, changes affecting the length of, e.g., element and attribute names, cause much less byte moving on pages. We fill pages between 50% and 100%.

3.5   Indexing

We complement our AST/TA data structure with various kinds of indexes to improve query performance. In *XEE* we basically provide indexes on both ASTs and TAs. Hence, we distinguish indexes on both structure and content of XML documents; this is analogous to [7]. We apply indexes among other things to element names, attribute names, attribute values, comments, processing instructions, and structural paths. In addition, we use indexes known from information retrieval for content-based indexing such as, e.g., *String B-Trees* [3]. Hereby, we cover the "traditional" requirements for indexes on XML documents as demanded, e.g., in [12].

Furthermore, we provide indexes notably for *entities, CDATA sections*, and *XML namespaces*. Entities refer to physical components rather than to the logical structure of XML documents. We map the information about replacement texts of parsed entities to additional structures—*entity indexes*, since our AST/TA data structure refers to logical structure only. Entries for such indexes may look like as follows: *<name of the entity> <text surrogate value>*, in which the text surrogate value refers to values in the corresponding AST. We propagate this concept to *CDATA section indexes* and *XML namespace indexes* as well. XML namespaces are valid for complete subtrees. Text surrogate values help to find namespace declarations in charge of an arbitrary AST vertex very quickly based on inclusion relationships. Eventually, we also take a look at issues like, e.g., how we can make indexes on structure and on content interact with one another.

3.6   The Internal Interface and Data Models Supported

The *Internal Interface* merely brings together and combines functionality provided by the diverse data structures of AST, TA, and additional indexes. We implement the *XQuery 1.0 and XPath 2.0 Data Model* [16] and the *Document Object Model (DOM)* [14] using the Internal Interface. In addition to these *de facto* data models, we experiment with the *Proximal Nodes Model* [7], which is designed for structured documents in general and integrates the aspect of querying documents with respect to both structure and content. With such a document model integrated, our system naturally enables the support of information retrieval and structural queries in equal rank. In *XEE* we support such a diversity of models to get more insight how models may interact with our data structure.

3.7   The Document Processor

The *Document Processor* provides the interface to the *XEE* system for users and external applications. The main component of the Document Processor is the *Query Processor*. The Query Processor allows the user to query both the structure and the content of XML documents. We experiment with several implementations of query processors. For example, we use a processor that may implement *XQuery* [15] for querying the structure of documents. For queries on content, we currently design a query language based on the *matching sublanguage* [7], *PAT expressions* [9], and *IRQL* [4].

Besides querying documents, it must also be possible to manage XML documents. That is, the Document Processor must provide functionality to create, remove, and update documents. Another important facility must support the import and export of documents to or from the system as usually supported by DBMSs. We map such "additional" functionality to the *Extended Interface* of our AST/TA data structure, whereas we map functionality for querying to the interfaces of the supported data models. We investigate these mappings based on our *XEE* system.

4.   Related Work

This section gives a brief overview of existing management concepts for structured documents that are related to our work: *Structured Mul-*

timedia Document DBMS (*SMD DBMS*) [2], *HyperStorM* (Hypermedia Document Storage and Modeling) [13], the *Proximal Nodes Model* [7], and NATIX (Native XML Repository) [5].

The concept we use in our AST/TA approach, i.e., considering the text content as contiguous string and representing the logical structure of documents in a separate hierarchy has already been introduced earlier. To the best of our knowledge, this approach was only used twice, i.e., in the framework of SMD DBMS and in the Proximal Nodes Model.

An object-oriented MMDBS was developed for storage of SGML documents in the presence of DTDs within the framework of the SMD DBMS [2]. Their approach is not well documented with respect to storage design; only few implementation issues are discussed in [8].

The Proximal Nodes Model is a model for querying document databases on both content and structure [7]; it regards documents as being static objects and does not refer to XML documents directly. Since the PN model is a purely logical model, it does not mandate any specific implementation.

The objective of the HyperStorM project was to build an application database framework for storing structured documents in a system coupling an object-oriented DBMS and an information retrieval system [13]. The authors of [1] advocate the *hybrid approach* as the favorite strategy for representing SGML documents in object-oriented databases. The hybrid approach is a trade-off between storing each logical document component as an individual database object and storing complete documents as BLOBs in databases.

NATIX is a repository for the storage and management of large tree-structured objects, preferably XML documents [5]. NATIX stores generic XML documents that do not depend on any schema information. The main idea of NATIX is to map the logical structure of an XML document directly into the corresponding physical structure. Such trees may be split up among several pages in storage. Hereby, the text content of documents is interspersed with structural data, e.g., element and attribute names and is thus fragmented within pages.

5. Conclusion

This paper introduces the XML Query Execution Engine (*XEE*), which we currently design and implement. The focus of the *XEE* system is to provide a testbed for the storage and retrieval approach for XML documents that is brought in by our AST/TA data structure. That is, we investigate a storage and retrieval approach, in particular with respect to updates, that has been neglected so far in the past. We are convinced this is a promising approach for bringing together database and information retrieval technology to improve storage, retrieval, and querying of large XML document collections.

We give insight into the concept of the *XEE* components and the current state of the system by introducing the system architecture. For example, we introduce our concept of efficiently implementing AST's for persistent storage based on the design of our main memory ASTs. Moreover, we carefully review the interdependence between the AST and the TA data structures for possible improvements, namely we apply diverse indexes to these structures. We propose indexes such as the *entity index* and the *XML namespace index* that are specific to our system. We provide efficient handling of large scale XML document collections on secondary storage. Another issue of interest is to provide a suitable interface that enables convenient access to XML documents managed by the *XEE* system. Therefore, we implement a persistent DOM based on persistent AST/TAs and map query languages to the AST/TAs. We provide access to XML documents both by an API for programming languages and by query languages. As for the mapping of query languages, the integration of both the concept of database query languages and the concept of information retrieval data plays an important role in the framework of *XEE*.

References

[1] Böhm, K., Aberer, K., and Klas, W. Building a Hybrid Database Application for Structured Documents. Multimedia Tools and Applications, January 1999, 8(1):65–90.

[2] Database Systems Research Group (Univ of Alberta). Multimedia Data Management.
http://www.cs.ualberta.ca/~database/multimedia/multimedia.html, 1998.

[3] Ferragina, P. and Grossi, R. The String B-Tree: A New Data Structure for String Search in External Memory and its Applications. J. of the ACM, 1999, 46(2):236–280.

[4] Heuer, A. and Priebe, D. IRQL – Yet Another Language for Querying Semi-Structured Data? Technical Report Preprint CS-01-99, Universität Rostock, 1999.

[5] Kanne, C.-C. and Moerkotte, G. Efficient Storage of XML Data. In Proceedings of ICDE, San Diego, California. IEEE Computer Society, 2000.

[6] Kha, D.D., Yoshikawa, M., and Uemura, S. An XML Indexing Structure with Relative Region Coordinates. In Proceedings of ICDE, 2001, Heidelberg, Germany, IEEE Computer Society, 2001, pp. 313–320.

[7] Navarro, G. and Baeza-Yates, R.A. Proximal Nodes: A Model to Query Document Databases by Content and Structure. Information Systems, 1997, 15(4):400–435.

[8] Özsu, M.T., Szafron, D., El-Medani, G., and Vittal, C. An Object-Oriented Multimedia Database System for a News-on-Demand Application. Multimedia Systems, 1995, 3(5-6):182–203.

[9] Salminen, A. and Tompa, F.W. PAT Expressions: An Algebra for Text Search. Acta Linguistica Hungarica, 1992-93, 41(1-4):277–306.

[10] Scheffner, D. Access Support Tree & TextArray: Data Structures for XML Document Storage. Technical Report HUB-IB-157, Humboldt Universität zu Berlin, 2001.

[11] Scheffner, D. and Freytag, J.-C. The XML Query Execution Engine (XEE). Technical Report HUB-IB-158, Humboldt Universität zu Berlin, 2002. avail. at: http://dbis.informatik.hu-berlin.de/publications/techreports.html.

[12] Schöning, H. Tamino - A DBMS designed for XML. In Proceedings of ICDE, 2001, Heidelberg, Germany, IEEE Computer Society, 2001, pp. 149–154.

[13] Volz, M., Aberer, K., and Böhm, K. An OODBMS-IRS Coupling for Structured Documents. Data Engineering Bulletin, 1996, 19(1):34–42.

[14] World Wide Web Consortium. Document Object Model (DOM) Level 2 Core Specification, Version 1.0. Technical Report REC-DOM-Level-2-Core-20001113, W3C, November 2000.

[15] World Wide Web Consortium. XQuery 1.0: An XML Query Language. Technical Report WD-xquery-20011220, W3C, December 2001.

[16] World Wide Web Consortium. XQuery 1.0 and XPath 2.0 Data Model. Technical Report WD-query-datamodel-20010607, W3C, June 2001.

OFFERING USER PROFILE AS AN XML WEB SERVICE

Anne Marie Hartvigsen
AgderUniversity College, Norway amihartvi@stud.hia.no

Tore E. Jønvik
Unik, University of Oslo, Norway, torejoen@ifi.uio.no

Do van Thanh
Telenor R&D, Norway, thanh-van.do@telenor.com

Abstract   In telecommunications, the User Profile is used to capture the user's preferences, settings and personal data such as address/telephone lists, bookmarks, family photos, encryption keys, etc. In order to make the User profile available to any desired application or service at the same time as to allow the user to access and modify it at anytime anywhere and on any terminal, we propose in this paper to offer the User Profile as an XML Web service. As an XML Web service, the User Profile will be accessible from any application over the operator's borders and firewall, and without the need for specific middleware platforms. Ubiquitous and customised access to applications and services can thus be a reality. The paper proposes an early outline of how the User Profile can be defined as an XML Web service.

Keywords: XML Web services, Web technology, user profiles, distributed computing, ubiquitous service access, service customisation, preferences and settings

H.-M. Haav and A. Kalja (eds.), Databases and Information Systems II, 95–108.

1.   Introduction

The success of mobile communication expressed by the explosion both in the number of mobile phones and the number of mobile subscriptions can only be explained by the user's demand for freedom and flexibility. The fact of being able to communicate anytime and anywhere is in itself very valuable to the users. Such a demand will soon be extended to comprise other services than just voice communication. In fact, after experiencing exciting data applications on the Internet the user will inevitably expect to be able to access them anywhere at anytime and on any terminal, both fixed and mobile. She will probably expect to access the same application or at least be able to recognise the application that she is familiar with at home. The functionality, the behaviour, the presentation, the look and feel, the preferences and settings, etc. should preferably be the same or as close as possible to what she is used to. Of course, it is always possible for a skilled user to set up and customise an application to her taste, and to restore the original settings after use. However, it is a boring and time consuming task that she would prefer to be exempt from. For a non-technical user such a task can neither be expected nor accepted.

In telecommunications, the User Profile is used to capture the user's preferences, settings and personal data such as address/telephone list, bookmarks, family photos, encryption keys, etc. In order to make the User profile available to any desired application or service at the same time as to allow the user to access and modify it at anytime anywhere and on any terminal, we propose in this paper to expose the User Profile to third parties as an XML Web service – a Web service realised using eXtensible Markup Language (XML) and XML protocols.

As an XML Web service, the User Profile will be accessible from any application over operator's borders, firewall and without the need of a specific middleware platform, such as Common Object Request Broker Architecture (CORBA), Remote Method Invocation (RMI), Distributed Component Object Model (DCOM), etc. With such a User Profile, ubiquitous and customised access to applications and services can be a reality. It would enhance a user's mobility between different terminals, applications and services because different services and applications would be able to share the same user data, and because the same or similar services could be configured according to user settings, even if the user changes device. For example a user would only have to keep one set of addresses and phone numbers, accessible from any application on any device.

The paper starts with a description of related work, followed by a brief overview of the XML Web service concept. The User profile is described in details before we discuss the main focus, which is how the User Profile can be realised as an XML Web service. In the conclusion, further works and activities are proposed.

2. Related Work

2.1 Distributed Computing

Distributed Computing is not a new research area. It was addressed already by CORBA, RMI, DCOM, etc. However these technologies have some deficiencies, both in terms of interoperability and in terms of compliance with the Internet and the Web. Complex implementation, symmetrical requirements and firewall problems have held back the expansion of these technologies, and there is an outspoken demand for simpler protocols that can be used more widespread. That is why the Object Management Group (OMG), the organisation behind CORBA, has recognised XML Web services as an alternative to CORBA/IIOP, and why we propose to realise our service using XML Web services.

2.2 User Profiling

There is a lot of work going on concerning the utilisation of user profiles to enhance services, and particularly in the area of mobility management for wireless and mobile networks [12], most often focusing on conveying situational context information about the environment, device and network, and only to a lesser extent personal preferences and needs. [3] identifies four categories of context: Computing context, user context, physical context and time context – our contribution regards mainly the user context, focusing the user's profile in terms of preferences and settings.

The CC/PP [17] (Composite Capabilities/Preferences Profiles) defines a way to specify what a user agent is capable of doing, in order to provide a generic content negotiation solution for Web clients. CC/PP is intended to provide information necessary to adapt the content and the content delivery mechanisms to best fit the capabilities and preferences of the users and their browsers, and mainly defines information about hardware and software platform and user agent application (typically a Web browser). See e.g. [14, 20] for implementation and evaluation of CC/PP, and [13] for an example of how CC/PP can be used with P3P to enhance privacy. CC/PP is focused on the configuring of services according to different browsers and termimnals, and as such is very limited compared to our proposed User Profile service.

3GPP's Virtual Home Environment [1] (VHE) aims at making networks supporting mobile users capable of provide them the same computing environment on the road that they have in their home or corporate computing environment. VHE is part of IMT-2000 and UMTS, but specifications are far from complete. The goal is that with VHE, a foreign network emulates the behaviour of the user's home network, providing portability for a user's personal service environment. For VHE to be realised there need to be consensus between all operator's, and even then it would be limited to services on 3G mobile networks.

.NET myServices is a Microsoft project still under development, offering users the capability to store personal information, which can be retrieved by applications through an XML Web services interface. The concept relies heavily on .NET Passport service for single sign-on. While similar to parts of our proposed User Profile service, and also using the same means for exposing the information to any type of application, our framework goes beyond the scope of .NET myServices, which focus on storage and exposure of personal data such as calendar, contacts, alerts, etc.

3.   Using XML in Distributed Computing

As previously mentioned, several technologies already exist for distributed computing. What XML web services additionally offer is an XML based access via transparent Internet protocols like HTTP, relieving distributed computations from the need of middleware platforms and enabling the use of services across company borders, firewalls, infrastructures and technologies.

One might classify Web Services as services that are available from a Web server for Web browsers or other Web connected programs. However, the word has lately taken on a more specific meaning, especially when XML and XML defined standards are used to provide universal interoperability. Thus, with XML Web services we here mean self-contained, modular applications that can be described, published, located, and invoked over a network [10]. They don't offer user interfaces, instead they are programmatically accessible to other applications. Specifically XML Web services use XML [18] for data description, *SOAP* [19, 7, 8] (Simple Object Access Protocol) for messaging (invocation), *WSDL* [4] (Web Service Description Language) for service description (in terms of data types, accepted messages, etc) and *UDDI* [16] (Universal Description, Discovery and Integration) for publishing and discovery.

These are all universal, open protocols, and are the de facto Web service standards today, adopted by e.g. Microsoft, IBM and Sun, and governed by the World Wide Web Consortium (W3C) and other standards organisations through standards specifications[1]. This is in conformance with the Web Service Interoperability Organisation, WS-I (http://www.ws-i.org/). Figure 1 shows the protocol architecture.

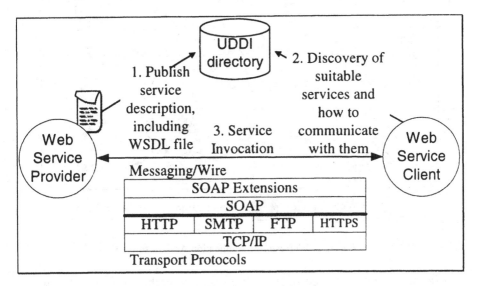

Figure 1. Web Service Protocol Architecture

As long as these standard protocols are used, the applications themselves can be implemented in any language and on any platform, and should be able to interact with other services and applications regardless of what platforms and languages they are built on. Also, the protocols are designed to be independent of other layers in the architecture, so that while e.g. the SOAP protocol can (and usually does) run on HTTP, there is nothing wrong with running SOAP over any other transport protocol, e.g. Telnet or FTP.

The idea with XML Web services is that one application should be able to dynamically exploit the functionality of other applications, which is exposed as Web services. The applications offering Web services might themselves consume other Web services, either for accessing content and business logic, or to utilise supporting services such as security, billing, orchestration, etc. [9].

Consider for example a purchasing application that automatically obtains price information from different vendors, and lets the user select a vendor, submit the order, and then track the shipment until it is received. The vendor applications must of course expose services on the Web, and might also use

---

[1] At the time of writing only XML has reached standard status, while SOAP and WSDL are in Working Draft state. UDDI is this far handled by UDDI.org and not by W3C

other Web services to perform credit check, charge the customer's account and set up the shipment with a shipping company [9].

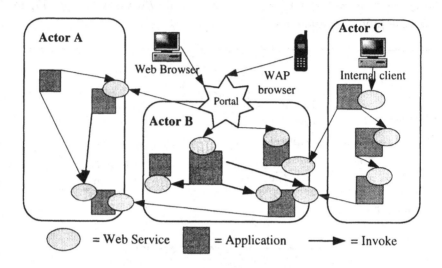

Figure 2. Web Service Application Architecture

Figure 2 shows how complex a Web service architecture can be, when several applications are linked together through Web Services and eventually serving the content either externally or internally. In *Figure 2* all actors use Web services for internal integration of systems. Actor A exposes two Web services, one which actor B uses directly in his Web/WAP portal together with Web services from internal systems, and one which actor B uses in an internal application. Actor C uses two Web services from Actor B, which themselves may rely on a Web Service from actor A. This complexity requires loose coupling and asynchronous communication, which is an important XML Web services characteristic.

4. What is a User Profile?

In telecommunication systems, in order to allow the customisation of services, a User Profile is introduced to capture the preferences and settings of the users as in the case of UPT (Universal Personal Telecommunication) [11] and in TINA (Telecommunications Information Networking Architecture) [15]. In GSM (Global System for Mobile Communications), such a User Profile is called Subscriber Data or Subscriber Profile [6]. The User Profile contains information, which is required for service provisions, identification, authentication, routing, call handling, charging, subscriber tracing, operation, and maintenance purposes. Unfortunately, the User Profile as defined has many limitations. The User Profile is intended for the customisation of the main service, namely voice communication or telephony, and its supplementary services, e.g. call forwarding, call answering, etc. It is also stored deep inside the operator's system and is hardly available to 3rd party applications or services.

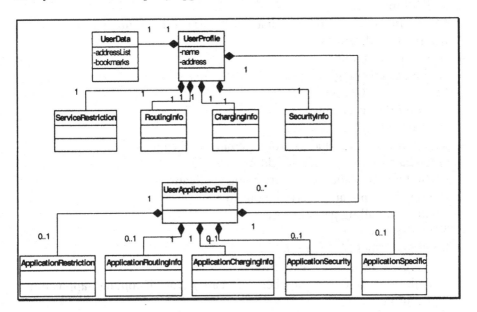

Figure 3. The User Profile structure

In order to allow the users access to multiple applications and services anytime, anywhere and on any terminal, the content of the User Profile needs to be extended to fulfil the following requirements:

- For each user the User Profile must be expandable to incorporate the preferences and settings for any additional application or service that the user requires.
- For each application the User Profile must contain the information necessary for the presentation of the application on the terminal types requested by the user.
- For each application the User Profile must contain usage restriction
- The User Profile must incorporate also user's data such as address book, telephone list, bookmark or favourite link list, etc.

We propose a structure for the User Profile in UML in *Figure 3.*

The UserProfile has six components: *UserData, ServiceRestriction, RoutingInfo, ChargingInfo, SecurityInfo* and *UserApplicationProfile*. *UserData* contains for example addressList, bookmarks, etc.

ServiceRestriction has attributes such as:
- Roaming restriction
- Time restriction
- Credit limit
- Maximum number of terminal addresses for group registration for incoming applications
- Incoming screening
- Outgoing screening
- List of subscribed services
  RoutingInfo has attributes such as
- Forwarding activation status
- Registered terminal address for incoming applications
- A linked-registered terminal address
- Default terminal address for incoming applications
- Routing by applications originating area
- Routing by calling party identity
- Time-dependent routing
- Routing on "busy" condition
- Routing on "no answer" condition
- Default duration (or number of calls) for incoming applications registration
  ChargingInfo has attributes such as
- Default charging reference location
- Charging option selected
- Temporary charging reference location
- Advice of charge activation status
  SecurityInfo has attributes such as
- Authentication procedures subscribed
- Security options subscribed
- Type of authentication procedures activated
- Max number of failed authentication attempts
- Password

The *UserProfile* may contain zero or more *UserApplicationProfiles*. The *UserApplicationProfile* component is to enable customisation of an application. For each application (run in a service session), there may hence be assigned zero or one *UserApplicationProfile*. The *UserApplicationProfile* may contain zero or one *ApplicationRestriction, ApplicationRoutingInfo, ApplicationChargingInfo, ApplicationSecurityInfo* and *ApplicationSpecInfo*.

It is therefore possible to specify the restrictions, routing, charging, and security options for each application. The *ApplicationSpecInfo* is a component that contains application specific data. Greater flexibility is achieved in this way. An application must, however, not have its own *UserApplicationProfile*. For applications that do not have their own profile the main *UserProfile* is applied at the initiation of the application.

The user should have access to a service, which permits him to interrogate and modify some of the attributes of his *UserProfile*. His access rights are linked to and used by the access control procedure.

5. User Profile as an XML Web Service

Several issues need to be addressed in the design of the User Profile Web Service (UPWS):
- Storage and retrieval of user profile data
- User access to and modification of user profile data
- 3rd party application access to user profile data

To manage the data retrieval and providing the UPWS we need a small application, here called the User Profile Manager (UPM). This application acts as a layer between the data itself and the user terminal or application.

5.1 Storage and Retrieval of User Profile Data

When deciding how to store and manage XML data there are at least four alternative ways to do it: In a file system, in a native XML database, in a modified object database or in a relational database. File systems and native XML databases are appropriate when one is storing XML *documents* rather that XML *data*, the latter being more structured. Object databases have been identified by several observers as a natural storage for XML, but have yet to prove their usefulness in this context. When storing structured data, it is generally recommended to use a relational database and then extract the information from the database to XML when needed.

Structured data will benefit from the relational model when it comes to retrieval, searching and aggregation of data. While this forces a need to transform the original XML document, decomposing an XML document to persist it to a relational database is not all that difficult. Also, many relational database vendors are implementing thin XML wrappers that enable them to generate XML documents on demand from relational data. So even if data will be coming in and going out as XML, e.g. in the form of SOAP messages, they can be stored as relational data. The technology for relational databases is mature, stable and ubiquitous, and a whole range of tools exists. The UPM will extract the relational data into XML documents before providing applications and users access to them. It will also have to extract the data from XML documents and update the database. Depending on the implementation, more or less of this functionality can reside in the database itself.

5.2   User Access to and Modification of User Profile Data

The user must be able to access her profile to read and modify settings for existing terminals and add new terminals. This should be done through any kind of terminal, e.g. Web browser, mobile phone, PDA, etc. This means that functionality for reading from and updating the database information must be exposed to the user and a suitable user interface must be provided.

The UPM can apply eXstensible Stylesheet Language Transformations (XSLT) style sheets to XML documents in order to transform the documents into HTML (XHTML) or WML (or any other desired mark up) according to what type of device is calling the service. See [2, 5] for more details on possible architecture and implementation.

Figure 4 shows a user accessing the user profile through a WAP interface.

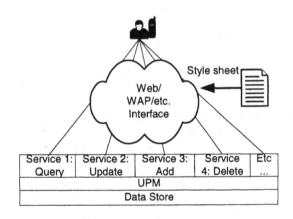

Figure 4. User updating the User Profile through a dynamically created user interface

5.3   3rd Party Application Access to User Profile Data and Functions

The end user application provided by any 3rd party must get access to the UPWS in order to configure according to the settings defined in the profile. The application should not have access to the whole profile, merely the parts relevant for the type of terminal and service in use, and according to user specifications. Conforming to de facto Web service standards, the UPWS uses the SOAP protocol for wrapping data to be exchanged between the user profile and the application. Based on the information retrieved from the profile service, the application can provide the user with a personalised service, as shown in *Figure 5*.

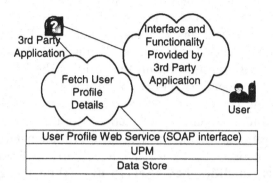

Figure 5. Application using the UPWS for personalisation of its services to the end user

It would be desirable that the user be able to modify the profile through the 3rd party application. The functionality required is the same as if the user accessed the profile directly, but the UPM does not need to provide any user interface, since that will be taken care of by the 3rd party application. However, a SOAP interface must be provided so that the 3rd party application can interact with the services. Figure 6 shows a user interacting with the UPM through a 3rd party application.

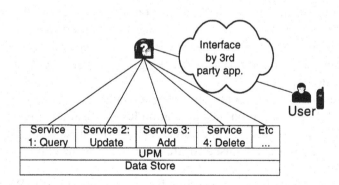

Figure 6. User updating the User Profile through a 3rd party application

5.4 Scenarios

1. **The user accesses the profile through a mobile phone**. After the user logs in through the UPM, the UPM extracts the correct user profile data from the database and wraps them in XML. Since the terminal is a WML browser, a WML style sheet is used to create WML pages that displays the desired parts of the XML document that constitutes the user's profile. Through the UPM the user gets access to the data and can update the User Profile. All needed functionality is disclosed to the user through the WAP interface.

2. **The user uses an application that utilises the UPWS**. In order to provide a personalised service to the user, the 3rd party application contacts the UPWS and fetches the necessary user data. These are then used to configure the interaction with the user. The user never has to worry about the profile, since all communication with the UPWS is between the UPWS and the 3rd party application.

3. **The user modifies her User Profile while using a 3rd party application.** In this scenario the application must be able to update the database, using the *same* functions as in scenario 1, but this time the interface is not WML, but SOAP. The user performs the same functions, but through the user interface provided by the application, instead of the interface provided by the UPM.

5.5 Security

Given the nature of the service, the most important security aspect will be to ensure the privacy and integrity of the sensitive user data. Mechanisms for authentication, authorisation and encryption must therefore be in place. Secondly it is very important that the service has uninterrupted availability, since other applications will depend on this service. Mechanisms such as load balancing, packet filtering, virus checking, fail over and backup must therefore be in place.

Data security arrangements can be implemented either on transport level (HTTP, SMTP, IP, etc.) or on the application level. Assuming that the UPWS will use HTTP for transport, basic authentication, forms authentication, SSL and client certificates can be used for transport level security on the data that are being transferred.

Security on the application level involves modifying the SOAP messages, e.g. passing credentials in the SOAP messages themselves. Different XML security specifications are emerging, such as XML signature, XML encryption, P3P (Platform for Privacy Preferences) and SOAP Security

Extensions – Digital Signature. It would also be possible to use Kerberos and ticket-based authentication, used by e.g. Microsoft's Passport service.

6.   Conclusion

We have suggested that it can be useful for telecom operators to offer user profiles as XML Web services in order to provide 3rd party applications access to user data, preferences and settings. This way the application providers can offer customised services to the user anytime, anywhere and on any device, without the user having to maintain the same data in several applications.

Our work is in an early stage, and further work must be done in order to decide on implementation details. Security is an important concern, and further details of how sensitive user information is to be secured will be crucial for successful implementations. Choice of platform (J2EE based or .NET) is another significant decision to be made. When considering platforms and other implementation details, interoperability issues inevitably become an important aspect, as does issues concerning reliability and performance.

Further refinement of the user profile's data model is necessary, and in this work compliance with existing standards, such as CC/PP, P3P and VHE should be regarded as a desirable goal.

References

[1]   3GPP TS 22.121 v5.1.0.
[2]   Biancheri, C., Pazzaglia, J.-C., Peddeu, G. EIHA?!? : deploying Web and WAP services using XML Technology. Sigmond Record. Vol. 30, Issue 1, 2001, pp. 5-12.
[3]   Chen, G., Kotz, D. A survey of context-aware mobile computing research. Dartmouth Technical report TR 2000-381, November 2000.
       http://www.cs.dartmouth.edu/reports/abstracts/TR2000-381/
[4]   Christensen, E., Curbera, F., Meredith, G., Weerawarana, S. W3C Note "Web Services Description Language (WSDL) 1.1". 2001. [Online]. Available:
       http://www.w3.org/TR/2001/NOTE-wsdl-20010315 [2002, 15. March]
[5]   Coyle, F.P. Breathing Life into legacy. IT Professional. Vol. 3, Issue 5, 2001, pp. 17-24.
[6]   ETSI/3GPP – GSM- Digital cellular telecommunications system (Phase 2+) Organization of subscriber data (Release 1998) TS 03.08 V7.4.0 (2000-09)
[7]   Gudgin, M., Hadley, M., Moreau, J.-J., Nielsen H.F. W3C Working Draft "SOAP Version 1.2 Part 2: Adjuncts". 2001. [Online]. Available:
       http://www.w3.org/TR/2001/WD-soap12-part1-20011217/. [2002, 14. March]
[8]   Gudgin, M., Hadley, M., Moreau, J.-J., Nielsen, H.F. W3C Working Draft "SOAP Version 1.2 Part 1: Messaging Framework". 2001. [Online]. Available
       http://www.w3.org/TR/2001/WD-soap12-part1-20011217/. [2002, 14. March]

[9] Hagel, III, J., and Brown, J.S. Your Next IT Strategy, Harward Business Review Vol. 79, Issue 9, 2001, pp.105-113.

[10] IBM Web Services Architecture Team. Web Services Architecture Overview. [Online] http://www-106.ibm.com/developerworks/library/w-ovr/, 2000 [2001, 18. Dec.]

[11] ITU-TS Universal Personal Telecommunication (UPT) Service Description, version 10 editio, January 1994. Draft recommendation F851, version 10

[12] Lin, Y.-B. Reducing Location Update Cost in a PCS Network IEEE/ACM Transaction on Networking, vol. 5, no. 1, Feb 1997, pp. 25-33.

[13] Nilsson, M., Lindskog, H., Fischer-Hübner, S. Privacy Enhancements in the Mobile Internet. presented at the WAP Forum & W3C Joint Workshop on Mobile Web Privacy, Munich/Germany, 7-8 December 2000.

[14] Okada, W, Kato, F., Kitagawa, K., Hagino, T. Applying CC/PP to User's Environmental Information for Web Service Customization. Tenth International World Wide Web Conference, May 1-5, 2001, Hong Kong

[15] TINA Consortium – Service Architecture – version 5.0 – 16 June 1997 - http://www.tinac.com

[16] UDDI.org. UDDI Version 2.0 Specifications. 2002. [Online]. Available: http://www.uddi.org/specification.html [2002, 15. March]

[17] W3C. CC/PP Working Group. 2002. [Online] Accessible: http://www.w3.org/Mobile/CCPP/ [2002, 15 March]

[18] W3C. Extensible Markup Language (XML) 1.0 (Second Edition)W3C Recommendation 6 October 2000. [Online]. Available: http://www.w3.org/TR/2000/REC-xml-20001006 [2002, 21. March]

[19] W3C. SOAP version 1.2. Part 0. 2001. [Online]. Available: http://www.w3.org/TR/soap12-part0/ [2002, 14. March]

[20] Yasuda, K., Asada, T., Hagino, T. Effects and Performance of Content Negotiation Based on CC/PP. Second International Conference on Mobile Data Management January 8-10 2002, Hong Kong

SHARED CONCEPTUALISATION OF BUSINESS SYSTEMS, INFORMATION SYSTEMS AND SUPPORTING SOFTWARE

Albertas Caplinskas, Audrone Lupeikiene
Institute of Mathematics and Informatics
Akademijos 4, 2600 Vilnius, Lithuania
{alcapl, audronel}@ktl.mii.lt

Olegas Vasilecas
Vilnius Gediminas Technical University
Sauletekio al. 11, 2600 Vilnius, Lithuania
Olegas.Vasilecas@fm.vtu.lt

Abstract   This paper discusses a shared conceptualisation of business systems, information systems and supporting software. The main idea is to think of all above listed systems as different kinds of an abstract operational system. The paper proposes also a shared conceptualisation of business engineering, information systems engineering and supporting software engineering processes on the basis of systems engineering. The proposed approach enables to define all above listed systems in unified manner and to develop unified enterprise engineering environment that increases the reliability of design of enterprise systems because of the possibility to check consistency between business, information and software systems.

Keywords: conceptualisation, enterprise engineering, information systems, information systems engineering, ontology, systems development

1.   Introduction

An enterprise system can be viewed as a three-layered system: business systems, information systems, and supporting software. In other words, any information system is a component of an enterprise system and any

H.-M. Haav and A. Kalja (eds.), Databases and Information Systems II, 109–120.

supporting software is an essential component of a particular IS. So, architecture of any IS should be aligned with business goals and mission, architecture of supporting software should be aligned with goals and mission of the supported IS. Consequently, an enterprise system is effective only then all layers of this system are integrated properly. Concepts should be mapped rightly from higher-level system to lower level systems and lower level systems should be constrained by rules governing processes in higher level systems. Lower level systems should be aware of higher-level systems and all changes should be propagated correctly from top-level system to bottom-level one. Even systems of the same level should be aware of each other. So, it is strongly preferable that a shared systems development environment should be used to develop systems of all three layers. In this paper the term "systems development environment" refers to an arrangement of software tools, repositories, techniques, and technologies used to support the system development process.

Although research in this field was very fruitful during recent decades, systems development environment supporting the development of the whole enterprise system still does not exist. Existing environments usually support either IS development or software engineering only. What is more, any systems development environment does not really support the design of business itself. At the moment, business process frameworks (e.g., [15, 22]) are also not proper tools for this aim. It now seems, however, that the development of shared systems development environment is already possible. But do we really need systems to design business itself?

It is rather exceptional case that the development of the whole enterprise system starts from the scratch. Usually, at least one business system and a number of information and business software systems already exist. However, a rapidly changing environment challenges enterprises. As a result, incremental changes and continuous improvement of business processes and even complete reengineering of the whole business systems are currently rather a natural state than something occasionally forced onto the enterprise [5], what is very complex task. Without mentioning whole business system, even most of business processes are very complex. In addition, business processes should be developed very consciously, keeping a number of functional requirements and non-functional constraints in mind and the development of these processes should be strictly controlled. Therefore organisations are often unable to change their business processes, because they do not know how it can be done [10]. For these reasons the systems development environment supporting the design of business itself is very desirable. Such environment is very useful even if enterprise engineering is limited to the development of supporting software because it supports domain modelling and facilitates transformation of the domain architecture to the software architecture.

The development of an environment, which supports the development of the whole enterprise system, first of all requires that systems operating at different layers should be based on the shared conceptualisation. Further, it is necessary that system development processes for systems operating at different layers were conceptualised in uniform manner, too. This paper aims to propose the principles how to build both mentioned conceptualisations. It is based on research done in AGILA project. The project is in progress. It aims to unify approaches used to model business processes, information systems and software systems and to create an environment that facilitates the development of the whole enterprise system. The main contribution of the paper is the proposed conceptual framework that enables to conceptualise business systems, information systems and supporting software systems in uniform manner.

The rest of the paper proceeds as follows. Section 2 explains our conceptual framework. Section 3 describes the conceptualisation of an enterprise system. Section 4 describes conceptualisation of a system engineering process. Section 5 summarises the proposed approach.

2. Conceptual Framework

To make it easier to understand the essence of this paper, it seems useful to clarify the position from which we start. First of all, we aim to clarify the terminology because there is a variety of approaches in the field of enterprise, IS and software engineering and different approaches use different terminology. So, we present short glossary of essential terms, which explains our conceptual framework. We hope that our choice of terms and their definitions will enlighten certain aspects of the proposed approach.

Researchers in the information systems and related areas discuss the nature of ontologies already in the last few decades. However, any common accepted agreement about where is the boundary between ontologies, conceptualisation and other related approaches does not exist. We are generally following the point of view presented in [18, 8] (Fig. 1), and think of a conceptualisation as a system of categories. Here the word "category" is used to refer to "division or class in a complete system or grouping" [11]. For the purposes of this paper we adopt the following terminology related to the conceptualisation:

Conceptualisation: the formal structure of reality as perceived and organised by an agent [9] using a particular system of compatible categories.

Generic conceptualisation: a conceptualisation of universe of discourse. Generic conceptualisation is "top-level" conceptualisation that introduces very generic categories, which reflect underlying theory about nature of being or kinds of existence and are indented to be used to build lower level conceptualisations.

Domain conceptualisation: a conceptualisation of a partial (generic) domain of discourse (e.g., enterprise). Domain conceptualisation introduces categories, which are specific for this domain and reflect underlying domain theory. Specific categories are introduced by specialising the generic categories. Domain conceptualisation may be used further to build conceptualisations of partial subdomains. On the other hand, it is intended to use it to conceptualise a particular application domain (e.g., certain individual enterprise).

Process conceptualisation: a conceptualisation of a generic process (e.g., business process). Process conceptualisation introduces categories, which are specific for this process and reflect underlying process theory. Specific categories are introduced by specialising the generic categories. Process conceptualisation may be used further to build conceptualisations of partial subprocesses. On the other hand, it is intended to use it to conceptualise processes in a particular application domain.

Problem conceptualisation: a conceptualisation of a particular application. Problem conceptualisation introduces categories, which are specific for this application, characterise roles played by domain entities while performing certain process. Specific categories are introduced mainly by specialising both, domain and process categories.

Conceptualisation of representation: a conceptualisation behind a certain modelling formalism (e.g., predicate calculus, semantic networks, frame formalism, etc.) intended to be used to represent a kind of conceptualisation. Sometimes a modelling formalism may also be used to represent the conceptualisation behind itself.

Conceptual model: a set of claims about reality (universe of discourse, domain of discourse, process, application, formalism, etc.) expressed in categories of particular conceptualisation and represented using certain representation formalism of the conceptual level.

Ontology: a linguistic artefact that defines a shared vocabulary of basic terms used to describe a particular conceptualisation of the reality (universe of discourse, domain of discourse, process, application, formalism, etc.) and specifies what precisely those terms mean.

It should be noticed that our point of view slightly differs from these presented in [18, 8]. In our opinion the claim that conceptualisation is neutral language is not so obvious. Our experience with English, Russian, Polish and Lithuanian terminology shows that the language significantly affects each conceptualisation in sufficiently rich domains, for which it is impossible to build formal ontology because of amount of required efforts. One should express its categories in vocabulary of certain representation language, in order to explain certain conceptualisation. In case of natural languages conceptualisations behind the languages are quite different. Therefore, it is impossible to map conceptualisation categories to language categories directly. Often it is impossible to express intended meaning exactly in the terms of particular vocabulary at all. Most evident examples are English terms like "hardware", "software", "middleware", "courseware", "robot", "softbot", etc. So, one should extend vocabulary. Sometimes it can be done by adopting the word from another vocabulary (e.g., English). Often, however, one should invent a new word and do this following the conventions behind the language. In the context of particular social reality, including the history of particular language, the invented term suggests additional, not intended relations and meanings. It affects the agent's perception of the domain of discourse (conceptualisation) and even socially constructed reality itself. Other authors have also done similar observations. For example, A. U. Frank notes [7] that software designers and programmers from the U.S.A. sometimes produce software, which rest on concepts distinct from those used in many other countries.

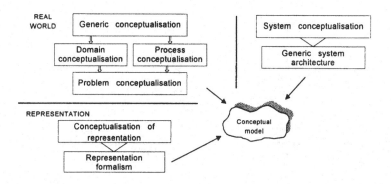

Figure 1. Conceptual modelling of real world systems

Another group of terms explains our understanding of an enterprise (Fig. 3) and an information system (Fig. 2):

Operational system: a set of interrelated processes performed by a certain processor (or by a certain network of processors) to achieve certain goals while producing particular outcome.

Enterprise: one or more organisations sharing a definite mission, goals, and objectives to offer an output such as product or service [12]. Enterprise is thought as a set of functional entities (organisational structures, software systems, machines, etc.) capable to execute functional operations (atoms of work to be performed by enterprise).

Organisational process: a process used to establish or maintain organisational structures.

Enterprise system: a kind of operational system. Enterprise system is thought as a collection of interrelated business systems supported by a number of information and software systems.

Business system: a subsystem of enterprise system. Business system is thought as a set of interrelated business processes performed by an enterprise to achieve certain, usually, long duration goals while producing particular products or/and services delivered to clients.

Business process: a set of interrelated activities, which manipulate (acquire, create, store, transform, transport, deliver, etc.) instances of particular business entities. Business process is governed by a set of business rules, implements particular functionality and meets a number of certain non-functional constraints ensuring the rational usage of recourses, reliability and other preferable properties of this process.

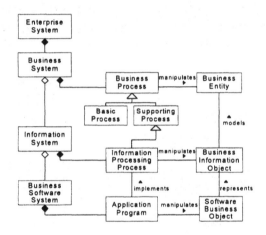

Figure 2. Business system, information system and business software system

Basic process: a business process that is used in business system directly to produce products or/and services delivered to clients.

Supporting process: a business process that is used to support directly or indirectly basic business processes in business system.

Business entity: anything (thing, process or event, e.g., resource, customer, etc.) that is of interest to the business.

Business rule: a directive, which is intended to influence or guide business behaviour [20].

Information system: a subsystem of business system. Information system is thought as a set of information processing processes performed by enterprise functional entities in order to provide a number of information services required to support business processes.

Information processing process: a kind of supporting process. Information processing process is thought as a set of interrelated activities, which manipulate (create, copy, store, transform, transport, disseminate, etc.) particular business information objects. Information processing process is governed by a set of information processing rules (a kind of business rules, e.g., accounting rules).

Business information object: a kind of business entity. Business information object is thought as a piece of business knowledge (including business rules) or as a record of socially constructed reality [4].

Business software system: a component of information system. Business software system consists of application programs, information resources (databases, knowledge bases, document bases, etc.), user interfaces, protocols, middleware, and other components. It may be used to implement (partly at least) a particular functional entity or a particular tool (e.g., word processor), which is used to manipulate software business objects.

Software business object: business information object represented in digital format.

Systems development environment: a collection of tools, languages, documents, repositories, services and other means, which are used to develop a system.

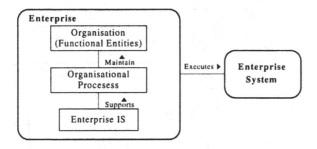

Figure 3. Enterprise and enterprise system

We strongly separate enterprise and enterprise system (Fig. 3). The relation between an enterprise and its system is similar to one between hardware and software. We see an enterprise as the collection of functional entities capable to do certain work. Enterprise is created and maintained by organisational processes. Organisations are characterised by time-independent (static) rules, such as hierarchies or enterprise topologies [15].

Human resource management is an example of organisational process. Organisational processes are supported by enterprise information system. Although enterprise information system and business information system supporting some business processes are interrelated they should be thought as autonomous entities. Such approach decreases coupling between more static processes that are concerned with maintaining organisational structures and processes supporting business itself. In this paper we deal with issues related with the design of enterprise systems only. Issues related to design of enterprise is out of the scope of this paper.

It should also be noticed that an information system is usually thought as a set of applications centred around a database (IS in a narrow sense). However, this point of view is unproductive in our case. We use the term "*information system*" in other sense to refer to the real world system that provides information services required to support certain business system (IS in a broad sense). We use the term "*business software system*" to refer to an IS in a narrow sense.

3. Conceptualisation of an Enterprise System

The development of an environment, which supports the development of the whole enterprise system (Fig. 4), requires that systems operating at all enterprise levels (business, information processing, and software) shared a common conceptualisation first of all.

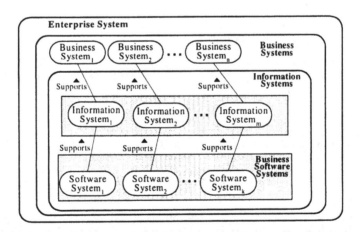

Figure 4. The structure of enterprise system

In order to build such conceptualisation, we should consider the notion of a system as a universe of discourse. The generic conceptualisation for this universe of discourse either may be the same as for "real world" or may be not. Further we define the domain of discourse "operational system" and its subdomains "business system", "information system" and "business software system". We consider an abstract operational system as the upper-level system and think of business systems, information systems, and business software systems as different kinds of operational system (Fig. 5). So, conceptualisation of any of these systems can be defined on the basis of upper-level conceptualisation. The enterprise system is also a kind of operational system. Its conceptualisation can be defined on the basis of upper-level conceptualisation, too. On the other hand, business systems, information systems, and business software systems are subsystems of the enterprise system. Consequently, we have shared conceptualisation for all considered kinds of systems, including system development projects, which can be seen as a kind of business systems.

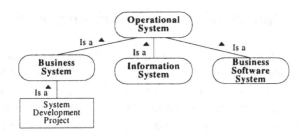

Figure 5. Taxonomy of components of enterprise system

The conceptualisation of an abstract operational system is based on the point of view that an operational system is a goal-driven system that can be characterised by resource model, product model, and process. The appropriate ontology is still under development. The firsts results of this activity are presented in [3].

It should be noticed that we do not aspire to develop this ontology from the scratch. Our goal is rather to systemise well-known results of conceptualisation of enterprise, business systems, information systems and software systems (e.g., [1, 5, 6, 12, 13, 14, 15, 16, 19, 21, 22]) using above presented conceptual framework.

We seek to develop such ontology that could serve for several purposes [17]. Firstly, it should assist the process of identifying requirements and defining a specification for a system under development. The use of the ontology as the basis for domain analysis should facilitate analysis process and increase reliability of analysis results. Secondly, in design phase the ontology should serve as the basis for formal encoding of entities, attributes, processes and their inter-relationships. The ontology should define what modelling constructions (in our case, UML [2] constructions) are meaningful and what are meaningless, and thus enable the automation of consistency checking. Thirdly, ontology should serve as a semantic index used to index contents in the project repository. Finally, use of ontologies should enable system documentation improvement and reduce its maintenance costs (according to our approach, the repository and, consequently, ontology should be a part of operating enterprise system, too).

In our opinion, the possibility to develop fine-grained ontology [8] complete in the sense of [4] is questionable. The domain is far too rich and the task is too difficult. Consequently, we only aim at building a coarse ontology, which is a kind of generic domain ontology. Many aspects of business systems, information systems and software systems are generic and independent of the particular social reality. Namely, these generic aspects should be defined by our ontology.

4. Conceptualisation of a Systems Engineering Process

Enterprise system development is a kind of project. According to [12], each engineering project (project enterprise entity) is "an enterprise (often with a short life history) which is created for the one-off production of another entity". So, business systems, IS, and business software systems development projects can be thought as kinds of business systems (Fig. 5).

From this point of view enterprise system conceptualisation is the conceptualisation of a product produced by systems development environment (Fig. 6). In other words, the sketched ontology describes only the conceptualisation of a system under development. In order to build environment that facilitates the development of the whole enterprise system, we also need to develop shared conceptualisation of business engineering, information systems engineering and software systems engineering processes. We build such conceptualisation on the basis of systems engineering (Fig. 6).

We thought of systems engineering as a generic engineering discipline, which introduces very generic concepts, such as analysis and synthesis, abstraction and decomposition, perspectives and perspective integration, system conceptualisation, identification of information needed to analyse domain of discourse, fact finding and information analysis techniques, requirement engineering, quality models, design approaches, system integration, etc. According to our approach, business engineering, information systems engineering, and software systems engineering are particular kinds of systems engineering.

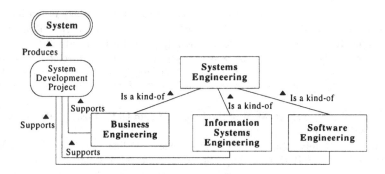

Figure 6. The role of systems engineering in the engineering of enterprise system

5. Conclusions

Changes in business, reengineering of the whole business and even enterprise itself is currently rather a natural state of affairs. These changes affect information systems and supporting software. Consequently, systems development environment that could be used to design and redesign in a uniform way the whole enterprise system including business, IS and supporting software is urgently demanded. In order to develop such environment, uniform conceptualisation of business, information and software systems and uniform conceptualisation of business engineering, IS engineering and supporting software engineering is required. Conceptualisation of business, information and software systems can be based on generic concept of operational system, and conceptualisation of business, information systems and software engineering can be done on the basis of general systems engineering. The usage of the ontology describing both proposed conceptualisations enables implementation of tools that increase reliability of design because of the possibility to check consistency between business, information and supporting software systems.

References

[1] Bernus, P., Mertins, K., Schmidt, G. (eds.). Handbook on Architectures of Information Systems. Springer, 1998.

[2] Booch, G., Rumbaugh, J., Jacobson, I. The Unified Modeling Language. User Guide. Addison Wesley, 1999.

[3] Caplinskas, A., Lupeikiene, A. Intelligent system engineering: review of problems. Proceedings of the Conference IT'2001, Kaunas University of Technology, Kaunas, Technologija, pp. 200-205, (in Lithuanian).

120

[4] Colomb, R.M., Weber, R. Completeness and quality of an ontology for an information system. N. Guarino (ed.), Formal Ontology in Information Systems. Proceedings of FOIS'98, Trento, Italy, 6-8 June 1998. Amsterdam, IOS Press, pp. 207-217.

[5] De Weger, M. Structuring of Business Processes: an Architectural Approach to Distributed Systems Development and its Application to Business Processes. CTIT Ph. D-thesis series, no. 98-17, CTIT P.O. Box 217, 7500 AE Enschede, The Netherlands, 1997.

[6] Ericksson, H.-E., Penker, M. Business Modeling with UML. Business Patterns at Work. John Willey & Sons, Inc., 2000.

[7] Frank, A.U. Ontology: a consumer's point of view. On-line paper. Research Index, NEC Research Institute, 1997, URL: http://citeseer.nj.nec.com/94212.html.

[8] Guarino, N. Formal ontology and information systems. N. Guarino (ed.), Formal Ontology in Information Systems. Proceedings of FOIS 98, Trento, Italy, 6-8 June 1998. Amsterdam, IOS Press, pp. 3-15.

[9] Guarino, N., Welty, Ch. Conceptual Modelling and Ontological Analysis. The AAAI-2000 Tutorial, URL: http://www.cs.vassar.edu/faculty/welty/aaai-2000/.

[10] Hammer, M., Champy J. Reengineering the Corporation. HarperCollins, 1993.

[11] Hornby, A.S. Oxford Student's Dictionary of Current English. Special edition for the USSR, Moscow, Prosveshenye Publishers, Oxford, Oxford University Press, 1984.

[12] Industrial Automation Systems. Requirements for Enterprise-Reference Architectures and Methodologies. ISO/TC 184/SC 5, Draft International Standard, 1999-08-20, Web version: WG1 N431, URL: http://www.mel.nist.gov/sc5wg1/.

[13] Martin, J. Information Engineering, Book II: Planning and Analysis. Englewood Cliffs, 1990.

[14] Olle, T.W. et al. Information Systems Methodologies: A Framework for Understanding. Second edition, Wokinham, 1991.

[15] Scheer, A. -W. ARIS - Business Process Frameworks. Second edition, Springer, 1998.

[16] Sowa, F., Zachman, J.A. Extending and formalizing the framework for information systems architecture. IBM System Journal, 31(3), 1992, pp. 590-619.

[17] Uschold, M. Knowledge level modelling: concepts and terminology. Knowledge Engineering Review, 13(1), 1998, pp. 5-29.

[18] Uschold, M., King, M. Towards a Methodology for Building Ontologies. Technical report AIAI-TR-183, The University of Edinburgh, 1995.

[19] Uschold, M., King, M., Moralee, S., Zorgios, Y. The enterprise ontology. The Knowledge Engineering Review, 13 (special issue on putting ontologies to use, Uschold. M. and Tate. A. (eds.)), Cambridge University Press, 1998, pp. 31-89.

[20] What is the business rules? On-line publication. Business Rules Group, 2001, URL: http://www.businessrulesgroup.org/brgdefn.htm.

[21] Williams, T.J. The Purdue Reference Architecture. Purdue Laboratory for Applied Industrial Control, Purdue University, West Lafayette, Indiana 47907, USA, March, 1992.

[22] Zelm, M., Vernadat, F.B., Kosanke, K. The CIMOSA business modelling process. Computers in Industry, 21(2), 1995.

CONCEPT OF INTELLIGENT ENTERPRISE MEMORY FOR INTEGRATION OF TWO APPROACHES TO KNOWLEDGE MANAGEMENT

Janis Grundspenkis
Systems Theory professor's group, Riga Technical University, Riga, Latvia
E-mail: jgrun@cs.rtu.lv

Abstract   A number of knowledge management definitions have been explored and their classification is proposed using such criteria as formal aspects, process aspects and organisational aspects. Two knowledge management tracks - people track knowledge management and information technology track knowledge management are discussed in details. To focus on possible role of modern paradigms of artificial intelligence for bridging gaps between two tracks it is shown that knowledge management systems have their roots in information and knowledge based systems. The role of intelligent agents and multiagent systems for present and future solutions in knowledge management system development is outlined. A novel multilevel model of intelligent enterprise memory is proposed as an integration tool of different approaches.

Keywords: knowledge management, intelligent agents, multiagent systems, intelligent enterprise memory

1.   Introduction

Nowadays we can observe rapid evolution from the industrial age to the information age that influences all kinds of organisations. Modern organisations are under the pressure to create a new type of workplace due to the progress of computing technology that causes dramatic change in work environment and emerging of a new type of intellectual work, so called, "knowledge work". The essence of knowledge work is turning information into knowledge through the interpretation of available non-standardised information for purposes of problem solving and decision making. Organisations realise that knowledge is their most important asset. In other

H.-M. Haav and A. Kalja (eds.), Databases and Information Systems II, 121–134.
© *2002 Kluwer Academic Publishers.*

words, organisations realise that they must be more conscious of their vast knowledge resources. Knowledge is recognised as a strategic resource and a critical source of competitive advantage [13]. At the same time the question is still open why such service organisations as, for example, higher education or health care organisations are "information rich" but "knowledge poor". One of the main reasons is lack of systematic and formal methods to capture, represent, store, convert and transfer both types of knowledge called tacit and explicit knowledge as defined in [12]. There is a growing need for the new type of systems, namely, knowledge management systems (KMS) that focus on knowledge discovering, representation, preservation, aggregation, analysis, application, distribution and sharing. Knowledge management (KM) has become a new way of capturing and efficiently managing an organisation's knowledge.

There are hundreds of books and articles as well as specialised journals concerning issues of KM and related problems (more than 300 titles can be found on Web). At the same time main concepts of KM are not generally accepted and unambiguously used even inside the KM community. Moreover, two different tracks exist in KM [15], namely, information technology track KM and people track KM. The gap between these tracks is rather wide due to the different education of communities representing each particular track, and, what is even more crucial, due to the different point of view on the real nature of knowledge. Representatives of people track strongly believe that only humans possess knowledge [5]. Representatives of information technology track have a broader viewpoint and argue that there are natural knowledge possessors and artificial knowledge possessors [7]. It looks like that this point of view is more perspective and will help to narrow the gap between two tracks of KM.

In this paper possible ways are outlined how to bridge gaps between different approaches to KM. They are based on advanced information technology (IT) and modern approach to artificial intelligence (AI). We have neither an intention nor the space to cover in detail all methods, techniques and technologies that already are or may be borrowed from IT and AI fields for KM purposes. Rather, we will try to focus on potential of these techniques and technologies for the development of KMS. It is worth to stress that perspectives of modern trends in IT and AI frequently are underestimated and even denied.

The paper is organised as follows. In the next section details about two KM tracks are given. The purpose of this section is to show the differences of both tracks and to stress the necessity of integration of traditional KMS and modern IT and AI techniques. The third section is devoted to the information and knowledge-based systems that are considered as roots of KMS. The role of intelligent agents and multiagent systems in KM is described in this section, too. A novel multilevel model of intelligent enterprise memory is proposed in the fourth section. Conclusions outline the perspective of the proposed model and the future work on its implementation.

2. Characteristic of Knowledge Management and two Tracks in it

Knowledge management is a concept that has emerged explosively over recent years. Is this concept of KM really new? Answer is not really! The discipline of KM is only fifteen years old. Remember that Karl Wiig coined the term *"knowledge management"* in 1986. It is not easy to find a widely recognised definition of KM. At present there is much debate, and little consensus, about exactly what in fact is KM. The perceptions of KM depend on the person and his/her speciality [14]. For example, information professionals (librarians and archivists) emphasise document management, information technologists stress hardware, software, network and telecommunications. Scientists, state or local government, specialists in education, health care, industry, business, agriculture etc., have different viewpoints reflecting their interests in knowledge management.

Generalisation of known opinions allows concluding that KM is the amalgamation of earlier experience. This experience includes past and current systems such as data base management systems, business process reengineering, management information systems, decision support systems, total quality management, knowledge-based systems, artificial intelligence, software engineering, human resource management and organisational behaviour concepts [10, 14].

Exploration of KM definitions given by different authors [11, 15, 17] initiates their division into three classes. The proposed classification is based on three criteria: formal, process and organisational aspects.

If *formal aspects* are stressed then KM is the formalisation of and access to experience, the systematic, explicit, and deliberate building, renewal and application of knowledge and expertise to maximise an enterprise's knowledge-related effectiveness and returns from its knowledge assets.

If focus is on *process aspects* KM is the process of capturing an organisation's collective expertise and the process through which organisations create, store and utilise their collective knowledge.

In case if *organisational and management aspects* are brought to the forefront KM means exactly the explicit control and management of organisational knowledge aimed at achieving the objectives and for generating a competitive advantage.

Quite different opinion on KM is connected with an attempt to define KM by looking at what people in this field are doing [15] Two tracks of activities, namely, *information technology track knowledge management* and *people track knowledge management* are distinguished. Because of their different origins, these two tracks use different languages that frequently cause confusion. The first track corresponds to management of information field where researchers and practitioners tend to have their education in computer, systems and/or information science. They are involved in construction of document and information management systems, decision support systems, artificial intelligence, reengineering, groupware, etc. To them knowledge means objects that can be identified and handled in information systems. The focus of artificial intelligence specialists and E-specialists is on the individual, while focus of reengineers is on the organisation. This track is new and is growing very fast at this moment due to new developments in information technology [15]. Information technology track KM has become a new way of capturing an organisation's expertise and knowledge addressing factors such as:

– Knowledge infrastructure for just-in-time knowledge and global access
– Enhancing the amount and visibility of knowledge in an organisation
– Sharing knowledge both within an organisation and with external clients
– Capturing tacit knowledge and experience of knowledge workers, and promoting transformation of tacit knowledge into explicit knowledge for global access.

A wide variety of technology components constitute the infrastructure of KMS. The list includes browsers, Web site interfaces and documents, skill directories, maps of people's competencies and interests, and collaborative work tools. Video conferences, electronic forums, digital white boards and libraries, wrapper tools, knowledge repositories, electronic data exchange, data mining, data warehouses, just-in-time inventory management, total quality management, enterprise resource planning, intelligent agent tools, and many other components must be added to this list as well.

People track KM corresponds to management of people. Researchers and practitioners in this field tend to have their education in philosophy, psychology, sociology and/or business and management. They are primarily involved in assessing, changing and improving human individual skills and/or behaviour. To them knowledge means processes, a complex set of dynamic, constantly changing skills, know-how, etc. They are traditionally involved in learning and in managing these competencies on an organisational level like, the so-called organisational theorists, i.e., philosophers and sociologists, or on an individual level like psychologists. They are convinced that knowledge is not something that can be managed.

For them KM is the art of creating value from an organisation's intangible assets. This track is very old, and is not growing so fast [15].

Due to their different origins both tracks use different languages and to a certain extent even do not recognise each other's successful solutions. For example, organisational theorists claim that information technology has never addressed the tacit knowledge, and that information technology approach is a purely mechanistic solution of information issues that can be considered as naively promoting software and hardware packages to resolve KM problems. They argue that the user inputs the knowledge, not the "knowledge manager" or "knowledge engineer" [9]. As a consequence, people track community is very cautious about successes of IT and AI, in particular, in efforts to capture and structure the tacit knowledge to make it accessible. On the contrary, those who represent IT track are focusing their efforts on how to achieve knowledge flow because numerous case studies manifest that knowledge growth is impossible without the knowledge flow. They look at KM from the point of view of systems analysis, design and implementation. Their approach may emphasise one or several areas, in particular, knowledge storage and access, telecommunications, application software packages, knowledge processing and distribution. Thus, any technological advances that help to promote knowledge flow are considered as KM tools. In fact, the real synergy can be achieved if there will be balanced approaches to KM taking into consideration advantages and drawbacks of both tracks. It is quite obvious that if more knowledge is captures and made accessible, the organisation is richer of knowledge, and vice versa. This is very important for organisations that are operating in rapidly changing environments and for service organisations that are under permanent pressure from the business world, and, as a consequence, are facing danger to lose a part of their knowledge if somebody leaves the organisation. In this case knowledge capturing, storage, processing and usage are the most relevant activities to keep organisation's intelligent capital up to date. Advanced information systems and modern paradigms of AI are very promising to manage these activities. Information system and AI areas are more or less interdisciplinary and have borrowed many fruitful ideas from philosophy, psychology, sociology, organisational theory, economics, linguistics, mathematics, and computer science, and have worked out concepts of intelligent information systems, intelligent agents and multiagent systems. The use of these concepts in knowledge management may produce the synergy effect reaching balance between both tracks of knowledge management.

3. Roots of Knowledge Management Systems and Impact of Distributed Artificial Intelligence

Knowledge management systems centre on the organisation, codification and dissemination of knowledge in organisations. It represents a collaborative work environment in which organisational knowledge is captured, structured and made accessible to facilitate a more effective decision making. KMS have their roots in various kinds of prior information and knowledge-based systems as it is depicted in Figure 1.

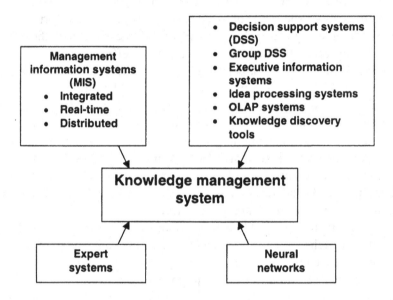

Figure 1. Knowledge management system and its roots

Today's KMS are influenced by past and current management information systems such as *integrated, real-time* and *distributed management information systems* [16]. All management information systems centre on periodical reports and give a periodical answer what should have been done.

Systems where a viewpoint of decision-maker is added are called *decision support systems*. These systems are designed to support problem-finding and problem-solving decisions of the manager. Nowadays we can observe evolution of decision support systems towards *group decision support systems* that combine computers, data communication, and decision technologies to support problem finding and problem solving for managers and their staffs. Technologies such as groupware, electronic boardrooms equipped with large screen projectors or electronic whiteboards, local area networks, Web and video conferencing, group process technologies (voting tools, brainstorming tools, etc.), decision support software have promoted an interest in these systems. *Executive information systems* are an extension of decision support systems. Executive information systems bring together relevant data from various internal and external sources. *Idea processing systems* are a subset of group decision support systems and are designed to capture, evaluate, and synthesise ideas into a large context that has real meaning for decision-makers. Related to previous kinds of systems are *on-line analytical processing (OLAP) systems*. These systems centre on the question "what happened" and provide a multidimensional view of summarised data. As such, they provide a starting point for knowledge discovery within a knowledge management system's operating mode [16]. *Knowledge discovery tools* are the next step beyond OLAP systems for querying data warehouses, and as the prerequisite for interpretation and dissemination of knowledge, and discovering of new knowledge.

Knowledge acquisition and usage typically have been implemented in *expert systems*, i.e., knowledge-based systems. These systems are designed to imitate problem-solving abilities of experts in a particular problem domain. In the knowledge management context expert systems can be thought of as knowledge transfer agents [16]. The real problem with expert system is that if the query is about something outside the expert system knowledge domain, it cannot respond. This is where *neural networks* can help. Neural networks learn the human decision-making process by examples. Thus, neural networks do not require a complete knowledge base and extensive interpretation of it by an inference engine. Neural networks are effective in processing fuzzy, incomplete, distorted, and "noisy" data. They are suitable for decision support under conditions of uncertainty, and extremely useful in data mining and other database specialised tasks.

Recent trends manifest that there is a transition to a combined environment of KMS and advanced AI techniques, such as, for example, *virtual reality* and *distributed artificial intelligence* (multiagent systems) [8]. The integration of KMS with virtual reality allows decision makers to think from a different perspective and to enhance their skills using sophisticated interactive computer graphics, special clothing and fibber optic sensors. This allows treating of system-generated objects almost as real things.

These developments to a large extent are related with the appearance of the notion "*cyberspace*" as the environment for both humans and intelligent agents [1] to support interactive users. These developments promote new exciting results of AI and new promising applications as well. Intelligent software agents, in particular, offer an ideal technology platform for providing data sharing, personal services, and pooled knowledge [3].

Where and how intelligent agents can be used in KM already today and what are the perspectives of single agents and multiagent systems in this field in the future? Nowadays agents prove to be good at performing lists of tasks when specified triggers evaluate true [8]. The triggers can be such events as, for example, report completed, fax received, and so on. Agents can also serve for monitoring and collecting information from data streams and taking action on what they encounter. In this case multiple agents are responsible for network access, searching and filtering, i.e., for information gathering and filtering. They are designed for information handling in information environments like wide-area and local area networks, for instance, the Internet, organisation's intranet, etc. These agents are most commonly used due to the fact that for most people navigating and using network systems is an increasingly difficult and time-consuming task. In [8] descriptions of various agents can be found. The most interesting classes of agents that may be used for KM purposes are depicted in Figure 2.

All classes of agents may be developed using environments that effectively support agent building and execution [8]. Smalltalk and Java have a tremendous potential as agent languages however they are not yet ready to provide a standardised agent execution environment and architecture (theoretically agents could be built in assembly language, C, or COBOL). Generally speaking, all technologies that incorporates an object-oriented (OO) language and development environment can be successfully used for building agents. For example, Visual Basic, Power Builder, Delphi, FoxPro, Excel and Word can access OLE Automation objects allowing to use OLE Automation's ability to support dynamic invocation of interfaces of COM objects from scripting languages to invoke CORBA objects while mobile agent technologies require Telescript [8].

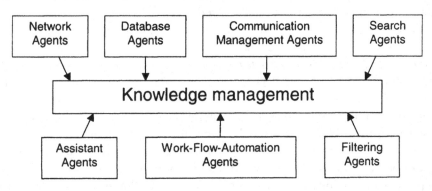

Figure 2. Intelligent agents for knowledge management support

To conclude this resume, let us point out that the described classes of agents may be included into a groupware, that is, hardware and software technology to assist interacting groups [4]. *Computer Supported Co-operative Work*, in its turn, is the study how groups work, and how it is possible to implement this technology to enhance group interaction and collaboration that is particularly important to achieve the goals of KM. There are many groupware systems such as systems that allow group (concurrent) editing and reviewing documents, computer aided software engineering (CASE) and computer aided design (CAD) tools, workflow management systems, meeting co-ordinators and group decision support systems, desktop conferencing systems (audio and video), distance learning systems, and so on. Besides groupware modules, which are relevant for operating of the entire groupware system, frequently modules are needed that perform specialised functions and involve specialised domain knowledge. The latest modules are called *team agents* [4]. Examples of team agents are user interface agents, "social mediators" within an electronic meeting, and appointment schedulers that allow scheduling a meeting among a group of people by selecting a free time slot for all participants.

From the discussion above follows that nowadays there is a wide variety of systems (information management systems, knowledge-based systems, agent-based systems) that are already used as components of KMS to extend their effectiveness in organisation's everyday operations and achieving of organisation's strategic goals.

Some authors [8, 3] foresee that in future the role of agent-based systems in KM will grow rapidly and steadily. The next step in agent technology is to use *smart agents*. They exhibit a combination of all capabilities that are characteristic for *co-operative agents* (communicate with other agents), *adaptive agents* (behave differently in given situations), *personal agents* (serve individual users), *proactive agents* (initiate actions) and *collaborative agents* (co-operate with other agents). Smart agents will be able to collect information about database and business applications, as well as to acquire, store, generate and distribute knowledge. The future evolution of suitable agents for KM is connected with information agents and their extension – *knowledge agents* that will be able to learn from their environments and from each other as well as to co-operate with each other. They will have access to many types of information and knowledge sources and will be able to manipulate information and knowledge in order to answer queries posed by humans and other knowledge agents. So, more and more activities performed by humans will be automated that allow to replace at least part of humans that now provide information and knowledge base services by intelligent agents and their communities. That, in turn, will crucially impact evolution of KMS making them more and more intelligent.

4.   Concept of Intelligent Enterprise Memory

Working together components of KMS provide the *knowledge environment,* that is, creation (acquisition, inference, generation), preservation, storage, aggregation (creation of meta-knowledge), use, reuse, and transfer (distribution, sharing) of all knowledge. It is obvious that knowledge can be reused, processed and transformed only if it is captured and stored in some kind of memory. Traditional memories used in KM are *organisational, corporate* and *enterprise memories* [2, 6, 18]. Due to the focus of this paper only enterprise memory will be discussed in this section. Let only remark that an organisational memory refers to stored information from an organisation's history but a corporate memory focus on the persistence of knowledge in an organisation.

Enterprise memory is considered as a structure that can support the sharing and reuse of individual knowledge worker's and enterprise-wide knowledge, experience and lessons learnt. It can be created through processes of acquisition, capturing and representation of tacit (informal) and explicit (formal) knowledge coming from different sources. Structurally the enterprise memory is very similar to the organisational memory. One can look at the enterprise memory as a systematic merging of various knowledge bases. The enterprise memory is designed to provide the functionality to identify, acquire, store, distribute, and reuse all captured knowledge for future use. To a certain extent, the enterprise memory promotes enterprise learning and adaptation. Knowledge about past cases (experience) serves as stimulant for learning and leads to expertise transfer and distribution. Though, despite of the fact that concept of enterprise memory is very knowledge centred, known models lack "intelligence" [6].

In this paper we propose an intelligent multilevel enterprise memory model based on the sequence of seven phases of knowledge life cycle. This model is depicted in Figure 3. If one looks at the proposed model from the point of view of four phases of knowledge life cycle [12], several paths of knowledge transformations can be followed. Tacit knowledge sources are individual knowledge workers and problem domain experts. All knowledge acquisition methods and tools of the second level support the externalisation process. Explicit knowledge sources are listed at the first level. This knowledge is captured at Levels 3 and 4. Knowledge processing tools (Level 5) support combination of existing explicit knowledge, i.e., the process of generation of new explicit knowledge which is implemented in tools depicted at the six level. Consultation and advisory service (Level 7) supports the internalisation of knowledge, i.e., the conversion process of explicit knowledge into new individual tacit knowledge.

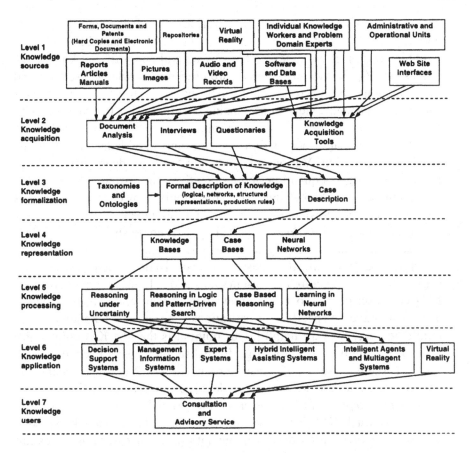

Figure 3. Model of intelligent enterprise memory

Relationships between KM process and the levels of the proposed intelligent enterprise memory model are reflected in Table 1. This table represents mapping of components of KM process on corresponding levels of intelligent multilevel enterprise memory model.

Table 1. Mapping

Components of knowledge management process	Levels of enterprise memory model
Knowledge identification and creation	1, 2, 5
Knowledge acquisition, inference and generation	2, 5
Knowledge storage	3, 4, 5
Knowledge aggregation	5
Access, analysis, use-reuse of knowledge	5, 6, 7
Knowledge distribution and sharing	6
Consultations	7

Now let look at the proposed model in more details.

- *Knowledge Source Level* consists of various knowledge sources of tacit and explicit knowledge. Knowledge at this level is tangible and non-tangible as well. It is possessed both by natural and artificial knowledge possessors [6]. Knowledge sources are used for knowledge creation and identification. These activities are supported by several KM technologies such as, for instance, video conferencing and discussion forums.
- *Knowledge Acquisition Level.* The main purpose of this level is to facilitate systematic acquisition of relevant knowledge in a given application situation. Various methods and tools are developed in AI to make knowledge acquisition more effective, for instance, interviews, questionnaires and knowledge acquisition tools. However, till now it is the bottleneck of knowledge-based system development.
- *Knowledge Formalisation Level* is a prerequisite for efficient representation and processing of explicit knowledge. The AI community has developed four different classes of formalisation languages, namely, logic, networks, structured representations and rules as well as languages for case description. To make knowledge formalisation more effective and to avoid case-specific formalisations, appropriate taxonomies and ontologies may be very helpful. Our opinion is that the KM community pays little attention to knowledge formalisation aspects even in the IT track (except issues of case descriptions). Very promising is amalgamation of case description methods used in AI and KM.
- *Knowledge Representation Level* is the crucial level in information technology track KM. This level provides bases for explicit knowledge processing when knowledge is stored into a knowledge base, cases are stored in a case base or the structure of neural network is determined. Recent trends manifest implementation of hybrid systems where different knowledge representation schemas are used. The AI community, as a rule, asserts that transformation of formalised knowledge from one scheme to another is not a problem at all. Unfortunately, in practice interface problems usually arise if different formalisation languages are used for development of an organisational or enterprise.
- *Knowledge Processing Level.* This level may be considered as "explicit knowledge flow engine" in KM process which provides knowledge combination. A plethora of reasoning and machine learning methods has been offered and may be used in KM. Knowledge flow is supported also by many KM technologies; knowledge repositories, digital libraries and Internet search engines are only few examples. Integration of different technologies promises higher effectiveness of combination and internalisation processes of organisational knowledge life cycle.
- *Knowledge Application Level.* This is the second relevant level for knowledge flow in organisation. Such activities as knowledge reuse and

transfer depend on the quality of systems used. Many technologies are proposed in KM, for example, workflow, groupware and helpdesks. Well known knowledge-based systems, namely, decision support systems, management information systems and expert systems must be added as instruments for easy access, analysis, use, reuse and distribution of captured organisational knowledge. We predict that the role of hybrid intelligent assisting systems based on the intelligent agent paradigm and different kinds of models and simulation tools will increase very quickly.

- *Knowledge Users Level.* User's level provides consulting and advisory services to organisation's knowledge workers or the public. To intensify the knowledge distribution nowadays modern IT facilities are used in rapidly increasing numbers. Among those tools the most popular ones are Web and video conferencing, collaborative work tools and intranets of organisations. Explanation modules of knowledge-based systems also can fulfil mission of knowledge dissemination.

In future a lot of work must be done to make the proposed intelligent multilevel enterprise memory a reality. To the large extent it depends on advanced AI technologies.

5. Conclusions

The hard obstacles towards an integrated approach to KM are rather clearly outlined differences between the two tracks, namely, people knowledge management and information technology knowledge management that exist like two large "knowledge islands". In this paper the role of modern approaches to information systems and AI is outlined for bridging gaps between two isolated fields. Amalgamation of intelligent agent paradigm with KM approaches may give a synergy effect. This paper has several objectives. First, KM definitions are classified into three classes on the bases of such criteria as formal, process and organisational aspects. Second, it is shown that KMS have the roots in information and knowledge-based systems. Third, the impact of distributed AI on present and future solutions for KMS is discussed. At last, but not least, a novel multilevel model of intelligent enterprise memory as a tool for integration of concepts used in KM and AI is proposed.

Regardless of future work needed to achieve a considerable amalgamation of KM and AI technologies, we see a potential for using proposed model to develop a general approach that will make the intellectual capital of an organisation to work as an effective knowledge engine. The intelligent enterprise memory offers a systematic approach to knowledge creation, capturing, representation, use/reuse, and transfer of organisational

134

knowledge. Practical implementation of the proposed model is the major topic of the future work. It would serve as a platform for researchers to investigate the effectiveness and efficiency of integrated interdisciplinary approaches to knowledge management.

References

[1] Bradshow, J.M., et. al. Terraforming cyberspace. Computer, July, 2001, pp. 48-56.
[2] Brooking, A. Corporate Memory: Strategies for Knowledge Management. International Thompson Business Press, 1999.
[3] Case, S., Azarmi, M., Thint, M., Ohtani, T. Enhancing e-communities with agent-based systems. Computer, July, 2001, pp. 64-69.
[4] Ellis, C., Wainer, J. Groupware and computer supported cooperative work. In Waiss, G. (ed.). Multiagent Systems. A Modern Approach to Distributed Artificial Intelligence, The MIT Press, 2000, pp. 425-458.
[5] Galiers, R.D., Newell, S. Back to the future: from knowledge management to data management. In Smithson, S. et. al. (eds.). Proceedings of the 9th European Conference on Information Systems, University of Maribor, Slovenia, 2001, pp. 609-615.
[6] Grundspenkis, J. Concepts of organizations, intelligent agents, knowledge and memories: towards an interdisciplinary knowledge management. In Wang, K., Grundspenkis, J., Yerofeev, A. (eds.). Applied Computation Intelligence to Engineering and Business, Riga Technical University Press, 2001, pp. 173-193.
[7] Kirikova, M., Grundspenkis, J. Using knowledge distribution in requirements engineering. In Leondes, C. T. (ed.). Knowledge Based Systems, Techniques and Applications, Vol. 1, Academic Press, 2000, pp. 149-184.
[8] Knapik, M., Johnson, J. Developing Intelligent Agents for Distributed Systems. Mc-Graw Hill, 1998.
[9] Koenig, M.E.D., Srikantaiah, T.K. The evolution of knowledge management. In Srikantaiah, T.K., Koenig, M.E.D. (eds.). Knowledge Management for the Information Professional, ASIS Monograph Series, 2000, pp. 23-36.
[10] Liebowitz, J. Building Organizational Intelligence: A Knowledge Management Primer. CRC Press, 2000.
[11] Liebowitz, J. Knowledge Management Handbook. CRC Press, 1999.
[12] Nonaka, I., Takeuchi, H. Knowledge Creating Organizations. Oxford University Press, 1995.
[13] Piccoli, G., Ahmad, R., Ives, B. Knowledge management in academia. Information Technology and Management, 1, 2000, pp. 229-245.
[14] Srikantaiah, T.K. Knowledge management: a faceted overview. In Srikantaiah, T.K., Koenig, M.E.D. (eds.). Knowledge Management for the Information Professional, ASIS Monograph Series, 2000, pp. 7-17.
[15] Sveiby, K-E. What Is Knowledge Management? http://www.sveiby.com.au/KnowledgeManagement.html
[16] Thierauf, R.J. Knowledge Management Systems for Business. Quorum Books, 1999.
[17] Tiwana, A. The Knowledge Management Toolkit. Prentice Hall, 2000.
[18] Walsh, J.P., Ungson, G. R. Organizational memory. Academy of Management Review, 16(1), 1991, pp. 57-91.

KNOWLEDGE REPRESENTATION IN ADVISORY INFORMATION SYSTEM OF CRIME INVESTIGATION DOMAIN

Dale Dzemydiene
Law University of Lithuania
Ateities 20, 2527 Vilnius, Lithuania
Institute of Mathematics and Informatics
Akademijos 4, 2600 Vilnius, Lithuania
E-mail: daledz@ktl.mii.lt

Egle Kazemikaitiene, Rimantas Petrauskas
Law University of Lithuania
Ateities 20, 2527 Vilnius, Lithuania
E-mail: eglek@ltu.lt, rpetraus@ltu.lt

Abstract   New information technologies take new possibilities in detecting criminals and investigation of crimes. The paper considers the methods of knowledge representation helpful in the management of repository of criminalistics information system. The development of advisory system in crime investigation domain deals with incomplete and uncertainty information from the broad variety of data sources ensuring many forms of intellectual analysis and situation evaluation methods. New possibilities of knowledge representation are examined for the purposes to prepare the qualitative intelligent systems for crime investigation. The unified approach of integrating different databases and knowledge representation techniques for aiding advisory processes in relevant patterns recognition and crime investigation is proposed.

Keywords: advisory information system, knowledge representation, databases, case-based reasoning, crime investigation.

H.-M. Haav and A. Kalja (eds.), Databases and Information Systems II, 135–147.

1. Introduction

The advisory-consultative systems in law enforcement offer additional advantages that facilitate the decision-making process in complex situations of crime recognitions. Such systems use artificial intelligence techniques to draw conclusions from facts presented by the crime investigator. Developments in the field of information technology provide the crime investigation processes with a vast quantity of data, from different sources, reflect criminal events and their relationships [15]. Relevant patterns are not easy to extract from this huge quantity of data. Moreover, the available data are often incomplete and uncertain; for instance, all criminal events are not reported to the police; the date and time of a particular event are generally not precisely known; and traces collected are often fragmentary. Dealing with imperfect data reflecting complex-evolving phenomena is very common to criminal investigation and crime analysis [13, 14]. Legal and organizational barriers, the proliferation of methods for collecting and interpreting data, and the consequent variety of incompatible recording systems make comparisons difficult, when performed. Poor analysis of similar offences crossing different areas is recognized as one of the major weaknesses pertaining to information systems; this has been called 'linkage blindness'.

The aforementioned reasons create the necessity to seek for the methods of display that would allow avoid these disadvantages: case-based learning strategy is integrated with the experts' experience in the MODELER system [20]. Some systems employ case-based learning for the design of knowledge base optimising system [2]. The opportunities of conceptual clusters of machine learning are presented, by use of case-based method for testing and assessing a real time complex system knowledge base [7, 22].

The main purposes of our advisory system under construction are to assist in crime-solving processes, creating of suspect profiles by giving computer-aided instructions, planning and situation recognition techniques. The use of advisory systems may also improve legal training, for example, providing police with advice on the type of information required by prosecutors to reduce the rate of case attrition.

A key part of law enforcement is to understand those activities, through the development and use of methods, models and tools for collecting and then interpreting the large volume of data available in real time [6, 11]. Consequently, intelligence programs have been developed, leading to recognition of a field of activity called crime analysis, which has been described as 'the identification of and the provision of insight into the relationship between crime data and other potentially relevant data with a view to police and judicial practice' [21]. The artificial intelligence methods are very important in the development of judicial, consultative, expert systems. This caries over to disagreement on what the content of our research should be.

Moreover, technological means provide the opportunity to solve problems involving strategic data recording and integrating it with the automatic situation detection and management system. The system offers several ways of making decisions, based on the situation evaluation [6, 8, 10]. The knowledge acquisition methods have the properties of representing of deep knowledge [1].

The purpose of this research is to develop the coherent framework of intellectual information systems for supporting crime investigation processes. The questions of how to integrate the different pieces of data into warehouse and how to manage knowledge for complex situation recognition has become an important topic of our research. Patterns reflecting fraudulent activities are therefore always more difficult to reveal from the huge quantity of data scattered in files across independent police and legal structures. Increased mobility and new communication channels give criminals the capacity to better plan and organize their activities over large geographical areas. The tasks for development of advisory decision-support system and the methods of implementation are being considered. The paper addresses the problem of interoperability of independent heterogeneous information resources in a crime investigation domain.

2. Problems and Purposes of Crime Analysis

The crime investigator and the crime analyst are of increasing importance to provide the best use not solely of new techniques but also of scientific attitudes during the whole investigation process. Traditionally, each scene of crime is seen as an independent 'complete' set of data from which the intelligent investigator can find the signature of the offender. Links between cases are often interred through police investigation in a separate process; cases are also compared through the use of physical evidence collected at the scene of crime.

Thoroughly the crime analysis aims at the deciphering the knowledge used by experienced investigators to identify and formalize concepts and notions, and the methods used by them to manage their information. As well we deal with the conceiving new methods of treating data, and adapting existing ones, given that computer tools can improve the analysis process in a way that was not previously possible. Normalizing language and symbols are used in the course of the analysis in order to facilitate teamwork on complex problems, and to disseminate the results of the analysis in a way that is easy to interpret.

Using those methods the advisory system under development must produce relevant conclusions or hypotheses that can help towards concrete actions.

A broad variety of analysis forms could be defined. For instance, crime pattern analysis, profile analysis, case analysis (course of events immediately before, during and after a serious offence), comparative case analysis, etc.

As a consequence:

• New structures could be created to exchange of information across countries;

• New intelligence structures within the organizations could be created, with an important part dedicated to crime analysis;

• Structured and normalized methods of analysis of data could be developed.

For these purposes a broad variety of computerized tools have been introduced (geographic information systems, meta-modelling of repositories, statistical analysis, qualitative management of data warehouses, etc.).

3. Knowledge Representation of Crime Investigation Application Domain

The development of intelligent system in crime investigation domain requires the application of additional methods, their task being the description of situations, revealing relationships between people, scenes of crimes and objects, as well as helping to develop working hypotheses and decision support. When analysing the components of intellectual information systems, the attention is paid to the opportunities: how to display legal information, which methods to use for the decision-making in crime investigation, what procedures are used in judicial systems, etc. For that reason we are trying to define the purposes of applying these methods, including decision making problems in judicial system.

The specificity of judicial system fields most frequently involves the problems of structuring and describing the phenomena formalised. The structural analysis of system becomes an interesting problem when analysing the steps of developing intelligent informational system. The knowledge that enables us to understand how to apply the methods of decision preparation is of special importance. Means of reasoning, methods of proof are among the concepts used in the intelligent informational systems. Intellectual information systems have the additional properties that enable structuring and storing data in the system, modelling situations, making and explaining hypotheses [2, 7, 8, 16]. In most instances the complex structure of legal information and knowledge can't be expressed by single formal means. Other possibilities for the integrated use of these methods have to be sought.

An important task is the development of a common computer-based working dictionary of the law enforcement system. In order to become familiar with the principles underlying the development of such working dictionary, the methods that enable the definition of the concepts and associations used in judicial system as well as the level of concord between concepts and their equal comprehensibility are discussed. The methods of developing the legal ontology and presenting it in computer network play an important role in the solution of this problem [18]. The ontology of crime investigation domain is under construction in our advisory system. The ontological view based on object-oriented model using UML [4] helps us to reveal knowledge and examine main principles and substantiation of the "game" rules. An example of representation of crime characteristic is shown in Figure 1. An example of crime hierarchy is presented in Figure 2.

In addition, the knowledge system must be able to abstract information and data about the current situation and to have the possibilities of retrospective analysis and prognoses [10, 9].

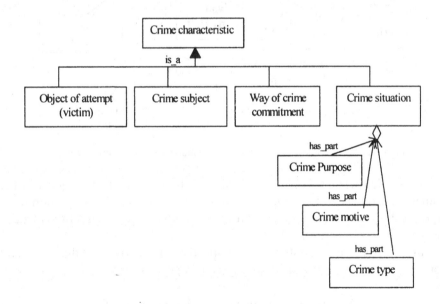

Figure 1. An example of representing crime characteristic model

Automatic selection and management of the rules, suitable for the assessment of a particular situation, is performed in the expert systems. Core and shell mechanisms of the expert system ensure the presentation, sorting and selection of the rules [5, 7]. As a result, the user is given a simple interface to enter the primary rules in a suitable natural format, e.g.

IF <situation$_i$ ∨ conditions$_k$> THEN <situation$_j$ ∨ conclusions$_n$>

Image enhancement by computer has emerged as a forensic examination method in its own right. In latent print examination, quantitative digital image processing relative to automated fingerprint identification systems (AFIS) has been proceeding for over 20 years [12].

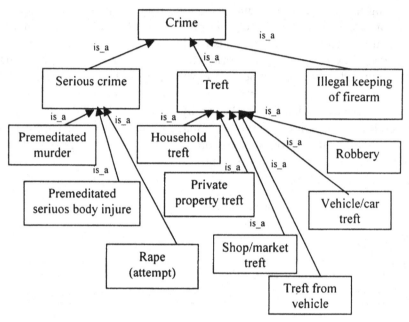

Figure 2. An example of representing crime hierarchy in the ontological layer

If deep knowledge is revealed, the causal structure of the objects in the domain is examined. Qualitatively expressed knowledge is the predominant type of deep knowledge. There are certain advantages of qualitative deep knowledge representation:

• as a rule, the qualitative perspective is narrower than general considerations about physical or psychological processes, which are to be modelled;

• the values of numerous parameters are not necessary for the completion of a model;

• computer-based implementation of qualitative modelling is less intricate than multiple modelling of instances;

• qualitative modelling can be used to explain various mechanisms of the system.

In addition, the model itself is visually more lucid as opposed to multiple enumerations of instances. The model may be used to automatically generate the instances of various course of action by the application of thorough qualitative imitational modelling.

Long-term use of the rule-based knowledge representation method in the expert systems has unveiled some of their disadvantages and certain limitations of expert practice expression. The exploitation of the rule-based system is aggravated when the knowledge base is large. The expression of the rules, generalising the use of rules, i.e. meta-rules, is quite complicated. There are certain limitations of displaying the deep knowledge. It is difficult to supplement the knowledge base with experience and exceptional cases [19]. Most systems have relatively simple explanation capabilities, by displaying rule sequences based on their use to draw a particular conclusion. It is rather difficult to encode knowledge by means of strictly defined rules in some applied fields.

Case-based reasoning is a computer-based method, which analyses the solution of formal solved problems based on analogy or associations with the solution of a current problem [2]. Case-based reasoning has several advantages over productive systems: case-based reasoning is closer in nature to the factual processes of human-made solutions; the expert, having been presented with a problem, initially compares this problem with formerly solved problems, determines its separate similar parts. Should the case-based system fail to arrive at a desired conclusion, new rules are to be made and added to the knowledge base.

4.   Integrating Components of Data and Knowledge in the Framework of Crime Investigation Processes

The main purpose of the criminal information system has been to assist all officials and agencies of the criminal justice system in the fulfilment of their varied responsibilities on a state-wide basis by providing round-the-clock access to needed information.

The unified national criminal information system could be created based on crime characteristics (corpus delicti), which include the object of attempt (victim), the crime subject (criminal), the crime situation and way of crime commitment [14]. The criminal information system has to provide the information about similar crimes, which were committed before, have to connect the new crime with already committed [19]. The criminal characteristics consist of information about the object of attempt (victims); information about the crime subject (criminals); information about the way of crime commitment; information about the crime situation. The types of situation can be provocative, conflict, and accidental, etc.

The forensic intelligence process starts with the collection of data and ends with the integration of results into the analysis of crimes under investigation (Figure 3).

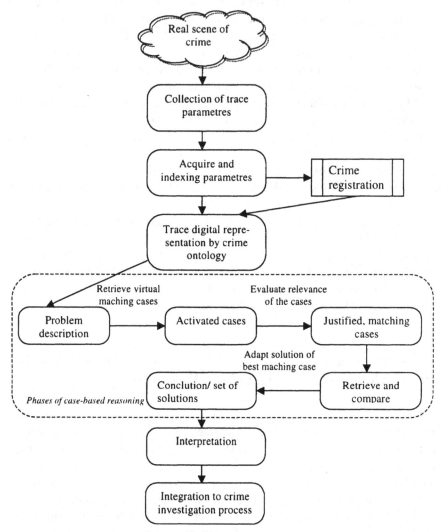

Figure 3. Forensic intelligence process from the collection of data to the dissemination of results

In this process, important intermediate steps may be described as follows:

- the acquisition of new data in order to transform it into a digital or symbolic form suitable for searching for similar items in the database, and to memorize it in a way that will allow retrieval when needed;
- the search and matching process;
- the interpretation/verification of the returned result.

Introducing model of reasoning from past cases subsumes knowledge–intensive case–based reasoning. Such model can be viewed as containing three phases:

(1)   *Activation phase*: retrieve a set of cases that matches the current problem according to some criteria.

(2)   *Explanation phase*: evaluate the applicability of retrieved cases to the current problem. This involves looking for contradictions, checking constraints, generating and testing expectations set up by the retrieved case.

(3)   *Adaptation phase*: adapt the solution of the case to the new problem. A modification process would typically involve a generalization of the past solution followed by a specialization satisfying constraints on the current problem.

Similarities found between accessible information can lead to inferences on the profile of offenders, their mode of action and the means they have used. The identification of recidivists is the better-known form of this basic scheme. Knowledge base can assist, but not replace, the decision-making process by providing access to more timely and accurate information on individual cases, for example, in scheduling cases and assigning them to investigators and in preparing decisions on bail and sentencing. Computerisation can also provide investigators with rapid access to reference material, such statutes and case law.

From a new situation or a new case, the purpose is to identify known offenders from their antecedents. The search for links between cases is another elementary activity that falls within the same framework; it allows groupings that delineate criminal events. Finally, when objects are found or perpetrators identified, all the cases in which there participation or presence can be supposed should be extracted. This process is traditionally incomplete because links may not systematically be searched before the offender has been arrested. It could be that identifying an offender for a crime is sufficient to put him or her behind bars, without being charged with other offences that could be difficult to prove. This is something that real-time crime analysis avoids. These steps have been partially reproduced in computer applications; the best-known illustrations are AFIS (automatic fingerprint identification systems) and DNA databases [14]. For instance, from a DNA point of view, it includes the application of the analytical techniques used to identify markers of a sample, together with encoding into the system the obtained values in the form of numbers.

Histogram equalization: radiometric enhancement wherein concentrations of radiometric intensities in the histogram of an image are reassigned values, effectively spreading out those intensities to increase contrast and clarity. The values of the required variables are scanned in the information module, which is the main component of the monitoring (i.e. real-time recording of data) system. Thus, if a finger mark, even fragmentary, found at the scene of a crime is compared with the content of a database, a restricted number of similar fingerprints will be given to the experts who interpret them. The histogram equalization is radiometric enhancement wherein concentrations of radiometric intensities in the histogram of an image are reassigned values [12].

Most information is gathered through a device that is interfaced with a computer, like a scanner or various types of camera. The image obtained is then treated to extract relevant features for encoding. This operation is computerized to different degrees, depending on the trace and its quality. Potentially, all the other marks transferred, or the information left by the offender (from clothing or accessories), could be analysed in a similar way.

Computer systems in forensic intelligence can be classified into two groups. Investigative methods are essentially based on analogy. Consequently, it is not surprising that most existing computer systems recognized as forensic intelligence systems can be viewed as an aid to performing this type of reasoning process. The second class of system pertains to collections that help classify evidence by the type of object that could have transferred a trace.

Unified criminal information system consists of separate databases, which are ruled of different departments. The main centred databases (DB) are: DB of population of Republic of Lithuania (information about citizens – all data of identification card and/or passport); DB of transport vehicles registration); DB of firearms (information about registered firearms and owners); DB of wanted persons as criminals and missing persons; DB of stolen vehicles; DB of stolen firearms; DB of committed crimes and criminals.

Police preventively records and collects the information about persons who is susceptible to violate, registered numbered objects, information about administrative violations of law, automated fingerprint identification system (AFIS), others criminal collections of traces, which were put from crime scene [13, 21]. Databases function in computers with UNIX operating system. The information loading, recognition, proofreading and searching programs accomplished ORACLE SQL*Forms program measures, switched in user menu SQL*Menu. The loading of information could be fulfil by regime SQL*Loader.

Retrieval and matching collection of data at the scene of crime is always incomplete and imprecise, and collected marks are often fragmentary, even if the investigation is careful and thorough. An object that caused a trace can evolve, and marks or prints can be distorted. The match between recorded data and collected evidence (in its digital form) is therefore generally only partial. A human operator must always interpret a limited set of possible solutions at the end of the chain.

A broad range of retrieval and matching algorithms using various techniques are actually implemented to compare the data automatically. From a practical point of view, DNA and fingerprints provide extreme examples; the problem of matching two DNA markers is very simple from a computing perspective, as the match is generally determined by an 'exact' comparison. It is not claimed that the implementation of the whole process, from the collection of data to its storage in the system, is easy, but the 'retrieval and matching problems' themselves are not difficult.) A retrieval algorithm can be implemented directly with simple computer development tools. The Lithuanian criminal information system network operated by teleprocessing specialists provides direct terminal access to computerized databases maintained by Lithuanian agencies.

5. Conclusions

The knowledge representation methods play an important role in solving decision-making problems for development of the advisory system in crime investigation processes.

The unified approach of integrating different data bases with knowledge for aiding advisory processes in relevant patterns recognition and crime investigation is proposed. A key part of this approach enforcement is to understand those activities, through the development and use of methods, models and tools for collecting and then interpreting the large volume of data available in real time for crime investigation. The ontological view based on object-oriented model helps us to reveal knowledge and examine main principles of the domain. Consequently the main principles of creating knowledge intensive framework have been developed, leading to recognition of a field of activity called crime analysis, which has been described as 'the identification of and the provision of insight into the relationship between crime data and other potentially relevant data with a view to police and judicial practice'.

References

[1] Aamodt, A. A Knowledge-Intensive, Integrated Approach to Problem Solving and Sustained Learning. Knowledge Engineering and Image Processing Group. University of Trondheim. 1991, pp. 27-85.

[2]   Barletta, R. An Introduction to Case-based Reasoning. AI Expert. 1991, pp. 43-49.

[3]   Bennett, J.S. ROGET: a Knowledge - based Consultant for Acquiring the Conceptual Structure of Expert System. Report HPP. Computer Science Dept., Stanford University, 1983.

[4]   Booch, G. Object Oriented Analysis and Design with Applications. The Benjamin Cummings Publishing Co. Inc. Second Edition, 1994

[5]   Bratko, I., Kononenko I. Learning Diagnostic Rules from Incomplete and Noisy Data. In B. Phelps (Ed) AI methods in statistics. London. Gower Technical Press. 1987.

[6]   Čaplinskas, A. General Introduction to Artificial Intelligence. In K.Wang, H.Pranevicius (Eds.) Lecturer Notes of the Nordic-Baltic Summer School on Applications of AI to Production Engineering. KTU Press. Technologija. Kaunas. 1997, pp. 1-38.

[7]   Chaturvedi, A.R. Acquiring Implicit Knowledge in a Complex Domain. Expert Systems with Applications. 1994. Vol. 6. No. 1, pp. 23-36.

[8]   Dzemydiene, D. A Basis for Evaluation Environmental Pollution Characteristics. In Proceedings the Forth International Baltic Workshop "Databases and Information Systems '2000". A.Čaplinskas (ed.). Vilnius. Vol. 2, 2000, pp. 139-151.

[9]   Dzemydiene, D. Conceptual Architecture for Dynamic Domain Representation. Mathematical Modelling and Analysis. R. Čiegis (ed.). Vol. 5, Vilnius, Technika, 2000, pp. 55-66.

[10] Dzemydiene, D. Representation of Decision Making Processes for the Ecological Evaluation System. In Intern. Journal "Annals of Operation Research". Vol. 51. Baltzer Science Publishers. Netherland. 1994, pp. 349-366.

[11] Dzemydiene, D. Temporal Information Management and Decision Support for Predictive Control of Environment Contamination Processes. In Procc. of Fifth East-European Conference 'Advances in Databases and Information Systems' ADBIS'2001. (Eds.) A. Capliskas, J. Eder. Vilnius. Technika. 2001. Vol.1, pp. 157-172.

[12] German, E.R. Computer Image Enchancement of Latent Print and Hard Copy Output Devices. In: Proceesings of International Symposium on Latent Print Examination. U.S. Government Printing Office. Washington, D.C. 1987, pp. 151-152.

[13] Hebenton, B., Terry, T. Criminal Records. – Brookfield USA, 1993.

[14] Kazemikaitiene, E., Petrauskas, R. Unified Criminalistic Information System for Investigation of Crimes and Violations of Law. In Procc. of Fifth East-European Conference 'Advances in Databases and Information Systems' ADBIS'2001. (Eds. A. Capliskas, J. Eder. Vilnius. Technika. 2001. Vol.2, pp. 45-54.

[15] Kovacich, G.L., Boni, W. High - Technology – Crime Investigator's Handbook: Working in the Global Information Environment. Butterworth-Heinemann. 2000, pp. 115-136.

[16] Kuipers, B. Qualitative Simulation of Causal Explanation. IEEE Trans. On Systems, Man and Cybernetics. Vol. SMC-17, No.3, 1987, pp. 432-444.

[17] Lee, H. C., Gaensslen, R.E. Advances in Fingerprint Technology. New York: Elsevier, 1991.

[18] Maskeliunas, S. Ontological Engineering: Common Approaches and Visualisation Capabilities. Informatica. Vol. 11. No. 1. 2000, pp. 41-48.

[19] Saferstein R. Criminalistics: An Introduction to Forensic Science. Fourth Edittion. - USA: Prentice Hall Career & Technology Englewood Cliffs, New Jersey 07632, 1990.

[20] Vellore, R.C., Vinze, A.S., Sen A. MODELER: Incorporating Experience to Support Model Formulation – a Case-based Planning Approach. Expert Systems with Applications. 1994. Vol. 6, No.1 , pp. 37-56.

[21] Weston, P.B., Wells, K.M. Criminal Investigation: Basic Perspectives, 2 Ed. Englewood Cliffs, NJ: Pretence Hall, 1990.

[22] Zeleznikow, J., Hunter D. Building Intelligent Legal Information Systems. Representation and Reasoning in Law. Computer Law Series 13. Kluwer Law and Taxation Publishers. Deventer, the Netherlands. 1994.

SEMANTICS FOR MANAGING SYSTEMS IN HETEROGENEOUS AND DISTRIBUTED ENVIRONMENT

Guntis Arnicans and Girts Karnitis
University of Latvia, Riga, Latvia

Abstract   The problem of legacy systems collaboration is being solved. Particularly we look at the collaboration as workflow in a distributed and heterogeneous environment. Attention is paid to the description of semantics for workflow process definition languages. There are many solutions how semantics can be decomposed into logical fragments, but the problem of obtaining reusable components that are easy to compile into desired specific semantics still remains. We evolve the division of semantics by semantic aspects whose description is based on abstract data types (pre-built components) and connectors (meta-programs to produce the glue code) between them. This paper offers a way in which semantic aspects are linked with the intermediate representation of a program, and performing of semantics is provided. We mix together various semantics aspects to get a desirable semantics.

Keywords: workflow, programming language specifications, semantics, interpreter, compiler, reusable components, domain specific languages, tool generation.

1.   Introduction

Nowadays new technologies are emerging in the government sector allowing to speak about the e-Government. The processes are one of the core components of e-Government [11]. We stated that there is practically no automation of processes in the governmental institutions that organize collaboration between legacy systems among various organizations and institutions. Document flows are manual, or by email. The automated workflows have to be introduced to make the document turnover faster and to improve the provided service for citizens.

H.-M. Haav and A. Kalja (eds.), Databases and Information Systems II, 149–160.

In [8] workflow is defined as "the automation of a business process, in whole or part, during which documents, information or tasks are passed from one participant to another for action, according to a set of procedural rules."

The workflow management system is defined as "a system that defines, creates and manages the execution of workflows through the use of software, running on one or more workflow engines which is able to interpret the process definition, interact with workflow participants and where required, invoke the use of IT tools and applications."

In the latest years many researchers and developers have paid attention to a problem how to organize the collaboration between legacy systems, and the exploitation of workflow is one of the most popular solutions [27, 28]. Various workflow process definition languages have been created which can be considered as domain specific languages.

The workflow implementations commonly are based on one fixed semantics, like most of the programming languages. We are interested in various semantics for a particular workflow, for example, common workflow semantics, a statistical data gathering semantics, a semantics for debugging and simulating purposes or its composition, therefore we need not only a compiler or an interpreter, but the necessity for specific supporting tools becomes a burning question due to demands for high software quality. An interesting topic is changing of semantics for active instance of workflow on the fly.

In our approach semantics are connected to syntax elements via semantic connectors that naturally allow linking legacy systems into collaborative workflow and allow to define or to execute multiple different semantics simultaneously. Actually, each semantic implementation is a tool, similarly to the principle in [10]. We present fragments of semantic description for simple programming language to demonstrate usefulness of this approach for a wide class of programming languages, and ideas how to implement a simple workflow description language.

2.   Implementation of Domain-Specific Language

According to Kinnersley's investigation [13], there were more than 2000 exploited languages in 1995, and most of them were classified as domain-specific language (DSL). Together with the growth of DSL many implementations and maintenance problems arise (e.g. [6] analysis of common problems and large annotated bibliography; [25] particular languages and problems). Unfortunately, formal semantics descriptions lose their position because of a weak support to solve practical problems [15, 20, 22].

Like natural language, the programming language definition consists of three components or aspects [21, 24]: syntax deals with questions of superficial form of a language, semantics deals with the underlying meaning of a language, pragmatics deals with the practical use of a language. The syntax and semantics of a language can be formalized, and both formalizations together form formal specification of a programming language.

The formalisms for dealing with the syntax aspect of a programming language are well developed. The theory of scanning, parsing and attribute analysis provides not only means to perform syntactical analysis, but to generate a whole compiler as well. There is a lot of problems with practical use of semantics formalisms. Recently the criticism of classical formalism has arisen from the difficulty of using formal methods. The main problem to use widely in practice the formal specifications of programming languages is that specifications become too complex, too abstruse to manage them, often it is impossible to express all needs, and in the end – who verifies and proves the correctness of the specification?

Summarizing the best practices in compiler construction we can declare that most of commercial compilers (interpreters or other tools that deal with programs) are written without using any formalisms or only the first phases (scanning and parsing) to exploit some formalisms [15].

Let us look at the language description again, try to divide it into smaller parts and see, what we can obtain from that. Traditionally the first decision is to separate syntax from semantics, and semantics consists of two parts: static semantics and dynamic (run-time) semantics. But we should divide syntax and semantics further, eliminate reusable components and provide a mechanism to stick all things together.

Syntax components are more or less visible: basic elements (for instance, terminals and nonterminals, if we parse program) connected with some relations (for instance, edges in the parse tree or abstract syntax tree).

To divide semantics into pieces we offer to split it by semantic aspects. Here are some examples of semantic aspects: program control flow management (e.g. loops, conditional branching), execution of commands or statements (e.g. basic operations, assigning), dealing with symbols (e.g. variables, constants), environment management (e.g. scopes of visibility), pretty printing of program, dynamic accounting of statistic, symbolic execution, specific program instrumentation, etc.

We are interested in any formalism to deal with syntax, because we want to make intermediate representation (IR) of program or structured information. The situation is clear what refers to conventional programming languages. But our goal is a workflow implementation, and we have to take into account other languages, for instance, diagrammatic visual languages (e.g. Petri nets, E-R diagrams, Statecharts) and the state-of-art in this field (e.g. [7]).

Our approach has borrowed some principles from attribute grammars, for instance, the ways to link semantics with syntax [20], modular decomposition and reuse of specification [12], distributed computing in real time (e.g. Communicating Timed AG [16]).

We found out that many formalisms of semantics use abstract data types (ADT). ADT is a collection of data type and value definitions and operations on those definitions which behave as primitive data type. This software design approach decomposes problem into components by identifying the public interface and private implementation. A typical example is Stack, Queue, Symbol table [1, 24].

Recently one of the simple and popular methods to build some simple tool for a programming language has become parse and traverse principle [5] that means to build intermediate representation (IR) of program or information, traverse IR and make appropriate computations at each node. This method is similar to the Visitor Pattern [9]. Other useful patterns are also developed [14, 19]. Besides, there exist also nontraditional traversal strategies [e.g. 4]. Many solutions can be obtained from Component collaboration [e.g. 18].

We have taken into account our experience in building prototypes of multi-language interpreter [2]. A Multi-Language Interpreter (MLI) is a program which receives source language syntax, source language semantics and a program written in the source language, and then it performs the operations on the basis of the program and the relevant semantics.

3. Principles of Semantic Definition and Implementation

3.1 Runtime Principles

Let us assume that we have fixed some formalism to describe the syntax of our language (e.g. BNF). Now we can define the language syntax and develop a language parser (e.g. by using Lex/Yacc). The parser creates intermediate representation (IR) of program (e.g. Parse tree), and IR is based on a desirable structure and contains any needed information about the syntax (e.g. node type (nonterminal), name (name of nonterminal), value (terminal value) etc.).

To perform semantics at runtime we choose a principle of parse and traverse. The Traverser that realizes our chosen traversing strategy (e.g. left-depth tree traversing) has to be created for our IR representation. The computations that have to be done at each node visited by the Traverser are defined in Semantic Connectors (SC). They use predefined data structures with operations to establish the cooperation between Legacy Systems (LS) (Figure 1).

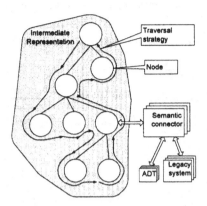

Figure 1. Runtime correspondence between syntax and semantics

Actually, most of work performing semantics is done via operations over various Abstract Data Types (ADT). In such a way we hide most of implementation details and concentrate mainly on logic of semantic aspect. The consequence of this approach is that we can choose the best physical implementation of ADT for the given task. For instance, Stack can be implemented in a contiguous memory or in a linked memory. The instances of ADT can be distributed objects in a heterogeneous computing network.

A concept of a *semantic connector* or simply *connector* is introduced to connect the instances of ADT and LS in a desirable environment. Connector is a meta-program that introduces a concrete communication connection into a set of components, i.e. it generates the adaptation and communication glue code for a specific connection. This concept is adopted from similar problem: how to connect pre-built components in a distributed and heterogeneous environment [3].

3.2   Semantic Definition Principles

Similarly to patterns in [20] we choose a correspondence *Nonterminal with visiting aspect = Semantic connector* to establish the relationship between syntax and semantics. *Nonterminal with visiting aspect* means that we distinguish computations performed at nonterminal node considering an aspect of node visiting (e.g. PreVisit or PostVisit). Any connector can see any instance of ADT or LS of the semantic aspect it (connector) belongs to.

The main problem is to find a good way to define semantics and obtain semantic connectors for the definition. After exploring various approaches

154

how semantics can be described and organized, we suppose that semantic aspect is a good basic component for constructing whole semantics according to our goals. The conceptual components of a semantics description and relationships with other concepts are represented in Figure 2.

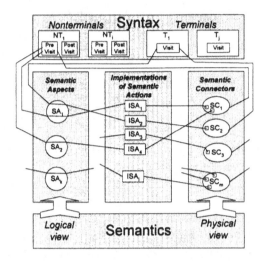

Figure 2. The conceptual schema of semantics.

Semantics can be observed from two different sides – a logical definition view and a physical runtime view. From the logical viewpoint semantics consists of Semantic Aspects (SA). The SA states what syntax elements (terminals, nonterminals) are involved, and what actions have to be performed traversing internal representation and visiting the corresponding node to implement the semantic aspect. Let us define the concept *Semantic Action* that denotes the action performed to implement SA while visiting a corresponding node, and the concept *Implementation of Semantic Action* (ISA) that denotes a meta program which implements the semantic action. In our example SA_1 involves nonterminal NT_1 and terminal T_1, and ISA_1 is performed while *previsiting* NT_1 and ISA_2 – while *visiting* T_1.

The example of semantic aspect INDEFINITE LOOP is given in Figure 3. There are various nonterminals and terminals organized by some syntax description. The arrows represent a traversal strategy. The small circles represent the semantic actions, and the rectangles connected to the circles contain the implementation of semantic action (meta program). A left circle into nonterminal stands for PreVisit, and a right circle - for PostVisit. All used abstract data types (ADT) are defined within semantic aspect. Another example of semantic aspect is given in Figure 4.

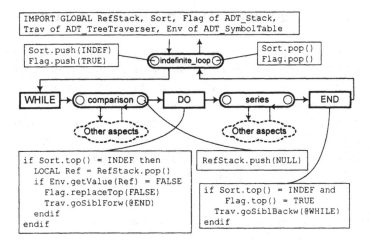

Figure 3. Semantic aspect INDEFINITE LOOP. It "goes through" series and back to WHILE until the comparison sets NULL reference or reference with value FALSE

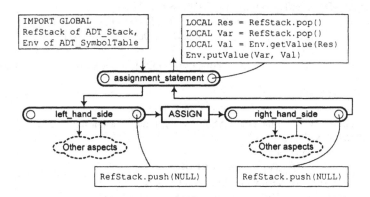

Figure 4. Semantic aspect ASSIGNMENT. It takes reference to a variable and reference to a value from the stack, and assigns the value to the variable. Pushing of references is simulated, real references will be pushed by other aspects and simulating will be excluded

Let us look at the physical view. The semantic connector contains all corresponding semantic actions having to be executed while visiting syntax element (IR node). For instance, visiting any node with the name T_1 we have to execute the semantic connector SC_2 that contains the implementation of the semantic action ISA_2. Similarly, SC_1 is some composition of ISA_1 and ISA_4.

156

3.3   Obtaining Semantics from Semantic Aspects

From the logical point of view semantics is a composition of semantic aspects with concrete linking to instances of abstract data types, legacy systems and traverser that performs a traversal strategy over fixed intermediate representation of program or structured information. We cannot simply stick all SA together risking to get senseless semantics. A composition of semantic aspects is operations over a set of implementations of semantic actions with the aim to get one set of connectors that correspond to the new mixed semantic aspect (Table 1).

Table 1. Fragment of semantics description for simple imperative language
compatible with ir_type ParseTree, traverser_type ParseTreeTraverser

...

syntax elements (program, expression, VARIABLE, ...)
semantic actions (<PROGRAM> program PreVisit {ENV.prepareProgEnv()},
        <PROGRAM> program PostVisit {...}, ...)

...

global Trav of ADT_TreeTraverser, Env of ADT_SymbolTable
create DataStack, OperatorStack, CanCreateVar, LoopSortStack, LoopCounterStack,
LoopFlagStack, IfFlagStack of ADT_Stack, InputFile, OutputFile of ADT_FILE

...

compose aspect <COMPOSED SA>   // composes semantic aspects from predefined aspects
(<PROGRAM>)
append (<ELEMENT>
  replace RefStack with DataStack // replaces stack for collaborating work
  rename INTEGER Visit with CONSTANT Visit) // renames according to PAM syntax
append (<ASSIGNMENT>
  replace RefStack with DataStack
  rename left_hand_side PostVisit with VARIABLE Visit,
      right_hand_side PostVisit with expression PostVisit
  ignore left_hand_size PostVisit)   // ignore pushing of NULL reference
append (<INDEFINITE LOOP>
  replace RefStack with DataStack,
    Sort with LoopSortStack, Flag with LoopFlagStack)

...

end compose aspect
... // other aspect are defined and composed together
link for <COMPOSED SA> Trav to TreeTraverser, Env to SymbolTable
use aspect <COMPOSED SA> with traverser TreeTraverser

The obtaining of semantics for the fixed syntax is achieved in several steps: 1) select predefined semantic aspects or define new ones for desired semantics, 2) rename syntax elements and traversing aspect in the selected semantic aspects with names from fixed syntax and traversing strategy, 3) rename instances of abstract components to organize the collaboration between semantic aspects, 4) make composition from semantic aspects, 5) specify the runtime environment and translate the meta-code to the code of the target programming language, and 6) compile the semantics.

After obtaining meta-semantics (Table 1) meta-code is translated into the target programming language, taking into account the target language (e.g. C++), the implementation of abstract components (e.g. Stack), the operating system (e.g. Unix), the communications between components (e.g. CORBA), runtime components type (e.g. DLL), etc. The translation may be done by hand or automatically (desirable in common cases).

By replacing ADT names we achieve an independent working for some semantic aspects or collaboration between them through common instances of ADT. Another way to get a new semantics is to combine semantic aspects as whole black-box unit. Self-evident method is to execute several semantic aspects sequentially, for instance, we perform static semantics first and dynamic one after that. Instances of ADT can be shared and one semantic aspect can use the results of others. More complex is a parallel execution of many semantics where we need to organize synchronization via instances of ADT.

4.   Workflow Case Study

To demonstrate our approach we use a very simple workflow definition language that syntax is described with BNF (Table 2). We have two types of generic statements for describing tasks in a workflow – universal statements and specific statements.

Table 2. Fragment of BNF for simple workflow definition language

workflow	-> series
series	-> statement I series ; statement
statement	-> generic_stm I cond_stm
cond_stm	-> IF compar THEN series ELSE series FI
compar	-> expr relation expr
expr	-> const I var
generic_stm	-> universal_stm I specific_stm
universal_stm	-> u_stm_type name
u_stm_type	-> DCOM I CORBA I WEBSERVICE I MANUAL
specific_stm	-> s_stm_type name
s_stm_type	-> ASK I ANSW

The *universal statements* are used to collaborate with external applications. The universal statement type describes the connection type: DCOM, CORBA, WEBSERVICE means automatic processing, but

158

MANUAL means, that a human handles this operation. The *specific statement* is used to communicate with a person – usually with a citizen who uses the particular service. There are two types of specific statements. ASK gets information from a person, ANSW sends some information to a person.

Lets us take a look at the following simple workflow:

WEBSERVICE Application_writing_and_submitting
ASK Communication
DCOM Application_data_control_and_update
IF Is_data_control_and_updating_successful = True THEN
    DCOM Printing_of_passport
    ANSW Positive_answer
    MANUAL Passport_handing_out
ELSE
    ANSW Negative_answer
FI

The purpose of this workflow is to issue a new passport for a person. The workflow has the following activities - a citizen fills in an application form and submits it to the official. It can be a paper form or a web based application. The official or the application asks from the person the communication type and address, and records data into workflow environment. Then the official verifies the correctness of the citizen's filled in form with the data in the Population Register, and if all data are correct, then the passport is issued and delivered to the citizen. Otherwise a negative answer is sent to the citizen. An example of one semantic aspect of this workflow is given in Figure 5.

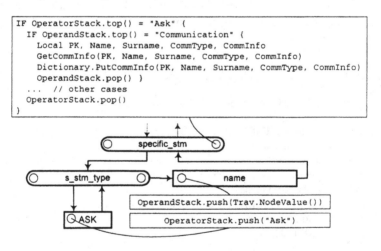

Figure 5. Semantic aspect SPECIFIC STATEMENT ASK

5.   Conclusions

We have presented ideas for establishing a framework to deal with different collaboration problems between legacy systems. The problem is reduced to describing the collaboration (e.g. workflow) by DSL and building various tools (various semantics) for this DSL.

There are many application generators that automatically produce conventional compiler and interpreter, but we need not only those ones. It is necessary to obtain various supporting tools that are based on the language text processing. The existing formal semantics are not well accepted by language or tool designers. We have made an attempt to search for a compromise to minimize this gap. The latest related works in this field to establish tool-oriented approach are mentioned in [10, 17, 23].

We have offered ideas how semantics can be decomposed into reusable parts, and specific semantics can be composed from them, and how execution is organized. We delegate most of the actual work for semantics to pre-built components (ADT). Our approach allows minimize semantics descriptions for an easier management and provides good implementation in, possible parallel, distributed and heterogeneous environment. Our approach is based on the experience received by constructing prototypes of a multi-language interpreter for conventional programming languages.

Due to practical needs, we lose some precision and benefits of classical semantic formalisms. The next step is to finish the formalization of our approach and to compare it with other formalisms, especially with attribute grammars. Other activities have to be the designing of useful collection of abstract data types.

References

[1] Aho, A.V., Sethi, R., and Ullman, J. D. Compilers: Principles, Technigues, and Tools. Addison-Wesley, 1986.

[2] Arnicane, V., Arnicans, G., and Bicevskis, J. Multilanguage interpreter. In H.-M. Haav and B. Thalheim, editors, Proceedings of the Second International Baltic Workshop on Databases and Information Systems (DB&IS '96), Volume 2: Technology Track, pages 173-174. Tampere University of Technology Press, 1996.

[3] Aßmann, U., Genßler, T., and Bär, H. Meta-programming Grey-box Connectors. Proceedings of the Technology of Object-Oriented Languages and Systems (TOOLS 33), 2000, pp. 300-311.

[4] Biswas, B. and Mall, R. Reverse Execution of Programs. ACM SIGPLAN Notices, April 1999, 34(4):61-69.

[5] Clark, C. Build a Tree – Save a Parse. ACM SIGPLAN Notices, 34(4):19-24, April 1999.

[6] Deursen, A., Klint, P. and Visser, J. Domain-Specific Languages: An Annotated Bibliography. ACM SIGPLAN Notices, June 2000, 35(6):26-36.

160

[7] Ferrucci, F., Napolitano, F., Tortora, G., Tucci, M., and Vitiello, G. An Interpreter for Diagrammatic Languages Based on SR Grammars. Proceedings of the 1997 IEEE Symposium on Visual Languages (VL '97), 1997, pp. 292-299.

[8] Fischer, L. (ed) The Workflow Handbook 2001, Published in association with the Workflow Management Coalition, 2000

[9] Gamma, E., Helm, R., Johnson, R., and Vlisides, J. Design Patterns: Elements of Reusable Software. Addison-Wesley, 1995, pp. 331-334.

[10] Heering, J. and Klint, P. Semantics of Programming Languages: A Tool-Oriented Approach. ACM SIGPLAN Notices, March 2000, 35(3):39-48

[11] Karnitis, E. E-Government: An Innovative Model of Governance in the Information Society. Baltic IT&T Review, 1, 2001

[12] Kastens, U. and Wait, W. M. Modularity and reusability in attribute grammars. Acta Informatica 31, 1994, pp. 601-627.

[13] Kinnersley, W. (ed), The Language List. 1995. http://wuarchive.wustl.edu/doc/misc/lang-list.txt

[14] Kühne, T. The Translator Pattern – External Functionality with Homomorphic Mappings. Proceedings of the Tools-23: Technology of Object-Oriented Languages and Systems, 1997, pp. 48-59.

[15] Louden, K.C. Compilers and Interpreters. In Tucker [28], pp. 2120-2147.

[16] Matsuzaki, T. and Tokuda, T. CTAG Software Generator Model for Constructing Network Applications. Proceedings of the Asia Pacific Software Engineering Conference, 1998, pp.120-127.

[17] Mernik, M., Lenič, M., Avdičauševič, E., and Žumer, V. Compiler/Interpreter Generator System LISA. Proceedings of the 33rd Hawaii International Conference on System Sciences – 2000, 2000, pp. 10.

[18] Mezini, M. and Lieberherr, K. Adaptive Plug-and-Play Components for Evolutionary Software Development. SIGPLAN Notices, 33(10):97-116, 1998. Proceedings of the 1998 ACM SIGPLAN Conference on Object-Oriented Programming, Systems, Languages & Applications (OOPSLA '98).

[19] Ovlinger, J. and Wand, M. A Language for Specifying Recursive Traversals of Object Structures. SIGPLAN Notices, 34(10):70-81, 1999. Proceedings of the 1999 ACM SIGPLAN Conference on Object-Oriented Programming, Systems, Languages & Applications (OOPSLA '99).

[20] Paakki, J. Attribute Grammar Paradigms – A High-Level Methodology in Language Implementation. ACM Computing Surveys, June 1995, 27(2):196-255.

[21] Pagan, G.P. Formal Specification of Programming Languages: A Panoramic Primer. Prentice-Hall, 1981.

[22] Schmidt, D.A. Programming Language Semantics. In Tucker [28], pp. 2237-2254.

[23] Sloane, A.M. Generating Dynamic Program Analysis Tools. Proceedings of the Autralian Software Endineering Conference (ASWEC'9), 1997, pp. 166-173.

[24] Slonneger, K., and Kurtz, B.L. Formal Syntax and semantics of Programming Languages: A Laboratory Based Approach. Addison-Wesly, 1995.

[25] Special issue on domain-specific languages. IEEE Transactions on Software Engineering, 25(3), May/June 1999.

[26] Tucker, A.B. (ed) The computer science and engineering handbook. CRC Press, 1997.

[27] Workflow Standards and Associated Documents, http://www.wfmc.org/standards/docs/Stds_diagram.pdf

[28] Workflow/BPR Tools Vendors http://www.waria.com/databases/wfvendors-A-L.htm

ONTOLOGICAL INTERMEDIATION BETWEEN BUSINESS PROCESS MODELS AND SOFTWARE COMPONENTS

Thorsten Teschke

Oldenburg Research and Development Institute
for Computer Science Tools and Systems (OFFIS)
Escherweg 2, 26121 Oldenburg, Germany
thorsten.teschke@offis.de

Abstract   Research and practice on software reuse have devised a variety of software retrieval techniques. For these techniques to be efficiently usable, a common understanding regarding the terminology used in requirements documents and descriptions of available software artefacts is required.

We propose to use an ontology for semantic intermediation between requirements formulated in business process models and solutions characterised by component descriptions. A basic ontology of natural language propositions is complemented with domain specific vocabulary. Propositions about the domain are then used to specify comparable business process models and software components.

Keywords: ontology, controlled languages, reuse, component, business process.

1.   Introduction

Flexible software architectures on the basis of software components facilitate the adaptation of application software systems in response to dynamically changing requirements. Szyperski defines a software component (further on only referred to as component) as "[...] a unit of composition with contractually specified interfaces and explicit context dependencies only. A software component can be deployed independently and is subject to composition by third parties" [15]. This definition takes into account the idea of (re-)use by third parties, where third parties may include developers within the same company (intra-organisational reuse) and from different companies (inter-organisational reuse).

Research on software reuse has devised a variety of software retrieval techniques, ranging from free text analysis over faceted classification and

H.-M. Haav and A. Kalja (eds.), Databases and Information Systems II, 161–173.

signature matching to behavioural conformance checking (for a comprehensive survey cf. [10]). For any of these techniques to be efficiently usable, a common understanding regarding the terminology used in requirements documents on the one hand and descriptions of available software artefacts on the other is indispensable. If at all, such a common understanding mostly is present within intra-organisational software reuse processes only. As soon as communication transcends organisational borders, standardisation measures need to be applied to the terminology used for problem and solution description.

Within the scope of the research project KOSOBAR (Component-Based Software Development Based on Reference Models), we are concerned with the retrieval of components from internet-based component markets. We focus on domain components, i. e. "vertical" components that offer relevant services in a particular application domain, and refer to the comprehensive requirements knowledge captured in business process models in the retrieval process. In order to achieve semantic comparability between business process models and components, we pursue a linguistic approach and employ an ontology of propositions for the representation of application domain knowledge. Business process models and component descriptions, respectively, are assigned their semantics by associating the individual steps of a business process model and the methods offered by a component and its contained classes with simple propositional sentences.

The structure of our paper is as follows. In section 2, we analyse the semantic expressiveness of business process models and method declarations, and introduce the notion of ortho languages as a disciplined linguistic approach to the representation of application domain semantics. Based on three simple grammatical patterns we borrow from ortho languages, section 3 defines an ontology of propositions about arbitrary application domains. Section 4 briefly introduces the approach of business process oriented component retrieval and outlines the application of the ontology. Finally, section 5 summarises our contribution and lists future work.

2.   A Linguistic Perspective on Application Domain Semantics

In computer science, semantics is often defined formally (e. g., using predicate logic) or semi-formally (e. g., using the UML). While rigorous mathematical definitions are difficult to understand for domain experts, semi-formal notations often do not provide the required precision.

2.1   Requirements to the Description of Application Domain Semantics

In our work on component retrieval, we strive for a representation of application domain semantics that may act as an intermediation layer between business process models and component descriptions. Therefore, we analyse the expressiveness of business process models and the semantics of method declarations in component descriptions.

The Business Process Modelling Perspective.   In the field of business process modelling, a number of techniques have been developed, each of which has particular strengths and weaknesses. We focus on two popular business process modelling techniques, namely event-driven process chains (EPCs) [6] and UML activity diagrams [11]. The purposes EPCs and activity diagrams have been devised for may differ, yet both techniques share a common core of expressiveness. In linguistic terms, they allow to model individual steps of process execution through *actors*, the *action* that is to be carried out by the actor (specified by a *predicate* and a *direct object* the predicate refers to), and an arbitrary number of *indirect objects* that may be input factors to the action or its outcome, respectively. Figure 1 illustrates these parallels between activity diagrams and EPCs using a simple example.

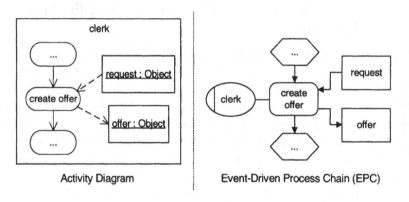

Activity Diagram   Event-Driven Process Chain (EPC)

Figure 1.   Parallels between activity diagrams and event-driven process chains

In both models, the term "offer" is used twice: in the identifier of the action and as the name of an object. Thereby, both models explicitly distinguish an intensional view on the "offer" (the action identifier refers to the abstract concept denoted by the term) and an extensional view on the "offer" (the object refers to an instance of the concept). We may disregard the intensional meaning of "offer" and formulate the semantics captured by both models as "a clerk creates an offer with a request".

The Component Software Perspective. In literature, the specification of method semantics using pre- and postconditions has often been advocated (cf. [5, 9, 7]). Apart from this formal approach, we may also conceive the meaning of a method in the object-oriented paradigm as a natural language proposition: each time the method is invoked, the proposition is uttered. The method's identifier corresponds to an *action* (again specified by a *predicate* and a *direct object* that the predicate refers to), and the method's in and out parameters are represented by an arbitrary number of *indirect objects*. We regard a method's owner, i.e. an object or a component, as the *actor* involved in the execution of the method. This generic syntactic pattern is applicable to arbitrary object-oriented method declarations. As an example, confer the following declaration of a method in OMG IDL:

```
interface SalesDepartment {
        Offer createOffer(in Request request);
}
```

The invocation of this method can be regarded as the utterance "a sales department creates an offer with a request". Here, similar deliberations regarding the intensional and extensional use of the term "offer" apply as in the case of business process models.

2.2 Linguistic Reconstruction of Application Domains

The analysis of the expressiveness of business process models and component declarations seems to suggest the use of natural language for the description of application domain semantics. Natural language is well understandable for domain experts, yet has deficiencies such as ambiguity and lack of precision. Controlled languages such as *Attempto Controlled English (ACE)* [3] represent an approach to remedy these defects of natural languages. They consist of a simplified grammar defined by specific patterns for the construction of sentences and a controlled vocabulary over which sentences may be constructed.

Ortho languages are a particular form of controlled languages [12]. They are developed by methodically reconstructing (i.e. newly defining the grammar and vocabulary of) the natural language that is deployed in some application domain. Ortho languages in general allow arbitrary patterns for the construction of sentences. TAOS (Terminology-Based Approach to Object-Oriented Specification) [13], e.g., a framework for the development of object-oriented software specifications, defines a comprehensive set of sentence construction patterns for the specification of object-oriented software systems. In our work on semantic intermediation, however, we only use the generic pattern [N | π | P | O_1 | O_2 | ...] to express the semantics captured in business process models and methods (cf. section 2.1). Here, N denotes the subject of the sentence (nominator), π represents the copula "do", P is the predicate, O_1 denotes the direct object, and $O_i (i > 1)$ are indirect objects. The predicate P is always used in the simple present tense third person singular. Adverbs or adjectives are not allowed in this sentence construction pattern. An exemplary sentence constructed using this pattern is clerk π add orderline to-order (read "[a] clerk does add [an] orderline to [an] order"). In this example, the indirect object "order" is supplemented with the preposition "to".

The ability to build meaningful sentences requires some vocabulary (material) which could be used in order to breathe life into a sentence construction pattern (the formal framework). Ortho languages employ a controlled vocabulary (lexicon) providing a body of methodically reconstructed terms. Individual terms are defined using explicit definitions such as "an order is a legal agreement between a customer and a retailer ... ", while semantic relationships between terms are reduced to ortho language propositions. In this context, the sentence construction pattern [N_1 | ϵ | N_2] (ϵ represents the copula "is-a" denoting the generalisation relation) allows one to express that "customer ϵ business_partner" or "Miller ϵ customer". Part-of relationships are formulated using the pattern [N_1 | ν | N_2] (ν stands for the copula "has" denoting the part-of relation). As an example, confer the proposition "order ν order_position". The latter two sentence construction patterns enable us to reconstruct the static structure of an application domain, i.e. to define the relevant concepts of a domain and their semantic relationships. The first pattern allows us to describe the behaviour of a system in that domain, i.e. the observable interactions between concept instances [12].

3. An Ontology of Propositions

The term "ontology" is often assigned two different meanings: first, it is used to denote some representation vocabulary and the underlying conceptualisation, and second, it refers to a body of knowledge about a domain [1]. We pursue a two-level approach that makes use of both meanings:

- On the *conceptualisation level*, we specify a general, domain independent vocabulary for the representation of propositions.

- Based on the conceptualisation level, the *core knowledge level* defines a body of knowledge of the domain under consideration.

3.1 The Conceptualisation Level

The conceptualisation level of the proposition ontology is derived from the three sentence construction patterns introduced in section 2.2. Figure 2 depicts a UML class diagram specifying the conceptual structure of the ontology. Starting from a general notion of abstract *terms* we

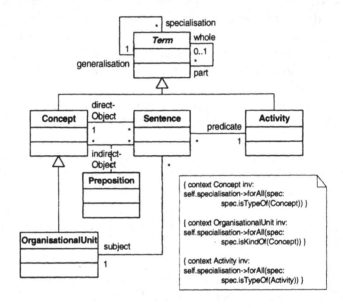

Figure 2. Conceptualisation level of ontology of propositions

distinguish *activities* such as "create" or "modify", and *concepts* such as "order" which may be objects that are affected by an activity. *Organisational units* are a special kind of concepts: they may not only be affected by, but also carry out an activity (e. g. "clerk"). Terms in general may be specialised, provided that an instance of a term subclass is only specialised by instances belonging to the same or a more special term subclass (cf. the OCL expressions in figure 2). This means in particular that an organisational unit must not be specialised by a concept. Moreover, the conceptualisation level permits the definition of part-of relationships between terms.

Sentences are syntactic structures for the representation of propositions. They conform to the syntactic conventions defined by our first sentence construction pattern. Therefore, a sentence is made up of an organisational unit acting as its subject, an activity representing its predicate, and concepts acting as direct and indirect objects. Indirect objects are associated with the predicate by means of a *preposition* such as "to" or "with".

3.2   The Core Knowledge Level

The core knowledge level defines taxonomies of concepts and activities that may be used for the construction of sentences (and thus propositions) in some domain. These taxonomies define, e.g., that "order" is a "transaction" and that "production order" and "customer order" are specialisations ($\leq$) of "order". Similarly, "create", "change", and "delete" can be defined as specialisations ($\leq$) of the activity "modify". Moreover, the core knowledge level defines semantic restrictions on the use of concepts and activities in sentences. These restrictions prohibit the construction of sentences such as "customer (does) create clerk". They are defined by a set of core sentences that give examples of "correct" propositions and a rule for the derivation of new sentences from these sentences: a new proposition may be derived, if the underlying sentence specialises a sentence contained in the core knowledge level, and if it does not violate the restrictions defined by some other sentence on the core knowledge level.

The general idea underlying the specialisation relationship between sentences is to demand that all constituents of the more general sentence are specialised by their counterparts in the more special sentence. Having in mind that we intend to compare business process models and component descriptions, we restrict ourselves to a simpler version where only predicates and direct objects are regarded:

Definition 1 (Specialisation Relationship) *Let S_1 and S_2 be two sentences specified by tuples (P_{S_1}, O_{S_1}) and (P_{S_2}, O_{S_2}) where P represents the predicate and O the direct object. Then,*

S_1 *is a specialisation of S_2 ($S_1 \leq S_2$)*

$$\iff \quad P_{S_1} \leq P_{S_2} \wedge O_{S_1} \leq O_{S_2},$$

where the specialisation relationship between predicates and direct objects is defined in the activity and concept taxonomies, respectively.

For a derived sentence to be valid, it does not suffice to specialise some core sentence. We additionally demand that the derived sentence respects the restrictions defined by other core sentences:

Definition 2 (Valid Specialisation) *Let CS be the set of core sentences and $S = (P_S, O_S)$ a sentence. Then,*

S *is a valid specialisation with respect to CS*

$$\Longleftrightarrow \quad \exists S_C \in CS : S \leq S_C$$
$$\wedge \quad \forall S_C' \in CS, S_C' \leq S_C, S_C' \neq S :$$
$$\neg (P_S \leq P_{S_C'} \vee O_S \leq O_{S_C'}).$$

A new sentence represents a valid specialisation of a core sentence, if and only if there is no other specialising core sentence that further constrains the use of the sentence's predicate or direct object. An example might illustrate this validity rule. Suppose that "organisational unit (does) do thing" is the only core sentence. Provided that the concept and activity taxonomies are defined accordingly, we would then be able to derive sentences such as "clerk (does) plan order" and "clerk (does) plan invoice". In order to express that we only want orders (or more special concepts) to be planned, we could further specialise the above core sentence by adding a sentence "organisational unit (does) plan order" to the set of core sentences. Then, "clerk (does) plan invoice" does not represent a valid specialisation of the first core sentence, since $\neg(\text{plan} \leq \text{plan} \vee \text{invoice} \leq \text{order}) = false$ (cf. 2nd part of definition 2). Clearly, this sentence does not constitute a valid specialisation of the second core sentence neither.

3.3 Related Work on Ontologies

Due to space limitations, we are not able to cover related work on ontologies for the representation of domain knowledge and semantic intermediation in the desirable depth. Nevertheless, we briefly mention some interesting efforts.

Within the Process Specification Language (PSL) project, the National Institute of Standards and Technology (NIST) is addressing the issue of sharing semantics between process-related applications in the manufacturing domain [14]. The TOVE (TOronto Virtual Enterprise) enterprise ontology constitutes an integrated enterprise model that comprises ontologies for activities, states and time, organisation, resources, and products to name but a few [2]. Within the scope of the Enterprise Project the Enterprise Ontology, a comprehensive collection of terms and definitions relevant to business enterprises, has been defined [18]. The Meta Data Coalition (MDC) Open Information Model (OIM) is a specification of core meta data types found in enterprises [8]. The semantic definitions package accommodates conceptual models of user information using linguistic expressions. In September 2000, the Meta Data Coalition has ceased to exist.

In their work on component retrieval with the OntoSeek system, Guarino et al. combine a content representation language of limited expressiveness with a large ontology for content matching [4]. The BALES methodology (Binding Business-Applications to Legacy Systems) [19] represents an approach to the reuse of legacy objects and processes in modern business applications.

4. An Application of the Proposition Ontology

In this section, we briefly introduce the approach of business process oriented component retrieval on component markets and outline the application of the proposition ontology for determining semantic matches between business process models and components.

4.1 Business Process Oriented Component Retrieval

Domain components often implement a specific business logic that constrains the possible sequences of method invocations. An order management component, e.g., may require that an order is approved before it is executed. The goal pursued by business process oriented component retrieval is to find those components whose interaction protocol, i.e. the order in which its methods may be invoked and the branching structure defined by alternatives, complies with (parts of) a business process model. Business process oriented component retrieval comprises the following phases:

1 *Offer Phase*: Component vendors publish component descriptions in a component repository. We employ *CDL* [17], a component description language that represents an abstraction from popular component models such as Enterprise JavaBeans (EJB) or Component Object Model (COM) and its successors.

2 *Request Phase*: Users interested in the retrieval of components specify their requirements in the shape of business process models.

3 *Matching Phase*: The component broker compares the behavioural requirements encoded in a business process model with the interaction protocols of available components. We apply the principle of behavioural subtyping to the problem of determining such behavioural matches: a candidate component is required to represent a behavioural subtype of the requested business process model [16].

4 *Results Presentation / Evaluation Phase*: Graphical and textual representations of retrieved components and metrics for the quality of the matches allow the user to evaluate the retrieval results.

So far, we have primarily been concerned with the syntactic and behavioural levels of correspondence between business process models and

170

component descriptions [16]. Through the proposition ontology, we are now able to extend our approach to the semantic level of correspondence.

4.2 Extending Business Process Oriented Component Retrieval to the Semantic Level

In this section, we outline the application of the proposition ontology to the phases above. For illustrational purposes, figure 3 shows excerpts from a business process model, a CDL component description of a component **SalesComponent**, and an instance of the proposition ontology.

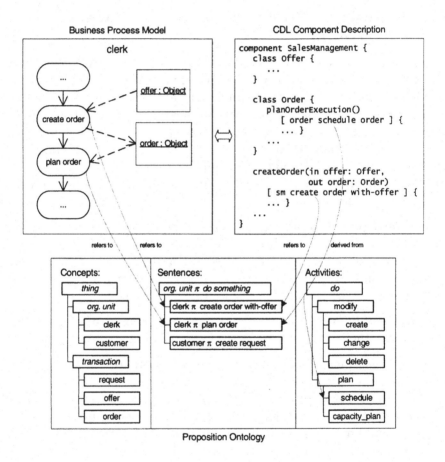

Figure 3. Intermediation between business process models and components

1 *Offer Phase*: As indicated in section 2.1, the semantics of methods may be expressed using the sentence construction pattern [N | π | P | O$_1$ | O$_2$ | ...]. Since this pattern represents the foun-

dation of the proposition ontology, we may define the semantics of a method using (derived) sentences from the proposition ontology.

In figure 3, the method `createOrder` of the `SalesManagement` component is assigned the semantics "sales management (does) create order with-offer" (in brackets). This sentence represents a valid specialisation of the sentence "clerk (does) create order with-offer" defined in the ontology (cf. definition 2). Similarly, the method `planOrderExecution` of the contained class `Order` is assigned the semantics "order (does) schedule order". This sentence represents a specialisation of the sentence "clerk does plan order".

2 *Request Phase*: The common core of expressiveness of business process modelling techniques pointed out in section 2.1 is covered by the same sentence construction pattern. Therefore, we may use (derived) sentences from the proposition ontology for the specification of a business process model's processing steps.

The steps of the business process model depicted in figure 3 are defined by sentences provided by the proposition ontology.

3 *Matching Phase*: The relationship between business process models and components is determined by the conformance of their interaction protocols on the one hand and the semantic relationship between the sentences that have been assigned to processing steps and methods on the other. While the former issue has been discussed in [16], we are now concerned with the latter. Following the principle of behavioural subtyping, we are interested in specialisation relationships between sentences: for a semantic match, we demand that a method is more special than a processing step.

In our example, the component's method `createOrder` matches the initial processing step of the business process model since—according to definition 2—its semantics is a valid specialisation of "clerk (does) create order with-offer" (the semantics of the initial processing step). Similarly, the method `planOrderExecution` of the contained class `Order` represents a specialisation of the processing step "clerk (does) plan order" since the activity "schedule" is defined as a specialisation of the required activity "plan".

4 *Results Presentation / Evaluation Phase*: The use of the proposition ontology improves the understandability of component descriptions for domain experts. Apart from technical aspects, the presentation of a components can be accompanied by text generated from the sentences assigned to a component's methods.

The analysis of semantic relationships between business process models and components represents work in progress.

5. Concluding Remarks

In this paper, we have proposed to use a linguistic ontology for intermediation between business process models and components on component markets. Starting out from linguistic perspectives on the semantics of business process models and components, we have devised a basic ontology of natural language propositions. While the domain independent conceptualisation level of this ontology specifies the syntactic characteristics of simple propositions, semantic relationships between terms and constraints on the usage of terms in sentences are defined on the domain specific core knowledge level. A simple specialisation relationship between sentences permits the derivation of new, valid propositions from the ontology. Finally, we have outlined the application of the proposition ontology to business process oriented component retrieval.

Future work will be concerned with elaboration on the usage of the proposition ontology for component retrieval. We are especially interested in the definition of an instance of the proposition ontology for customer care in the telecommunications services domain, and in the evaluation of our concepts and implementation by means of EJB components for customer care in the telecommunications services domain.

References

[1] Chandrasekaran, B., Josephson, J. R., and Benjamins, V. R. What are ontologies, and why do we need them? IEEE Intelligent Systems, vol. 14, no. 1, 1999, pp. 20–26.

[2] Fox, M., Chionglo, J., and Fadel, F. A common sense model of the enterprise. In 2nd Industrial Engineering Research Conference, (Norcross GA: Institute for Industrial Engineers), 1993, pp. 425–429.

[3] Fuchs, N. E. and Schwitter, R. Attempto controlled english (ACE). In The First International Workshop on Controlled Language Applications (CLAW 96), (Katholieke Universiteit Leuven), 1996.

[4] Guarino, N., Masolo, C., and Vetere, G. OntoSeek: Content-based access to the web. IEEE Intelligent Systems, vol. 14, no. 3, 1999, pp. 70–80.

[5] Hoare, C. A. R. An axiomatic basis for computer programming. Communications of the ACM, vol. 12, no. 10, 1969, pp. 576–583.

[6] Keller, G. and Teufel, T. SAP R/3 Process Oriented Implementation: Iterative Process Prototyping. Addison Wesley, 1998.

[7] Liskov, B. H. and Wing, J. M. A behavioural notion of subtyping. ACM Transactions on Programming Languages and Systems, vol. 16, no. 6, 1994, pp. 1811–1841.

[8] Meta Data Coalition. Open Information Model, Version 1.1 (Proposal). August 1999.

[9] Meyer, B. Applying "design by contract". IEEE Computer, vol. 25, no. 10, 1992, pp. 40–51.

[10] Mili, A., Mili, R., and Mittermeir, R. A survey of software reuse libraries. Annals of Software Engineering, vol. 5, 1998, pp. 349–414.

[11] Object Management Group. Unified Modeling Language Specification, Version 1.4, September 2001.

[12] Ortner, E. Methodenneutraler Fachentwurf (in German). B. G. Teubner Verlag, 1997.

[13] Schienmann, B. Objektorientierter Fachentwurf (in German). Vol. 20 of *Teubner-Texte zur Informatik*. Stuttgart, Leipzig: B. G. Teubner Verlag, 1997.

[14] Schlenoff, C., Gruninger, M., Tissot, F., Valois, J., Lubell, J., and Lee, J. The process specification language (PSL): Overview and version 1.0 specification. Technical report NISTIR 6459, National Institute of Standards and Technology (NIST), 2000.

[15] Szyperski, C. *Component Software - Beyond Object-Oriented Programming*. Addison-Wesley, 1998.

[16] Teschke, T. Using business process knowledge for software component retrieval. In Proceedings of 11th Annual BIT Conference, Manchester, 2001.

[17] Teschke, T. and Ritter, J. Towards a foundation of component-oriented software reference models. In Generative and Component-Based Software Engineering (G. Butler and S. Jarzabek, eds.), vol. 2177 of *Lecture Notes in Computer Science*, Springer, 2000, pp. 71–85.

[18] Uschold, M., King, M., Moralee, S., and Zorgios, V. The enterprise ontology. The Knowledge Engineering Review, vol. 13, Special Issue on Putting Ontologies to Use (M. Uschold and A. Tate, eds.), 1998.

[19] Van den Heuvel, W.-J. Integrating Modern Business Applications with Objectified Legacy Systems (to appear). Ph.D. thesis, Tilburg University, 2002.

EXTENDED USE OF A TRACEABILITY TOOL WITHIN SOFTWARE DEVELOPMENT PROJECT

Martins Gills, Mihails Bogdanovs
Riga Information Technology Institute, Kuldigas iela 45, LV-1083 Riga, Latvia
{Martins.Gills, Mihails.Bogdanovs}@dati.lv

Abstract   This paper describes the implementation of the traceability tool TraceIt that was applied in a commercial software development project to support the requirement maintenance, the testing, the problem management and the help-desk activities. The tool was developed to improve the cooperation between various activities of the software development process. Its primary goal was to keep trace information between any type of project items. The architecture of this tool allows to maintain nformation about various types of relations between project items. Relations may vary from a strong dependence to a weak link. Successful configuration features allowed it to serve also as problem tracking database, as help-desk system or repository for all the testing information. The integration of these two capabilities proved to be almost irreplaceable during the critical stages of the development project. Paper examines how the configurable traceability models were used in two projects, and lessons are analysed.

Keywords: quality assurance, traceability, testing

1.   Introduction

Formally, the existence of the traceability as a mechanism or process property within the software development life cycle is required by many industry standards like ISO/IEC 12207 [10]. A good software life cycle control requires a well-developed traceability mechanism [16]. Also, the interpretation of the standard ISO 9001:2000 for software development TickIT Guide Issue 5.0 in a number of requirements includes the traceability issue [3] identifying the tracing from the requirements up till final test report.

H.-M. Haav and A. Kalja (eds.), Databases and Information Systems II, 175–186.

In some particular areas there exists a problem related to notion what exactly is understood and practiced within the term "traceability", and thorough reviews have been made (e.g. the classical study by Gotel and Finkelstein [6]). The general definition for requirements traceability is identified as: the ability to describe and follow the life of a requirement, in both a forwards and backwards direction. It is essential for developing software systems of a high quality. Generally accepted classification is concerned with pre-RS (requirement specification) and post-RS traceability. Pre-RS reflects a real-life concept into RS, but post-RS deals with the relation of RS to the project artefacts. There could be also distinction between vertical (determines how one artefact is derived from another) and horizontal (tracks each artefact through various iterations) traceability [5]. In some cases traceability could be extended to trace personnel contributing the engineering of requirements [7].

Above mentioned principles of dependency on requirements determine that implementation and testing processes are two areas where traceability can be applied at large extent. The most typical problem is to find the way to implement in real-life software development projects the well-known traceability principles. Also, the surveys within software projects indicate the necessity for improved traceability in projects [25, 26].

This paper reflects experience of defining the requirements for project information traceability tool, and its implementation in form of tool TraceIt. It also shows the lessons learned from its usage in development projects.

The paper's main contribution is its demonstration that the mechanism of the traceability tool TraceIt is applicable for keeping requirement definition, testing and problem report information in one united repository. Our most important results are:

1. In a commercial development project of more than 25 team members involved TraceIt served as the primary place where the up-to-date requirements and their interrelations were kept. It was the only repository to hold the test specifications and test logs. TraceIt was used most extensively as problem tracking database, maintaining links to respective functions or tests where problem was detected.

2. This tool provided also as a link between user reported informal suggestions and formal requirements.

3. TraceIt architecture allows implementing different methodologies for each separate project.

In this paper, we present the methodological basis for the traceability tool (Section 2). Section 3 outlines the implementation concerns of the tool TraceIt. In Section 4 we share the experience from application of the tool in the real software development projects. In Section 5 we compare and contrast our approach with related work in requirements traceability domain. In Section 6 we present some concluding remarks.

2. Tracebility Tool Concept

2.1 Project Items and Their Relationships

The initiative to develop a traceability tool did not appear as sole wish to create some new software system. A software process improvement group in a software development company DATI analysed the most important processes and properties of the projects, producing the guidelines for software development process. One of the conclusions was related to improvement of traceability mechanism. For it to be functional, it must fit with the large variety of project types present in the company. Also, the traceability has to fit naturally within the project everyday tasks.

We focused on a broad notion of the project item. It may describe the intended product, and the project information as well. We declared that the project items could be the information of almost any character, but the main criterion is its relation to project development or subject under development, e.g. requirement, design item, function, module, test, problem report, change request. Thus there is both pre-RS and post-RS involved. Currently we mostly focused on the vertical traceability support, leaving the refinement of horizontal traceability for further research.

2.1.1 Evolution-provoked Relations

Typical evolution-provoked relations are those, which connect a given object with its refinement, or it transformed (improved, reflected into other terms, etc.) content. For example, the standard J-STD-016 [8] states the necessity to perform traceability between various elements of the project information. Here the project items are the elements of various defined documents. They all correspond to certain development life cycle phases, and are primary constituents of the requirement traceability.

2.1.2 Event-provoked Relations

There is a class of project items that are produced as a response to project events like test execution, problem detection and reviewing of items. Obtained records are not evolutionary continuation of the respective project items (like requirements or tests), but are rather separate statements. Project items like test logs, problem reports or review reports document project life events. The modification of a related item does not provoke a necessity modify the related one. There are no restrictions of what item types may be involved into such type of relations.

2.1.3   Relation Types

Two types of relations are defined: **Strong relation** - the relation between two items where the item that refers to the first one could be potentially changed (there is such a risk present). **Weak relation** - the relation that is used just to show that in principle there is some link, reference, similarity or belonging to a group.

There is not equivalence between terms weak relation and event-provoked relation. For example, there may be a relation "is part of" that is weak relation, but at the same time it is an evolution-provoked relation. In this case there is a narrowed view on relation types comparing to a more general classification presented as part of reference model for requirements traceability [21]. We found this rather simple classification to be more appropriate.

2.1.4   Graphical Interpretation

To represent the relation, an arrow symbol is used. The end from which the arrow goes out is related to the item it points to. The situation is similar to structure/object with pointer to another structure/object in programming languages. Strong relations in graphical notation are shown by solid line, weak relations - with dotted line (see Fig. 1).

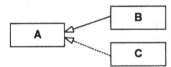

Figure 1. Strong (A-B) and weak (A-C) relation.

2.2   Traceability Model Definition

Relatively to the item, the relation that goes from the given item to another, we can call "from" relation, and the incoming - "to" relation. Also, in some particular cases where a strong dependency or inheritance (e.g. from requirement to design item) takes place we can informally call A as "parent" relative to the "child" B. The notation is slightly similar to the one used in specification language UML [18]. In UML diagrams, the generalization or inheritance is shown by means of an arrow symbol that comes from the child (class or object that inherits) to parent element (base class or object). Although there is no inheritance in the classical sense, the usage of these symbols characterizes the dependencies or evolutionary development order. Traceability model defines the relations that can exist (are allowed) between the project items. The project can treat only the defined of item type relations. At implementation level, the traceability model serves as a meta-model for traceability tool functionality.

Another role of the traceability model is to help project members to understand the information structures inside the project.

The resulting traceability model has to correspond to a connected directed graph where vertices are items and edges are relations. Each item may have one or more several items that reference to it ("incoming relations"), and it may reference to one or more other items ("outgoing relations"). There may exit also multiple paths through different relations between two items.

3.   Implementation

For implementation we chose a relational database approach. To increase compatibility of platforms, the interface with end-user is organized via web browser. To increase the platform independence on server side, we used PHP scripting language and MySQL database. Multiple user support is built-in. The functionality covers configuration, administration, work with items and relations, change review, analysis, import/export.

Configuration and administration. The configuration provides means to define and modify the traceability model. Types of item types and relation types can be defined. Item types can be compared to classes in UML diagrams. For each item type, the information structure has to be defined. An allowed relation definition sets the links within the traceability model. This model can be updated during the life cycle of a project.

Work with items and relations. Work with items and relations supports storage and retrieval of the traceability information. All functions are processed according to the traceability model. Items can be viewed under various filtering conditions. For each item and relations insert/update/delete operations are present. There are special functions for basic and advanced traceability information analysis like displaying of the relation hierarchy in a form of a tree; identification of all relations between any two item types, etc.

The tool stores history of changes for items and relations. This allows following their development over time and "undo changes" function.

Change review. The change review mechanism consists of the identification of items that are connected with a strong relation to some "parent" that is being changed. When the "parent" changes, all dependant "children" items are marked as "pending". They have to be reviewed by user. The user can either approve to leave existing content of an item (or presence of relation) or change something. At the same time, as pending items are identified, the items that could be next after the current pending ones (as the change wave propagates) are marked as "pending candidates" that signifies that they potentially are of one change's impact.

4. Project Experience

4.1 Project A

Project A was a commercial software development project. More than 25 persons were involved, duration - 5 months. This project had a classical incremental life-cycle model. There was a preceding system analysis phase. The following item types were defined: Requirement, Window, Test, Test log, Problem report/Change request (the fixation of the observed problem, or the initiation of a change in requirements or design. May be a direct result of the test execution, or it could be observed or initiated outside it), Help desk record. The traceability model is shown in Fig. 2.

4.1.1 Initial Set-up of the Traceability Model

At the beginning of the implementation phase the only problem was the dependency between various requirements and design items. These dependencies had a hierarchical character, therefore there was a relation name "contains" used.

The next phase was the parallel definition of the tests and implementation, producing the windows. The latter could be regarded as design item subtype, but due to convenience needs it was separated from type Requirement. In many cases we observed many-to-many relations between requirements and windows. Tests were defined with various detail levels. Each test record contained predefined fields, but they were filled upon the context. Every test record could be either of the type the set of tests or concrete test. In the first case there is no detailed information given. For the concrete tests that in some cases were with the detail level of test cases there were two classifying fields: Input data class and Test type.

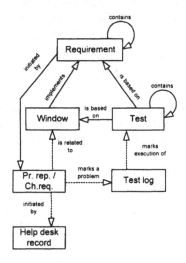

Figure 2. Traceability model for project A.

4.1.2 Test Execution Phase

When test execution phase started, test log and problem report documenting became active. Both these item types due to their event-provoked nature have weak relations with the tests and between themselves. We defined a possibility to link it with the window where the problem was found when the problem was discovered outside a defined test. Ruling by the experience from previous projects problem reports and change requests were kept in the same list. Because of this, there is also a possibility to reference some requirement to a given change request. The TraceIt capability to support features of the problem tracking tool proved to be a critical for project decision to use this one tool for several purposes. Basic benefits outside the traceability issue were the possibility of keeping track of the requirements, for maintaining test specifications, to log the test data, and most fundamentally, also to track the problem reports and change requests.

4.1.3 Further Support

Along with the first distributed releases to customer there was a Help desk record type defined. The tool TraceIt allows registering the question, observation or suggestion in a separate form. Project system analyst evaluates whether it could a source to some problem report or change request. If the answer is positive he or she creates a problem report or change request (the latter is least likely case).

The above described mechanism clarifies some doubts about the possible reference loops between the items. There may be cycle reference among several item types, but it is not among the concrete items - every time the items will be different.

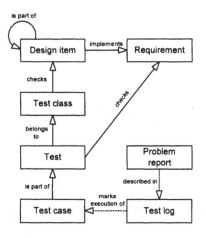

Figure 3. Traceability model of the project B.

4.2 Project B

In contrast with the project A, the traceability tool in project B was applied at the beginning of testing phase. The information about requirements and design was kept in the documentation of many different forms, mostly text documents. Design was documented poorly and these documents had no complete information. There were some problems concerning the information integrity.

After TraceIt was introduced into the project, this information was manually extracted, classified and put in the traceability database, also clarifying several issues concerning system requirements and design thus improving the overall project quality.

The traceability model of project B is shown in Fig. 3.

4.3   Common Issues

Along with application of the tool TraceIt in projects, we collected the responses from project members. The most typical questions that were put towards the traceability were: What are the direct relations between some two items? Are all requirements covered? Are all requirements tested (at all or in a particular version)? What is the status of problem reports? Where do problems originate from (requirement, window)?

Also, the lists that contained complete item information were extensively used for working with their contents, e.g. test specification or problem description. In some cases, tool also proved to be useful for following the development or testing progress. We found it useful to modify the traceability model as the project develops.

Main problems with the usage were associated with the selection of the appropriate methodology. In fact, this problem is outside tool itself, but it is a part of traceability problem. We saw that it is important to select the right way of how to define the traceability model. At the same time the model without a tool could be difficult to implement.

5.   Related Work

Our result is related to area of traceability tools. Commercial requirements management tools generally contain traceability as one of the features [9]. In many cases these tools are tied to some particular project workflow and methodology, e.g. tools, like TOOR, are made as part of the research projects that support definition of requirements, linking them to other project objects [19]. Some requirements engineering environments, like PRO-ART, are mainly oriented to pre-RT [20]. There are tools that help to extract traceability link information from the system's source code and design objects [24], to recover the links between source code and its free text documentation [2], to maintain traceability links between different versions of the same source code over the pace of evolution [1]. The usage of requirements management tools in context of automatic update of documents also is a research topic [11]. Methodology has been developed for improving the effectiveness of requirements management and traceability [14]. Traceability can improve requirements that contain various description types, e.g. scenarios [4].

Important area for traceability information maintenance (especially horizontal traceability) is in configuration management [15]. Our tool in its current implementation is primarily oriented to relation maintenance among different project artifacts, but the historical information is being kept only along with the given item. Traceability analysis can play a vital role in change management [13].

Another related area is problem management. In software engineering, there are well-established requirements towards problem reporting and handling [12, 23]. Authors have some experience with other comparable tools, including the problem tracking tools [22, 17]. Basic features are similar to the ones in TraceIt, but our tool provides more flexibility to configure the items and has the traceability concept natively built in. Commercial tools are more mature than TraceIt, but they mainly lack the traceability supporting functions. They also are more testing-specific, whereas TraceIt is designed to serve for all project life-cycle phases.

6.   Conclusions

The approach and the tool here presented provide organization of the project items into a structured form. We propose an approach that is based upon complete traceability principle between any two project items like requirements, tests, problem reports, etc. Project processes like testing become more measurable in terms of answering the basic questions of completeness and influence of change.

Traceability model definition helps to understand the software development process within the project. Project management and quality assurance staff can transform and optimize the existing model to satisfy the vital quality criteria of the project.

The integration of the problem tracking tool with the traceability tool allows to identify the dependencies and possible consequences.

Complete testing information from test specification to problem test logs and reports can be placed and maintained in TraceIt database. No need in external testing documentation unless some specific deliverables in a separate document form are required.

The tool TraceIt is not tied to a particular methodology, but rather serves as environment to build it in. We have selected the approach not to define global constraints on relation types, but rather to adapt to specific needs of every software development project.

As the tool gives a freedom of item type and traceability model definition, there has to be a high competence of software development processes for the person who defines them.

The implementation of the tool in a form of a web-based application provides many advantages in terms of information sharing among the team members, and intranet technology usage could be regarded as one of requirements for other future project tools with a project team as target audience.

References

[1] Antoniol, G., Canfora, G., De Lucia, A. Maintaining Traceability During Object-Oriented Software Evolution: a Case Study. Proc. IEEE Int. Conf. on SW Maintenance, 1998. 9 p.

[2] Antoniol, G., Canfora, G., Casazza, G., De Lucia, A. Inf. Retrieval Models for Recovering Trac. Links betw. Code and Doc./ Proc. IEEE Int. Conf. on SW Maint. (ICSM'00), 10 p.

[3] British Standards Institution. The TickIT Guide Issue 5.0, 2001

[4] Cesar, L.J., Rossi, G., Balaguer, F., Maiorana, V., Kaplan, G., Hadad, G., Oliveros, A. Enhancing a Requirements Baseline with Scenarios. Proc.of the 3rd IEEE Int. Symp. on Req. Engn.. (RE'97), pp. 43-53.

[5] Corriveau, J.-P. Trac. Process for Large OO Proj. Computer, Sept.1996, pp. 63-68.

[6] Gotel, O.C.Z., Finkelstein, A.C.W. An Analysis of the Requirements Traceability Problem. 1994. http://citeseer.nj.nec.com/78573.html

[7] Gotel, O., Finkelstein, A. Extended Requirements Traceability: Results of an Industrial Case Study. Proc. of the 3rd IEEE Int. Symp. on Reqs Engineering (RE'97), pp. 169-178.

[8] IEEE, J-STD-016-1995. Std for IT Software Life Cycle Processes. 1995.

[9] INCOSE, The International Council on Systems Engineering. Tools Survey: Requirements Management Tools. http://www.incose.org/tools/tooltax.html, 1998-2001.

[10] ISO. Standard ISO/IEC 12207. Standard Information Technology - Software Life Cycle Processes, 1995.

[11] James, L. Automatic Requirements Specification Update Processing From A Requirements Management Tool Perspective. Proceedings of the 1997 Workshop on Engineering of Computer-Based Systems (ECBS '97), pp. 2-9.

[12] Kaner, Cem et. al. Testing Computer Software, John Wiley & Sons, 1999. p 480.

[13] Lam, W., Shankararaman V., Jones, S., Hewitt, J., Britton, C. Change Analysis and Management: A Process Model and Its Application within a Commercial Setting. 1998 IEEE Workshop on Application - Specific Software Engineering and Technology, 6 p.

[14] Lavazza, L., Valetto, G. Enhancing Requirements and Change Mangmnt through Process Modelling and Measur.. Proc. of the 4th Int. Conf. on Reqs Engr. (ICRE'00), 10 p.

[15] Lindsay, P., Liu, Y., Traynor, O. A Generic Model for Fine Grained Config. Mangmnt Incl. Version Cont. and Trac. Proc. of the Austral. SW Engn. Conf. (ASWEC '97), 10 p.

[16] Luqi, G.J. A. Formal Methods: Promises and Problems. IEEE Software, January 1997, pp. 73-85.

[17] Merant PVCS Tracker. http://www.merant.com/

[18] Object Management Group. Unified Modeling Language. http://www.uml.org

[19] Pinheiro, F.A.C., Goguen J.A. An Object-Oriented Tool for Tracing Requirements. IEEE Software, March 1996, pp. 52-64.

[20] Pohl, K. PRO-ART: Enabling Requirements Pre-Traceability. 1996 IEEE Proceedings of ICRE '96, pp. 76-84.

[21] Ramesh, B., Jarke, M. Toward Reference Models for Requirements Traceability. IEEE Tansactions on SW Engineering, Vol.27, no1., pp. 58-93.

[22] Rational ClearQuest. http://www.rational.com

[23] Sabourin, R.A. The Effective SQA Manager: Getting Things Done. Proceedings of Software Quality Week 2001 conference, p 50.

[24] Tryggeseth, E. and Nytrø, Ø. Dynamic Traceability Links Supported by a System Architecture Description. Proc, of the 1997 Int. Conf. on SW Maint. (ICSM'97). 8 p.

[25] Weidenhaupt, K., Pohl, K., Jarke, M., Haumer P. Scenarios in System Development: Current Practice. IEEE Software, March/April 1998, pp. 34-45.

[26] Woodward, S. Evolutionary Project Management. Computer, October 1999, pp. 49-57.

MEASUREMENTS AND RISKS BASED METHOD TO SUPPORT SOFTWARE DEVELOPMENT PROCESS PLANNING

Baiba Apine
Riga Information Technology Institute, Kuldigas iela 45, LV-1083 Riga, Latvia
Baiba.Apine@dati.lv

Abstract   This paper describes the way in which software development process measurement data together with results of risk analysis are used for software development project planning. The Measurements and Risks Based Method (MERIME) to support software development process planning is proposed. The first results of using this method are announced.

Keywords: software development process planning, software development process measurements, risk analysis.

1.   Introduction

Software development is rather complex process, consisting of different activities. It is often said that software development is very hard to manage and projects are out of schedule and out of budget. Planning of the development process is very important activity. The software development process is dependent on skills level of different specialists as well as on usage of different technologies. A lot of various factors must be kept in mind while planning the software development process. Therefore any information submitted to support full-cycle software development process planning as well as short-term planning is helpful.

There are two software development supporting processes providing useful information for planning: risk analysis and measuring. Several methods are used in software development companies for planning using the information produced by these two processes. For instance, analytical

H.-M. Haav and A. Kalja (eds.), Databases and Information Systems II, 187–198.

software development cost estimation methods like COCOMO II [1], Experience Pro [4], which use statistical data about many software development projects probably developed in different companies. The results are used to forecast effort and schedule for software development projects. It is recommended to adjust the results given by formal analytical methods using software development process measurement information collected within the company [4], as formal results are might be too general and might not meet the specific project needs.

We have six-year experience of using COCOMO II method for software development effort and schedule planning. As well as the Measurement program is implemented as a set of activities on the company level to measure software development process. Gathered measurement data are used to adjust results of formal methods to our software development projects for more than two years. We often face the following drawbacks:

1. Analytical software development process effort and schedule estimation methods available are used to estimate the whole software development process only. It would be very useful for project short-time planning to forecast, for instance, the distribution of effort or any other project characteristic.

2. It is quite easy to gather the measurement data, but it worth nothing if not appropriately used. The effective usage of software development measurement data is a key success factor of Measurement program [3, 6]. It has to be shown continuously that measurement data are analysed properly and used efficiently.

To find the way how to use software development process measurement data for software project short-term planning, we started to use them together with results of risk analysis. This paper describes Measurements and Risks Based Method (MERIME) developed to support software development process planning. The method formalizes the experience of software managers and developers in such a way it could be spread among other software developers and used for software development planning.

Initially lets have a look at the method as a "black box" (see *Figure 1*) and discuss results expected from the usage of MERIME method for planning and input data necessary to apply the method.

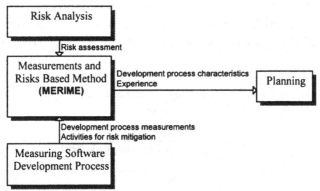

Figure 1. Measurements and Risks Based Method relationships with other processes

2.   Output of the Method

There are two results from using MERIME method:

- Development process characteristics for planning: the percentage of effort had to be spent on developments as well as on different activities within software development process for next months. For instance, the result could be the following forecast: work amount spent on project documentation for the project with unstable software requirements will be 6% of total project development work amount for next month.
- Tips based on experience from other projects of software development risk mitigation activities. For instance, consider that the live risk for the project under development is instability of software requirements. The tip could be: "Establish project level control structure: change request board consisting of two developers and two customers".

These results could be used for project short-term planning. Nevertheless it must be kept in mind that these are forecasted characteristics and recommendations only, so these results must be treated carefully.

3.   Input of the Method

There are two software development support processes creating input data for MERIME method: software development risk analysis and software development process measurement.

There are no special restrictions how to organize the software development process risk analysis. It is possible to use any software development risk analysis method, for instance, standards IEEE P1540/D11.0

[7] or CMMI [10] for software development process risk analysis. Nevertheless the results of risk analysis must satisfy the following criteria:

1. Results of the risk analysis must be summarized regularly. For instance, monthly.
2. Each identified risk must be graded. For instance, using grades from 1 (the lowest mark) to 5 (the highest mark) according to grading scale given in *Table 1*, which is used in our company.

Table 1. Risk grading scale

Risk Grade	Criteria for Choosing Risk Grade
1	Risk is not applicable to this project.
2	The probability that the risk will have negative influence to the development process is very low. It is not necessary to plan any activities for risk mitigation.
3	The probability that the risk will have negative influence to the development process is quite low. It is necessary to think about special activities for risk mitigation.
4	The probability that the risk will have negative influence to the development process is high. It is necessary to plan special activities for risk mitigation and monitor the risk continuously.
5	The risk will have negative influence to the development process. It is necessary to plan special activities for risk mitigation, monitor the risk continuously and involve top management in risk mitigation activities.

There are risk analysis methodologies grading separately risk probability and impact [8, 9] by assigning grades from 1 to 3. Total risk exposure is calculated by multiplying probability and impact. Although it is allowed to choose other risk grading scales, all the development processes, which are using MERIME method for planning, must be graded using one and the same risk grading scale.

MERIME method uses risk sequences as input data. Lets have a look at the sample. Risk analysis results suitable as input information for MERIME method are given in the *Table 2*, where risk analysis grades are chosen according to the criteria given in the *Table 1*.

Another software development supporting process producing information suitable for planning is measuring. Even if the official Measurement program doesn't exist at a company level, there are some traditions in each software development company regarding the software development process measuring. And again, like in the case with risk analysis data, MERIME method doesn't set any limitations on measurement information gathered in the company, the only restriction is that all the processes using MERIME method for planning must be measured according one and the same measurement methodology. This could be ensured by implementing Measurement program at a company level.

Table 2. Sample of risk analysis results (risk sequences)

Risk	Jan-00	Feb-00	Mar-00	Apr-00	May-00
Unstable software requirements	2	3	2	3	4
Schedule shortage	1	1	2	4	4

Lets have a look at the Measurement program sample, which results are suitable for using in MERIME method.

Software development process measurement activities have to be planned along with software development project planning. Each project gathers the following measurement data:

1. The amount of functionality has to be implemented (function points, lines of code etc.).
2. Work amount spent on different activities within software development process.

Each project developer writes down work hours spent on software development at the end of each working day.

3. Planned activities for risk mitigation.

During risk analysis, if the grade for the particular risk exceeds the accepted risk gap, risk mitigation activities are planned. For instance, if the grade for risk "Difficult communication with customer" increases 3, possible activity is "Conduct regular meetings on the project management level. It would be better to conduct these meetings on the customer site. If it isn't possible to meet, customer has to be informed about project development by phone or via e-mail." This is recorded by the project team member whose responsibility is project level risk management.

The head of Measurement program performs initial analysis of the measurement data by forming reports suitable for input data of MERIME method.

It is highly recommended that measurement data about problem reports are gathered and analysed also, but this is out of scope of this paper.

4. How does It Work ?

The idea of the method is to store risk analysis and measurement information (hereinafter risks and measurements) in MERIME information base and use it for new projects' planning (hereinafter current projects). MERIME method searches for relationships between risks and measurements in MERIME information base to find software development projects, which are similar to the current project, and therefore their measurement information could be used as guidelines for current project.

To illustrate how risks and measurements are stored in the MERIME information base, lets have a look at its meta-model [2] (see *Figure 2*):

1. *Project* is software development project, which risk analysis and measurement information is stored in the MERIME information base. *Project* attributes are name, development environment, problem area, etc.

2. *Risk* is, analysed and graded risk. "Unstable software requirements" and "Lack of knowledge in problem area" are samples of *Risk*. Name is an attribute of the *Risk*.

3. *Measurement* is project development process measurement information. "Percentage of work amount spent on documentation", "Average response time to problem report (days)" are samples of *Measurement*. Name is an attribute of the *Measurement*.

4. *Activity* is activity for risk mitigation. "Establish change request board", "Close project" are samples of *Activity*. Name is an attribute of the *Activity*.

5. *Sequence* is a sequence of measurement information or risk grades. For sample see *Table 2*. Name of the risk, month, for which risk is graded, grade and length of the sequence are attributes of the *Sequence*.

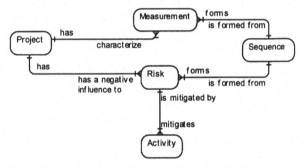

Figure 2. Meta-model of the MERIME method information base

Process diagram in *Figure 3* illustrates steps of using MERIME method for project development planning.

The first task is **Store risk analysis results**. To use MERIME method for new project planning (for current project), the following activities must be carried out:

1. Perform current project risk analysis and store results in MERIME information base for at least three months following the guidelines given in chapter "3 Input".

2. Perform current project risk analysis for the next time period. For instance, if MERIME method is used for planning for next two months, risk analysis must be performed for next two months also.

The results of the task **Store risk analysis results** are stored in the MERIME information base.

Task **Store measurement information** shows, that measurement data for new project must be gathered, summarised and stored in the MERIME information base for at least three months. The result of **Store measurement information** is stored in the MERIME information base.

Storing risk analysis and measurements information for current projects guarantees, that MERIME information base is updated continuously.

The next task is **Search for similar projects**, where all the projects satisfying the following criteria are found in MERIME information base:
1. Approximately the same amount of functionality must be implemented. The amount of functionality could be measured in function points, lines of code etc.
2. Software development projects follow the same software development life-cycle.
3. Have at least one risk sequence similar to the risk sequence of the current project.

In MERIME method two risks' sequences are considered as similar, if they are of equal length and there are no corresponding risk grades difference more than one. For instance, risk sequence $V1=1,2,3,3,2$ and $V2=1,3,3,2,1$, are similar. Sequence $V3=3,2,3,3,2$ is similar to neither $V1$ nor $V2$, because the first element of $V3$ differs from the first element of $V1$ and $V2$ for two.

The result of the **Search for similar projects** is *Risk and measurement sequence for sample project* satisfying the criteria defined above. The sample projects are considered as similar to the current project and will be used to generate guidelines for current project planning.

Example in *Figure 4* illustrates how to apply the criteria to find the sample projects. PROJ_4 is current project, but PROJ_1, PROJ_2 and PROJ_3 are sample projects found in the MERIME information base. The PROJ_4 satisfies the following requirements:
1. The same amount of functionality must be implemented.
2. Software development projects follow the same software development life-cycle.
3. PROJ_4 risks' sequence of length 5 is similar to PROJ_1, PROJ_2 and PROJ_3 appropriate risks' sequences.

The next task is **Process characteristics forecast**. Process characteristics are forecasted to keep the measurement sequences for the current project the same as for sample projects. *Process characteristics* are the result of the usage of the MERIME method.

194

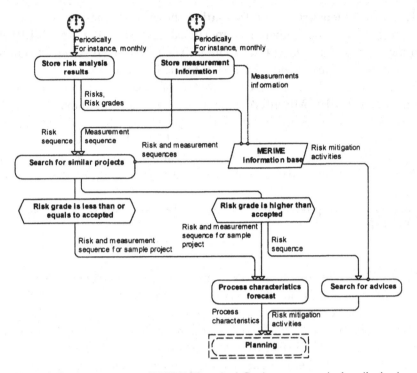

Figure 3. Business process of MERIME method. Business process is described using
GRAPES/BM business modelling language [5].

Have a look at the sample in the *Figure 4* once more. We shall forecast
the work amount spent on documentation for the next month for PROJ_4.
The sample projects used are PROJ_1, PROJ_2 and PROJ_3. The work
amount for documentation for the next time period for PROJ_4 will be 7.8%
from work amount spent on project development (see *Figure 4*). This value is
chosen as the closest for keeping measurement sequence for the PROJ_4
within the range of measurement sequences of PROJ_1, PROJ_2 and
PROJ_3.

The last task is **Search for advices**. This task is executed only in the case
when the risk grade in the sequence is higher than accepted. *Risk sequence* of
the current project is used for searching in the MERIME information base.
All projects having at least one risk sequence similar to the risk sequence of
the current project and having the last risk grade in the sequence quite high
are considered as sample projects. For instance, if the scale for risk grading
given in *Table 1* is used, high-risk grades are 4 or 5. The result is the list of
Risk mitigation activities stored in the MERIME information base.

5.   Application of the MERIME Method

Although MERIME method is still under development it is already used for planning for three software development projects within one software development company for half a year. The MERIME method information base contains risk analysis and measurement information about seven projects.

This software development company focuses on development of large tailored information systems for customers in Latvia and Western Europe, where short-term planning is very important and might be rather complex activity.

There are already established risk analysis traditions in the company, but risk analysis procedure is not formally defined yet. All the project level risks (unstable requirements, lack of knowledge in the problem area, squeezed development schedule etc.) are discussed weekly on the project level meetings.

There are some measurement traditions established in the company. The following measurement information is captured on the regular basis:

1. All development teams capture information about defects, usually including identifier, description, function and version where defect fixed, defect fix date, severity, current defect status, status fix date etc.
2. Some development teams capture information about time spent on different activities during project development.

There is accepted Software development measurement program in the company concentrating on usage of the existing data captured in different software development projects. These measurement data are gathered and analysed monthly. Standard set of measurement data reports is generated monthly and provided to the software developers. The measurement program is discussed in [3] in more details.

The first step was to fill data into the MERIME information base. Seven software development projects from approximately 40 currently running projects were chosen having the following advantages:

1. Project development teams have captured information about time spent on different activities during software development process.
2. Project manager loyalty to usage of formal methods to support software development planning.

Amount of functionality						
PROJ_1	1221	Function points				
PROJ_2	802	Function points				
PROJ_3	964	Function points				
PROJ_4	1008	Function points				
Month	**1**	**2**	**3**	**4**	**5**	**6**
Life cycle activity						
PROJ_1	Design	Design	Implement.	Implement.	Implement.	Testing
PROJ_2	Design	Implement.	Implement.	Implement.	Implement.	Testing
PROJ_3	Design	Design	Implement.	Implement.	Testing	Testing
PROJ_4	Design	Design	Implement.	Implement.	Implement.	
Risk: unstable software requirements						
PROJ_1	3	2	3	3	3	2
PROJ_2	2	3	2	2	2	3
PROJ_3	2	2	3	4	3	3
PROJ_4	2	2	2	3	2	
Risk: difficult communication with customer						
PROJ_1	2	2	2	1	1	1
PROJ_2	2	1	2	2	2	3
PROJ_3	2	2	1	1	1	1
PROJ_4	1	2	2	1	2	
Risk: lack of knowledge about development environment and technologies used						
PROJ_1	4	4	4	4	4	3
PROJ_2	3	2	2	2	2	3
PROJ_3	4	3	2	2	2	2
PROJ_4	4	4	3	3	3	
Measurement: percentage of work-amount spent on documentation						
PROJ_1	37.8%	20.0%	17.3%	13.3%	3.0%	6.3%
PROJ_2	4.5%	4.3%	5.4%	2.9%	4.8%	1.0%
PROJ_3	20.0%	17.3%	13.3%	10.9%	6.3%	3.5%
PROJ_4	12.2%	11.0%	11.8%	**7.8%**		

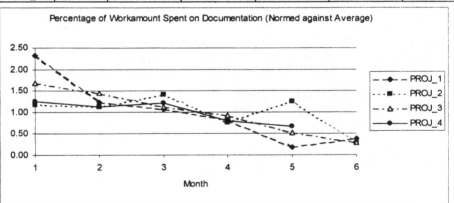

Figure 4. Searching for sample project in the MERIME information base

Questionnaires were provided to these five project managers asking to restore the risk sequences for their projects' risks following the scale given in *Table 1*. One month was chosen as a frequency period for the grading of risks, because measurement information is summarised monthly also. The results of the questionnaires were filled into the MERIME information base.

Measurement information for the initial filling into the MERIME information base was taken from the Measurement program reports. The following measurements information about each project was stored in the MERIME information base:

1. Percentage of work amount spent on development of the concept of operation, requirements specification, design, implementation, testing, deployment, maintenance, documentation, quality assurance, management, and training.
2. Average response time to problem reports generated by customers.
3. Activities for mitigation of risks having grade higher than 3.

The next step was to test the method for the projects under development. Three projects were chosen having the same advantages as those seven projects already stored in MERIME information base. Questionnaires were provided to project managers asking to restore the risk sequences for their projects' level risks following the scale given in *Table 1* from the beginning of the project. The results of the questionnaires for the first 4 months of projects' development were filled into the MERIME information base. MERIME method was used to get the measurement values forecasts for the next two months regarding the work amount spent on different activities during software development. The results were compared with real measurement values of the projects.

6. Conclusions and Further Work

The following conclusions can be made:

1. Method gives rather precise forecasts for the values of development process supporting activities: documentation, quality assurance, management and training. The average error of forecasts is 19.89% with deviation 15.02%.
2. Usage of this method shows that measurement information is used continuously and effectively, which is key success factor of the Measurement program successful implementation.
3. It is possible to use incomplete measurement and risk analysis data. It is very important that the first benefits from gathering measurement and risk analysis data could be obtained after first three months.

4. It is possible to use this method even if there are no data available about large number of software development projects. This is very important for software development companies in small countries like Latvia. Another reason why it is not possible to use large number of software development projects as a source for forecasting is rapid changes in technologies. Even in large companies and countries with high IT development level statistical data gathered becomes obsolete because of rapid changes in software development technologies and skills level of staff.

5. The method is very flexible as it determines neither risk analysis nor measuring process. It is possible to use this method in different software development companies with different software development process traditions.

Acknowledgement

This paper is partly supported by the Latvian Science Council programme No. 02.0002.

References

[1] Abts, C., Boehm, B., Clark, B., Devnani-Chulani, S. COCOMO II Model Definition Manual,_University of Southern California, 68 p.

[2] Apine, B., Apinis, I., Krasts, O., Sukovskis, U. Meta-model Based and Component Based Approach for Information Systems Design, Proceedings of the 4th IEEE International Baltic Workshop: Baltic DB&IS '2000, 2000, Vilnius, Lithuania, pp. 78-83.

[3] Apine, B., Smilts, U., Sukovskis, U. Software Measurement Practice to Address Customer Satisfaction, Scientific Proceedings of Riga Technical University, Applied Computer Systems. – 1st thematic issue, 2000, pp. 11–18.

[4] Experience Pro, http://www.sttf.fi, 03.02.2002

[5] GRADE Business Modeling. Language reference. INFOLOGISTIK GmbH., 1998

[6] Hetzel, B. Making Software Measurement Work. New York: John Wiley & Sons, Inc., 1993.

[7] IEEE P1540/D11.0, Draft Standard for Software Life Cycle Processes-Risk Management, IEEE Standards Department, 2000.

[8] Informācijas sistēmu riska analīzes metodika, http://www.lddk.lv, 03.02.2002.

[9] Microsoft, material No: 1516ACP, Principles of Application Development

[10] Paulk, M.C., Curtis B., Chrissis, M.B., Weber, C.V. Capability Maturity Model for Software, Version 1.1, Software Engineering Institute, CMU/SEI-93-TR-24, February 1993.

REDUCTION OF UML CLASS DIAGRAMS

Girts Linde

University of Latvia,
Raina bulvaris 29, LV-1459, Riga, Latvia
glinde@acm.org

Abstract   One and the same "real world" can be modeled by different UML class diagrams, which in such a case can be considered "intuitively equivalent". A formalization of this "intuitive equivalence" of class diagrams is proposed. An algorithm is constructed that for two class diagrams determines if they model the same "real world". This algorithm can be used in CASE tools to compare alternative models of a system, and for diagram "compression" to facilitate understanding of large diagrams.

Keywords: UML, CASE tools

1.   Introduction

As object modeling gains popularity, starting from the pioneering work [8], a need emerges for methods of handling and evaluating models. Object models are used in various stages of system development - from requirements definition to system design. One problem is to validate the model as it gets transformed and refined in the lifecycle of system development. Research is already being done on this topic [2, 3, 1, 4]. A more general problem is to compare several alternative object models of the same "real world".

Our goal is to formalize this "intuitive equivalence" for object models represented with UML class diagrams. Consider the class diagrams modeling directed graphs shown on Figure 1.

Formally, we have here 3 totally different class diagrams. Each of them describes different instance diagrams. But intuitively we know that all these 3 diagrams describe the same "real world" - directed graphs.

We formalize this "intuitive equivalence" as *reduction*, which is based on introduction of new *concepts* as composite classes containing the existing classes as parts. If using such new concepts one class diagram can

H.-M. Haav and A. Kalja (eds.), Databases and Information Systems II, 199–208.
© *2002 Kluwer Academic Publishers.*

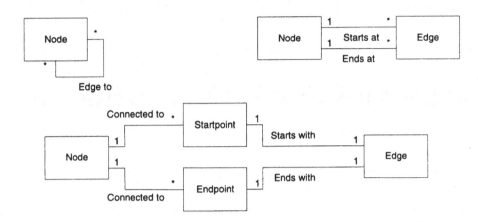

Figure 1. Three class diagrams of a directed graph

be reduced to another smaller class diagram then we can say that these diagrams are "intuitively equivalent".

Another application of reduction could be "compression" of class diagrams, i.e., representing a large class diagram with a smaller one that describes the same thing, but which is easier to understand. As noted in [7], there are at least two cases when such compression can help:

- when a reader who is not familiar with the application domain wants to learn a class diagram, it is often easier to start with a smaller one that contains only the most important concepts, and then to drill down into more detail,

- when dealing with really large class diagrams, for example, a diagram resulting from automated reverse engineering of legacy software.

In [7] a "syntactic" technique is proposed that allows some classes to be hidden under other classes, but in most cases the resulting diagram is not a valid UML class diagram any more. Our approach, however, produces a valid UML class diagram that is semantically derived from the original class diagram.

Our approach is based on the notation of a composite class. which is briefly outlined in Section 2. In Section 3 the reduction problem is described in more detail. In Sections 4 and 5 we present two algorithms that allow the construction of reduced class diagrams. In Section 6 these two algorithms are combined with the diagram equivalence check from [5] to form our main algorithm, which for two given class diagrams determines if one of the diagrams can be reduced to the other one.

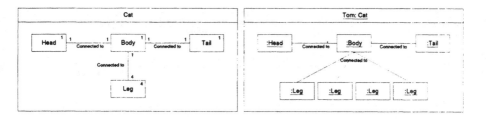

Figure 2.   A composite class and its instance

2.   Composition in UML Class Diagrams

Composition is a strong form of aggregation, which requires that a part instance be included in at most one composite at a time and that the composite object has sole responsibility for the disposition of its parts, as described in [6, 9]. The parts of a composition may include classes and associations. The meaning of an association in a composite object is that any tuple of objects connected by a single link must all belong to the same container object. One of the ways of showing composition is by graphical nesting of the symbols of the elements for the parts within the symbol of the element for the whole. A nested class element may have a multiplicity within its composite element. The multiplicity is shown in the upper right corner of the symbol for the part. An example of a composite class "Cat" and its instance are shown in Figure 2. (The other notation for the composition is a line with a black diamond connecting the whole with the part.)

Actually, any class diagram can be regarded as the content of the composite class "World" where every class has multiplicity 0..* if no other multiplicity is specified.

The equivalence problem for composite class diagrams is studied in [5], and it is proved that the problem can be solved algorithmically. We will use these results in our reduction algorithm.

In this paper composite classes are the basic elements of the reduction technique. We will introduce new concepts in class diagrams as composite classes with the existing classes as parts of the composition.

3.   The Reduction Problem

In this paper we consider the reduction problem only for simplified class diagrams that consist of classes and simple binary associations with four most popular multiplicities: 1..1, 0..1, 1..*, 0..*.

We will not give a formal definition of reduction, but rather explain it informally on an example. Consider two class diagrams shown in Fig.

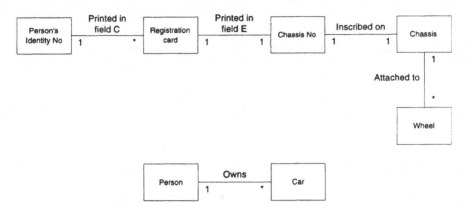

Figure 3. Two different class diagrams for "A person owns a car"

3. It is clear that these two diagrams describe the same (a person owns a car), but in different levels of detail.

We define the reduction of the more detailed diagram to the less detailed one by introducing a set of *concepts*.

Every concept is represented with a composite class – it is added to the class diagram as a box enclosing some of the existing classes and associations, and assigning multiplicity constraints to the enclosed classes (Fig. 4). The set of new concepts must cover all the classes of the class diagram – every class must be included in a concept, and the concepts cannot overlap. The multiplicity constraints assigned to the contained classes must guarantee that all instances of the composite classes are internally connected to each other (i.e., all part objects of a single composite object are connected by links of the internal associations of the composite class). This condition is natural, since all parts of a concept must be somehow conceptually linked together.

The set of new concepts also introduces a new association between the new concepts for every association of the original class diagram that is not included in any of the new concepts.

Consider, for example, the association Owns in Fig. 4 – if an instance diagram says that the registration card RC1 has the chassis number 83456WP234 printed in the field E, then there must also be a link of the association Owns between the Person object containing the registration card RC1 and the Car object containing the chassis number 83456WP234.

More precisely:

For every association R between classes C and D that are parts of different composite classes X and Y, respectively, (or if X = Y, but R itself is

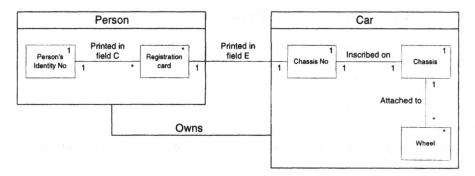

Figure 4. New concepts (Person and Car) marked out as composite classes

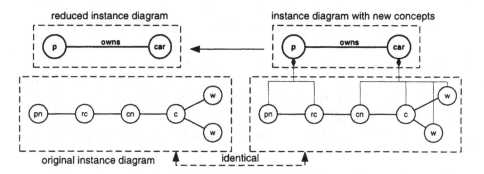

Figure 5. Instance diagrams: original, extended and reduced

not included in X) we define a new association Q between the composite classes X and Y as follows:

in any instance diagram of the class diagram there is a link of association Q between the object ox of class X and object oy of class Y iff there is a link of association R between the object of class C (part of ox) and the object of class D (part of oy).

The class diagram produced by adding new concepts as composite classes and associations between them we will call the *extended class diagram*.

With some luck we can construct such a set of new concepts, that the class diagram naturally decomposes into these new concepts, that is, the sets of instance diagrams of the original class diagram and the extended class diagram (with new concepts as composite classes) are identical (naturally, leaving out the instances of the new associations and composite classes) (Fig. 5). In such a case we will say that this set of new concepts is *correct for the given class diagram*.

4.   The Correctness Problem

A question arises – does there exist an algorithm that can determine if a given set of new concepts is correct for a given class diagram. In this section we propose such an algorithm (Algorithm 1).

Let A be a fixed class diagram, and let A' be the extended class diagram produced from A by extending it with a fixed set of new concepts S. To determine, if the set S is correct for the diagram A (i.e., the instance diagram sets of A and A' are identical), we need to check if the multiplicities of classes in the composites do not overconstrain the multiplicities of the original associations.

Algorithm 1. The algorithm consists of two steps:

1 Determine the *natural multiplicity in the composite* for every class C by the following rules:

- if there is another class in the composite, from which there is no path to C that has only multiplicity 1..1 or 1..* in the direction of C, then the lower bound of the multiplicity of C is 0, else 1,

- if the composite contains a cycle of associations, then the upper bound of the multiplicity of C (and also all the other classes of the composite) is *,

- if the composite does not contain any cycles of associations and if there is another class in the composite, from which in the direction of C some association has multiplicity 1..* or 0..*, then the upper bound of the multiplicity of C is *, else 1.

2 Check – if there is no such class in A' for which its composite multiplicity (marked in the upper right corner of the class box) is stronger than its "natural" multiplicity, then the set of concepts S is correct for the class diagram A, otherwise it is not correct.

To prove the correctness of the algorithm, we need to show that if there is no such class in A' for which its composite multiplicity is stronger (more restrictive) than its "natural" multiplicity, then the instance diagram sets of A and A' are identical, and vice versa. The proof of this fact is based on "representative instances for the multiplicity" from [5] and is rather complicated, so we will omit it here.

Let's demonstrate this algorithm on the class "Registration card" in Fig. 4.

1 There is only one other class in the composite ("PIN"), and on the path from it to "Reg. card" (which is composed of one association) there is only multiplicity 0..* in the direction of "Reg. card" – no paths with multiplicities 1..1 or 1..*. So, the lower bound of the "natural" multiplicity of "Reg. card" is 0.

2 Again there is another class in the composite ("PIN"), and on the path from it to "Reg. card" (which is composed of one association) there is only multiplicity 0..* in the direction of "Reg. card". So, the upper bound of the "natural" multiplicity of "Reg. card" is *.

That makes the "natural" multiplicity 0..*, which in this case is the same as the composite multiplicity for this class.

5. Construction of the Reduced Class Diagram

From an instance diagram of the extended class diagram a new instance diagram can be constructed, taking only the instances of the new associations and composite classes (in Fig. 5 – a person, a car and a link between them). We will call it *the reduced instance diagram*.

Let A be a fixed class diagram and S be a fixed set of new concepts that is correct for the diagram A.

We define *the reduced class diagram* as a class diagram that describes the set of reduced instance diagrams determined by the class diagram A and the set of concepts S.

In this section we present an algorithm (Algorithm 2) that constructs the reduced class diagram for the class diagram A and the correct set of concepts S.

Algorithm 2. The new classes and associations for the reduced class diagram are already present in the extended diagram A' and are taken from there. The main problem here is to assign multiplicities to the new associations.

The multiplicity of an end of a new association is calculated as the union of two multiplicities:

- the multiplicity of the corresponding end of the original association,
- the multiplicity of the class that is connected to the other end of the original association.

For example, in Fig. 6 we get the multiplicity of "how many cars a person can own" by combining the multiplicity of "registration cards per person" and the multiplicity of "chassis numbers in a registration card".

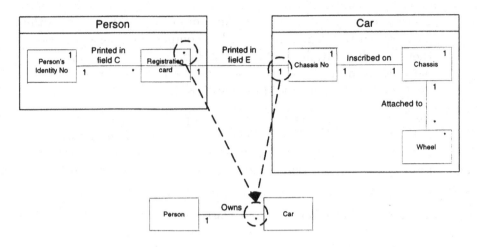

Figure 6.   Calculation of a multiplicity for a new association

The proof of this algorithm is not complicated and is based on the semantics of multiplicities.

6.   Final Result

The main result of this work is the following.

Theorem 1 *There exists an algorithm that for two given class diagrams determines if one of the diagrams can be reduced to the other one.*

We propose the following algorithm (Final Algorithm), which satisfies the theorem. This algorithm is based on the algorithms 1 and 2 presented above.

Final Algorithm. Let A and B be fixed class diagrams. We want to determine *if A can be reduced to B.* To do it:

- we generate all possible sets of new concepts for A,
- for every set of new concepts S we check if it is correct for A (Algorithm 1),
- for every correct set of concepts S we create the corresponding reduced class diagram A* (Algorithm 2),
- every reduced class diagram A* we check for equivalence with the diagram B (with the algorithm described in [5]).

If the diagram A can be reduced to B, then we will find the set of concepts that makes it possible. If we don't find any suitable set of concepts, then the diagram A cannot be reduced to B.

It must be noted that the algorithm completes in finite time – there is a finite number of different sets of new concepts for a given class diagram and all the operations on class diagrams in the algorithm are performed in finite time.

7.   Conclusion

In the paper we propose a formalization of "intuitive equivalence" of class diagrams as reduction, which is based on introduction of new concepts as composite classes. An algorithm is presented, which for two given class diagrams determines if one of the diagrams can be reduced to the other one. It is based on two other algorithms introduced in this paper and some results from [5].

This algorithm can be used in CASE tools to compare alternative models of a system. Another use of this algorithm could be diagram "compression" to facilitate understanding of large diagrams resulting, for example, from automated reverse engineering of legacy software.

The research on class diagram reduction will be continued to include richer notational elements, such as generalization and multiplicity constraints, other than those four basic multiplicities included in current formalization. An interesting extension would be composite associations, which could be defined in a similar way as composite classes.

The current formalization allows only to reduce a more detailed class diagram to a less detailed one. But it could also be improved to take into account the symmetric nature of "intuitive equivalence". One possible definition could be: two class diagrams A and B are "intuitively equivalent", if there exists a more detailed class diagram C that can be reduced to both A and B. And again a question arises, if this problem can be solved algorithmically.

References

[1] Evans, A.S. Reasoning with UML class diagrams. WIFT'98. IEEE CS Press, 1998.

[2] Evans, A.S., France, R.B., Lano, K.C., Rumpe, B. The UML as a Formal Modelling Notation. UML'98. LNCS, Vol. 1618, Springer, 1999.

[3] Lano, K., Bicarregui, J. Semantics and Transformations for UML Models. UML'98. LNCS, Vol. 1618, Springer, 1999.

[4] Lano, K.C., Evans, A.S. Rigorous Development in UML. FASE'99, ETAPS'99. LNCS, Vol. 1577, Springer, 1999.

[5] Linde, G. Equivalence Problem of Composite Class Diagrams. FCT 2001. LNCS, Vol. 2138, Springer, 2001.

[6] Object Management Group. OMG Unified Modeling Language Specification, version 1.4. http://www.rational.com/uml, 2001.

[7] Racz, F., Koskimies, K. Tool-Supported Compressing of UML Class Diagrams. UML'99. LNCS, Vol. 1723, Springer, 1999.

[8] Rumbaugh, J., Blaha, M., Premerlani, W., Eddy, F., Lorsen, W. Object-oriented modeling and design. Englewood Cliffs, NJ: Prentice Hall, 1991.

[9] Rumbaugh, J., Booch, G., Jacobson, I. The Unified Modeling Language Reference Manual. Addison-Wesley, 1999.

INCORPORATING MOBILITY INTO AN AGENT INTEROPERABILITY-BASED ENVIRONMENT

Mihhail Matskin
Department of Computer and Information Science, Norwegian University of Science and Technology, N-7491 Trondheim, Norway, Mihhail.Matskin@idi.ntnu.no

Arkady Zaslavsky
School of Computer Science & Software Engineering, Monash University, Melbourne, Australia, a.zaslavsky@monash.edu.au

Abstract   Software agents are currently considered as a promising paradigm for many distributed applications. Basic features of such agents include autonomy, goal-oriented behaviour, ability to learn and ability to communicate with other agents (interoperability) for problem solving. These features are mainly considered in intelligent agents research community. However, there is another agent feature – mobility – which refers to agents ability to migrate from one host to another and it is mostly considered in mobile agents research community. In spite of mutual interest of the above-mentioned communities in integrating their work most of agent-based systems are still divided by their affiliation either to intelligent or mobile agents communities. In this paper we present our solution to incorporating mobility issues into agent interoperability framework. In particular, we propose a scripting language, which allows expressing both interoperability and mobility constructs. The language can be used for description of agent behaviour and serves as an input to agent machinery component. The proposed language is a result of combining two earlier developed languages and systems Agora and ITAG where, correspondingly, agent interoperability and mobility were implemented. Both systems are compliant to FIPA and MASIF proposals and present a level of abstraction where FIPA and MASIF concepts are utilized.

Keywords: mobility, interoperability, ontology, software agents

H.-M. Haav and A. Kalja (eds.), Databases and Information Systems II, 209–224.

1.   Introduction

Software agents are considered at present as a promising paradigm for many distributed applications. Basic features of such agents include autonomy, goal-oriented behaviour, ability to learn and ability to communicate with other agents (interoperability) for problem solving [2, 17, 24]. The above-mentioned features are mainly considered in intelligent/software agents research community. However, there is another agent feature – mobility – which refers to agents ability to migrate from one host to another and it is mostly considered in mobile agents research community. In spite of mutual interest of the above-mentioned communities in integrating their work most of agent-based systems are still divided by their belonging either to intelligent [3, 4, 5, 8, 16, 18] or mobile agents communities [10, 19, 21, 22, 23]. One of the significant attempts to integration till now is done by FIPA initiative, which proposes Agents Communication Language (FIPA ACL) where a language for agents interoperability is specified [7]. FIPA also defines some basic requirements to agent environment. However, agent mobility is not considered at the interoperability level in FIPA. From the other hand, the MASIF [15] proposal specifies interfaces that provide functionality needed to manage and locate mobile agents. However, the MASIF interfaces do not address agent communication issues in depth and they are defined at the system level rather than at the agent level.

In this paper we present our solution to incorporating mobility issues into agent interoperability framework. In particular, we propose a scripting language, which allows expressing both interoperability and mobility constructs. The language is used for describing agent behaviour and serves as an input to agent machinery component. The proposed language is the result of combining two earlier developed languages and systems Agora [13, 14] and ITAG [11, 12] where, correspondingly, agent interoperability and mobility were implemented. Both systems are compliant with FIPA and MASIF proposals and present a level of abstraction where FIPA and MASIF concepts are utilized.

The rest of the paper is organized as follows. First, we present basic concepts and architecture of the Agora and ITAG systems and briefly describe the scripting languages they use. Next we present a proposal to unified language where both interoperability and mobility issues can be presented. Then we consider an example where the proposed scripting language is used. Finally, we present conclusions and future work.

2. The Agora System

2.1 General Introduction to the Agora System

The Agora system is a multi-agent system environment, which provides support for cooperation between agents. The system is based on the Agora concept [13, 14] which is implemented as a cooperative node where agents participating in a cooperative activity can register themselves and get support for communication, coordination and negotiation. Basic functionality of the Agora node is presented in Figure 1.

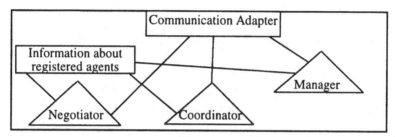

Figure 1. Agora functional structure

Agents in the Agora system can communicate in Agent Communication Language, which is compliant with both FIPA ACL [7] and KQML [6]. Communication can happen directly between agents or indirectly via Agora where they are registered. Agents in the system are generated by an agent deployment block and, by default, they have a functionality shown in Figure 2.

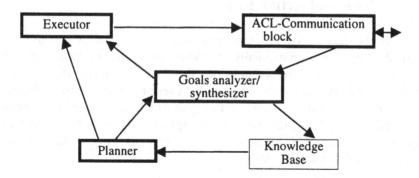

Figure 2. Default agent architecture

Each component of the agent architecture has a default implementation, which can be overridden by a user via attaching specific functional components to the agent deployment block (for example, by attaching a proprietary planner). However, if there is no need in modifying the default agent functionality then a simple agent generation process can be applied (see Figure 3).

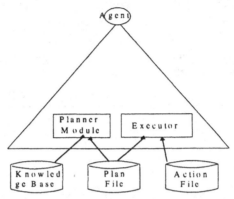

Figure 3. Simple agent generation

By this process, a user describes only a plan-file, action-file and, if necessary, Knowledge Base content for the agent. The Knowledge Base is needed for advanced usage of the agent when, for example, planning component is involved. However, an agent can already operate with plan- and action-files only and we consider only such minimal case in this paper. For more details about the Agora system we refer to [9, 13].

2.2   Plan- and Action Files

In the Agora system, agent behaviour is specified by a plan-file. The plan-file can be written manually (by the user) or generated automatically by the agent planner. Here we consider the first case only where plans are written manually. The plan-file contains a set of actions to be performed by the agent and a control structure defining in which order the actions should be performed. Plans are presented in a scripting XML-based language called Agora-ACL. Basic DTD (Data Type Definitions) [9] for the Agora-ACL language are shown in Table 1.

Table 1. Plan file format

```
<!DOCTYPE plancollection[
<!ELEMENT plancollection                      (name,plan+)  >
<!ELEMENT plan            (id,category,startstep,step+)  >
<!ELEMENT step         (id,action?,iteratecount?,accept+)  >
<!ELEMENT case        (postcondition,(nextstep|nextplan))>
<!ELEMENT postcondition       (performative,ontology)  >
<!ELEMENT nextstep                           (#PCDATA)  >
<!ELEMENT performative                       (#PCDATA)  >
<!ELEMENT ontology                           (#PCDATA)  >
<!ELEMENT name                               (#PCDATA)  >
<!ELEMENT id                                 (#PCDATA)  >
<!ELEMENT iteratecount                       (#PCDATA)  >
<!ELEMENT category                           (#PCDATA)  >
<!ELEMENT startstep                          (#PCDATA)  >
<!ELEMENT action                             (#PCDATA)  >
<!ELEMENT nextplan                           (#PCDATA)  >
]>
```

Each step in the plan-file has an action to be performed and post-conditions. Post-conditions are described as a reaction of the agent to a communicative act received from another agent, from Agora or from itself after performing the action. If the action is skipped then the agent in this step may just wait for receiving a communicative act. If the post-conditions are skipped then after performing the action, the agent starts performing the next step in the plan-file without waiting for a response. The next agent's step is specified in the field "nextstep". Otherwise (when "nextstep" is skipped) it is the next-by-order step in the agent plan-file. Steps can be performed iteratively by specifying a number of iterations or a condition for exit from the execution loop. An example of a fragment of a plan-file for a product seller agent [9] is presented in Table 2.

Table 2. A fragment of a plan file for a seller agent

```
<plancollection>
  <name>Sell electronics</name>
  <plan>
  <id>1</id>
  <category>Shopping</category>
    <step>
    <id>register_at_agora</id>
      <action>register_at_agora</action>
      <case>
        <postcondition>
           <performative>accept-proposal</performative>
           <ontology>AgentRegistration</ontology>
        </postcondition>
        <nextstep>advertise_product</nextstep>
      </case>
      <case>
        <postcondition>
           <performative>reject-proposal</performative>
           <ontology>AgentRegistration</ontology>
        </postcondition>
        <nextstep>TERMINATE</nextstep>
      </case>
    </step>
    <step>
```

```
<id>advertise_product</id>
  <action>advertise_product</action>
  <case>
    <postcondition>
        <performative>confirm</performative>
        <ontology>Product</ontology>
    </postcondition>
    <nextstep>wait_answer</nextstep>
  </case>
  <case>
    <postcondition>
        <performative>refuse</performative>
        <ontology>Product</ontology>
    </postcondition>
    <nextstep>TERMINATE</nextstep>
  </case>
</step>
```

It is not necessary to describe the whole plan in one plan-file. Instead, "nextstep" can refer to another plan-file. Actions also need not be specified explicitly in the plan-file and they can be described separately in action-file(s). Each action is described as a communicative act in the FIPA /KQML style and such communicative act may contain performative, ontology, receiver, content, language and some other fields specified in [6, 7].

A fragment of action file for a seller agent is presented in Table 3.

Table 3. A fragment of action file for a seller agent

```
<actionset>
  <action>
    <id>register_at_agora</id>
    <wrapper>
      <performative>propose</performative>
      <receiver>hifiShopAgora</receiver>
      <ontology>AgentRegistration</ontology>
    </wrapper>
  </action>
  <action>
    <id>advertise_product</id>
    <wrapper>
      <performative>inform</performative>
      <content>sell(dvd,black,sony)</content>
      <language>Prolog</language>
      <ontology>Product</ontology>
    </wrapper>
  </action>
                . . .
```

When a communicative act is received by an agent, an implemented meaning of the act is selected. Selection of the implemented meaning is based on combination of performative and ontology in the received communicative act. This means that the acts with the same performative may cause selection of different implementations for different ontology and the user may use different ontology for different applications. In particular, one of such ontology is the Mobility ontology that we describe in Section 4.

The "content" of the communicative act can be presented in different languages and this may cause invocation of different interpreters by the agent executor (at the moment we implemented support for content written in Java and Prolog).

3. The ITAG Language

The ITAG language is developed for mobile agent applications. It is based on the itinerary algebra proposed in [11]. The language and algebra are briefly outlined below.

3.1 Algebra of Itineraries

We assume that mobile agent is specified as follows:
$$mobile\_agent = state + action + mobility$$
State refers to an agent's state (run-time variables defining execution state, execution environment and context). Action refers to operations the agent performs to change its state or context. Mobility refers to operations modifying an agent's location, including moving its state and code from the current location to another host. While mobility assumes that an agent moves voluntarily the itineraries may be viewed as a specification or a plan of agent movements.

We assume that agents are capable of cloning, that is, replicating themselves with the same state, functionality and code. Also, agents can exchange messages to synchronize their activities, and the agent's code is portable across all locations it visits.

Let **A**, **O** and **P** be finite sets of agents, actions and places, respectively. An arbitrary itinerary denoted by I can now be formed as a sequence of one or more activities representing the null activity, atomic activity, parallel, sequential, nondeterministic, conditional nondeterministic behavior, and have the following syntax:

$$I ::= 0 \left| A_p^a \right| (I \parallel \oplus I) \left| (I \bullet I) \right| (I \mid I) \left| (I :_\Pi I) \right.$$

where $A \in \mathbf{A}$, $a \in \mathbf{O}$, $p \in \mathbf{P}$, $\oplus$ is an operator which merges an agent with its clone to form one agent with combined states, after a parallel operation causes cloning, and Π is an operator which returns a Boolean value to model conditional behavior. We specify how $\oplus$ and Π are used but we assume that their definitions and hence functionality are application-specific.

We assume that all agents in the itinerary have a starting place (which we call the agent's *home*) denoted by $h \in P$. Given an itinerary I, we shall use *agents(I)* to refer to the agents involved in I. The operations on agents are summarized below.

- **Agent Movement** (A_p^a). A_p^a means "move agent A to place p and perform action a". This expression is the atomic mobility abstraction. It involves one agent, one move and one action at the destination. The underlying mobility mechanism is hidden. So are the details of the action, which may change the agent state or the context in which it is operating at the destination place:

   $a:$ *states(A)* $\times$ *states(p)* $\rightarrow$ *states(A)* $\times$ *states(p)*

   In this agent model, each action is a method call of the class implementing A. The implementation must check that a is indeed implemented in A.

- **0** represents for any agent A, the empty itinerary A_{here}^{id} where the agent performs the identity operation $id \in O$ on the state at its current place *here*.

- **Parallel Composition** ($\|$). Two agent expressions composed by "$\|$" are executed in parallel. For instance, ($A_p^a \| B_q^b$) means that agents A and B are executed concurrently. Parallelism may imply cloning or replicating of agents. For instance, to execute the expression ($A_p^a \| A_q^b$), where $p \neq q$, cloning is needed since agent A has to perform actions at both places p and q in parallel. In the case where $p = q$, the agents are cloned as if $p \neq q$. In general, given the itinerary (I $\|$ J) the agents in *agents(I)* $\cap$ *agents(J)* are cloned and although possibly having the same name are in fact different agents. When cloning has occurred, the reverse operation (de-cloning) is needed, i.e. clones are combined (or merged or aggregated) using an associated application-specific operator (denoted by $\oplus$ as mentioned earlier). For example, given the expression ($A_s^d \| A_t^e$) $\bullet$ A_u^f and suppose that after the parallel operation $\|$, the agent community contains clones. Then, de-cloning is carried out before continuing with A_u^f. The resulting agent from de-cloning resides in the original departure place s. We have associated the de-cloning operation with this operator instead of the sequential operator because this seems to be more intuitive and natural [11].

- **Sequential Composition** ("$\bullet$"). Two expressions composed by the operator "$\bullet$" are executed sequentially. For example, ($A_p^a \bullet A_q^b$) means move agent A to place p to perform action a, and then proceed to place q to perform action b. Sequential composition is used when order of execution is important. In the example, agent state changes from performing activity a at place p must precede the agent's move to place q. Sequential composition imposes synchronization and partial ordering among agents. For example, in the expression $(A_p^a \parallel B_q^b) \bullet A_u^f$ the composite action $A_p^a \parallel B_q^b$ must complete before A_u^f starts. Implementation of such synchronization requires message-passing mechanism between agents at different places.

- **Independent Nondeterminism** ("|"). An itinerary of the form $(I \mid J)$ is used to express nondeterministic choice: "It doesn't matter which itinerary is executed, I or J". If $agents(I) \cap agents(J) \neq \varnothing$, no clones are assumed, i.e. itineraries I and J are treated independently. It is an implementation decision whether to perform both actions concurrently with terminating one or the other when either one succeeds. Such implementation decision may involve cloning but clones are destroyed once a result is obtained and the clones are merged. Alternatively, it is possible to try one itinerary at a time. In this case order may matter.

- **Conditional Nondeterminism** (":"). Independent nondeterminism approach does not specify any dependencies between its alternatives. We introduce conditional nondeterminism, which is similar to simple evaluation of boolean expressions in programming languages such as C. We first introduce *status flag* and *global state function*. A status flag is part of the agent's state, written as $A.status$ for agent A. Being part of the state, $A.status$ is affected by an agent's actions. $A.status$ might be changed by the agent as it performs actions at different places. A global state function Π need not be defined in terms of status flags but it is useful to do so. For example, we can define Π as the conjunction of the status flags of agents in a set Σ: $\Pi(\Sigma) = \wedge_{A \in \Sigma} A.status$. We can view Π as producing a global status flag. From the implementation viewpoint, agents in Σ communicate to compute Π. An itinerary of the form $I :_\Pi J$ means first perform I, and then evaluate Π on the state of the agents. If Π evaluates to true, then the itinerary is completed. If Π evaluates to false, the itinerary J is performed (i.e., in effect, we perform $I \bullet J$). The semantics of conditional nondeterminism depends on some given Π, expressed by writing ":$_\Pi$".

3.2 Implementation Syntax

To allow the programmer to type the itinerary expressions into the computer, we provide an ASCII syntax and a Controlled English version. The translations are given in Table 4.

Table 4. ITAG translations

Symbol	ASCII	Controlled English
A_p^a	[A, p, a]	Move A to p do a
•	.	Then
:Π	:{op}	Otherwise using op
				Or
$\|_\oplus$	#{op}	In parallel using op

When the operators are used without op, we assume a pre-specified system default one, i.e. op is an optional clause.

Hence, $A_p^a \bullet A_q^b \bullet A_r^c$ can be described as follows: "(move A to a do p) then (move A to b do q) then (move A to c do r)."

Apart from the above-mentioned basic elements of the language, we define the following five phrases that map down to more complex expressions:

1. A_h^a is translated as return A do a.
2. $A_p^a \bullet A_q^a \bullet A_r^a \bullet A_s^a$ is translated as tour A to p,q,r,s in series do a.
3. $A_p^a \parallel A_q^a \parallel A_r^a \parallel A_s^a$ is translated as tour A to p,q,r,s in parallel do a.
4. $A_p^a \mid A_q^a \mid A_r^a \mid A_s^a$ is translated as tour A to one of p,q,r,s do a.
5. $A_p^a : A_q^a : A_r^a : A_s^a$ is translated as tour A if needed to p,q,r,s do a. Similarly, we also have $A_p^a :_\Pi A_q^a :_\Pi A_r^a :_\Pi A_s^a$ translated as tour A if needed to p,q,r,s do a using Π.

4. Combination of Interoperability and Mobility in the Script Language

In order to combine properties of the Agora-ACL and ITAG languages we develop a special ontology, called Mobility. We also introduce a Mobility Manager Agent into the system and allow other agents to send communicative acts to the Mobility Manager Agent using the Mobility ontology. The Mobility Manager Agent can be activated by sending it a communicative act specified in a plan-file written in the Agora-ACL language. In particular, such communicative act can be sent anytime when the agent decides to migrate to another host. The "content" part of this act may contain itinerary written in the ITAG language. Upon receiving a communicative act, the Mobility Manager Agent performs actions depending on combination of the performative and ontology. If the Mobility ontology is used then the interpreter of the ITAG-language is invoked and migration of the agent can be performed. If another ontology is used then the Mobility

Manager Agent performs plans and actions non-related to mobility and use the Agora-ACL interpreter.

In order to be able implement the above-mentioned combination of the Agora-ACL and ITAG languages we need to satisfy the following requirements:

- The commands of the ITAG-language should be presented as performatives of a special ontology for the Agora-ACL interpreter
- The ITAG-interpreter should be able to accept plan-files as actions to be performed by migrating agent after/before the migration
- There should be an agent in the system which can invoke ITAG-interpreter

The first requirement is the most important from the integration point of view. In order to satisfy it we develop the Mobility ontology which fragment is presented in Table 5.

Table 5. A fragment of the Mobility ontology

Performative	Ontology	Implemented Meaning
Request	Mobility	Ask for migration to specified hosts
request-whenever	Mobility	Ask for migration whenever the condition is true
request-when	Mobility	Ask for migration when appropriate
Propose	Mobility	Ask for registering new host list
accept-proposal	Mobility	Remote host agrees to accept agent migration
reject-proposal	Mobility	Remote host denied agent migration.
query-ref	Mobility	Request for available hosts
Refuse	Mobility	The Mobility Manager Agent refuses to move the agent to a specified host
Failure	Mobility	The Mobility Manager Agent can't help right now, but may help later.
Inform	Mobility	The Mobility Manager Agent informs about available hosts

Implementation of the ITAG operations is done as follows:

- The upper index in A_p^a expression is understood as a name of Agora-ACL plan-file which agent A takes with it when migrating to the place p (by default it is the current plan-file which the agent executes at the moment of migrating)
- Parallel Composition is implemented via the "request" performative in the Mobility ontology. Content field of a communicative act containing "request" may include a list of places where the agent should migrate to. The action corresponding to this communicative act has semantics of Parallel Composition operator from the Section 3. It is possible that only one place name is presented in the list of places and this corresponds to a single migration of the agent to the specified place

- Sequential Composition is expressed as a sequence of steps in a plan-file. The steps contain actions, which send performative "requests" with only one place name in the content field to the Migration Manager Agent. In this case the implementation of the Migration Manager Agent performs only a single migration of the agent to a place specified in the content part. The next migration place is defined in the next step of the plan-file

- There are two ways of implementing Conditional Nondeterminism in the system:
  - o Conditional Nondeterminism can be expressed in the same way as the Sequential Composition with the following difference. After each migration the post-condition is fired as a communicative act, which is sent to the migrating agent. Depending on a post-condition the next step is selected by the agent. In this case the agent has full control over condition handling
  - o Conditional Nondeterminism can be implemented via sending communicative act with "request-whenever" performative to the Mobility Manager Agent. In this case control over condition handling is embedded into implemented meaning of the action corresponding to the performative-ontology combination

- Independent Nondeterminism is implemented via sending a communicative act with "request-when" performative and Mobility ontology to the Mobility Manager Agent.

The Mobility Manager Agent can be implemented as any other agent in the Agora system. However, in addition to standard Agora agents the Mobility Manager Agent implements MASIF specified interfaces, it can invoke ITAG interpreter and it performs agent migration related operations. A prototype implementation of the Mobility Manager Agent in the Agora system was done in [1].

5.   An Example

We consider a modified voting example from [12]. According to this example there is a list of voting agents and there is an agent, which organizes voting and announces results (this can also be considered as a variant of the Contract Net Protocol [20]). In the original example, the organizing agent migrates sequentially from host to host in order to collect votes, then tabulates votes and then announces results to all voters in parallel (by parallel migration to voters hosts). We decided that migration for collecting results may be inefficient compared to just communication with the voter agents and we replace the sequential migration of the organizing agent by sequential communication. However, announcing results can be done by parallel migration in order to keep announcing fairness for all voting agents. Fragments of plan-file and action-file for the organizing agent are presented below.

Table 6. Fragment of plan file

```
<plan>
<id>Voting example </id>
  <step>
  <id>ask-for-voters</id>
    <action>ask-for-voters</action>
    <case>
        <postcondition>
            <performative>inform</performative>
            <content>potential-voters-list</content>
            <ontology>Mobility</ontology>
        </postcondition>
        <nextstep>collect-votes</nextstep>
    </case>
  </step>
  <step>
  <id>collect-votes</id>
    <action>collect-votes</action>
    <case>
        <postcondition>
            <performative>accept-proposal</performative>
            <content>voting-result</content>
            <ontology>Voting</ontology>
        </postcondition>
        <nextstep>collect-votes</nextstep>
        <postcondition>
            <performative>reject-proposal</performative>
            <ontology>Voting</ontology>
        </postcondition>
        <nextstep>advertise-results</nextstep>
    </case>
  </step>
  <step>
  <id>advertise-results </id>
    <action>advertise_results</action>
    <case>
        <nextstep>TERMINATE</nextstep>
    </case>
</plan>
```

And action file is as follows:

Table 7. Fragment of action file

```
<actionset>
  <action>
    <id>ask-for-voters</id>
    <wrapper>
        <performative>query-ref</performative>
        <receiver>Mobility-Manager-Agent</receiver>
        <ontology>Mobility</ontology>
    </wrapper>
```

```
    </action>
    <action>
      <id>collect-votes</id>
      <wrapper>
          <performative>call-for-proposal</performative>
          <receiver>next-potential-voter</receiver>
          <ontology>Voting</ontology>
      </wrapper>
    </action>
    <action>
      <id>advertise-results</id>
      <wrapper>
          <performative>request</performative>
          <content> voting-agents-itinerary</content>
          <receiver>Mobility-Manager-Agent</receiver>
          <ontology>Mobility</ontology>
      </wrapper>
    </action>
  </actionset>
```

In the postcondition of the "ask-for-voters" step the Mobility Manager Agent returns a list of potential voters in the "content" field as a reply to "query-ref" performative of the organizing agent. Then the organizing agent asks each agent from the "potential-voters-list" to submit a vote. From those agents who submitted their votes the organizing agent forms a "voting-agents-itinerary" (using the parallel composition operator) in the ITAG language syntax and sends "request" performative to the Mobility Manager Agent for performing migration.

6.   Conclusions

Combining mobility and interoperability can be done at different levels. In this paper we consider only language support for agents who might perform both a high-level language communication and migration. We demonstrate that usage of a unified scripting language provides a good basis for expressing different agent actions including mobility. We also reckon that implementing migration related constructs via a special ontology is a practical and natural way of dealing with agent mobility.

Our future work is focused on other levels of mobility and interoperability integration. In particular, we continue working on the following issues:

- Architectural support of interoperability and mobility. We have a prototype implementation where the Agora system is extended with mobility support components. Now we would like to develop a more advanced implementation
- Combining interoperability and mobility on conceptual level. In particular, we are interested in investigating conditions for migration vs.

interoperability and vice versa. In other words, when it is more efficient and secure for an agent to migrate instead of performing communication and when communication is more preferable compared to migration.

In our work we will keep our tools and methods compliant with existing standards such as FIPA and MASIF

Acknowledgements

This work is partially supported by the Norwegian Research Foundation in the framework of the Information and Communication Technology (IKT-2010) program - the ADIS project and in the framework of Distributed Information Technology (DITS) program – the ElComAg project. We would like also to acknowledge contribution of Dr Seng Wai Loke (RMIT University) into developing the original ITAG scripting language.

References

[1] Andenæs, E.M. Implementing Mobility in the Agora System. Diploma Thesis, Department of Computer and Information Science, Norwegian University of Science and Technology, Trondheim, 2001.

[2] Bradshaw, J.M. (Ed.). Software Agents. Menlo Park, CA: AAAI Press/The MIT Press, 1997.

[3] Bradshaw, J.M., Dutfield, S., Benoit, P., Woolley, .J.D. KAoS: Toward an Industrial-Strength Open Agent Architecture. In: G. M. O'Hare, N. R. Jennings, (eds.), Foundations of Distributed Artificial Intelligence, John Wiley & Sons, 1996, pp. 375 - 418.

[4] Cohen, P., et al. An Open Agent Architecture. In: Readings in Agents, M.N. Huhns and M.P. Singh, Editors. 1998, Morgan Kaufmann Publishers: San Mateo, CA, pp. 197-204.

[5] Ferguson, I.A. Touring Machines: An Architecture for Dynamic, Rational, Mobile Agents, in Clare Hall,. 1992, University of Cambridge: Cambridge, UK

[6] Finin, T., Labrou, Y., and Mayfield, J. KQML as an Agent Communication Language. In: J. M. Bradshaw (ed.), Software Agents. AAAI Press/The MIT Press: Menlo Park, CA. (1997), pp. 291-316.

[7] Foundation for Intelligent and Physical Agents (FIPA). URL: http://www.fipa.org/repository/bysubject.html

[8] Graham, J.R., and Decker, K.S. Towards a Distributed, Environment-Centred Agent Framework. In N. Jennings and Y. Lesperance (eds.), Intelligent Agents VI – Proceedings of ATAL-99, Lecture Notes in Artificial Intelligence, Springer-Verlag, Berlin, 2000.

[9] Kirkeluten, O.J., Krossnes, S.B., and Sæle, Ø. Shells for Multi Agent Applications. Diploma Thesis, Department of Computer and Information Science, Norwegian University of Science and Technology, Trondheim, 1999.

[10] Lange, D.B and Oshima, M. Programming and Deploying Java Mobile Agents with Aglets. Addison Wesley, 1998.

[11] Loke, S.W., Schmidt, H., and Zaslavsky, A. Programming the Mobility Behaviour of Agents by Composing Itineraries. In P. Thiagarajan and B. Yap, editors, Proceedings of

the 5th Asian Computing Science Conference (ASIAN'99), volume 1742, LNCS, Springer-Verlag, pp. 214-226.

[12] Loke, S.W., Zaslavsky, A., Yap, B., and Fonseka, J. An Itinerary Scripting Language for Mobile Agents in Enterprise Applications. Proceedings of the Second Asia-Pacific Conference on Intelligent Agent Technology (IAT-2001), Maebashi Terrsa, Maebashi City, Japan, October 23-26, 2001, World Scientific, 2001.

[13] Matskin, M., Kirkeluten, O.J., Krossnes, S. B., and Sæle, Ø. Agora: An Infrastructure for Cooperative Work Support in Multi-Agent Systems. T. Wagner, O. Rana (eds.) Infrastructure for Agents, Multi-Agents, and Scalable Multi-Agent Systems. Springer Verlag, LNCS, Volume 1887, 2001, pp. 28-40.

[14] Matskin, M. Multi-Agent Support for Modelling Co-operative Work. In: T. Yongchareon, F. A. Aagesen, V. Wuwongse (Eds.) Intelligence in Networks. The Fifth International Conference SMARTNET'99, Thailand, Kluwer Academic Publishers, 1999, pp. 419-432.

[15] Mobile Agent System Interoperability Facility (MASIF). URL: http://www.fokus.gmd.de/research/cc/ecco/masif/

[16] Nwana, H.S., Ndumu, D.T., Lee, L.C., and Collos, J.C. ZEUS: A Tool-Kit for Building Distributed Multi-Agent Systems. Applied Artificial Intelligence Journal, Volume 13 (1), pp. 129-186.

[17] Nwana, H.S., Software Agents: An Overview. The Knowledge Engineering Review, 1996. 11(3): pp. 1-40.

[18] O'Hare, G.M. Agent Factory: An Environment for the Fabrication of Multi-agent Systems. In: G. M. O'Hare, N. R. Jennings, eds. Foundations of Distributed Artificial Intelligence. John Wiley & Sons, 1996, pp. 449 - 484.

[19] ObjectSpace Voyager, General Magic Odyssey, IBM Aglets: A Comparison. ObjectSpace, Inc., Jun. 1997. Technical White Paper.

[20] Smith, R.G.: The Contract Net Protocol: High-Level Communication and Control in a Distributed Problem Solver. IEEE Transactions of Computer Science, 29(12). (1980), pp. 1104-1113.

[21] Strasser, M., Baumann, J., and Hohl, F. Mole - A Java based Mobile Agent System. In M. Muehlhaeuser, editor, Special Issues in Object Oriented Programming. dpunkt Verlag, 1997.

[22] Voyager Core Package: Technical Overview. ObjectSpace, Inc., Mar. 1997. Technical White Paper.

[23] Webhopper and Grasshopper: URL: http://www.grasshopper.de

[24] Wooldridge, M. and Jennings, N. Intelligent Agents: Theory and Practice. The Knowledge Engineering Review, 1995, 10(2): pp. 115-152.

AN EXTENSIBLE STORAGE MANAGER FOR MOBILE DBMS

Erik Buchmann, Hagen Höpfner, Kai-Uwe Sattler

Otto-von-Guericke-University of Magdeburg

P.O. Box 4120, D-39016 Magdeburg

Germany

{buchmann | hoepfner | sattler}@iti.cs.uni-magdeburg.de

Abstract   The increasing usage of mobile devices like PDAs, laptops, or embedded devices results in a new type of application which must especially consider the strict limitations of the used mobile hardware. One aspect of the application development is the storage and retrieval of data. For non-mobile application this is often efficiently realized with database management systems, which offer standardized interfaces and can be easily integrated into the applications. For mobile devices DBMS are also already available. But existing solutions are not extensible, and therefore, limited to the builtin functionality. That means also, that they include functions which are not always necessary. The optimal DBMS for mobile database systems must allow for the special requirements of its applications in order to reduce the hardware requirements. Thus, it must offer core funtionality which can be extended by additional required features. In this paper, we present a core component of such a customizable DBMS – the storage manager – and describe the architecture as well as the main modules. Furthermore, we show how this modules can be combined in order to address different requirements.

Keywords: mobile computing, storage management, customizable DBMS

1.   Introduction and Motivation

Due to the increasing usage of mobile computer equipment a new type of application – mobile applications – emerges in importance in comparison to the classical desktop and client server applications. Software for mobile devices must especially consider the limitations (e.g. less memory, small display size, limited power supply) of the mobile devices. On the other hand, users and application developers of such systems want to get nearly the same functionality and comfort like working with non-mobile systems.

H.-M. Haav and A. Kalja (eds.), Databases and Information Systems II, 225–238.
© 2002 *Kluwer Academic Publishers.*

An important issue in many applications is efficient data management. Though modern operating systems for mobile devices provide some kind of database support by allowing applications to store records in permanent Flash ROM, often more advanced techniques are required. This includes standard interfaces like JDBC or ODBC, a declarative query and manipulation language, index support for fast access and replication with an enterprise database. Therefore, most DBMS vendors offer smaller versions of their systems for mobile devices, e.g. Oracle 9i lite and IBM DB2 Everyplace. These products mostly provide reduced but fixed functionality, i.e., they are not extensible and customizable. So, some of the offered functions are not necessary for a specific application, and others – non-implemented functions – would be essential.

Specific requirements of mobile database applications exist at several levels of a DBMS. For instance, some applications require query processing. In other applications encryption of stored data is needed, which could be performed transparently by the DBMS. Further examples are transaction support, synchronization with a central database and support for special data types (e.g. geographical objects). If the device offers different types of storage, e.g. Flash ROM or a Microdrive, specific adaptable access modules could increase the performance and reduce the power consumption at the same time.

Obviously, a general "all in one" DBMS cannot fulfill all these requirements, in particular for small devices with limited resources. A viable approach could be a customizable DBMS allowing to choose and combine required modules from the set of available components. Although this idea is not really new – database generators and toolkits have been studied in database research since several years – it plays an important role for mobile DBMS. However, this requires rethinking the functionality of the individual components of a DBMS considering the requirements of the mobile devices.

In this paper, we present first results of our work towards an extensible and customizable DBMS for small devices. We describe the storage manager component of ELORDESS – our *extensible lightweight object-relational DBMS for embedded and small systems*. This storage manager consists of a set of modules which can be combined depending on the requirements of the application. In addition, new modules can be easily plugged in without affecting the application. In this way, storage management functionality can be customized in a wide range and even for individual relations.

The remainder of this paper is structured as follows: After briefly presenting related work, we discuss in section 3 the specific requirements and in section 4 the different approaches for customizable DBMS. Section 5 presents the architecture of the storage manager and section 6 describes the combination of the individual modules for a given example configuration. Finally, we summarize our approach and outline future work.

2. Related Work

There are different approaches to solve the challenges of limited resources, extensibility, modularity and flexibility. Many problems are already addressed in other contexts. Researches in respect of a storage manager providing the features described above overlap with main memory DBMS, extensible database systems, and mobile applications in general.

A hierarchical memory architecture with fast RAM on top and slower harddiscs as secondary storage media have been established on stationary workstations or servers. In contrast embedded or mobile devices often use battery-backed RAM or Flash-ROM in various architectures [9]. Therefore, technologies used in modularized main memory storage managers [4, 6] are playing a prominent role. Some hardware components differ in speed, quantity and in their handling. Especially Flash devices need dedicated writing policies to achieve maximum lifetime [8]. Variable power requirements of components used in mobile or embedded devices lead to new problems for query processing. For instance, queries can be executed on external servers [13] or can be optimized considering the energy consumption [1].

Most applications do not use the whole, but a reduced, varying function set. This kind of applications can be supported by a general purpose database management system which is heavyweight, feature-laden and costly in installation and maintenance, or otherwise by a lightweight, customized system. On lightweight appliances the resource requirements forbid the use of general purpose DBMS.

The classical way extends a DBMS by inserting external supplementary layers on top of the external layer of the three tier architecture presented in [5]. But neither requirements of application-specific access methods nor hardware-specific optimizations are satisfied by extending the external layer. Therefore, other approaches introduce a widespread range of extensible architectures allowing the customization of both, internal and external database management system layers by introducing new data types [14] or storage methods.

KIDS [11] uses a broker/services model. A service represents a task or a part of it, which has to be provided by the DBMS. A broker reacts on events and satisfies requests for services. Add-ons for services or brokers provide the extensibility. Another concept introduces a RISC-style DBMS library [7]. A DBMS consisting of an application specific set of RISC-style lightweight components will be faster and needs a smaller amount of memory (like RISC-processors) than other system concepts. Some approaches use small, lightweight database cores like "Single Schema DBMS" [3] and offer interfaces to enhance the core features. DBMS suppliers like Oracle or IBM, which are established with well known products in the database server market, prefer the not extensible and not customizable concept of a small "general purpose" DBMS for lightweight appliances [12].

The integration [10] of these approaches into database systems is a relevant challenge. One solutionr is to use transformations or generator systems [2, 15]. Another way is the use of toolkits of reusable components [7] with the ability to be assembled with custom software modules to an application specific system.

This requires to identify different functionality domains which are needed or can be omitted. [16] describes – without the claim of completeness – the distinct functionality domains concurrency control, checkpoints and recovery, the ability to use raw devices instead OS files, persistence, databases larger than primary storage, the support for the client/server model or distributed databases, and the computing of dynamic queries, set-oriented queries or joins.

Recapitulating, there are several applicable approaches dealing with extensibility, limited resources and modularity. But none tries to transfer the suitable concepts to an open, lightweight, mobile database management system. We try to close this gap with ELORDESS.

3. Requirements on a Storage Manager for Mobile DBMS

Beyond the general needs for a DBMS, both technical and application specific demands come up for a storage manager applicable on mobile or embedded devices. As shown in section 2, highly different applications need many varying functions in all layers of a DBMS. Database-driven mobile applications can be distinguished between two distinct fields:

Personal information management This field of activity means the "classical" applications for PDA or organizers. Mostly, there is no cooperative work with other users on the same piece of data. The amount of data on the mobile device is usually small, and is at most edited on the mobile device itself. The main challenge for mobile databases for personal information management is *flexibility*.

Replication of large databases The replication of large databases or parts of them – large in the context of mobile, lightweight appliances, e.g. not more than 1 GB – is characterized by the cooperative use of the same data by numerous users. Data are mainly managed and manipulated by DBMS on stationary servers, only a few or no changes are performed on the mobile device. Business applications, geographic information systems or multimedia are typical applications. The most important challenges for mobile databases in this field are *specializability performance.*

Technical requirements result from quality and quantity of the relevant ressources *CPU, memory, network* and *power supply.* The differences between stationary and mobile devices can be described by the following issues:

Quantity In order to meet restictions in weight, size and price, mobile devices are offering significantly less ressource capacities. Therefore, programs for small, lightweight devices must not depend on consuming large amounts of CPU-, memory-, battery- or network resources. Otherwise, if large quantities of some resources are available, they can be used to enhance the quality of service.

Customizability Stationary devices are customizable for the needs of their applications with a broad range of exchangeable hardware components. In contrast mobile devices are at most upgradable with an expansion slot.

Heterogenity Mobile devices are equipped with very heterogeneous resources. For instance, a personal computer uses a x86-CPU, and harddiscs as secondary storage devices. In contrast, mobile devices use completely different central processing units like MIPS, Strong-ARM or DragonBall, and as secondary storage battery-backed RAM, Flash-ROM, hard discs, network interfaces and so on. The use of heterogeneous hardware requires a flexible, portable architecture that can be customized to deal in an optimal manner with most different devices.

In order to achive a compact system architecture, an ideal storage manager must offer abstract, generalized interfaces which are specializable to any kind of application and hardware component, providing interoperability of existing modules.

4. Approaches for Customizable DBMS

In our approach we decided to create a *toolkit system* to obtain a sufficient compromise between flexibility, extensibility, adaptability and maintainability. A DBMS implementor will be able to assemble a few existing modules very quick to a running system, but also to enhance all modules with extended functionality.

Other concepts lack some features needed by lightweight appliances. The *add-on layer approach* uses a nearly complete DBMS and maps all functionality added to a layer on top of the system with the underlying DBMS. This leads to poor runtime performance and large memory consumption.

Customizable approaches to create database management systems utilize a parameterizable DBMS which can be adjusted by parameters or modified on code level to change its behavior. For this reason very detailed knowledge concerning the specific DBMS and DBMS technology in general is mandatory.

Kernel systems offer a public interface supporting common functionality and hide all other system architectures. Extending the system has to be done by implementing new layers on top of the kernel. New functionality cannot be included in the kernel. Therefore, kernel systems leads to suboptimal database systems.

Generator systems should always produce code which uses resources and satisfies application needs at its best. But unfortunately, generator systems are unable to support a broad range of applications, and extending generator systems itself is a hard task.

We introduce a concept consisting modules. Every module implements one or more distinct services which provide a part of database management system functionality. Because communication across module boundaries leads to some inevitable resource consumption, the suggested modularized architecture offers the option to implement more than one service in a single module.

A module may depend on distinct methods implemented in other modules. For instance an access path module that provides tries needs attributes which implements access on designated parts of the key value. Therefore, a module is characterized by its methods – realized as a Java class – and some interfaces.

The set of modules must be small but applicable to a broad range of DBMS appliances. Components have to be reusable in most usecases. Hence, components are not allowed to be too complex and specific, but rather generally adaptable. Using a large amount of very small modules leads straightforward to reduced CPU performance because extensive parameter passing and method calling. In contrast, defining only a few modules implies poor reusability. For this reason, the only applicable way is obtaining an acceptable compromise.

5. The Storage Manager of ELORDESS: Architecture

Some tasks of general purpose DBMS should be taken into distinct modules, others have to be implemented in all modules. *Meta-data management* is often described as special task performed by the database catalog. But it is a cross section task that is used by most other tasks. Therefore, we decided to put this functionality in all affected modules.

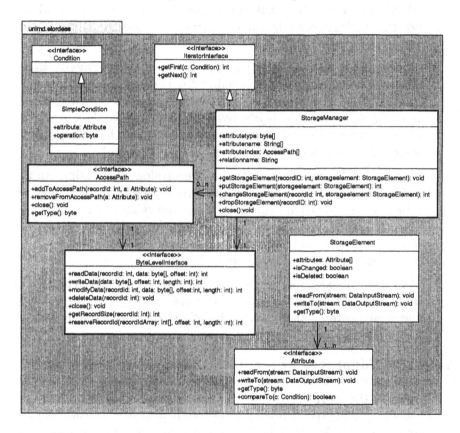

Figure 1. Main Classes

In a similar way, *transaction management* is utilized in a couple of different tasks and cannot be realized as a separate module. Mobile or distributed transaction management requires flags or time stamps attached on every internal record to solve the concurrent transaction problem. For local transaction processing, every storage module has to be thread-safe and needs methods to delay or release writing of internal records concerned with *commit* and *abort* commands. Because of this, we currently do not implement transaction support.

The architecture is based on three major module interfaces, which are adequate to describe any kind of service supported by ELORDESS. These interfaces are shown as bold-boxed classes in Figure 1 and described as follows:

StorageManager The `StorageManager`-Module has two distinct tasks: first the module transforms data objects of `StorageElement` containers passed through application level to untyped data bytes, which are written to `ByteLevelInterface`, and vice versa. Methods for storing, retrieving and removing data objects perform this task.

Every object held by ELORDESS is typed as `StorageElement`. These objects provide functionality for reading and writing their content from a byte stream. This arrangement is sufficient to obtain the needs of object-oriented database models. For providing object-relational or relational database models, the `StorageElement` class is extended by an array of `Attribute`-objects.

Second, the StorageManager holds the catalog information. In the case of relational database architectures the module manages relation names, relation types, attribute names and attribute types. Object-oriented or object-relational DBMS architectures provide names and types for root- and dependent objects. Furthermore, index information has to be accessible.

Stored database objects are only handed out by `RecordID` or in undetermined order for sequential scans. To fetch an object with specified content, an access path defined on the distinguished attribute is required.

AccessPathManager The `AccessPathManager` describes an interface that allows to apply hash-tables, trees, tries or other index structures to the storage system. The interface specifies abstract methods for adding and removing `Attribute` objects to the access path and retrieving `RecordID`'s for a given condition. The module itself stores all hash-buckets or tree-nodes like other modules using the `ByteLevelInterface`.

Each `AccessPathManager` requires `Attribute` objects implementing special interfaces. The methods specified by these interfaces are used to integrate keys into access paths. For example, B-trees need *lower-than* comparison methods. Hash-indexes require every key independent of its type to be transformed to an integer value which can be used as input for hash function. Tries are unable to perform their job without the ability to obtain a part of the key. Figure 2 shows an example which extends two attributes by supporting methods for hash- and trie-based indexes.

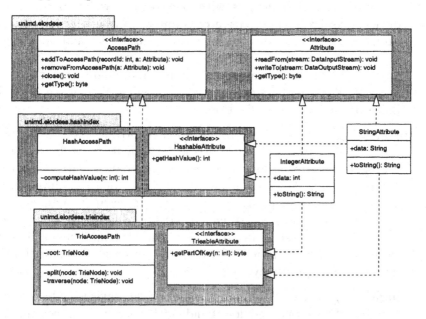

Figure 2.   Implementing different access paths.

ByteLevelInterface This describes an API which works on untyped byte arrays. Methods for reading, writing, deleting and modifying records are provided. Because under certain circumstances – for caching purposes, in disconnected network state, etc. – scheduled or delayed computing of requests will be required, a method for reserving `recordID` enables transparent time-shifted writing.

Every implementor of `ByteLevelInterface` has the permission to split or join given byte pages, as long as it performs the repartitioning transparently for other modules. This may be necessary for cryptographic algorithms which are vulnerable when handling a small amount of data, for mass storage devices with a static block size, or for network protocols with a fixed frame length.

In order to decrease the number of interfaces, tasks like caching, cryptography, or compression working directly on data bytes are specified by the same interface. The interface defines methods for reading, writing, updating and deleting byte arrays. These arrays are read and written to the stable memory by a `PersistenceManager`-class and handled by a couple of different modules like `CachingManager`, `CryptoManager` and `PackingManager`.

CachingManager As described above, supported storage devices show a broad range of characteristics. A `CachingManager` module can be used to support devices with slow read or write speed. Some devices like IBM's microdrive consume a lot of energy by waking up from suspend mode, but sometimes less on normal operations afterwards. This suggests to safe energy by collecting read- or write-requests and performing them in batch mode. In such cases, a special `CachingManager` implementation can be chosen to maximize battery power utilization.

CryptoManager Some applications manage private data which are not allowed to be read by everyone. Particularly mobile devices are vulnerable to be lost or stolen. Hence data security becomes a prominent task on such kind of devices. In this approach an optional `CryptoManager` module supports security management by encrypting and decrypting all written or read data. Varying modules with the same interface can be used to implement distinct security levels by the use of different cryptographic algorithm or different encryption key lengths.

PackingManager On most mobile, lightweight devices only a small amount of memory and low bandwidth network connections are available. Therefore, data compression is an emerging task which will be realized by a separate `PackingManager` module. This module packs the volume of bytes while storing and unpacks it while receiving from other modules. Data compression depends on the processed data and uses different amounts of computing power and main memory. This leads to the need for different compression algorithms performed by different `PackingManager`-modules.

PersistenceManager The secondary storage interface, which works at operating system level, is hold by the `PersistenceManager`-Module. This module reads and writes internal records typed as `ByteArray` from or to persistent memory. Due to heterogeneity of supported hardware, the `PersistenceManager` is the only direct hardware dependent module class. The `PersistenceManager` offers methods for reading, writing and updating internal records identified by numerical keys named `RecordID`. Operations for opening and closing databases are implicitly invoked by creating or destroying the object instance. Various `PersistenceManager` modules realize persistent storage on networks, disc files, main memory blocks or expansion cards.

The complete set of system modules is shown in Figure 3. Optional modules are depicted as dotted boxes, required modules as solid ones. A minimal configuration required for a working system, consists only of objects of classes derived from **StorageManager** and **PersistenceManager**.

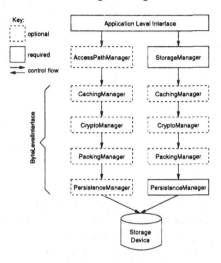

Figure 3. System Architecture

The module configuration is built by the database implementor at design time. At startup, assembling modules is done by the process using the services offered by the modules. This can be performed on static information "hard-wired" in the code. Otherwise, information stored into a designated schema information relation may be used to build up the modules architecture.

6.   System Configuration

Using the same interface for compression, cryptography and buffering enables some extended features. If not required, omitting modules is fully transparent on other levels. No request for non-existing functions will be performed on each operation. Secondly, some customization can be done only by changing the order, in which modules are connected among each others. For example, security-challenged applications are able to encrypt the content in the buffer by using the **CryptoManager** "above" to the **CachingManager**.

If used as a service requester to the **CachingManager**, the **CompressionManager** packs the buffer content and saves main memory space, but stresses the CPU resource. Otherwise, under equal circumstances more main memory is needed, but the CPU is utilized less than before. Every module is serving only one relation or one access path. If more than one is needed, more object modules have to be created. This concept was chosen to reduce the management complexity.

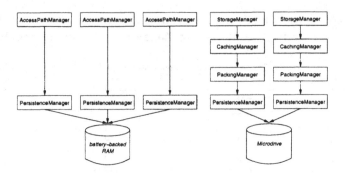

Figure 4. Example system architecture

Figure 4 shows an example system architecture. The hypothetical device offers a large amount of slow, energy-expensive memory on a small harddisc and a little but quick amount of battery-backed RAM. This is a typical constellation for PDAs with expansion slot. All data – in our example represented as two relations – were stored on the Microdrive. To save storage space and achieve better throughput, data will be packed and temporarily buffered. Because storing on harddiscs causes slow access times, indexes are put on battery-backed RAM without any buffering or packing.

To explain the functionality of the described system, the processing of a common request is shown. We assume a query on a given attribute using a system with B-tree based access structure. At first, the application process creates the object instances required by the storage manager. Then the application instantiates a condition object describing the requested data items and an empty **StorageElement** object. The condition object is taken as input for the **AccessManager** object. As far as objects exist which match the condition, every call of the **getNext()** method of this module returns a record identifier. This ID is given to the **StorageManager**. The **StorageManager** recursively gets the byte array associated with the record id from a **ByteLevelInterface** module. In fact the **PersistenceManager** is the last called **ByteLevelInterface** and returns the requested byte array. In this way, each module performs its own special task. Finally, the **StorageManager** transforms the given data bytes into typed variables stored in the obtained empty **StorageElement**. Figure 5 shows this process by a sequence diagram.

7.   Conclusion and Outlook

In many cases the specific requirements of mobile applications with regard to database support cannot be fulfilled by general purpose database

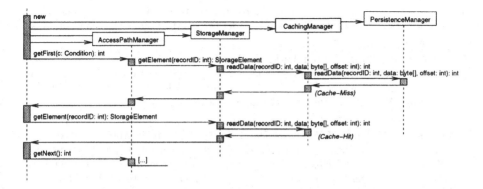

Figure 5. Set-up and performing sample request.

management systems which either try to offer all potentially required functionality or provide only a limited set of functions due to the resource restrictions. One promising approach for solving this problem is an extensible and customizable data management solution enabled to plug in or omit certain modules.

Following this idea, we presented in this paper the storage management component of our DBMS for small and embedded devices. We discussed the overall architecture of this component, which comprises several composable modules implementing specific functions like caching, exploiting access paths or encryption.

In addition, we are currently working on a query engine following a similar approach of customization. In future work, we plan to study techniques for configuration/customization by allowing developers to specify requirements as well as dependencies and using these informations for generating the final system.

References

[1] Alonso, R. and Ganguly, S. Query Optimization for Energy Efficiency in Mobile Environments. In Proceedings of the Fifth Workshop on Foundations of Models and Languages for Data and Objects, 1993.

[2] Batory, D. and Thomas, J. P2: A Lightweight DBMS Generator. Technical Report TR-95-26, University of Texas at Austin, Department of Computer Sciences, 1995.

[3] Batory, D. S., Das, D., Singhal, V., Sirkin, M., and Thomas, J. Database Challenge: Single Schema Database Management Systems. Technical Report CS-TR-92-47, University of Texas, Austin, 1992.

[4] Bohannon, P., Lieuwen, D. F., Rastogi, R., Silberschatz, A., Seshadri, S., and Sudarshan, S. The Architecture of the Dali Main-Memory Storage Manager. Multimedia Tools and Applications, 1997, 4(2):115–151.

[5] Burns, T., Fong, E., Jefferson, D., Knox, R., Reedy, C., Reich, L., Roussopoulos, N., and Truszkowski, W. Reference Model for DBMS Standardization. In ACM SIGMOD Record, 1986.

[6] Cha, S. K., Park, J., and Park, B. D. Xmas: An Extensible Main-Memory Storage System. In Golshani, F. and Makki, K., editors, Proceedings of the 6th International Conference on Information and Knowledge Management (CIKM-97), New York. ACM Press, 1997, pp. 356–362.

[7] Chaudhuri, S. and Weikum, G. Rethinking Database System Architecture: Towards a Self-Tuning RISC-Style Database System. In El Abbadi, A., Brodie, M. L., Chakravarthy, S., Dayal, U., Kamel, N., Schlageter, G., and Whang, K.-Y., editors, *VLDB 2000, Proceedings of 26th International Conference on Very Large Data Bases, September 10–14, Cairo, Egypt*, Los Altos, CA 94022, USA. Morgan Kaufmann Publishers, 2000, pp. 1–10.

[8] Chiang, M.-L. and Chang, R.-C. Cleaning policies in mobile computers using flash memory. The Journal of Systems and Software, 1999, 48(3):213–231.

[9] Douglis, F., Kaashoek, F., Li, K., Cceres, R., Marsh, B., and Tauber, J. A.

Storage Alternatives for Mobile Computers. In First Symposium on Operating Systems Design and Implementation, Monterey, Californie, US, 1994, pp. 25–37.

[10] Geppert, A. and Dittrich, K. R. Constructing the next 100 database management systems: like the handyman or like the engineer? SIGMOD Record (ACM Special Interest Group on Management of Data), 1994, 23(1):27–33.

[11] Geppert, A., Scherrer, S., and Dittrich, K. R. KIDS: Construction of Database Management Systems based on Reuse. Technical Report ifi-97.01, Department of Computer Science, University of Zurich, 1997.

[12] Karlsson, J., Lal, A., Leung, C., and Pham, T. IBM DB2 Everyplace: A Small Footprint Relational Database System. In 17th International Conference on Data Engineering (ICDE' 01), Washington - Brussels - Tokyo. IEEE, 2001, pp. 230–234.

[13] Rudenko, A., Reiher, P., Popek, G., and Kuenning, G. Saving Portable Computer Battery Power through Remote Process Execution. Mobile Computing and Communications Review, 1998, 2(1):19–26.

[14] Stonebraker, M. Inclusion of New Types in Relational Data Base Systems. In Proceedings of the International Conference on Data Engineering,, volume IEEE Computer Society Order Number 655, Los Angeles, CA. IEEE Computer Society Press, 1986, pp. 262–269.

[15] Sybase The Next Generation Database for Embedded Systems, 2000. Whitepaper.

[16] Thomas, J. and Batory, D. P2: An extensible lightweight DBMS. Technical Report CS-TR-95-04, The University of Texas at Austin, Department of Computer Sciences, Austin, Texas, 1995.

TOWARDS MULTI-AGENT MODELS OF DOMAIN-SPECIFIC LANGUAGES

Merik Meriste, Tõnis Kelder, Jüri Helekivi
University of Tartu, Estonia
E-mail: Merik.Meriste@ut.ee

Abstract   Framework for the appropriate development of domain-specific languages (DSL) is expected to provide conceptually clear tools for DSL modeling and implementation. Multi-agent systems are proposing a new design concept for software – the kenetic program design – based on the concepts of interactions and agents. On the basis of this conceptual view, the interactive attributed automata are considered as a potential framework for DSL development. Attributed automaton is a state transition machine introduced for knowledge structuring and conceptual specification on the basis of regular attributed structures. Distributed memory of an attributed automaton supports the decomposition of computational problems into a network of information nodes with attached communication and computation actions. Compositions of Attributed Automata (AA) serve as a structuring tool of AA as complex computational agents. Basic techniques of interactive AA are implemented in a development environment prototype.

Keywords: domain-specific languages, multi-agent systems, kenetic program design, interactive models of computation, attributed automaton.

1.   Introduction

An interesting aspect in DSL approach is that of formal models and frameworks for DSL design and for the development of appropriate models of linguistic notions and constructs. To what extent the formal methods applied support the reasonable structuring of information objects and problem solving actions, is a crucial aspect of modeling. The efficient implementation and accordance of the model with problem area specification language concepts are usually valued most in this process. A reasonable framework is expected to provide tools for DSL modeling and implementation on a

H.-M. Haav and A. Kalja (eds.), Databases and Information Systems II, 239–251.

conceptually clear basis. The variety of contextual views and application areas accentuate the complicated nature of the task. *The success of system modeling depends on the extraction of surface and/or deep (regular or contextual) substructures from the informational environment and their subsequent attachment to computational activities. Multi-agent systems are proposing a new design concept for software – the kenetic program design – based on the concepts of interactions and agents.* We consider that kind of modeling framework as a methodologically suitable basis for DSL design and development tools.

On the basis of this conceptual view the interactive attributed automata concept is considered as a potential particular framework for DSL modeling and implementation. Attributed automaton is a state machine introduced initially for purposes of structuring and the conceptual specification of knowledge on the basis of regular attributed structures [7, 8, 9, 10]. To support the decomposition of a specification problem or computational task into a network of information nodes, an attributed automaton has finite memory distributed to its states, as well as traditional computations and communication actions at transitions. Compositions of Attributed Automata (AA) serve as a structuring tool while treating AA as complex computational agents. Since the transformational AA appeared to be inadequate for interactive systems, interactive AA with communication channels as more appropriate were introduced [9]. Basic interactive AA techniques are implemented in interactive AA visual development environment prototype described in this paper. Attributed automaton and interactive attributed automaton were later on identified as a kind of Wegner's sequential interaction machine and multi-stream interaction machine respectively [15, 16, 17].

The integrated presentation and specification of knowledge will obviously remain a long-term research and technological development problem for DSL, too. Thus, on the one hand, the development of models for conceptual, expert and procedural knowledge, as well as of appropriate methods for knowledge presentation and management is essential for the successful use of definite DSL in practice. On the other hand, we would like to focus in this context on the domain-specific language as an environment for modeling and managing information objects and problem solving actions for the presentation of linguistic notions. The next section will consider different views of a domain-specific language – as a problem-solving environment (i.e., a community of practice), a collection of intelligent agents, and as an interaction machine. Section 3 will present the AA formal approach and describe the AA pilot applications practice. Section 4 will concentrate on the interactive AA approach as a potential DSL modeling tool based on the paradigm of interactive state machine with distributed memory.

2. Communities of Practice, Intelligent Agents and Interactive Models of Computation

The concept of *Community of Practice* (CP) is a central concept of the social theory of learning [18]. In this approach, the primary unit of analysis is neither the individual nor social institution but the informal community of practice that is formed for some activity. A domain-specific language forms a consensual language, a kind of problem solving environment for particular communities of practice. The particular problem-solving environment will serve as a handy tool to the extent that it simulates and supports the basic notions and principles and integrates the key components of these communities of practice.

Intelligent agents concept offers another viewpoint for modeling DSL as collections of intelligent agents, i.e. as distributed (artificial) intelligent systems. As proposed by Wooldridge and Jennings [19], an intelligent agent as a system has the following features – autonomy, social ability, reactivity, pro-activeness. In terms of interactive models, the computational agents and CP are a kind of interaction machines, as introduced by Peter Wegner. "Though interaction machines are a simple and obvious extension of Turing machines, this small change increases expressiveness so it becomes too rich for mathematical models. Interaction machines may have single or multiple interaction streams and synchronous or asynchronous actions and can differ along many other dimensions" [16].

Design and implementation methods for software-intensive systems have undergone a remarkable evolution during the last decades. Procedure and algorithm centric approach in software engineering and computer science has been substituted by interaction-centered paradigms. In artificial intelligence a similar shift, from logic-based to agent-based models, has taken place. Interaction-centered systems appear to be more powerful problem solvers than procedure and algorithm centered. It is also suggested that algorithmic models alone do not suffice to express certain expected aspects of behavior of today's systems – e.g. ability to self-organize the interaction of its components, to adapt its behavior to the changes in its environment, or in its goal function. Interaction-based computation involves, unlike algorithmic computation, infinite and dynamic input/output streams that may represent the behavior of a non-terminating program, or that of a collection of loosely interacting, repeatedly activated, terminating computational agents. A collection of components (agents) often displays a behavior that is rather complex and well organized, despite the simplicity of each single agent. This observation conforms perfectly to the software engineering empirical experience regarding the nature of system integration errors. With these observations in mind we will consider interactive attributed automata.

3.   Attributed Automata

Attributed automata were introduced as a model of executable specifications based on regular structures with attributes attached to structure nodes. Regularity is here treated in terms of formal languages – primitive items can be composed into a structure by means of concatenation, selection and iteration operations. Attributes serve for the presentation of contextual relations, as well as of properties and meaning of underlying concepts.

3.1   Conceptual View

Attributed automaton can be treated as a state machine with distributed finite memory at its states and specified at its transitions computations and communication actions. In this aspect, an attributed automaton is simply a generalization of a traditional finite automaton with attributes and computational relations attached to states and transitions of the automaton, respectively. By specializing the general definition of the finite attributed automaton one can easily obtain classical language recognition devices. For instance, attributed automaton without attributes is a classical finite automaton, an attributed automaton with stack as its only attribute in each of its state is a pushdown automaton. Attributed automata in terms of formal languages are considered as recognizers based on regular data structures, the respective class of formal grammars is that of regular attribute grammars. Furthermore, traditional input tape of a state machine can be treated as an attribute of all its states – it will lead to a transformational attributed automaton as a certain kind of transition network [9]. Transformational AA can be treated as a general model of (algorithmic) computation – every partially recursive function can be specified by a transformational attributed automaton [12].

3.2   Formal Approach: Finite Attributed Automata

The basic concept has been defined [9] as follows:

Definition *A finite attributed automaton M is a tuple*
$M = (I, S, A, \sigma, s_0, s_F)$, *where*

(a) *I is a finite alphabet of terminal symbols,*

(b) *S is a finite alphabet of states,*

(c) $A = \{A_s \mid s \in S\}$ *is a family of domains of attributes indexed over states,*

(d) $\sigma = \{\sigma_{ss'} \subseteq (A_s \times I^*) \times A_{s'} \mid s, s' \in S\}$ *is a family of transition relations indexed over pairs of states,*

(e) $s_0 \in S$ *is an initial state and*

(f) $s_F \in S$ *is a final state.*

The functioning of the automaton is considered as a change of its current state. Transitions start from the given initial state with the initial attribute value and the input string given. Automaton terminates if there are no more transitions possible. The termination is defined successful if the current state is one of final states. The remaining input, together with attribute value of the current state, forms the result of the work. Automaton fails in case the current state is not a final one.

An interesting aspect to consider in the context of DSL modeling approach is that of AA as language recognizers [7, 9, 12]. The notion of the accepted language has been defined as follows [9]:

Definition *Let M* $= (I, S, A, \sigma, s_0, s_F)$ *be an attributed automaton. The* language *accepted by the automaton M is defined as follows*

$$L(M, a_0) = \{w \in I^* \mid (s_0, a_0, w) \mapsto^*_M (s_F, a, \varepsilon), \ a \in A_{s_F}\}.$$

The final attribute value $a \in A_{s_F}$ can be interpreted as the *meaning* of the string w in the language $L(M, a_0)$.

Consider recognizers of binary numbers (Fig.1) and a context-sensitive language (Fig.2). Attributed automaton given in Figure 1 recognizes binary numbers and the final attribute value a represents the decimal value of the binary number. In another automaton (Fig.2) attributes are in a different role, they collect contextual information used in some states to select the next transition. As our examples demonstrate, there are two alternative possibilities to construct a data recognizer on the basis of an attributed automaton. Firstly, we can specify predicates at transitions, i.e. we select the next move in accordance with context conditions. Secondly, we can simply collect the contextual information we need at some state and specify by a predicate the acceptable context at that state. The second approach appears to be interesting from the methodological point of view, as it suggests a more systematic and modular way for building such attributed recognizers.

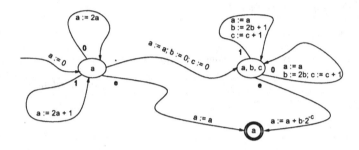

Figure 1. Recognizer of binary numbers.

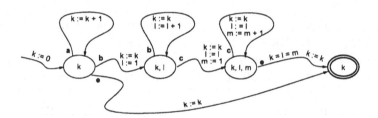

Figure 2. Recognizer of the language L = { an bn cn | n ≥ 0}.

3.3   Compositions of AA

State transition machines are widely applied in software engineering for modeling the behavior of systems. There exist several extensions of the concept of finite state machine with memory. Attributed automaton can be distinguished among them by distributed memory, i.e. by allocating memory to the states (of data processing). Distributed memory together with the local definition of data transformation functions helps to decompose/compose an attributed automaton. We would like to point out the following methodological aspect: in the examples of AA as recognizers we decomposed the problem of language recognition into two parts: the syntactic recognition of regular structures by a simple (i.e. without predicates on transitions) attributed automaton and the analysis of contextual relations of attributes by an accepting predicate. An accepting predicate can certainly be viewed as an attributed automaton with one transition labeled by that predicate. It leads us to a trivial serial composition of two AA of different kind. In general, the composition problem of attributed automata is the following: how and when can a complex attributed automaton be simulated by a network of simpler attributed automata; how are these component automata related to the attributed automaton under consideration? *Operational compositions* of attributed automata [9] are stated in state machine compositions in the usual manner:

- *serial composition* where two automata are connected by "pasting" together the final state of the first automaton and the initial state of the second one;
- *parallel composition* where two automata are connected by "pasting" together their initial states and final states;
- *hierarchical composition* where during a transition another (or even the same) attributed automaton is called

Note that hierarchical composition functions as a tool for the adequate modeling of hierarchical data structures and hierarchical computational structures (in addition to iterative and selective ones modeled by ordinary AA). This idea has its roots in the interpreting automata approach [13], applied by the Vienna method for defining programming languages.

For interactive AA, other types of composition can be applied, such as parallel compositions with some kind of synchronization, action hiding, etc. The method of *functional compositions* [11] has good compositional and algebraic properties and is therefore interesting from a pragmatic point of view. To conclude, AA model provides new tools for the restructuring of large systems in order to reduce their conceptual complexity.

3.4   Interactive Attributed Automata

In the modeling of interactive systems it appears important for the system to react adequately to the changes in its environment. These changes cannot be predicted in a system which will recognize changes by checking periodically whether particular events happen in the environment. Such a system is certainly *interactive*, i.e. it responds to changes in the environment by performing *internal* changes, which, in turn, will be registered by the environment as some internal events of the system. We call AA simulating interactive systems *interactive AA*. In these attributed automata, the sequence of internal events (transformations of attribute values) will be in some manner synchronized with external events in the environment. In the formal model events are presented by means of messaging primitives and communication channels [9]. Interactive attributed automata represent a

246

certain kind of *multi-stream interaction machines* introduced by Wegner [15, 16, 17].

For example, the parsing of Dyck languages [1] is solved by interactive AA as follows (Fig. 3). The regular structure of a string is represented by the moves of AA, counters of parentheses are represented as attributes. An interactive automaton is constructed for counting certain kinds of parentheses ('[]'. '()', '{}'). Automata interact with each other for recognition of a string of parentheses.

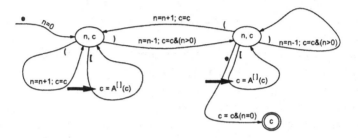

a) Accounting of parenthesis '(' and ')': c' = A$^{()}$ (c)

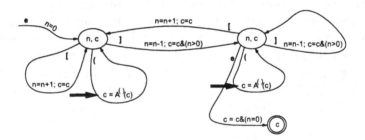

b) Accounting of parenthesis '[' and ']': c' = A$^{[]}$ (c)

Figure 3. Grammar: S —> SS I ( ) I (S) I [ ] I [S]

3.5 Experience

AA have been a useful engineering tool for software development. Pilot applications in medical signal analysis [3, 4, 6] were the first particular "problem solving environments" where AA served successfully as a problem modeling tool. These applications have significant results [2, 5] and a strong theoretical foundation. Analyzers of auditory brainstem responses and ECG are applied in the clinical practice of Finnish universities. We combined statistical and syntactic pattern recognition methods in the form of a particular interactive AA collection in our analyses of ECG signals. We considered the attributed model of the Alternating Bit Protocol (described briefly in [9]) as a pilot example where communicating objects were modeled by means of interactive AA. As our experience has shown, AA is a simple and suitable concept for organizing ideas when evaluating complex problems.

4.   Interactive AA as a DSL Modeling Tool

The experience described above led us to the design and implementation of a system for the visual development of interactive AA. Such a development environment will serve as an instrumental tool for the design, as well as for the implementation of various applied software. To quote Peter Wegner [16]: "The "negative result" that interactive behavior is not expressible by Turing machines determines a "positive challenge" to develop practical models of interactive computation". Moreover, we are encouraged by our pilot practice experience. Interactive AA compositions are expressive in solving non-algorithmic problems. Some algorithmic problems can be more efficiently solved by interactive non-algorithmic techniques.

The basic interactive AA composition techniques are implemented in a prototype system programmed in Java. The communication technique applied is that of Java Message Service (JMS). Automata are interacting by sending messages, both point-to-point and publish-and-subscribe methods are available. Sending a message is treated as a separate process that can affect the evaluation of attributes for the next state. A message can be accepted either in the synchronous mode – acceptance included in the selection process of the next state, or, in the asynchronous mode – an arriving message initiates a specific separate process of acceptance, which in its own turn may affect the values of attributes.

The collection of interactive automata designed to solve a problem forms a cluster, i.e. a multi-agent. Member agents of a cluster may be activated as one complete task on a computer or, as a distributed task. In the first case, automata can exchange information by common (cluster) attributes and messages, in the second case only by messages. In general, interactive computation involves, unlike algorithmic computation, infinite and dynamic input/output streams of computational agents involved [16, 17]. Such a computation can be considered as a kind of distributed control of information streams and agents activities in a dynamic environment [15]. A cluster of agents often shows a behaviour that is rather complex and organised, despite the simplicity of each single agent. In this aspect, application of interactive AA as interaction machines leads from systems with algorithmic behaviour to systems with either sequential interactive behaviour (a pair of interacting agents) or with multi-interactive behaviour. This observation conforms perfectly to the software engineering principles of programming-in-the-large and programming-in-the-small. Moreover, the agent-based approach in (domain-specific) languages design and implementation seems extremely intriguing in the context of these observations.

Our prototype system as an agent-based problem-solving environment is, in a sense, a system of programming where the software is constructed by means of collaborative (interacting) automata. Components constructed are saved as items of the common database of automata – agents. From the specification of agents of a particular task, a Java-program will be compiled. Notions and terms applied in an automaton are specified by means of the so-called *axiom-classes* (specific Java-classes, representing notions of an automaton are). Notions are implemented as particular *notion-classes* derived from axiom-classes. The application is derived from particular notion-classes and compiled in the context of constructs (terms and notions), specified by the user. Such a style of implementation supports the system's flexibility – by changes in notion-classes new properties can be introduced to the cluster as a whole. On the other hand, at some level, Java-programming is needed.

From the viewpoint of language implementation we take a 'notion view' of DSL design, in that a language is designed as a set of interrelated autonomous notions. The idea of agent-based programming is interpreted as follows: a language processor will be constructed as a cluster of interactive AA (agents) of language notions. An agent "represents" an instance of a particular notion, i.e. the notion's representation, its structure, properties and meaning. The task of the notion agent is to secure the appropriate translation/interpretation of every notion instance in its given specific context. The contextual and structural relations of the notions included in a language are specified in terms of the properties of the notion agent and its interactions with other notion agents. If necessary, the notion agents will apply other agents for traditional subtasks of syntax-directed translation and code generation. In other words, an implementation of a language is treated as a multi-stream interaction machine [15, 17]

As an example of the multi-agent approach for DSL in the framework of interactive attributed automata, let us consider a tiny interaction language for an online ticket sales system. The example problem is borrowed from [14]. Customers buy tickets from a ticket server. The server communicates only with sales agents. Customers can ask the agent for various services. These services include reserving tickets, paying for and getting the reserved tickets, and canceling reservations. The language of communication between the customers and agents consists of a couple of notions only, as given in figure 4. Implementation of the language by automata is given in figure 5.

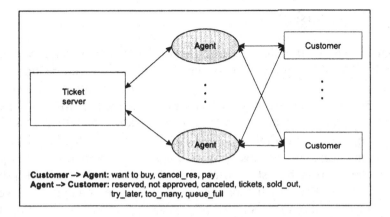

Figure 4. Interactions of customers and agents

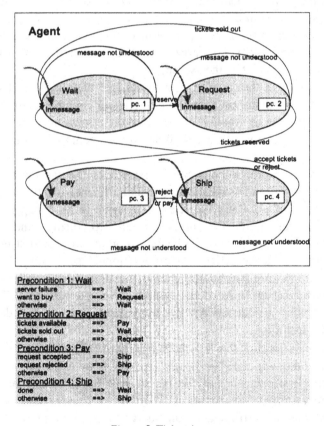

Figure 5. Ticket Agent

5. Conclusion

During the last decade the paradigm for designing software systems has gradually shifted from the algorithm-centred to the interaction-centred approach. A number of interaction-centred computational models has appeared, which makes the multi-agent paradigm naturally usable for designing software systems. The idea of building agent-based software engineering methods is rapidly spreading. The crucial methodological aspect of modeling software systems is to what extent the formal methods applied support the reasonable structuring of information objects and problem solving actions. For domain-specific languages, a reasonable framework is expected to provide, on a conceptually clear basis, tools for their modeling and development, preferably in terms of the problem domain.

The concept of smart components was introduced about thirty years ago to simplify the development and maintenance of continuously evolving non-homogenous open architecture based software intensive systems. Each smart component implements certain pre-defined functions, and carries out this function and the ability to carry it out by arranging (semi)-automatic interactions with the rest of the system.

Approximately at the same time, the notion of the multi-agent system was introduced into the distributed artificial intelligence research community. The concept of intelligent agents offers another viewpoint for modeling a compiler as a collection of agents. What about agents in practical language processing?

On the basis of these conceptual viewpoints the interactive attributed automata are considered as a feasible particular framework for the design and implementation of (domain-specific) languages in this paper. Attributed automaton serves here for purposes of structuring and conceptual specification of knowledge on the basis of regular attributed structures. The decomposition of a specification/computational task into a network of information nodes/computational agents is supported by distributed memory and the interaction abilities of interactive attributed automata. The notions and techniques of interactive AA are implemented in a visual development environment prototype.

Interactive models enable to create a semantically richer modeled world, also for the domain-specific languages. As any other artificial languages, the DSL, too, are first only partially designed, evolving gradually in the process of communication and observation. With these observations in mind, we consider interactive attributed automata (a) as an appropriate tool for the development of domain-specific languages, and (b) as a feasible basis for (agent-based) compilation techniques.

References

[1] Ginsburg, C., Greibach, S. Deterministic context-free languages. Inform. and Control, 9(6), 1996, pp. 620–648.

[2] Grönfors, T. Novel Methods of Syntactic Pattern Recognition for Peak Detection of Auditory Brainstem Responses. Doctoral Dissertation, University of Kuopio, Publications C. Natural and Environmental Sciences 28,1994.

[3] Grönfors, T., Meriste, M. Attributed Automata in Pattern Recognition of Digital Signals. Computer Methods and Programs in Biomedicine, 1993, pp. 763–785.

[4] Juhola, M., Meriste, M. An Attributed Automaton for Recognizing of Nystagmus Eye Movements. IAPR Papers on Structural and Syntactic Pattern Recognition, Bern, 1993, pp. 194–206.

[5] Koski, A. On Structural Recognition and Analysis Methods Applied to ECG Signals. Doctoral Dissertation, University of Turku, Computer Sci. Res. Reports R-97-1, 1997.

[6] Koski, A., Juhola, M., Meriste, M. Syntactic Recognition of ECG Signals by Attributed Finite Automata. Pattern Recognition, 28(12), 1995, pp. 1927–1940.

[7] Meriste, M., Penjam, J. Attributed Finite Automata. In: Proc. of Int. Workshop CC'92 on Compiler-Compiler, Reports of the University of Paderborn 103, 1993, pp. 48–51.

[8] Meriste, M., Penjam, J. Attributed Finite Automata. Res. Rep. CS23/91, Institute of Cybernetics, Estonian Academy of Sciences, Tallinn, 1991, 15p.

[9] Meriste, M., Penjam, J. Attributed Models of Computing. Proceedings of the Estonian Academy of Sciences. Engineering, 1(2), 1995, pp. 139–157.

[10] Meriste, M., Penjam, J. Toward Knowledge-based Specifications of Languages. In: J.Barzdins, D.Bjorner (Eds.), Baltic Computer Science, LNCS, 502, Springer Verlag, 1991, pp.65–76.

[11] Meriste, M., Penjam, J.,Vene, V. Models of Attributed Automata. Informatica, 9(1), 1998, pp. 85–105.

[12] Meriste, M., Vene, V. Attributed Automata and Language Recognizers. In: Proc. of 4th Symposium on Programming Languages and Software Tools. Visegrád, Hungary, June 9–10, 1995, pp. 114–121.

[13] Ollongren, A. Definition of Programming Languages by Interpreting Automata. Academic Press, London, 1974.

[14] Wang, W., Hidvégi, Z., Bailey A.D. Jr., Whinston, A.B. E-Process Design and Assurance Using Model Checking. Computer, 33(10), 2000, pp. 48–53.

[15] Wegner, P. Interactive Software Technology. In: Handbook of Computer Science and Engineering, CRC Press, 1997.

[16] Wegner, P. Why Interaction is more Powerful than Algorithms. Communications of the ACM, 40(5), 1997, pp. 80–91.

[17] Wegner, P., Goldin, D. Interaction as a Framework for Modelling. In: Chen et al (eds). Conceptual Modelling: Current Issues and Future Directions, 1999, LNCS vol. 1565.

[18] Wenger, E. Communities of Practice. Cambridge University Press, London, 1998.

[19] Wooldridge, M., Jennings, N.R. Intelligent agents: theory and practice. Knowledge Engineering Review, 10(2), 1995, pp. 115–152.

E-MATE: AN OPEN ARCHITECTURE TO SUPPORT MOBILITY OF USERS

Davide Carboni, Eloisa Vargiu, Claude Moulin, Stefano Sanna, Alessandro Soro, Gavino Paddeu

CRS4, Centro di Ricerca, Sviluppo e Studi Superiori in Sardegna
VI Strada OVEST Z.I. Macchiareddu,UTA, CA – Italy
gavino.paddeui@crs4.it

Sylvain Giroux

Dep. of Mathematics and Computer Science, University of Sherbrooke
Sherbrooke, Canada
sylvain.giroux@dmi.usherb.ca

Abstract   As the world gets connected, people need to access information anywhere, anytime, whatever the device is (laptop, cellular phone...). They look for situated services that identify and package relevant context-sensitive information. Situated services for mobile people must integrate 1) user profile: who the user is; 2) space: where the user is; 3) time: when the user needs the service 4) context: of which services the user is surrounded by. A situated service is multi-modal, geo-referenced and personalized. A multi-modal service is available through very different devices. A geo-referenced service selects information according to the physical position of the user. A personalized service chooses only relevant information. This paper presents the main elements of an architecture that fosters the design, implementation and deployment of situated services. These elements can be organized into three processes: personalization, deployment and access to a service. Personalization is the process that chooses the right information and presents it at the right time with the appropriate user interface. The deployment of services is supported through application servers that supports from fat-client to thin client distributed schemas. The access to service is done through portals that enables to get the client part of the service, a service viewer then uses an object

H.-M. Haav and A. Kalja (eds.), Databases and Information Systems II, 253–267.

renderer to generate on the fly the user interface according to the device profile, the service features and layout information.

Keywords: personalization, geo-referenced information, multi-modality, mobile computing, wireless networks, distributed systems, Jini, XML

1.   Introduction

An effective pervasive information system must identify which information is related to the current context of use and dynamically re-compose this information in a suitable and usable presentation. The convergence between networks and terminals encourages the development of location-aware and personalized services. Several standards define how to build networks of heterogeneous appliances and terminals. For one, Bluetooth supports wireless spontaneous networks within a radius of ten meters [4]. IEEE 802.11 standards allow the connection among wireless devices within a radius of 100 meters [8]. Market-available cellular phones can directly connect to the Internet and the majority of them are already equipped with a WAP micro-browser, on the other hand cellular phones can simply be exploited as wireless modems and connect laptops and Personal Digital Assistants (PDA) to the Internet.

The physical layer of the wireless internet is already capable to fully support the mobility of users; nevertheless, there are a number of factors that any clever information system architecture must take into account: the user profile, who the user is and which are his needs; the place, where the user is; the time, when the user wants to obtain the required information; the context, which services are available and which kind of terminal is available to the user.

This paper presents the nuts and bolts of e-MATE. e-MATE is a middleware for such services standing at the crossroad of personalization, mobility and location awareness. We coin this class of services as mobile, personalized and location-based services (MPLS).

This paper first extracts the issues and requirements of a MPLS by means of an application currently under development in the domain of travel and leisure (§3). Then we describe e-MATE as the combination of a middleware and a framework that supports MPLS. More precisely we show how e-MATE provides for original and integrated solutions to three processes: service personalization (§5),service deployment (§7) and service access (§6). Personalization is the process that chooses the right information and presents it at the right time with the appropriate user interface. To achieve it, we integrate user profiling, device profiling, persistent users sessions built from workspace and agents, geo-referenced information (for instance using GIS) and user physical location (GPS based). The deployment of services is supported through application servers that supports from fat-client to thin client distributed schemas. The access to services is done through portals that enable to retrieve the client part of the service, a service viewer then uses an object renderer to generate on the fly the user interface according to the device profile, the service features and layout information. Implementation relies on Java, RMI, Jini [3], XML [19] and RDF [5].

2. Related Works

A work as vast as e-MATE has a number of relationships and likenesses with other projects and research activities in disparate domains. GUIDE [6] is an application which thoroughly explores the issues related to a software tourist guide. It is basically a working prototype based on IEEE 802.11 network. It defines its own information model for situated objects and takes into account the usability of the system by means of user trials. Cyberguide[2] defines interesting scenarios and describes the experiences and the research carried out in this field drawing out a set of issues that are similar to those addressed by e-MATE.

In the field of device adaptive services, we found some useful concepts in the "Device Independence Activity" [18] carried out by W3C. Such a work gives an overview of principles - candidate to be the foundation of device independent systems - from three different perspectives: user perspective, author perspective and delivery context perspective. Closely related to device independency and adaptive content delivery, the CC/PP Working Group [17] at W3C is developing an RDF-based framework for the management of device profile information.

In the field of device independent user interfaces, our approach consists in the definition of a set of user interface abstractions that, at runtime, are translated into concrete components by appropriate "rendering engines". Such a technique falls into the vast category of model-based user interface development techniques whose the reader can find a valid discussion in [15].

3. A Travel Assistant: t-MATE

In order to assess e-MATE, we have designed scenarios in which mobility, multi-modality and geo-referenced information are decisive key elements. Three of these scenarios are currently under implementation as MPLS. The application domains are travel and leisure (t-MATE), risk management (evacuation of a city) and education (mobile lessons). The design and implementation of these scenarios provided and is still providing useful insights, hints and feedback on the specification and the design of e-MATE. The domain of travel and leisure is the ideal test-bench for a MPLS architecture like e-MATE. In this section, we sketch the t-MATE scenario. The scenario is divided in three phases: user profiling (§3.1), macro-planning (§3.2) and micro-planning (§3.3). Each phase focuses on a specific type of devices and on different time-frames. In the range of devices involved in this scenario are included internet-digital TV, desktop computers, cellular phones and personal digital assistant (PDA). The assistance to a traveler is personalized and position-aware. The variety of tasks and configurations is luxuriant. Some are performed when the user is disconnected. Some need him to be on-line. Some require thin-clients, others are better suited for fat-clients. Some involve the cooperation between distributed remote services. Other are stand-alone services written from scratch.

Thus, t-MATE will later be used throughout the paper as a source of concrete examples of the issues addressed by e-MATE and the solutions it provides.

3.1   User Profiling

The first phase of the scenario relies on user profiling while the customer is listening to interactive-TV. An off-line agent, called "Profile Manager", is loaded on the set-top box. This agent gathers information and refines continuously the user profile. The user profile structure is defined according to services ontologies and requirements. User profiles are refined either automatically in the background and/or at the explicit request of the user. The automatic profiling system makes inferences on preferences and interests according to the semantic information encoded in the video stream (MPEG4 and MPEG7 [11]). For instance, if the user spends most of the time watching TV series on angling, the system should refine the profile with this information. On the other hand the user can explicitly assign a score to a video content; for instance, if during a television documentary about Kenya the user marks the programme with the maximum score the system can infer interest about a Kenya sojourn. Thus, the user profiling is refined gradually over time. The "Profile Manager" connects periodically to the service servers to update the user profile available for a service.

Once ready to go on vacation, the customer requests proposals to his travel agency service. To build these proposal, the agency will use his profile built while he was listening to the TV. Obviously profiles may be built using information coming from multiples sources, electronic journals, web browsing, etc. The profiling engine indeed needs only a semantic encoding of information and a function that values the interest of a topic selected in the ontology. XML is the natural way to encode this semantic information.

3.2 Macro-Planning

The second phase of the scenario focuses on the macro-planning of the journey. It mainly involves personal computer, browsers and e-mails. During this phase the user connects to the planning agent service in order to plan a trip and submits, by means of the service user interface, his requirements about the travel such as the total budget for the tickets, the preferred hour of departure and so on. Hence, the planning agent will use his knowledge of the travel industry to plan an appropriate itinerary.

The current implementation of the planning algorithm is summarized as follows: (i) search the minimum route, (ii) repeatedly make queries to the database looking for the corresponding flights, (iii) remove the unavailable routes, and (iv) return the minimum-cost route.

The first phase is realized using an A*-like algorithm [12], the result of this phase is the list of cities and airports involved. The agent repeatedly makes queries to the database in order to find all the possible flights. Among the resulting flights the agent has to screen out flights that are unavailable at the given departure date. Finally, the agent sorts the flights with respect to the cost and returns the minimum-cost itinerary to the user.

The planning agent could also arrange hotel accommodation for the duration of the traveler's stay, and provide a selection of local attractions that might interest the traveler during his stay. Once the plan has been approved by the user, the planning agent keeps working off-line to handle any event or change that might affect the plan such as adverse forecast, strikes and so forth. The commercial transaction is completed with the usual security care.

3.3 Micro Planning

The last phase occurs while the user is on the road. The main devices involved are PDAs and cellular phones. Actually, once a travel package has been sold, an agency has few means to continue to interact with its customer. This part of the scenario shows how MPLS can extend and improve the notion of customer service relationships.

During the night, the traveler's personal agent achieves a micro-planning of the next day. For instance, the planning agent works off-line searching cultural events in order to fill the tomorrow agenda of its user. It uses weather forecasts to select the activities, museum if rain is expected, beach otherwise. As far as personalization is a concern, the agent needs to know the user preferences (user profile). Events are screened out by inquiring the profile manager and those matching the user profile are stored in the user personal agenda as appointments. The personal agenda notifies the user whenever an event is imminent by means of SMS messages. The personal agenda is a self-contained service accessible from any device in respect of multi-channel capabilities of e-MATE. Therefore, the user can connect to his agenda with his cellular phone and manage his appointments while he is in line for visiting a museum or if he's moving through the city by train. Furthermore, the agent can act as a tourist guide, providing information according to the physical position; for instance, the traveler may ask: "what is the name of the church I am in front of?" The traveler may point new interests to his agent. The agent will then search information related to these newly expressed interests and adapts the user's agenda accordingly. The travel agency may offer last minute promotions for shows to its customer through the customer's t-MATE. Applications, variations and possibilities opened by MPLS on the travel and leisure are infinite.

4. Mobile, Personalized and Location-Based Services (MPLS)

This section outlines the constraints and requirements on e-MATE architecture imposed by personalized services for people that are changing location, who continuously switches for connected and disconnected states and may use a wide variety of heterogeneous devices.

4.1 Implications of Mobility

The mobility of users implies that services and information systems should be visible from a number of different channels. The same information should be accessible from a web page, from a WAP site or from an Interactive Voice Responder (IVR) machine. Besides, a given channel can have more interaction modalities. For instance, a Windows-Icons-Mouse-Pointing (WIMP) desktop application can greatly improve the experience of some kind of users providing the possibility to dictate texts by means of a voice recognizer.

With respect to these implications, a service supporting mobility of users should be designed in a way such that the following principle will stand: design once, run anywhere. Nevertheless, multi-modality and multi-channel access are only the first step towards the result. In fact, even though a service is available for any device, the user can feel the interaction with the system rather uncomfortable. This occurs when the network is too slow, scarcely reliable and disconnections frequently occur. Moreover, some tasks can take long before their accomplishment and waiting on-line for the results is useless and expensive. In such a situation the user experiences the system as a hostile environment to work with. An approach that can greatly improve the user experience is through the management of user sessions and the scheduling of off-line agents. A session provides a workspace that can be either strictly personal or shared with other users. The former is a concrete base to build a wide range of services such as address book, agenda and home directory. The latter is more suitable for cooperative applications such as chat rooms and multi-player games.

Sessions can be joined and left at any time and by means of any device. Thus, a session created with a mobile phone can be joined in a later time with a palm computer or with a desktop-PC. Agents may be created, associated to sessions and committed to perform some tasks such as content-searches or cultural events notification when the user is off-line. We believe that the possibility to create agents and to join and leave sessions using different devices in different moments can really improve the interaction between the user and a distribute information system.

4.2   Implications of User Position

The user position is a new important parameter in the mobile computing. In fact, this parameter can be used to provide the right information at the right moment by 'position aware' systems. The precision required can vary according to the objectives. In fact, if we are designing an agent aimed to search cultural events such as concerts or football matches, it is important to screen out all events that will not be held in the city in which the user is standing. So the precision required is at city-level. On the other hand if the agent task is to notify the user whenever his position is nearby a monument or a museum the precision required should be about 100 meters.

There are several ways to obtain the position of the user. The most known is the Global Positioning System (GPS) [16] that is based on the terminal capability to connect to a network of satellites. Other systems are specifically based on mobile phone networks such as Enhanced Observed Time Difference (E-OTD) and Cell Global Identity (CGI). The precision of those systems can range from 10 meters, in the case of GPS, to 30 km in the case of CGI. See [7] for a complete discussion about positioning of mobile phones.

4.3   Implications of User Profile

A wide variety of applications, from graphical user interfaces to information filtering, can better serve users if they adapt to user wants and needs. The key to enable the adaptation and personalization of services are the "user models". User models can be successfully applied in: recommendation based systems, adaptive information retrieval systems, and systems for coaching/teaching users. It might be said that the notion of context-awareness.

4.4 Design Once, Run Anywhere: The e-MATE Architecture

e-MATE is a software architecture conceived and developed at CRS4, aimed to support the development and the deployment of MPLS. It defines a model of service and provides a framework that facilitates the development of new services available through multiple channels and position-aware. e-MATE is provided with a distributed middleware that meets the providers' needs concerning the deployment and the publishing of new services and allows the dynamic constitution of a federation of services. Besides, e-MATE addresses both the heterogeneous nature of access and the management of agents and user sessions. User terminals may differ considerably each other, some of them can load end run mobile code from the network, other can be programmed to communicate with online services exchanging data but not code, and many of them cannot be programmed but can access to information by means of pre-installed micro-browser or via voice-interfaces.

About user-system interaction, one should be able to interact directly with the service by means of an appropriate user interface in synchronous manner and to obtain immediately a result. On the other hand, the user would appreciate the possibility to schedule some kind of work, i.e. a search on the web, and to retrieve the results of such a job in a later time. The latter is an asynchronous way to interact with the service in which the user engages one or more agents to perform some tasks while the user is off-line.

5. Personalization

Personalizing the information is a process which involves many of the implications explained in this paper. The result of such a process is the ability for the system to provide the right information at the right time both in synchronous manner - i.e. when the user is connected and browsing between services - and in asynchronous manner, i.e. some agents keep searching any relevant data while the user is disconnected but he is reachable by means of Short Messaging Service (SMS) or Multimedia Messaging Service (MMS) [1].

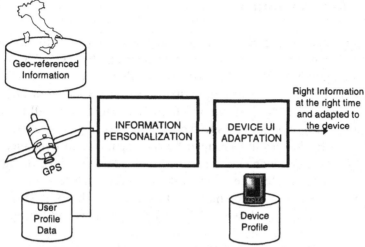

Figure 1. Information and device UI personalization process

Thus, the personalization process (Figure 1) is based on the integration of a number of elements such as agents' management, user sessions and workspace management, localization technologies, users' models and GIS systems [10]. Nevertheless, the personalized information must be presented in such a way that the human computer interaction causes the minimum effort for the user. Thus, the personalization process must be followed by a device-adaptation process based on the device-profile of the user terminal.

5.1 User Sessions and Agents

The e-MATE framework is provided with the core elements to build, activate and interrupt agents. Any agent can access to its user session workspace and perform tasks when the user is off-line. The number of agents that are running in the system varies according to the number of sessions. In the actual implementation of the e-MATE application server a new execution thread is forked whenever a new agent is started. This choice is not optimal if the number of agents grows a lot. In such a case a thread pooling implementation would be a more performing strategy.

6. Architecture for Heterogeneous Types of Access

Different devices have different features and this fact can deeply constraint how the service may be distributed to devices. This section describes a general and open infrastructure enabling a user to access a service whatever the device features are.

6.1   Categorization of Devices

A number of categorizations can be done according to the physical characteristics of devices. For instance, devices can be divided according to their computation power or according to their network interface type (Ethernet, PPP, etc.), or according to their input/output modalities (keyboard, touch screen, mouse, etc.). If one wants to take into account all the existing possibilities the number of cases to face up becomes unmanageable.

In e-MATE, devices are grouped by the capability to dynamically load and execute the mobile code of a service. We distinguish three fundamentals typologies of devices that need three different infrastructures.

Type 1: the device can download and execute mobile code. This category includes devices such as desktop-PC, Unix workstations and laptops (Figure 4).

Type 2: the device can execute local code and can download/upload data. Smart-phones and PDA programmable in Java fall into this category [13] (Figure 5).

Type 3: the device can only download/upload data and can visualize the information by means of some pre-installed applications like a browser. VoiceXML browsers, WAP phones and WEB kiosks fall into this category (Figure 6).

6.2   The Service Viewer

In e-MATE, services can be accessed by means of a base component called "Service Viewer" (SV). All SV are committed to perform the following tasks: authentication of the user, loading of the device profile, discovery of portals and lookup of services, dynamic loading and execution of mobile code, generation on-the-fly of the user interface.

With respect to these requirements, the building blocks of any SV are:

Device Profile: this module contains any device relevant information like keyboard/pen availability, display size, color depth and position. Once the device profile is loaded, it is stored in the execution context.

Lookup Component: this module searches all portals available across the network by either multicast or unicast discovery protocols and allows the user to access to the services published in the portals.

Object Renderer: A device-independent model, that we call "Human Machine Interaction" (HMI), is translated at runtime by an appropriate module called Object Renderer into a concrete user interface. More details about interaction modeling are provided in (§6.3)

There is one implementation of Service Viewer for each category of devices. Next sections will discuss these implementations.

6.2.1 Service Viewer for Devices of Type 1

In the Service Viewer for devices of type 1 the mobile part of the service runs on the terminal and the device profile is loaded from a local file. The devices that fall into this category normally can display services with WIMP user interfaces and connect to the GPS via serial interface. The SV is a local application containing all the building blocks cited above. It generates a concrete user interface provided with windows, buttons and keyboard/mouse input modality.

6.2.2 Service Viewer for Devices of Type 2

In a device of type 2 the device cannot run mobile code and cannot directly connect to the portals nor to services, therefore the SV must be two-tiered. The local tier is a part of e-MATE that must be installed in the device before it can be used. It loads the device profile and connects to the GPS via serial interfaces. It is also provided with an object renderer implementation that translates the HMI into a concrete user interface. The remote tier performs the discovery of portals, the lookup and the execution of the mobile code. The communication between local tier and remote tier uses XML as application level protocol and HTTP as transport protocol.

6.2.3 Service Viewer for Devices of Type 3

In a device of type 3 the developer can install none of the SV modules so all the SV building blocks are remote (*Figure 2*).

The pre-installed browser, that is a third-party application bundled with the terminal and not part of e-MATE, queries the SV via HTTP and the response is translated into the appropriate markup language on-the-fly by means of translation processors. This category of devices cannot connect to a GPS system and, unless particular cases, the device profile must be built by the remote SV using the HTTP header data or other relevant user agent information.

6.3 Device Independent User Interfaces.

A way to manage the complexity in the design of user interfaces is through the Model-View-Control design pattern [8]. Such a pattern decomposes the system in a set of models which are strictly bound to the data either persistent or transient that are managed by the system and shared with the user. For each model, the designer can provide one or more views that give the user the perception of data objects and, eventually, the possibility to edit them. A peculiarity of device independent user interfaces is that we can, indeed, define device independent models but cannot define device independent views. Views are concrete "interactors" and must be defined by composing widgets belonging to a specific toolkit such as Swing, AWT, Tcl/Tk and so forth. e-MATE provides a framework to define and compose models (i.e. a string value is a model of a text object and can be part of an enclosing model such as the model of a form). Therefore, such a composition can be mapped at runtime into a structure of concrete and interactive objects by means of a "rendering process", performed by the Object Renderer Engine. In such a process widgets such as text fields, radio buttons and more sophisticated controls, are deployed in place of data they refer: strings, booleans and more complex data types.

The advantage of this approach is that the same model can be used from any channel for which is available a rendering engine.

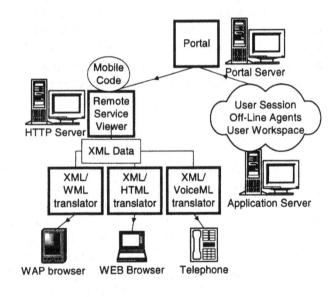

Figure 2. Service Viewer for devices of type 3

7. A Middleware to Deploy a Network of Services

The life-cycle of any e-MATE service comprises development, unit testing, deployment, and publication phases. Development is facilitated by the e-MATE service framework which allows the creation of new services by extension of core classes in such a way similar to the creation of a new Servlet starting from the Java Servlet API [14]. Once the service has been developed, it can be executed in a testing environment that provides a fake execution context, but nevertheless useful to accomplish the unit testing. Once the service has been tested, it is ready to be deployed and published by an appropriate serving unit called Application Server (AS) that provides the running environment for the service, the CPU time necessary to run the service itself and all its off-line agents, and the memory to manage the user sessions and to store persistently the session workspace.

Once the service is deployed, it must be published in order to be found by clients. An e-MATE network contains a number of servers dedicated to this scope that are called "portals". A portal can be discovered across the network by means of a multi-cast protocol or can be directly referenced using its host-name. The AS is committed to discover the portals and to publish the services that it runs. The portal metaphor allows making a weak categorization of services, and it is implemented in e-MATE exploiting a well known Java-based connection technology called Jini which implements multi-cast discovery, lookup protocols and dynamic code loading from remote hosts.

8. Conclusion

The rising pervasiveness of networks allows information system to provide to users the right information at the right time based on his physical location. In the paper, we first have identified issues raised by a very specific category of services. The services aimed at were mobile personalized and location-aware. Then we have described e-MATE. e-MATE provides original and open solutions to these issues. Mobility entails synchronous and asynchronous access to the services through heterogeneous channels and devices. The devices that are currently supported by e-MATE are desktop-computers, laptops, palm-top computers, and cellular phones. Personalization is implemented by algorithms and core objects that integrate user profile, the user location, geo-referenced information into a coherent perspective. Persistent user sessions enable to support asynchronous interactions. They are implemented as a workspace where agents may carry on their tasks even if the user is off-line. e-MATE also solved the issues related to the access to a MPLS through heterogeneous devices by personalization of the user interface according to user profile and device profile on the one hand, and by supporting various code distribution scheme, from fat-client to very thin ones, on the other hand. Tools and facilities are also available to service providers to deploy and publish their MPLS. Throughout the paper to make these issues more concrete and to give a glimpse to the solutions provided by e-mate, we used an application currently under implementation in the domain of "travel and leisure" in which the need for personalized and geo-referenced information seems to be critical. e-MATE is implemented in Java and XML. Presently we are designing and implementing the notion of dialogue into the user interface personalization process thanks to an abstract representation of the sequences of interactions. Other applications are also under investigation. We are also currently implementing the required middleware to provide for a service viewer for interactive digital TV.

Acknowledgements

The e-MATE project began in January 2000 at CRS4 and is funded by the Italian Government. Besides, we'd like to take this opportunity to thank all those people who have collaborated and supported this work: Manuela Angioni, Antonio Concas, Roberto Demontis, Emanuela De Vita, Massimo Deriu, Luc Hogie, Cristian Lai, Ivan Marcialis, Vladimiro Marras, Antonio Pintus, Andrea Piras, Raffaella Paola Sanna, Enrico Stara, Pietro Zanarini and Guido Zucconi.

References

[1] 3rd Generation Partnership Project; Technical Specification Group Terminals; Multimedia Messaging Service (MMS); Functional description; Stage 2 Release 1999

[2] Abowd, G.D., Atkeson, C.G., Hong, J., Long, S., Kooper, R., and Pinkerton, M. Cyberguide: A mobile context-aware tour guide. ACM Wireless Networks, 1997, 3:421-433.

[3] Arnold, K., (ed), The Jini(TM) Specifications. Addison-Wesley Pub Co, 2nd edition 2000; 688 pages

[4] Bluetooth. The Official Bluetooth Wireless Info Site. http://www.bluetooth.com

[5] Brickley, D., et al., RDF Specifications. Containing: Resource Description Framework(RDF) Schema and Resource Description Framework(RDF) Model and Syntax Specification, iUniverse.com; 2000, 136 pages, ISBN: 0595132308

[6] Cheverst, K., Davies, N., Mitchell, K., and Friday, A. Experiences of Developing and Deploying a Context-Aware Tourist Guide: The GUIDE Project. MOBICOM'2000, Boston, ACM Press., 2000.

[7] Drane, C., Macnaughtan, M., and Scott, C. Positioning GSM telephones. IEEE Communications Magazine, Volume: 36, Issue: 4 , April 1998, pp. 46 -54, 59.

[8] Gamma, E., Helm, R., Johnson, R., and Vlissides, J. Design Patterns: Elements of Reusable Object-Oriented Software. Addison-Wesley, Reading, MA, 1995.

[9] IEEE Standard for Information technology, Telecommunications and information exchange between systems, Local and metropolitan area networks, Specific requirements, Part 11: Wireless LAN Medium Access Control (MAC) and Physical Layer (PHY) Specifications, ANSI/IEEE Std 802.11, 1999 Edition

[10] Korte, G.B. The GIS Book. Onword Press. 414 pages. 1997.

[11] Moving Picture Expert Group. http://mpeg.telecomitalialab.com/index.htm

[12] Nilsson, N.J. Principles of Artificial Intelligence. Morgan Kaufmann Publishers, January 1994.

[13] Sun Microsystems, Inc. PersonalJavaTM Technology White Paper. August 1998. (Available at http://java.sun.com/products/personaljava/pj_white.pdf)

[14] Sun Microsystems, Inc. Java™Servlet Specification. Version: 2.2. Release: 12/17/99. (Available at http://java.sun.com)

[15] Szekely, P. Retrospective and Challenges for Model-Based Interface Development. In Proceedings of the 2nd International Workshop on Computer-Aided Design of User Interfaces, (Vanderdonckt, J. Ed.). Namur University Press, Namur, 1996.

[16] United States Department of Defense (1995). Global Positioning System Standard. Positioning Service Signal Specification. 2nd Edition, June 2, 1995.

[17] W3C. Composite Capabilities/Preference Profiles: Requirements and Architecture. Working Draft 21 July 2000. Available at:http://www.w3.org/TR/2000/WD-CCPP-ra-20000721/

[18] W3C. Device Independence Principles. Working Draft 18 September 2001. Available at: http://www.w3.org/TR/2001/WD-di-princ-20010918/

[19] W3C. Extensible Markup Language (XML) 1.0. 2nd Edition, October 6th, 2000.

SPECIFICATION AND IMPLEMENTATION OF MOBILE-AGENT-BASED DATA INTEGRATION

Peter Ahlbrecht and Jan Röver

Information Systems Group TU Braunschweig

P.O.box 3329, D-38023 Braunschweig

{p.ahlbrecht | j.roever}@tu-bs.de

Abstract   Mobile Agents provide a means of integrating heterogeneous data sources —different kinds of database systems as well as varying file types. In addition, they may be used to easily adjust a federation to incorporate new or dismantle old subsystems, to retrofit legacy systems and to adjust the schema of the federation. In this paper, we survey language constructs for the specification of mobile agent systems and use them to describe an architecture that demonstrates these features, illustrating it with an example application.

Keywords: data integration, mobile agents, distributed database techniques

1.   Introduction

A mobile agent is a proactive software object that has control over its own actions. It requires an execution environment which enables creation, execution, and migration of as well as communication between agents and other environments. It is able to sense its environment and can move from one location to another. In doing so, it is able to exploit some of the main characteristics of mobility: that separate locations possess different properties [27], and that barriers between these locations exist. Of course, these features apply to mobile systems in general [3], not only to mobile agents.

A lot of research has been done on how to integrate heterogeneous databases (e. g. [11, 18, 26]). However, already the point of whether it is possible to use such approaches to federate *databases* relying on different data models has been questioned [7], although this is considered possible [10]. Often inspired by WWW-related standards like HTML or XML, more recent work (e. g. [14, 22]) investigates means to integrate

H.-M. Haav and A. Kalja (eds.), Databases and Information Systems II, 269–283.

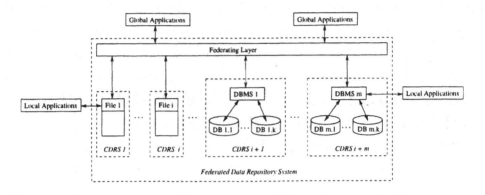

Figure 1. Basic architecture of a data repository system

heterogeneous *data sources.* We will follow this line and present an approach to extend integration to different data sources, namely databases and file types, based on mobile agents.

We will use *data repository systems* as the generic term to refer to database systems as well as to files. The basic architecture of a federated data repository system is shown in figure 1. Just like a federated database system it comprises several database systems, but, in addition, it also includes files of possibly different types. Assumptions and demands usually placed on federated database systems are adopted for federated data repository systems: the formerly stand-alone systems become component data repository systems (CDRSs) and make their data available to system-spanning applications. Nevertheless, they keep their autonomy to allow legacy applications to continue running.

Mobile agents provide a means of facilitating this continuity, as hosts for them may be added to indispensable legacy systems without intervening with the applications being used. Furthermore, qualities associated with mobile agents motivate their deployment: they adapt dynamically to their environment, they execute autonomously and asynchronously, they are naturally heterogeneous, and they encapsulate protocols [6, 17]. As we will see, these features ease augmenting and diminishing the federated system as well as adjusting its global schema.

In the next section, we will sum up features of mobile agents as well as approaches to data integration. Moreover, we shall also investigate language constructs for specifying mobile (agent) systems in order to establish the vocabulary and notation needed to describe the agent-based data integration system. Section 3 will deal with the architecture of the system, whereas section 4 will present a sample application. Finally, section 5 will conclude this survey and discuss future work.

2.   Preparatory Remarks

In the subsections of this section we shall give a brief overview of approaches to data integration. In doing so, we will focus on the terminology used. We shall also present preliminary material on agents and mobile agents, and survey language constructs for the specification of mobile (agent) systems in order to provide a suitable notation for mobile objects.

2.1   Approaches to Data Integration

When speaking of data integration in federated systems, first the types of data should be characterised. A first distinction is between *local data*, which only exists at a single component, and *global data*, for which related counterparts at other subsystems occur. This distinction can be refined to take into account whether the global, integrated entity subsumes all the attributes of all the local entities participating. Another difference can be made with regard to the question of whether the global data has to be available at every component, at exactly one, or at some but not at others. These features are sometimes referred to as *semantically equivalent, semantically disjoint* or *semantically overlapping* sets of objects, respectively [7].

Our application is concerned with integrating semantically equivalent sets of objects, where local entities do not match in all attributes, and we limited the integration to checking for equivalence constraints, i. e. the demand that, in case of replicated data, the values of the replicae be consistent.

According to [7], the main approaches to consistency protection [25] in data integration can be divided into two categories: one introduces an additional layer at each subsystem (e. g. [8]), and the other focuses on developing suitable protocols (e. g. [10]). The tasks of the additional layer are to maintain information on changes that need to be spread to other components via the federating layer, and to provide an interface to local applications that matches the one originally offered by the subsystem. The latter approach assumes a direct communication between components of the federation, for instance in the following way: the part responsible for the data repository at subsystem 1, *DR1*, informs the local communication facility, *CF1*, of a change $\Delta D1$ to the local data. *CF1* asks *CF2* to evaluate this change with respect to *CF2*'s local data, which passes the information to *DR2*, which in turn actually evaluates the query and returns the result to *CF2*. *CF2* passes the result on to *CF1* which raises an alarm in case the result indicates a violation of a global integrity constraint (*Indirect Remote Query* (IRQ) Protocol from [10]).

The $\Delta D1$ above represents all the modified data (inserted, deleted, or updated) at component 1. Similarly, $\Delta^+ D$ stands for all new values (inserts and after-images of updates) and $\Delta^- D$ for all old values (deletes and before-images) of some amount of data D.

2.2 Agents and Mobile Agents

With respect to the etymological meaning of "agent" as "a person who or thing which acts or exerts power" or "a person who acts for another in business, politics, etc." (e. g. [2]) two features are commonly associated with software agents and used to distinguish them from software objects. The first is *autonomy*, i. e. the capacity to control its own actions, and the second is *proactivity*, the ability to follow its own goals.

From the area of Artificial Intelligence concepts such as *belief, intention, desire* or *learning* are frequently related to agents [28], but as we are mainly interested in the impacts of mobility we refrain from these concepts and adopt an understanding of a mobile agent similar to the one in [16]: A mobile agent is a software object that has control over its own actions, is proactive, requires an execution environment, may sense its environment, and can move from one location to another. Non-mobile agents lack the last ability.

Mobile agents ultimately need a runtime environment supplied by *hosts*, which conform to some agent API or agent system. They enable creation, execution, and migration of and communication between agents and other hosts. In order to exploit mobility, usually a number of hosts will be used to provide a distributed agent environment. Useful and frequently found are logical groupings of several hosts into a superordinate unit, possibly corresponding to different agent systems being used, and of substructuring a host into distinguished subunits. A difference is often made between *strong* and *weak migration*, also referred to as *movement* and *remote execution*, respectively. The former is used to indicate that the mobile agent even retains its execution state when arriving at the target host. The latter signifies that only its operations and data will be identical, but execution has to start all over again—possibly governed by data values of the agent's attributes. For our application, however, we will not dwell upon this subject and merely use the term *migration*, knowing that IBM's Java-based ASDK API and Tahiti Aglet Server [16] used for implementation only support weak migration.

Another feature that distinguishes agents from software objects is "cloning". Apart from being known for objects, in the context of mobile agents it always denotes the method an agent uses to produce an exact copy of itself, i. e. including not only the same methods but also the same data and, if a distinction between strong and weak mobility is being made, also the same execution state. For *Properties* objects in Java, for example, the clone method does not copy the properties and their values to the clone.

2.3 Language Constructs for Specifying Mobile Systems

So far, most of the formal methods that treat the concept of mobility explicitly are process algebras, with the π-Calculus [20] being its most well-known representative. It adopts a notion of mobility that the area of movement is the space of linked processes in which the moving entities are the *links*. Instead of movement of processes the π-Calculus is rather concerned with the movement of *access* to processes.

A frequently mentioned argument in favour of mobile agents, however, is that in case a computation is expected to work on a large amount of data, it will be more efficient to move the computation to the data than to transfer the input to the computation and evaluate it locally [6, 17]. This argument may be extended to mobile systems in general: if performance of a system depends on its location then a model which captures mobility by movement of access may not be adequate. To represent such scenarios the Ambient Calculus [4] or the Algebra of Itineraries [19] seem to be better suited.

An ambient is a bounded named place where computation takes place. The boundary captures location-dependent qualities. Location is also explicitly represented in [19], which concentrates on providing means to model itineraries of movement in a flat structure of places. In contrast to this ambients can be nested. They may access each other when they are nested at the same level within the same super-ambient, and movement can be expressed by *capabilities* which allow them to enter, exit, and open another ambient if its name is known. The calculus distinguishes between subjective moves, which are initiated by the moving entity, and objective moves, which are imposed on it from outside.

This distinction allows to represent proactive movements of mobile agents as well as moves enforced on other objects. The Ambient Calculus can be used to encode the π-Calculus, and the latter has been shown to capture objects of object oriented languages and the way in which they interact [20], whereas other concepts of object orientation like inheritance, method overriding, and aggregation have not yet been covered.

The same applies to another formal approach, Mobile Unity [23], which is based on a computational model and proof system for parallel program design [5]. As in the Ambient Calculus, Mobile Unity provides means to explicitly represent location. In contrast to the former, this is achieved via a location attribute and constructs which reflect location dependency in communication, namely transient variable sharing and transient action synchronisation, which allow entities to share data and synchronise actions when in close proximity. It also extends the proof logic of [5], but does not cover features of object orientation at all.

As the currently most widespread semi-formal specification language, already the "basic" version of the Unified Modeling Language (UML) provides sufficient means to model mobile systems, as for example the package element can be used to group other elements like classes, objects etc. together, and the ≪become≫ stereotype is suited to express mobility [1, 13]. However, several extensions to the UML have been proposed to make the language more suitable for specifying agent and mobile agent systems and the special features ascribed to them, most of them elaborating new stereotypes and thereby exploiting the UML's extensibility mechanism [12, 21]. In order to be able to model features of both object orientation and mobile agents, we shall adopt this view and use the extensions and notations suggested in [15], which we will restrict and adjust to the features of mobile agents considered above.

The stereotype ≪mobile agent≫ characterises objects which may move between different locations that provide suitable environmental conditions to them, and these locations are marked with the stereotype ≪agency≫. Both are derived from the metamodel element *class*. Here, no further distinction between grouping facilities for agent environments is necessary.

The stereotype ≪migrate≫ corresponds to the ≪become≫ stereotype applied to the dependency symbol, with the additional meaning that the object's point in space which gives the source and target for the dependency is also a different one [1]. With respect to the ability of mobile agents to move as described above, we do not differentiate between strong or weak migration.

Finally, the ≪clone≫ stereotype characterises a dependency between a source and a target object in the way that the target represents an exact copy of the source. ≪clone≫ refines the *dependency* metamodel element as ≪migrate≫ does.

Figure 2.3 provides an overview of the extensions made to the UML and also shows the corresponding graphical notations.

Stereotype	Applies to symbol	Meaning	Graphical notation
mobile agent	class	Specifies a mobile agent class; a class, which instances can migrate from the system where they have been created to other systems that also provide an agency.	Agent name : Class
agency	class	Specifies a class that provides an execution environment for mobile agents; a context, where mobile agents can be created, destroyed, activated and deactived, where they can execute and migrate to and from.	Agency name : Class
migrate	dependency	Specifies that the target (B) is the same mobile agent as the source (A), but at a later point in time and a different point in space, possibly with different values, state, or roles.	A ⟶ B
clone	dependency	Specifies that the target (B) is an exact copy of the source (A), a mobile agent, with the same methods and identical values for its attributes.	A ⟶ B

Figure 2.   Extensions of the UML for modelling mobile agents

3.   Architecture

With the suitable vocabulary and notation at hand we shall now describe our architecture for facilitating data integration via mobile agents, and compare it to other approaches mentioned in the last section. As previously stated, we restrict our method to consistency constraints, namely equivalence constraints on replicated data. The frequently used example of keeping a company's address information up-to-date, with some employees managing their private files even though a corporate database, which is consulted by other employees, is available, should suffice to illustrate the potential of this application on the one hand, and the difficulties that have to be faced despite this restriction on the other.

As the fundamental part of the architecture an agent host has to be installed at every CDR of the federation. Next, an agent is set up at every component which computes the ΔDs for the replicated data stored at the local system and updates that data or rolls back such updates when requested to do so. In the following, we will refer to these agents as *Stationaries*, even though they are implemented as mobile agents. The rationale for this is that being mobile allows them to be created at one host and then be dispatched to another, while their main task requires them to stay put at the CDR they are sent to.

The requests to compute the ΔDs are sent to a *Stationary* by a truly mobile agent, *Traveller*, which migrates from host to host. As there is only one *Traveller* throughout the entire federation, miscoordinations are avoided—the architecture closely resembles a token ring structure.

The final part is taken by *Propagators*. An instance of this type of agent also has to be set up at every CDR. Once the *Stationary* has signalled the *Traveller* currently at its host that it has finished computing the updates, the *Traveller* informs the local *Propagator* instance. The latter then checks if updates need to be spread and, if so, sends clones of itself carrying that data to the other hosts. The *Propagator* receives the information about the target hosts from the *Traveller's* itinerary, and the *Traveller* keeps track of the *Propagators* leaving the site. Each clone transfers the data to its destination and informs the *Stationary* there about it. The *Stationary* then checks if relevant updates—which would need propagation—have also occurred locally in between, caused by local applications. If so, it informs the *Propagator* about it, which in turn passes the information on to the *Traveller* at the remote host. The *Traveller* then advises the other *Stationaries* to roll back the update last made and raises an alarm. This implies that any conflict has to be resolved by human interaction, which is, of course, feasible only if few changes raise a conflict. If no relevant updates are detected, the *Stationary* adopts the changes keeping $\Delta^- D$ (in case of a roll back, the $\Delta^+ D$ is provided by another *Propagator*), and the clone returns to the *Traveller*, informing it about the successful update. The *Traveller* adjusts its bookkeeping and disposes the *Propagator*. If all clones have returned, the *Traveller* moves on to the next target.

Figure 3 illustrates the propagation process for a successful update with a sequence diagram in the extended UML. It uses the notation suggested in [13] to express iteration in sequence diagrams: a repetition of messages is pooled together inside a rectangle, and a control expression for the loop is given at the lower part of it. In figure 3 this rectangle is merely adumbrated, as it would have to span all ≪agencies≫.

In our implementation the ΔDs are passed on from *Stationaries* to *Propagators* and back via files at the local host. However, a direct transfer from agent to agent or any other way should also be suitable. Also, instead of transferring the data *in* an agent some other way should suffice as well. We did not intend to develop any sophisticated new means, but as already the entire architecture was based on mobile agents, it seemed reasonable to try if they could be used for the transport, too. The approach follows a lazy group replication model: one replica is update and this change is propagated to other replicas asynchronously, and any CDRS can update its copy of a data item. According to [9], this will lead to performance problems as the system scales up.

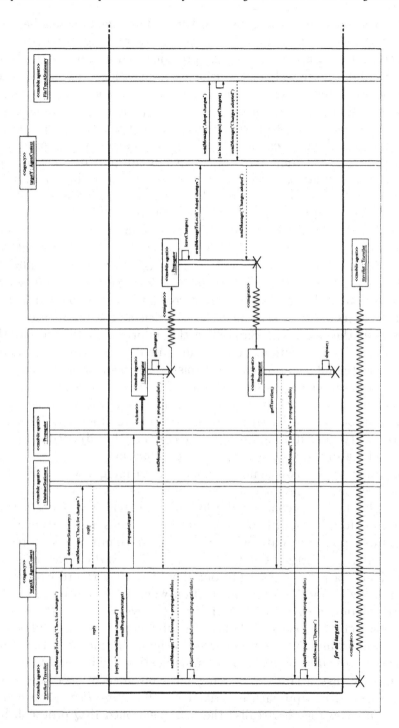

Figure 3. Sequence diagram of the propagation process for a successful update.

Our focus was to investigate whether mobile agents could be used to integrate different types of data sources, exploiting the feature of mobility that separate locations may provide separate properties. From the point of database technology, using an application program to check integrity constraints is clearly not a desirable method, but addressing files as data sources made it necessary. As [10] points out, components of a federation which do not provide a means to signal updates will require an additional polling mechanism to check for changes. Considering this and including files as sources of data, which do not provide a notification mechanism on updates, it was to be expected that a polling mechanism had to be implemented (the *Traveller*), and that a separate means to detect changes had to be developed (different *Stationaries*).

Nonetheless, the approach works, and it also allows to effortlessly adjust a federation to incorporate new or dismantle old component systems as well as to modify its schema through its mobile parts. As already mentioned, despite their names the *Stationaries* are mobile agents, which upon creation read information from a configuration file on which data source to access, which schema to use, which attributes to use as its key etc. In the same way they write this information to a file at the local host upon destruction. As they may be dispatched and retracted in between, the information can be adjusted when and where necessary. A *Stationary* can be disposed, leaving the federation-related information at its current location. The information can be changed, and a new *Stationary* can be created based on the modified data. Figure 4 illustrates this possibility. The itinerary of the *Traveller* may be adjusted similarly, and thereby also the targets for the *Propagator* clones.

Compared to the two main streams of data integration outlined in the last section, this architecture comprises elements of both ways, and accordingly should be considered a hybrid approach. The *Traveller* and *Propagators* form an additional layer which maintains information about transactions updating data which has related counterparts stored in other local repositories. On the one hand, the *Stationaries* can also be considered a part of the additional layer, as they record changes to local data by extracting that information when requested to do so. On the other hand, they form part of the local systems, directly providing access to data in case of file-based CDRs, computing the ΔDs, and partly establishing the communication facility. In addition, the *Traveller* and *Propagators* support the communication facility, and the *Traveller* directly instantiates the polling mechanism mentioned above for the protocol-based approach described in [10]. *Traveller, Propagators* and *Stationaries* together realise the aforementioned IRQ protocol, but

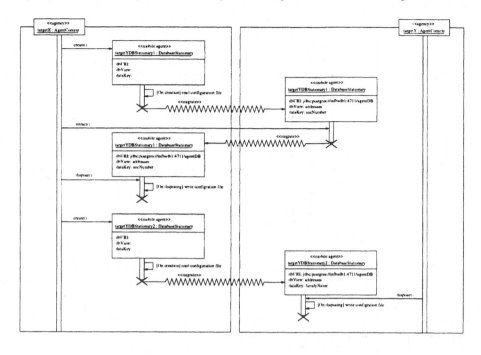

Figure 4. Sequence diagram of adjusting federation-related information.

the *Traveller*'s bookkeeping on the leaving and returning *Propagators* corresponds to the TBS and HC data structures of [8].

4.   Sample Application

As a sample application, we chose to integrate the information on special project and diploma theses, which are realised in cooperations between a university and some company of the industrial sector. A Postgres database is used to store the data on all the entities involved, while part of that data is also published via an HTML file, which also contains links to the theses themselves and additional sites. Due to these links on the one hand and the additional information kept in the database on the other, the implementation has to cope with semantically equivalent sets of objects with only partly matching attributes of the local object classes.

The area of application is that an institute of a university and a company cooperate, enabling students to do at least part of their student research project or diploma thesis outside the academic area. A thesis is usually related to one of the company's projects, which is realised by one or more of the company's organisational units. Various information

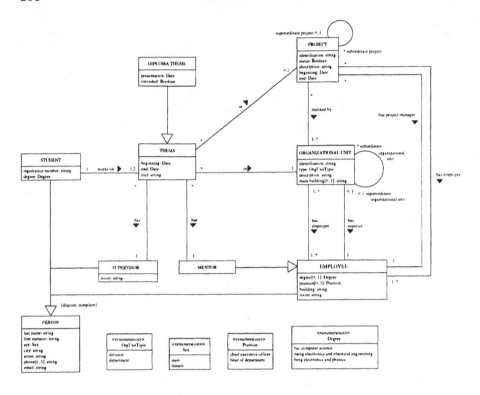

Figure 5. Class diagram for ThesisIS

need to be stored for the different entities, such as status, beginning, and end of a project or address information of the persons involved. Data on entities of the company might be relevant for students and supervisors of the university. Employees of the company might want to look up information on students involved in a project as well as on their supervisors, ranging from contact information for both students and supervisors to title and type of the students' theses.

An information system provides the different stakeholders with information about the other parties involved and supports the theses related work for the university tutors. Figure 5 shows the class diagram for the schema underlying the database. As a means of public relations, some of the information should also be published on the web.

The data of the HTML file and the database should be kept consistent, and admissible updates made to one should be propagated to the other. For example, the status will or the title of the thesis may change (up to a certain point). Thus, adjusting the web page (c. f. figure 6) should lead to a corresponding update of the database and vice versa.

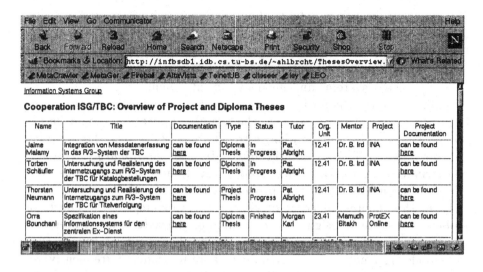

Figure 6. HTML file on Project and Diploma Theses

The implementation uses IBM's Java-based API Aglets Software Development Kit (ASDK) [16] and Tahiti Aglet Server, *aglet* being a portmanteau word combining *agent* and *applet*. The ASDK is not completely MASIF compliant, mostly because it uses its own protocol for agent transfer instead of CORBA. With regard to the development of mobile agents, Java supports two interesting features, namely object mobility via serialisation, and adaptability to changes via its reflection API. Moreover, ease of database access through JDBC [24] also promotes using Java, and the open source availability and ample documentation supported our decision to use the ASDK.

So far, we have implemented a *TravelAglet* and *TransportAglet* as the counterparts to the *Traveller* and *Propagator* of the architecture, respectively, and in order to access data a *DatabaseStationary, HTMLStationary,* and a *CsvASCIIStationary* (accessing files of comma separated values) have been realised.

The mechanism described in the last section allows to change the schema of the federation "on the fly", and also to add and remove subsystems, i. e. use any combination of database- or file-based components.

5. Conclusion and Future Work

The main contribution of this paper lies in introducing a way to federate heterogeneous data sources by mobile agents and showing that this approach also allows for effortless adjustments of the federation schema as well as augmenting or diminishing its member scope. We have provided a sample application using this architecture developed to keep HTML file and database data consistent. However, we have also summarised and illustrated possibilities of data integration, concepts related to mobile agent systems and means to specify them.

Similarly, our plans for future research are twofold. On the one hand, from the technical point of view, the sample application should be extended in order to provide dialogs to interactively adjust the itinerary and the schema. The possibilities of the *DatabaseStationary* should also be expanded. Up to now, it has used a view to access the database and is therefore limited to systems providing triggers or rule mechanisms.

From the theoretical point of view, we are looking at the effects of mobility on system design, i. e. determining characteristics of mobility, developing ways to represent them, and using these modelling techniques for mobile applications. For instance, another concept frequently related to mobile agents and mobile applications in general is *adaptability*, adjustment to changing environmental and communication conditions. Furthermore, a formal method that covers both features stemming from object orientation and mobility seems to be useful, too. One approach here may be to extend the Ambient Calculus accordingly.

References

[1] Booch, G., Rumbaugh, J., and Jacobson, I. The Unified Modeling Language User Guide. Addison–Wesley, 1999.

[2] Brown, L., editor. The New Shorter Oxford English Dictionary. Clarendon Press, 1993.

[3] Cardelli, L. Abstractions for Mobile Computing. In Secure Internet Programming, LNCS 1603, 1999.

[4] Cardelli, L. and Gordon, A.D. Mobile Ambients. In Foundations of Software Science and Computation Structures, LNCS 1378, 1998.

[5] Chandy, K.M. and Misra, J. Parallel Program Design: A Foundation. Addison-Wesley, 1988.

[6] Chess, D., Harrison, C., and Kershenbaum, A. Mobile Agents: Are They a Good Idea? LNCS, 1222, 1997.

[7] Conrad, S. Föderierte Datenbanksysteme. Springer, 1997. In german.

[8] Do, L. and Drew, P. Active Database Management of Global Data Integrity Constraints in Heterogeneous Database Environments. In Proc. of the 11th IEEE Int. Conf. on Data Engineering (ICDE'95). IEEE Computer Society Press, 1995.

[9] Gray, J., Helland, P., O'Neill, P., and Shasha, D. The Dangers of Replication and a Solution. In Proc. of the ACM SIGMOD Int. Conf. on Management of Data, 1996.

[10] Grefen, P. and Widom, J. Protocols for Integrity Constraint Checking in Federated Databases. Int. Journal of Distributed and Parallel Databases, 5(4), 1997.

[11] Heimbinger, D. and McLeod, D. A Federated Architecture for Information Management. ACM Transactions on Information Systems, 3(3), 1985.

[12] Heinze, C., Papasimeon, M., and Goss, S. Specifying Agent Behavior with Use Cases. In Design and Applications of Intelligent Agents, 2000.

[13] Hitz, M. and Kappel, G. UML@Work. dpunkt, 1999. In german.

[14] Kalinichenko, L.A. Integration of Heterogeneous Semistructured Data Models in the Canonical One. In Proc. of First Russian National Conference "Digital Libraries: Advanced Methods and Technologies, Digital Collections", 1999.

[15] Klein, C., Rausch, A., Sihling, M., and Wen, Z. Extension of the Unified Modeling Language for Mobile Agents. In Unified Modeling Language: System Analysis, Design and Development Issues. Idea Publishing Group, 2001.

[16] Lange, D.B. and Oshima, M. Programming and Deploying Java Mobile Agents with Aglets. Addison-Wesley, 1998.

[17] Lange, D.B. and Oshima, M. Seven Good Reasons for Mobile Agents. Communications of the ACM, 42(3), 1999.

[18] Litwin, W., Mark, L., and Roussopoulus, N. Interoperability of Multiple Autononous Databases. ACM Computing Survey, 22(3), 1990.

[19] Loke, S.W., Schmidt, H., and Zaslavsky, A. Programming the Mobility Behaviour of Agents by Composing Itineraries. LNCS, 1742, 1999.

[20] Milner, R. Communicating and Mobile Systems: the π-Calculus. Cambridge University Press, second edition, 2001.

[21] Odell, J., Parunak, H. v. D., and Bauer, B. Representing Agent Interaction Protocolls in UML. In Proceedings of AOIS-2000 at CAiSE*00, 2000.

[22] Pokorny, J. Integration and Interoperability of Data Sources: Forward into the New Century. In Proc. of BITWorld 2001, 2001.

[23] Roman, G.-C., McCann, P.J., and Plun, P.J. Mobile UNITY: Reasoning and Specification in Mobile Computing. In ACM Transactions on Software Engineering and Methodology 6, 1997.

[24] Saake, G. and Sattler, K.U. Datenbanken & Java: JDBC, SQLJ und ODMG. dpunkt, 2000. In german.

[25] Schewe, K.-D. and Thalheim, B. Achieving Consistency in Active Databases. In Fourth Int. Workshop on Research Issues in Data Engineering: Active Database Systems, 1994.

[26] Sheth, A.P. and Larson, J.A. Federated Database Systems for Managing Distributed, Heterogeneous, and Autonomous Databases. ACM Computing Surveys, 22(3), 1990.

[27] Thanh, D., Steensen, S., and Audestad, J.A. Mobility Management and Roaming with Mobile Agents. LNCS, 1818, 2000.

[28] Woolridge, M. and Jennings, N. Agent Theories, Architectures and Languages: A Survey. In Proc. of the ECAI-94 Workshop on Agent Theories, Architectures and Languages, 1995.

DATA MINING TECHNIQUES IN PREDICTING DEFAULT RATES ON CUSTOMER LOANS

Jozef Zurada

Computer Information Systems Department, College of Business and Public Administration, University of Louisville, Louisville, KY 40292, USA, email: jmzura01@louisville.edu

Abstract   The paper examines historical data from consumer loans issued by a financial institution to individuals that the financial institution deemed to be qualified customers. The data consists of the financial attributes of each customer and includes a mixture of loans that the customers paid off and defaulted upon. The paper uses three different data mining techniques (decision trees, neural networks, and logistic regression) and the ensemble model, which combines the three techniques, to predict whether a particular customer defaulted or paid off his/her loan. The paper then compares the effectiveness of each technique and analyzes the risk of default inherent in each loan and group of loans.

Keywords: neural networks, decision trees, logistic regression, loan-granting decision, credit worthiness, data mining, knowledge discovery, classification, prediction

1.   Introduction

Credit-risk evaluation decisions are inherently complex and unstructured due to the nonlinear relationships between independent variables that interact with each other and various forms of risks involved. The most harmful risk to the party approving credit is the nonpayment of obligations when they come due. Simultaneously, the payoff associated with a correct credit-risk decision is high. As a result, any improvement in making a reliable discrimination, between those who are likely to repay the loan and those who are not, would be highly desired.

This paper examines and compares the effectiveness of three data mining techniques and the ensemble model to predict whether a consumer defaulted or paid off a loan. From the original, highly unbalanced data set, which was dominated by good loans, we randomly selected several hundred good loans

H.-M. Haav and A. Kalja (eds.), Databases and Information Systems II, 285–296.
© 2002 *Kluwer Academic Publishers.*

and matched them with the same number of bad loans. As a result, the data set used in this study contained an equal mix of good loans and bad loans. The data mining techniques proved proficient at identifying both good loans and bad loans in the test set. The ensemble model, which combined decision trees, neural networks, and logistic regression techniques proved to be the most skillful at classifying the good loans and bad loans. The models were impressive at distinguishing good loans from bad loans given that the financial institution that provided the data considered all of the loans contained in the data set to be good loans warranting an extension of credit. The paper assesses and analyzes the probability of default on a single loan and a collection of loans.

The paper is organized as follows. Section 2 reviews the current literature. Section 3 covers decision trees, neural network, and logistic regression fundamentals. Section 4 describes the data sample used in this study. Section 5 presents the experiments and simulation results. Finally, section 6 concludes the paper and gives some recommendations for future work.

2.   Literature Review

The literature focusing on the usefulness of data mining tools and examining how these tools could be applied in a credit-risk assessment is abundant. For example, Barney and his colleagues analyzed the performance of neural networks and regression analyses in distinguishing between farmers defaulting on farmers Home Administration Loans [3]. Tessmer used decision tree-based inductive learning approach to refine the credit granting process based on the impact of Type I and Type II credit errors, as near misses, on the accuracy, stability and conceptual validity of the learning process [15]. Jagielska et al. used three data sets, including the credit approval data set, to investigate neural networks, fuzzy logic, genetic algorithms, rule induction software, and rough sets to automated knowledge acquisition for classification problems [8]. Piramuthu analyzed the beneficial aspects of using both neural networks and nuerofuzzy systems for credit-risk evaluation decisions [11]. In another paper, the same author proposed a new methodology based on the "blurring" measure for feature selection in the context of financial credit-risk evaluation decisions [12].

West investigated the credit scoring accuracy of five neural network architectures and compared them to traditional statistical methods [17]. Desai et al. explored the ability of neural networks and traditional techniques, such as discriminant analysis and logistic regression, in building credit scoring models in the credit union environment [5]. Adya and Collopy reviewed and evaluated the general effectiveness of neural networks at forecasting and prediction [1], and Thomas surveyed the techniques for forecasting financial risk of lending to consumers [16]. Glorfeld and Hardgrave presented a comprehensive and systematic approach to developing an optimal architecture of a neural network model for evaluating the creditworthiness of commercial loan applications [6]. Yang *et al.* examined the application of neural networks to an early warning system for loan risk assessment [18]. Finally, Zurada reported some preliminary results from investigating data mining techniques for loan-granting decisions [19], and Zurada *et al.* validated loan-granting decisions and predicted default rates on consumer loans [20].

3. Decision Trees, Neural Networks, and Logistic Regression Fundamentals

3.1. Decision Trees

Decision trees are particularly useful for classification tasks. Like neural networks, decision trees learn from data. Using search heuristics, decision trees are able to find explicit and understandable rules-like relationships among the independent and dependent variables. Search heuristics use recursive partitioning algorithms to split the original data into finer and finer subsets, or clusters. The algorithms have to find the optimum number of splits and determine where to partition the data to maximize the information gain. The fewer the splits, the more explainable the output is (there are less rules to understand).

Decision trees are built of nodes, branches and leaves that indicate the variables, conditions, and outcomes, respectively. The most predictive variable is placed at the top node of the tree. The operation of decision trees is based on the ID3 or C4.5 algorithms [10, 14]. The algorithms make the clusters at the node gradually purer by progressively reducing disorder (impurity) in the original data set. Disorder and impurity can be measured by the well-established measures of entropy and information gain borrowed from information theory. We briefly introduce these measures below.

Given a target attribute A taking on k different values from a collection of examples S, the entropy of S relative to this k-wise classification is defined as

$$Entropy(S) \equiv \sum_{i=1}^{k} - p_i \, log_2 \, p_i$$

The information gain, $Gain(S,A)$ of an attribute A, relative to a collection of examples S, is defined as

$$Gain(\,S,A\,) \equiv Entropy(\,S\,) - \sum_{v \in Values(\,A\,)} \frac{S_v}{S} Entropy(\,S_v\,)$$

where *Values(A)* is the set of all possible values for attribute *A*, and S_v is the subset of *S* for which attribute *A* has the value *v* (i.e., $S_v = \{ s \in S \mid A(s) = v \}$.

One of the most advantages of decision trees is the fact that knowledge can be extracted and represented in the form of classification if-then rules. Each rule represents a unique path from the root to each leaf. In addition, at each node, one can measure: the number of records entering the node, the way those records would be classified if these were leaf nodes, and the percentage of records classified correctly.

3.2. Artificial Neural Networks

Artificial neural networks are one of the most common data mining tools, and they have attracted the attention of researchers from business. Neural networks have a wide array of applications. They are particularly useful for the tasks of classification, prediction, and clustering. They try to emulate biological neurological systems. In other words, they try to mimic the way the human brain functions and processes information. Neural network models are characterized by three properties: the computational property, the architecture of the network, and the learning property [7].

Computational property. Neural networks are built of neurons or nodes, which are simple processing elements. Each neuron contains a summation node and nonlinear sigmoidal activation function of the form $f(\,n\,) = \dfrac{1}{1 + e^{-\lambda n}}$, where $n = \mathbf{Wp}$ is the output from a summation node; λ is the steepness of the activation function; $\mathbf{W}$ is a weight matrix and $\mathbf{p}$ is an input vector. Because a single neuron has a limited capability, neurons (sometimes hundreds) are organized in layers and are interconnected between layers using connections called weights. Each weight carries a numerical value that represents the strength of connection or expresses the relative importance of each input to the neuron.

Architecture. Neural networks come in several architectures. One of the most common architectures used in financial applications is a two-layer feed-forward network with error back-propagation. This network typically has only two layers, a hidden layer and an output layer. Signals propagate through these layers from input to output.

Learning. Neural networks use a variety of learning modes. These are supervised learning, unsupervised learning, and reinforcement learning. During supervised learning, which is the most common for the mentioned feed-forward networks, weights are initialized at small random values and training patterns are presented to the network (one at a time). The output produced by the training pattern is compared with the actual response provided by a teacher. The differences modify the weights of the network to make them closer to the actual output. This process is repeated for all training patterns contained in a training set until the cumulative error between the actual outputs and the network's output is reduced to a small value. Weights are crucial to the operation of the neural network because through their repeated adjustment the neuron (or network) learns. Knowledge of the network is encoded in its weights.

Features. Neural networks can be implemented as simple computer programs that build models or relationships from data by trial and error. Software that implements different learning architectures and learning algorithms is widely available on the market and became an integral part of the software packages used for data mining. The most attractive features of these networks are their ability to adapt, generalize, and learn from training patterns. These features are not present in modern conventional computers whose processing is based on precise algorithms converted to computer programs. One of the main drawbacks of neural networks is the fact that they produce black box outcomes. In other words, the results generated by a network cannot easily be explained or converted to if-then rules. Although neural networks can approximate very complex nonlinear functions, the explicit equation of these functions that the network learns to classify data is unknown.

3.3.   Logistic Regression Model

The purpose of the logistic regression model is to obtain a regression equation that could predict in which of two or more groups an object could be placed. The logistic regression also attempts to predict the probability that a binary or ordinal target will acquire the event of interest as a function of one or more independent variables. The logistic model is represented by the logistic response function $P(y)$ of the form:

$$P(y) = \frac{1}{1+e^{-z}}, \text{ where } z = b_0 + \sum_{i=1}^{m} b_i x_i.$$

The function $P(y)$ describes a dependent variable y containing two or more qualitative outcomes. z is the function of m independent variables x called predictors, and b represents the parameters. The x variables can be categorical or continuous variables of any distribution. The value of $P(y)$ that varies from 0 to 1 denotes the probability that a dependent variable y belongs to one of two or more groups. The principal of maximum likelihood can commonly be used to compute estimates of the b parameters. This means that the calculations involve an iterative process of improving approximations the estimates until no further changes can be made. For a more detailed explanation see [2, 4, 9].

Unlike neural networks, logistic regression models are designed to predict one dependent variable at a time. On the positive side, one can note that logistic regression output provides statistics on each variable included in the model. Researchers then can analyze these statistics to test the usefulness of specific information.

4.   Data Set Used in the Study

Desai *et al.* used 18 predictor variables and three data sets to assess the ability of neural networks and logistic regression to classify good and bad loans [5]. Each data set contained about 900 observations describing ordinary customers of three credit unions. West used German credit scoring data that contained 24 predictor variables and consisted of 700 examples of creditworthy applicants and 300 examples where credit should not be extended [17]. The Australian scoring data used by Quinlan are similar but more balanced with 307 and 383 examples of each outcome [13].

In our study we used similar qualitative variables to the ones used in the mentioned papers. We used a sample data set that contains 13 variables and 3364 observations provided by one of a money lending institution. The data set contains information about the customers whom a bank has extended a loan in the past. It consists of 3064 and 300 observations that represent good loans and bad loans, respectively. Out of 3364 applicants, about 9% have defaulted. There were no missing values in the data set. Out of these 13 variables, there were 12 independent variables and one dependent/target variable that we were going to predict.

Using this data set, we built a decision tree model, a neural network model, a logistic regression model, and a combined (ensemble) model to predict whether a future applicant will default on a loan. The independent variable, which was the target variable, could take values of 1 (client defaulted on loan or seriously delinquent) or 0 (loan repaid). For more details about the dependent variables, see [19, 20].

5.   Experiments and Results

From the original, highly unbalanced data set, we randomly selected 300 good loans from 3064 good loans and matched them with 300 bad loans. The sampling reduced the data set size to 600 cases equally divided into cases with good and bad loans. We allocated 60%, 20%, and 20% for the training, validation, and test set, respectively. We employed three data mining tools such as neural networks, decision trees, and logistic regression. Finally, to increase the reliability of the classification accuracy, we used an ensemble (combined) model by combining the three tools and measured its classification accuracy. The ensemble (combined) model is used to improve the stability of the three disparate non-linear models to form a potentially stronger solution. It averages the posterior probabilities for class target variable BAD from the three tools. Given the posterior probabilities, each case can be classified into the most probable class.

Table 1 shows the classification rates for the test set containing 120 observations in which the good and bad loans are almost equally represented. The ensemble model appeared to be the best in the overall classification accuracy (79.2%) and in classifying bad loans (79.7%). Generally, the regression model performed the worst. Two-tailed proportional z-tests found some significant differences in the classification accuracy rates between the regression and ensemble models, and the regression and decision tree models. The data in Table 1 reveal that the combined tool is effective in classifying bad loans as well as good loans.

Table 1. Classification accuracy rates for the four models. It shows the percentage and number of test cases classified correctly. * The ensemble model's overall classification rate was significantly better than logistic regression at $\alpha=0.1$. ** The decision tree classified good loans significantly better than logistic regression at $\alpha=0.05$.

	Decision Tree	Neural Network	Logistic Regression	Ensemble Model
"Overall"	76.7% (92/120)	72.5% (87/120)	70.8% (85/120)*	79.2% (95/120)*
"Good"	83.6% (51/61)**	73.8% (45/61)	68.9% (42/61)**	78.7% (48/61)
"Bad"	69.5% (41/59)	71.2% (42/59)	72.9% (43/59)	79.7% (47/59)

Because one can extract simple and understandable if-then rules from a decision tree and a money lending institution has to explain the reasons for which the loan was denied to the customer, the output from the combined tool may be complemented by the rules generated by the decision tree. Some of the rules based on the training data set generated by this decision tree are as follows:

(1) IF (Debt-to-income ratio $\geq$ 42.625) THEN
    (The loan good and bad 6.2% and 93.8% of the time, respectively)
(2) IF (Age of oldest trade line in months > 86.51) AND
    (Value of current property > \$47,546.5) AND
    (Number of delinquent trade lines < 0.5) AND
    (Debt-to-income ratio < 42.625) THEN
    (The loan was good and bad 80.6% and 19.4% of the time,
    respectively)

To evaluate the performance of the four methods on the test data set, it is advisable to use a combination of the following charts: the % cumulative and non-cumulative response chart, the lift chart, the response threshold chart, and the receiver operating characteristics chart. In addition to the classification rate of the four models presented in Table 1, these charts provide a valuable perspective that enables one to evaluate the strength of the models and perform a more thorough analysis of the results.

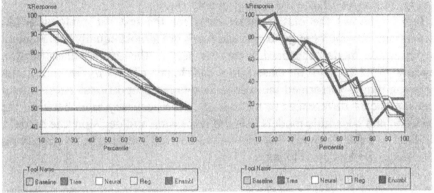

Figure 1. Cumulative (left) and Non-cumulative (right) Percent Response Charts for the four methods. Target event: 1 (bad loans).

The cumulative percent response chart (Figure 1) arranges defaulters into percentiles based on their predicted probability of response, and then plots the actual percentage of defaulters. (A defaulter is defined as an individual who defaults on a loan (BAD=1).) One sees that the neural network model is worse than the three remaining models. The first 10% decile contains a very large number of defaulters -- the three models predicted that between 92% and 95% of individuals had defaulted on their loans. In the top 20%, the ensemble model identified 98% of those who defaulted on a loan. The horizontal 50% line represents the percentage of defaulters that one would expect if one were to take a random sample. The non-cumulative plot shows the percentage of defaulters in each decile. The cumulative and non-cumulative lift charts (Figure 2) plot essentially the same information but on a different scale. The lift values vary from about 1.4 to 1.95 for the four models. The chart shows that the predicted power of the four models drops to the 50% baseline (lift=1) between the fifth and the seventh deciles. By the seventh decile the models permanently drop below the baseline's 50% default baseline and remain at roughly 0.5 lift value for the last three deciles.

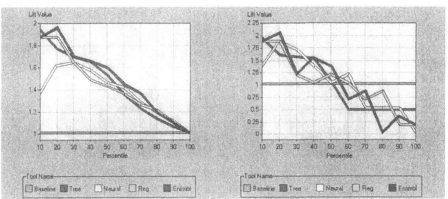

Figure 2. Cumulative (left) and Non-cumulative (right) Lift Charts for the four methods. Target event: 1 (bad loans).

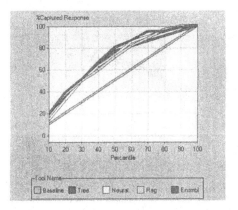

Figure 3. Cumulative Percent Captured Response Chart for the four methods. Target event: 1 (bad loans).

The % captured response chart (Figure 3) depicts the total number of defaulters in a particular bin. For example, if one wanted to eliminate the first and second deciles of customers, the total number of defaulters would drop by about 36-40%. The straight response line represents the response rate that one would obtain by not using a model (or the rate of defaulters that one would expect if one were to take a random sample). For example, if one takes a random sample of 50% of the data, one would expect to capture 50% of the defaulters. The choice of the final model(s) may depend on the proportion of individuals that one has chosen for action. When comparing several models on the same proportion of the data, the model with the higher lift is often preferred. The response threshold charts (Figure 4) display the prediction accuracy of the target event level across a range of threshold values. The threshold value is the cutoff value that is used to classify an observation based on the posterior probabilities of each event level. This type of assessment chart helps one to determine model consistency.

294

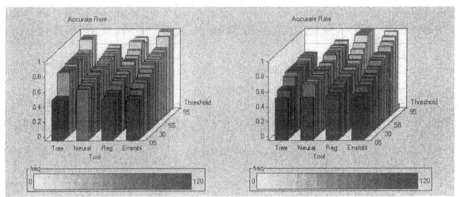

Figure 4. The Response Threshold Charts for the four Methods. Left chart: target event - 1 (bad loans). Right chart: target event - 0 (good loans).

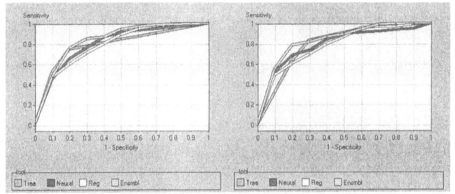

Figure 5. Sensitivity as a function of 1-specificity for the four methods. Left chart: target event - 1 (bad loans). Right chart: target event - 0 (good loans).

The performance quality of the models is demonstrated by the degree to which the receiver operating characteristics (ROC) curves push upward and to the left. The shapes of the ROC charts (Figure 5) indicate that the predictive power all four models (decision tree, neural network, regression analysis, and combined model), for differentiating between loans that will be paid off and loans that customer will default on, is good. The ensemble model seems to be the most effective in predicting good and bad loans, whereas the regression model appears to be the worst. For more detailed analysis of the results see [19, 20].

6.   Conclusion

Of the four models used, the ensemble model appears to be the best in classifying loans into good and bad loans. One must keep in mind that all of the bad loans included in the sample are close cases because these bad loans were granted to customers by the financial institution providing the data. In practice, faced with a mixture of clear-cut cases and close cases, the four models are likely to classify good and bad loans even more precisely. In addition to predicting whether a loan is good or bad, the data mining techniques also provided valuable statistical information that would allow a financial institution to adjust its lending policies to avoid groups of high-risk consumers. A financial institution would be able to determine the probability of default by a potential customer based on which decile that customer falls into and evaluate whether the risk of default justifies potential profit on the loan. Conversely, the bank could attract more low risk customers by offering more favorable terms to those customers who fall into the higher percentiles. The classification properties of the data mining tools presented in this article complemented by the statistical information derived from these data mining techniques provide a wealth of knowledge. This knowledge would allow a financial institution to cut losses by eliminating many bad loans and increase profits by instantly recognizing the risk presented by each customer in relation to potential gain.

References

[1] Adya, M., and Collopy, F. How Effective are Neural Networks at Forecasting and Prediction? A Review and Evaluation, Journal of Forecasting, 1998, Vol. 17, pp. 481-495.

[2] Afifi, A.A., and Clark, V.   Computer-Aided Multivariate Analysis, Van Nostrand Reinhold Co., New York, 1990.

[3] Barney, D.K., Graves, O.F., and Johnson, J.D. The Farmers Home Administration and Farm Debt Failure Prediction, Journal of Accounting and Public Policy, 1999, Vol. 18, pp. 99-139.

[4] Christensen R. Log-Linear Models and Logistic Regression, Springer, New York, 1997.

[5] Desai, V.S., Crook, J.N., and Overstreet, G.A. Jr. A Comparison of Neural Networks and Linear Scoring Models in the Credit Union Environment, European Journal of Operation Research, Vol. 95, pp. 24-37.

[6] Glorfeld, L.W., and Hardgrave, B.C. An Improved Method for Developing Neural Networks: The Case of Evaluating Commercial Loan Credit Worthiness, Computer & Operations Research, 1996, Vol. 23, No. 10, pp. 933-944.

[7] Hagan, M.T., Demuth, H.B., and Beale, M. Neural Network Design, PWS Publishing Company, 1996.

[8] Jagielska, I., Matthews, C., and Whitfort, T. An Investigation into the Application of Neural Networks, Fuzzy Logic, Genetic Algorithms, and Rough Sets to Automated Knowledge Acquisition for Classification Problems, Neurocomputing, 1999, Vol. 24, pp. 37-54.

[9] Manly, B.F. Multivariate Statistical Methods: A Primer, Chapman & Hall, London, 1994.

[10] Mitchell, T.M. Machine Learning, WCB/McGraw-Hill, Boston, Massachusetts, 1997.

[11] Piramuthu, S. Financial Credit-Risk Evaluation with Neural and Neurofuzzy Systems, European Journal of Operational Research, 1999, Vol. 112, pp. 310-321.

[12] Piramuthu, S. Feature Selection for Financial Credit-Risk Evaluation Decisions, INFORMS Journal on Computing, 1999, Vol. 11, No. 3, pp. 258-266.

[13] Quinlan, J.R. Simplifying Decision Trees, International Journal of Man-Machine Studies, 1987, Vol. 27, pp. 221-234.

[14] Quinlan, J.R. C4.5: Programs for Machine Learning, Morgan Kaufman Publishers, San Mateo, California, 1993.

[15] Tessmer, A.C. What to Learn from Near Misses: An Inductive learning Approach to Credit Risk Assessment, Decision Sciences, 1997, Vol. 28, No. 1, pp. 105-120.

[16] Thomas, L.C. A Survey of Credit and Behavioral Scoring: Forecasting Financial Risk of Lending to Consumers, International Journal of Forecasting, 2000, Vol. 16, 149-172.

[17] West, D. Neural Network Credit Scoring Models, Computers & Operations Research, 2000, Vol. 27, pp. 1131-1152.

[18] Yang, B., Li, L.X., Ji, H., and Xu, J. An Early Warning System for Loan Risk Assessment Using Artificial Neural Networks, Knowledge-Based Systems, 2001, Vol. 14, pp. 303-306.

[19] Zurada, J. Comparison of the Performance of Several Data Mining Techniques for Loan-Granting Decisions, The Proceedings of the Tenths International Conference on Information Systems Development, England, London, September 2001, (in press).

[20] Zurada, J., and Zurada, M. Validating Loan-Granting Decisions and Predicting Default Rates on Consumer Loans, accepted to The Review of Business Information Systems, Western Academic Press, Littleton, Colorado, USA, 2002.

EFFICIENT CONSTRAINT-BASED SEQUENTIAL PATTERN MINING USING DATASET FILTERING TECHNIQUES

Tadeusz Morzy, Marek Wojciechowski, and Maciej Zakrzewicz
Poznan University of Technology, Institute of Computing Science
ul. Piotrowo 3a, 60-965 Poznan, Poland

Abstract   Basic formulation of the sequential pattern discovery problem assumes that the only constraint to be satisfied by discovered patterns is the minimum support threshold. However, very often users want to restrict the set of patterns to be discovered by adding extra constraints on the structure of patterns. Data mining systems should be able to exploit such constraints to speed-up the mining process. In this paper we discuss efficient constraint-based sequential pattern mining using dataset filtering techniques. We show how to transform a given data mining task into an equivalent one operating on a smaller dataset. We present an extension of the GSP algorithm using dataset filtering techniques and experimentally evaluate performance gains offered by the proposed method.

Keywords: data mining, sequential patterns

1.   Introduction

Data mining aims at discovery of useful patterns from large databases or data warehouses. One of the data mining methods is sequential pattern discovery introduced in [2]. Informally, sequential patterns are the most frequently occurring subsequences in sequences of sets of items.

Among many proposed sequential pattern mining algorithms, most of them are designed to discover all sequential patterns exceeding a user-specified minimum support threshold. Some of them (e.g. *GSP* [8]) also allow users to specify time constraints to be taken into account when checking whether a given data-sequence contains a given subsequence.

H.-M. Haav and A. Kalja (eds.), Databases and Information Systems II, 297–309.
© 2002 *Kluwer Academic Publishers.*

However, very often users are interested in patterns that satisfy more sophisticated criteria, for example concerning size or contents of patterns. Data mining tasks involving various types of constraints can be regarded as data mining queries [5].

It is obvious that additional pattern structure constraints can be verified in a post-processing step, after all patterns exceeding a given minimum support threshold have been discovered. Nevertheless, such a solution cannot be considered satisfactory since users providing advanced pattern selection criteria may expect that the data mining system will exploit them in the mining process to improve performance. In other words, the system should concentrate on patterns that are interesting from the user's point of view, rather than waste time on discovering patterns the user has not asked for [4].

Very little work concerning constraint-driven sequential pattern discovery has been done so far. In fact, only the algorithms from the *SPIRIT* family [3] exploit pattern structure constraints in order to improve performance. These algorithms can be seen as extensions of *GSP* using advanced candidate generation and pruning techniques. In the *SPIRIT* framework, pattern constrains are specified as regular expressions, which is an especially convenient method if a user wants to significantly restrict the structure of patterns to be discovered. It has been shown that pushing regular expression constraints deep into the mining process can reduce processing time by more than an order of magnitude. Nevertheless, it appears that further research on constraint-based sequential pattern mining is needed.

We claim that techniques applicable to constraint-driven pattern discovery can be classified into the following groups:
- post-processing (filtering out patterns that do not satisfy user-specified pattern constraints after the actual discovery process);
- candidate filtering (application of pattern constraints to reduce the number of processed candidates);
- dataset filtering (restricting the source dataset to objects that can possibly support patterns that satisfy user-specified pattern constraints).

In the context of sequential pattern mining, candidate filtering techniques are represented by the *SPIRIT* algorithm family, whereas dataset filtering techniques have not been considered before. Dataset filtering techniques have been first proposed for efficient constraint-based discovery of association rules. However, due to different pattern constraints and the presence of time constraints, adaptation of these techniques to sequential pattern discovery is not straightforward.

In this paper we present new dataset filtering techniques to be used in the context of sequential pattern discovery. We identify pattern constraints that can be pushed down to dataset selection queries, which leads to a transformed data mining task on a smaller dataset but equivalent in terms of resulting sequential patterns. The proposed techniques can be integrated with any sequential pattern discovery algorithm. We present an efficient way of integrating the dataset filtering techniques with *GSP*, and experimentally evaluate performance gains in comparison with the original *GSP* algorithm.

1.1 Sequential Patterns

Let $L = \{l_1, l_2, ..., l_m\}$ be a set of literals called *items*. An *itemset* is a non-empty set of items. A *sequence* is an ordered list of itemsets and is denoted as $<X_1 X_2 ... X_n>$, where X_i is an itemset ($X_i \subseteq L$). X_i is called an *element* of the sequence. The *size* of a sequence is the number of items in the sequence. The *length* of a sequence is the number of elements in the sequence.

We say that a sequence $X = <X_1 X_2 ... X_n>$ is a *subsequence* of a sequence $Y = <Y_1 Y_2 ... Y_m>$ if there exist integers $i_1 < i_2 < ... < i_n$ such that $X_1 \subseteq Y_{i_1}, X_2 \subseteq Y_{i_2}, ..., X_n \subseteq Y_{i_n}$. We call $<Y_{i_1} Y_{i_2} ... Y_{i_n}>$ an *occurrence* of X in Y.

Given a sequence $Y = <Y_1 Y_2 ... Y_m>$ and a subsequence X, X is a *contiguous* subsequence of Y if any of the following conditions hold: 1) X is derived from Y by dropping an item from Y_1 or Y_m. 2) X is derived from Y by dropping an item from an element Y_i which has at least 2 items. 3) X is a contiguous subsequence of X', and X' is a contiguous subsequence of Y.

Let D be a set of variable length sequences (called *data-sequences*), where for each sequence $S = <S_1 S_2 ... S_n>$, a timestamp is associated with each S_i. With no time constraints we say that a sequence X is *contained* in a data-sequence S if X is a subsequence of S. We consider the following user-specified time constraints while looking for occurrences of a given sequence in a given data-sequence: minimal and maximal gap allowed between consecutive elements of an occurrence of the sequence (called *min-gap* and *max-gap*), and time window that allows a group of consecutive elements of a data-sequence to be merged and treated as a single element as long as their timestamps are within the user-specified *window-size*.

The *support* of a sequence $<X_1 X_2 ... X_n>$ in D is the fraction of data-sequences in D that contain the sequence. A *sequential pattern* (also called a *frequent sequence*) is a sequence whose support in D is above the user-specified minimum support threshold.

1.2 Review of the GSP Algorithm

The *GSP* algorithm, introduced in [8], exploits the following property: all contiguous subsequences of a frequent sequence also have to be frequent. *GSP* makes multiple passes over the data. During the first pass the support of each item is counted. At the end of the first pass, the set of frequent items (equivalent to the set of 1-element frequent sequences) is known. In each subsequent iteration, new potentially frequent sequences, called *candidate* sequences, are generated from the frequent sequences found in the previous pass. Each candidate sequence has one more item than frequent sequences from the previous iteration. In each iteration, the source dataset is scanned to evaluate the support of the candidate sequences and determine which candidates are actually frequent. The algorithm terminates when there are no candidates generated or if none of the candidates turns out to be frequent.

1.3 Related Work

Constraint-driven mining was extensively studied in the context of association rules [6, 9, 10]. The key step in association rule mining is discovery of frequent itemsets. Techniques of constraint-driven discovery of association rules proposed so far apply two kinds of optimizations: generating only frequent itemsets that can lead to rules satisfying the constraints, and restricting the source collection of sets to those which can contain such itemsets. However, because of the presence of time dependencies and time constraints in case of sequential pattern mining, direct adaptation of techniques proposed for association rules is not possible, or at least not sufficient.

Most of the research on sequential patterns focused on introducing new algorithms, more efficient than *GSP* (e.g. *PrefixSpan* [7]). However, the novel methods do not handle time constraints. Thus, *GSP* still remains the most general sequential pattern discovery algorithm and the reference point for new methods and techniques.

2. Pushing Pattern Constraints into Dataset Selection Queries

In constraint-based sequential pattern mining, we identify the following classes of constraints: database constraints, pattern constraints, and time constraints. Database constraints are used to specify the source dataset. Pattern constraints specify which patterns are interesting and should be returned by the query. Finally, time constraints influence the process of checking whether a given data-sequence contains a given pattern. The basic formulation of the sequential pattern discovery problem introduces three time constraints: max-gap, min-gap, and time window, and assumes only one pattern constraint (the minimum support threshold). We model pattern constraints as complex Boolean predicates having the form of a conjunction of the following basic Boolean predicates on patterns and pattern elements:

- π(**SPG**, α, pattern) - true if pattern support is greater than α, false otherwise;
- π(**SL**, α, pattern) - true if pattern size is less than α, false otherwise;
- π(**SG**, α, pattern) - true if pattern size is greater than α, false otherwise;
- π(**LL**, α, pattern) - true if pattern length is less than α, false otherwise;
- π(**LG**, α, pattern) - true if pattern length is greater than α, false otherwise;
- π(**C**, β, pattern) - true if β is a subsequence of the pattern, false otherwise;
- π(**NC**, β, pattern) - true if β is not a subsequence of the pattern, false otherwise;
- π(**SL**, α, pattern$_n$) - true if the size of the n-th element of the pattern is less than α, false otherwise;
- ρ(**SG**, α, pattern$_n$) - true if the size of the n-th element of the pattern is greater than α, false otherwise;
- ρ(**C**, γ, pattern$_n$) - true if γ is a subset of the n-th element of the pattern, false otherwise;
- ρ(**NC**, γ, pattern$_n$) - true if γ is not a subset of the n-th element of the pattern, false otherwise.

We believe that the above list of predicates is sufficient to allow users to express their pattern selection criteria. For simplicity's sake, in length and size predicates we consider only sharp inequalities.

Dataset filtering techniques consist in discarding data-sequences that cannot support any pattern satisfying pattern constraints specified by a user. There are two questions that have to be answered. Firstly, basic Boolean predicates concerning patterns or pattern elements whose presence in pattern constraints of a sequential pattern query leads to the possibility of dataset filtering have to be identified. Secondly, for each of the applicable basic Boolean pattern predicates, the corresponding predicate concerning data-sequences has to be provided.

Before we present theorems describing relationships between predicates concerning patterns or pattern elements and properties of data-sequences that can possibly support patterns satisfying these predicates, we have to introduce basic Boolean predicates concerning data-sequences to be used for dataset filtering:

- σ(**SG**, α, sequence) – true if the size of the data-sequence is greater than α, false otherwise;
- σ(**LG**, α, sequence) – true if the length of the data-sequence is greater than α, false otherwise;
- σ(**C**, β, sequence, maxgap, mingap, window) – true if the data-sequence contains the sequence forming the pattern β using given time constraints, false otherwise;

- $\sigma(\mathbf{CS}, \alpha, \text{sequence, window})$ - true if there exists a 1-element sequence of size α that is contained in the sequence with respect to the window-size constraint, false otherwise;
- $\sigma(\mathbf{CL}, \alpha, \text{sequence, maxgap, mingap, window})$ - true if there exists a sequence of length α that is contained in the sequence with respect to the max-gap, min-gap, and window-size constraints, false otherwise.

Theorem 1 Sequential patterns of size greater than k cannot be supported by a data-sequence whose size is not greater than k.

Proof: The proof is obvious since an occurrence of a pattern in a sequence must consist of the same number of items as the pattern.

Theorem 2 Sequential patterns of length greater than k, to be returned by a data mining query, can be supported only by data-sequences which contain some sequence of length $k+1$ using max-gap, min-gap, and window-size specified in the query.

Proof: Each sequential pattern of length greater than k has at least one contiguous subsequence of length $k+1$. If a data-sequence contains some sequence, it contains every contiguous subsequence of that sequence. Thus, if a data-sequence contains some sequence of length greater than k, it contains at least one sequence of length $k+1$.

Theorem 3 Sequential patterns, to be returned by a data mining query, containing a given sequence can be supported only by data-sequences containing that sequence using min-gap and window-size specified in the query, and max-gap of $+\infty$.

Proof: If a data-sequence contains some sequence using certain values of max-gap, min-gap, and window-size, it also contains every contiguous subsequence of the sequence, using the same time constraints. If max-gap is set to $+\infty$, a data-sequence containing some sequence contains all its subsequences.

Theorem 4 Sequential patterns, to be returned by a data mining query, whose n-th element has the size greater than k can be supported only by data-sequences which contain some 1-element sequence of size $k+1$ using window-size specified in the query.

Proof: Each 1-element subsequence of any sequence is its contiguous subsequence (from the definition of a contiguous subsequence). If any element of a sequence has the size greater than k, the sequence has at least one 1-element contiguous subsequence of size $k+1$. If a data-sequence contains some sequence, it contains every contiguous subsequence of that sequence. Thus, if a data-sequence contains some sequence whose n-th element has the size greater than k, it has to contain some 1-element sequence of size $k+1$.

Theorem 5 Sequential patterns, to be returned by a data mining query, whose n-th element contains a given set can be supported only by data-sequences which contain a 1-element sequence having the set as the only element, using time constraints specified in the query.

Proof: Each 1-element subsequence of any sequence is its contiguous subsequence (from the definition of a contiguous subsequence). If any element of a sequence contains a given set, a 1-element sequence formed by the set is a contiguous subsequence of the sequence. If a data-sequence contains some sequence, it contains every contiguous subsequence of that sequence. Thus, if a data-sequence contains some sequence whose n-th element contains a given set, it has to contain a 1-element sequence having the set as the only element.

The above theorems concern the basic Boolean predicates on patterns or pattern elements that can be used for dataset filtering and provide corresponding data-sequence predicates to be used in the filtering process. These predicates and their corresponding data-sequence predicates are presented in Table 1.

Table 1. Basic Boolean predicates on patterns or pattern elements and corresponding data-sequence predicates

Basic Boolean predicate on a pattern or n-th element of a pattern	Basic Boolean predicate on a data-sequence
$\pi(\mathbf{SG}, \alpha, \text{pattern})$	$\sigma(\mathbf{SG}, \alpha, \text{sequence})$
$\pi(\mathbf{LG}, \alpha, \text{pattern})$	$\sigma(\mathbf{CL}, \alpha+1, \text{sequence}, max, min, win)$
$\pi(\mathbf{C}, \beta, \text{pattern})$	$\sigma(\mathbf{C}, \beta, \text{sequence}, +\infty, min, win)$
$\rho(\mathbf{SG}, \alpha, \text{pattern}_n)$	$\sigma(\mathbf{CS}, \alpha+1, \text{sequence}, win)$
$\rho(\mathbf{C}, \gamma, \text{pattern}_n)$	$\sigma(\mathbf{C}, <\gamma>, \text{sequence}, max, min, win)$

In the above table, $<\gamma>$ denotes a 1-element sequence having the set γ as its only element, while *max*, *min*, and *win* represent values of max-gap, min-gap, and window-size time constraints respectively.

The presence of other basic Boolean predicates in pattern constraints of a sequential pattern query does not affect the filtering process since patterns having support greater than a certain value, size or length less than a certain value, size of the n-th element less than a certain value, as well as patterns not containing a certain sequence, or whose n-th element does not contain a certain itemset, can be supported by any data-sequence.

Example 1 Consider the following sequential pattern query (for the query we present time and pattern constraints, the specification of the source dataset is omitted for brevity): DMQ = {max-gap: 100, min-gap: 7, window-size: 0, π(**SPG**, 0.01, pattern) ∧ π(**SG**, 3, pattern) ∧ π(**LL**, 5, pattern) ∧ π(**C**, <(A)(B)>, pattern)}. The query returns sequential patterns having support greater than 1%, having more than three items but less than five elements, containing the sequence <(A)(B)>. The specified values of max-gap, min-gap, and window-size constraints are 100, 7, and 0 respectively.

Thus, according to the Table 1 (based on the Theorems 1 – 5), the following dataset filtering predicate has to be satisfied by a data-sequence containing a pattern satisfying pattern constraints: σ(**SG**, 3, sequence) ∧ σ(**C**, <(A)(B)>, sequence, +∞, 7, 0). The dataset filtering predicate says that only data-sequences having more than three items and containing the sequence <(A)(B)> with max-gap of +∞, min-gap of 7, and window-size of 0, have to be considered in the discovery process.

According to the Theorems 1 - 5, a sequential pattern query having one or more basic Boolean pattern predicates from the left column of Table 1 in its pattern constraints can be transformed into a query representing a discovery task on a potentially smaller dataset in the following way. Firstly, database constraints of the query have to be extended with appropriate data-sequence predicates. Secondly, the minimum support constraint has to be adjusted to the size of the filtered database. This step is necessary because the support of a pattern is expressed as the percentage of data-sequences containing the pattern. The Theorems 1 – 5 guarantee that the number of data-sequences containing a given pattern in the original and filtered dataset will be the same as long as the pattern satisfies pattern constraints. Thus, we have the following relationship between the support of a pattern p (satisfying pattern constraints) in the original and filtered datasets: $sup_F(p) = |D| * sup(p) / |D_F|$, where $sup_F(p)$ and $sup(p)$ denote the support of the pattern p in the filtered and original dataset respectively, and $|D_F|$ and $|D|$ denote the number of data-sequences in the filtered and original dataset respectively. After the patterns frequent in the filtered dataset have been discovered, their support has to be normalized with respect to the number of data-sequences in the original dataset according to the above formula.

Dataset filtering techniques can be combined with any sequential pattern discovery algorithm since they conceptually lead to a transformed discovery task guaranteed to return the same set of patterns as the original task. The transformation of the source dataset (by filtering out data-sequences that cannot contain patterns of interest) and conversion of pattern constraints concerning pattern support can be performed before the actual discovery process. However, in reality such explicit transformation might be impossible due to space limitations. Some sequential pattern discovery algorithms perform certain projections of the database (e.g. *PrefixSpan*) by nature, while others (e.g. *GSP*) do not transform the database in any way, which is a serious advantage if the database is large and the storage space limited. We believe that if the original algorithm has some desirable properties, any extension applied to the algorithm should preserve them.

3. Integration of Dataset Filtering Techniques with GSP

In this section we present an extension of the *GSP* algorithm (denoted as *GSP-F*) exploiting dataset filtering techniques to support efficient constraint-based sequential pattern mining. We chose *GSP* as the basis for implementing the dataset filtering techniques for two reasons. Firstly, *GSP* (and its extensions) is still the only sequential pattern discovery algorithm supporting time constraints, which affect the dataset filtering process. Secondly, *GSP* does not create any temporal structures to store portions of the source database and preserving this property may be a challenging task.

GSP iteratively generates candidate sequences and evaluates their support by testing their occurrence in each data-sequence from the source dataset. Since we do not want to materialize the filtered dataset, filtering has to be performed on-line in each iteration of the algorithm. Data-sequences that do not satisfy dataset filtering constraints derived from pattern constraints are excluded from the candidate verification process (conceptually the discovery process takes place in the reduced dataset). It should be noted that since we do not explicitly transform the data mining task into an equivalent one, the support conversions discussed in the previous section are not necessary.

The detailed *GSP-F* algorithm extending *GSP* with dataset filtering techniques is presented below. The algorithm takes a collection D of data-sequences as input, and returns all sequential patterns in D supporting user-specified pattern and time constraints.

Algorithm *GSP-F*
DF = dataset filtering predicate derived from pattern constraints;
scan D in order to:
1) evaluate minimum number of supporting data-sequences for
a pattern to be called frequent (*mincount*)
2) find L_1 (set of 1-sequences contained in at least *mincount*
data-sequences satisfying DF);
for $(k = 2; L_{k-1} \neq \varnothing; k++)$ **do**
begin
    C_k = apriori_gen(L_{k-1});   /* generate new candidate sequences */

```
    if C_k = ∅ then break;
    forall data-sequences d ∈ D do
        if d satisfies DF then
            forall candidates c ∈ C_k do
                if d contains c using user-specified time constraints then
                    c.count ++;
                end if;
            end if;
        L_k = { c ∈ C_k | c.count ≥ mincount};
    end;
    output patterns from ∪_k L_k satisfying pattern constraints;
```

The algorithm starts with deriving dataset filtering constraints from pattern constraints provided by a user. These dataset filtering constraints are used in each scan of the source dataset and data-sequences that do not satisfy them are excluded from the candidate verification process. When the discovery of sequential patterns in the filtered dataset is finished, a post-processing step filtering out patterns that do not satisfy user-specified pattern constraints is applied. This phase is required since dataset filtering itself does not guarantee that only patterns supporting pattern constraints are to be discovered. It should be noted that the support of patterns not satisfying user-specified pattern constraints, counted in the filtered dataset, can be smaller than their actual support in the original dataset, but it is not a problem since these patterns will not be returned to the user. Moreover, this is in fact a positive feature as it can reduce the number of generated candidates not leading to patterns of user's interest.

$GSP\text{-}F$ does not reduce the amount of data read from the database in each iteration in comparison to the original GSP algorithm. However, we expect it to be more efficient since data-sequences that do not satisfy dataset filtering constraints are excluded from the costly candidate verification process.

4.   Experimental Results

In order to evaluate performance gains offered by our dataset filtering techniques, we performed several experiments on a synthetic dataset generated by means of the GEN generator from the $Quest$ project [1]. The dataset contained 1000 data-sequences built from 50 different items, the average number of transactions per data-sequence was 5.5, and the average number of items per transaction was 1.2. Since GEN does not generate transaction times, we treated transaction identifiers as transaction times, thus the time gap between each two consecutive elements of each data-sequence was always equal to one time unit. The generated data-sequences were stored in a database table (a local *Oracle8i* database server was used).

We started the experiments with varying the constraints regarding pattern size, length, and contents for the fixed minimum support threshold of 1%, infinite max-gap, and min-gap and window-size equal to 0. Apart from measuring the total execution times of *GSP* and *GSP-F*, we also registered the time spent by *GSP-F* on dataset filtering, and the selectivity of dataset filtering constraints derived from pattern constraints (expressed as the percentage of data-sequences in the database satisfying dataset filtering constraints). Figure 1 presents the ratio of the execution time of *GSP-F* to the execution time of *GSP* for different values of selectivity of the derived dataset filtering constraints.

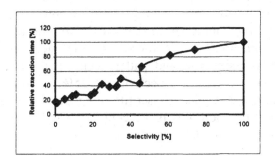

Figure 1. Performance improvements for different values of selectivity

As we expected, the experiments showed that the lower the selectivity of dataset filtering constraints, the better the performance of *GSP-F* is likely to be as compared to *GSP*. However, we observe that sometimes the performance improvement might be better for a query leading to a larger filtered dataset. This can be easily explained by the fact that performance of *GSP-F* depends not only on the number of data-sequences against which candidates generated in each iteration have to be verified but also on the number of the candidates, which depends on the data distribution within the filtered dataset. Nevertheless, dataset filtering reduces the processing time (usually several times), except for an unlikely situation when dataset filtering constraints derived from pattern constraints do not filter out any source data-sequences. However, even that unrealistic situation does not pose a problem since, according to our experiments, the time spent on extra dataset filtering operations constitutes less than 1% of the overall processing time.

The selectivity of dataset filtering constraints depends on the original pattern constraints but also on the actual contents of the database. In general, we observed that pattern constraints involving the presence of a certain

308

subsequence or subset led to much better results (reducing the processing time 2 to 5 times) than constraints referring only to pattern size or length (typically reducing the processing time by less than 10%). This is due to the fact that sequential patterns are usually smaller in terms of size and length than source data-sequences, and therefore even restrictive constraints on pattern size/length result in weak constraints on data-sequences.

In another series of experiments, we observed the influence of varying the minimum support threshold and time constraints on performance gains offered by dataset filtering. *GSP* encounters problems when the minimum support threshold is low or time constraints are relaxed (large max-gap and window-size, small min-gap) because of the huge number of candidates to be verified. In our experiments, decreasing the minimum support threshold or relaxing time constraints worked in favor of our dataset filtering techniques, leading to bigger performance gains. (Figure 2 presents the influence of varying the minimum support from 0.5% to 2% on the relative processing time of *GSP-F* compared to *GSP* for an example query with min-gap = 0, max-gap = +∞, win-size = 0 and pattern constraints resulting in dataset filtering constraint having the selectivity of 25%.) This behavior can be explained by the fact that since dataset filtering reduces the cost of candidate verification phase, the more this phase contributes to the overall processing time, the more significant relative performance gains are going to be.

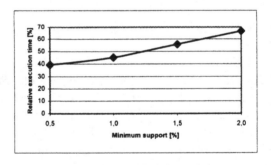

Figure 2. Performance improvements for different values of minimum support

5.   Concluding Remarks

We have discussed the application of dataset filtering techniques to efficient sequential pattern mining in the presence of various pattern constraints. We identified the set of pattern selection predicates that support dataset filtering and presented the method of pushing these constraints down to dataset selection queries. Dataset filtering techniques can be applied to any sequential pattern discovery algorithm since they conceptually lead to an equivalent data mining task on a possibly smaller dataset. We focused on the implementation details concerning integration of dataset filtering techniques with the *GSP* algorithm. Our experiments show that dataset filtering can result in significant performance improvements, especially in case of pattern constrains involving the presence of a certain subsequence or subset.

References

[1] Agrawal, R., Mehta, M., Shafer, J., Srikant, R., Arning, A., Bollinger, T. The Quest Data Mining System, In E. Simoudis, J. Han, U. M. Fayyad (Eds.), Proceedings of the 2nd KDD Conference, Portland, Oregon, AAAI Press, 1996.

[2] Agrawal, R., Srikant, R. Mining Sequential Patterns, In P. S. Yu, A. L. P. Chen (Eds.), Proceedings of the 11th ICDE Conf., Taipei, Taiwan, IEEE Computer Society, 1995.

[3] Garofalakis, M., Rastogi, R., Shim, K. SPIRIT: Sequential Pattern Mining with Regular Expression Constraints, In M. P. Atkinson, M. E. Orlowska, P. Valduriez, S. B. Zdonik, M. L. Brodie (Eds.), Proceedings of 25th VLDB Conference, Edinburgh, Scotland, UK, Morgan Kaufmann, 1999.

[4] Han, J., Lakshmanan, L., Ng, R. Constraint-Based Multidimensional Data Mining, IEEE Computer, Vol. 32, 1999; 8:46-50

[5] Imielinski, T., Mannila, H. A Database Perspective on Knowledge Discovery, Communications of the ACM, Vol. 39, 1996; 11:58-64

[6] Ng, R., Lakshmanan, L., Han, J., Pang, A. Exploratory Mining and Pruning Optimizations of Constrained Association Rules, In L. M. Haas, A. Tiwary (Eds.), Proceedings of the 1998 SIGMOD Conference, Seattle, Washington, ACM Press, 1998.

[7] Pei, J., Han, J., Mortazavi-Asl, B., Pinto, H., Chen, Q., Dayal, U., Hsu, M-C. PrefixSpan: Mining Sequential Patterns Efficiently by Prefix-Projected Pattern Growth, Proceedings of the 17th ICDE Conference, Heidelberg, Germany, IEEE Computer Society, 2001.

[8] Srikant, R., Agrawal, R. Mining Sequential Patterns: Generalizations and Performance Improvements, In P. M. G. Apers, M. Bouzeghoub, G. Gardarin (Eds.), Proceedings of the 5th EDBT Conference, Avignon, France, Springer, 1996.

[9] Srikant, R., Vu, Q., Agrawal, R. Mining Association Rules with Item Constraints, In D. Heckerman, H. Mannila, D. Pregibon (Eds.), Proceedings of the 3rd KDD Conference, Newport Beach, California, AAAI Press, 1997.

[10] Zakrzewicz, M. Data Mining within DBMS Functionality, In A. Caplinskas (Ed.), Proceedings of the 4th IEEE International Baltic Workshop on Databases & Information Systems, Vilnius, Lithuania, 2000.

A PARAMETRIZABLE TASK–ADAPTIVE NE–RECOGNITION SYSTEM

Jakub Piskorski
DFKI GmbH
Stuhlsatzenhausweg 3, 66123 Saarbrücken
piskorsk@dfki.de

Tilman Jäger
XtraMind Technologies GmbH
Stuhlsatzenhausweg 3, 66123 Saarbrücken
jaeger@xtramind.com

Feiyu Xu
DFKI GmbH
Stuhlsatzenhausweg 3, 66123, Saarbrücken
feiyu@dfki.de

Abstract   Robust Named–Entity Recognition software is an essential preprocessing tool for performing more complex text processing tasks in business information systems. In this paper we present a Framework for Domain and Task Adaptive Named–Entity Recognition. It consists of several clear–cut subcomponents which can be flexibly and variably combined together in order to construct a task–specific NE–Recognition tool. Additionally, a diagnostic tool for automatic prediction of best system configuration is provided, which speeds up the development cycle.

Keywords: named–entity recognition, text processing, information extraction

1.   Introduction

Nowadays, knowledge relevant to business of any kind is mainly transmitted through free–text documents. New trends in information technology such as *Information Extraction, Text Mining* or *Text Classification* could provide dramatic improvements in the process of converting the overflow of raw textual information into valuable knowledge. Since

H.-M. Haav and A. Kalja (eds.), Databases and Information Systems II, 311–326.

named entities (NE) constitute a significant part of business texts[1] , robust NE–Recognition software is an essential preprocessing tool for performing more complex text processing tasks in business information systems [1].

The NE task has formally been defined at the MUC conference [13] and consists of recognition of *entities* (organizations, persons, locations), *temporal expressions* (date, time) and *quantities* (monetary values, percentages). The recognition process is usually subdivided into delimitation, i.e. determination of the boundaries of the NE, and classification, in which the identified NE is assigned a more specific category. The question whether a phrase is a named entity and what name class it belongs to, might depend on both internal structure and surrounding context [7]. The "Inc." designator reliably shows the phrase "Financial Investments, Inc." to be a company name. The text fragment "Paco Raban" in the following example sentence can be recognized as a company name by utilizing the preceding word sequence "director of".

(1) Mr. Diagne would leave his job as vice–president of Yves Saint Laurent, Inc. to become operations director of Paco Raban.

However, "Paco Raban" could also be a person name. In this case, the problem of disambiguating the type of this NE seems to be intuitively simple, but generally a broader contextual knowledge is required in order to determine the type of the named entity correctly. An intuitive strategy for NE recognition one could think of is simply using dictionaries containing NEs. However, some NEs like for instance company names are too numerous to include them in dictionaries. Further they are changing constantly and may appear in many variant forms (e.g. subsequent occurrences might be abbreviated). Hence, such straightforward list–search approach would not perform well.

Most of the IE systems participating in the NE task in the recent MUC conferences were based on handcrafted approach [16] which use context–sensitive rules. Such contextual rules rely usually on tokenization and/or lexical information computed in the preprocessing phase. Recently, a variety of machine learning methods for solving NE task were introduced [2, 3, 6, 14]. Nevertheless, the handcrafted systems achieve on an average higher coverage than machine–learning based approaches. This is due to the fact that non–local phenomena are best handled by using regular expressions. For instance, the pattern [PER-

---

[1] According to [4] newswire texts may consist of up to 10 percent of proper names.

SON_NAME ∘ STRING:THE ∘ (POS:ADJ)* ∘ STRING:PRESIDENT OF ∘ ORG_NAME] which covers the following example phrase would be difficult to learn for an automated system because of the presence of a sequence of zero or more adjectives:

(2) Bill Gates, the young dynamic successful president of Microsoft

A broader overview of existing NE recognizers and current problems in this field are given in [3].

In this paper we describe a Domain and Task Adaptive Named–Entity Recognition Platform. In contrary to other tools, our platform comprises of several clear–cut submodules which can be flexibly and variably combined together in order to construct a task–specific NE–recognition component. The submodules include among others fine–grained tokenization, regular pattern matching, acronym recognition, gazetteer lookup, NE variant identification and lexical processing. The main advantage of the flexible workflow is that unnecessary computations might be avoided (e.g., specific IE tasks do not require lexical processing) and the best configuration for solving a particular real–world extraction task may be easily defined. Therefore an additional diagnostic tool for automatic evaluation and scoring of possible system configurations is provided, which means faster development cycle. Since it is important to process big quantities of texts efficiently, we make an exhaustive use of *finite–state technology* [9] in all subcomponents[2]. Currently, we have adapted the system for performing NE–Recognition for German. Additionally, we highlight frequent problems we encountered while processing real–world data which illustrate the indispensability of each system component. The presented system is a continuation of the work presented in [11].

2.   Architecture

The system consists of two main pools of resources: (1) *the linguistic resources*, which are maintained (and optimized) by the *Grammar Manager*, and (2) *processing resources* including Tokenizer, Pattern Matcher, Gazetteer Checker, Context Explorer, Lexical Processor and Acronym Finder. The processing resources can be flexibly and variably combined into a task–specific workflow schedule through the use of the *Resource*

---

[2]Computationally, finite–state devices are time and space efficient and from the linguistic point of view, local natural language phenomena can be easily and intuitively expressed as finite–state devices.

314

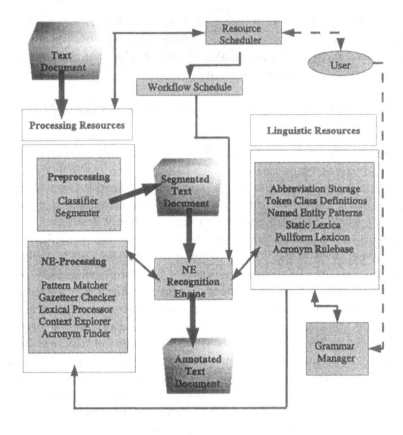

Figure 1. Architecture

Scheduler. The workflow schedule determines which components of the system are used and defines the order of their application and interplay.

Each text document is first preprocessed by the tokenizer which is an obligatory step in our NE–recognition system. The *Tokenizer* splits the text into word–like units called tokens and classifies them according to user–defined token–class definitions. The segmented text together with the workflow schedule constitute the input for the *NE–Recognition Engine* which performs the proper NE identification. The text fragments which are recognized by a certain module as NEs are by default not further consumed by the subsequent modules[3]. The extracted information may be redirected into a corresponding XML document or stream of feature structures.

---

[3]More complex configuration of the system allow for consuming previously recognized entities which will be discussed later.

We describe now briefly the functionality of the processing resources. The *Pattern Matcher* applies handcrafted rules representing patterns for NE recognition. The patterns rely on tokenization information and information computed by the *Lexical Processor* which is responsible for retrieving lexical information (including online compound recognition) for each unconsumed token. The task of *Acronym Finder* is the recognition of acronyms and identification of their corresponding definitions. The *Gazetteer Checker* uses static NE–lexica (e.g., geographical locations) in order to match unconsumed text fragments. Finally, the *Context Explorer* searches for associations between token sequences which do not exhibit strong named entity evidence (potential NE) with named entities which were recognized within a parametrizable context frame (e.g., different variants of the same NE).

A scenario–specific workflow schedule may include more than one instance of some of the processing resources. For instance, in some scenario the set of recognition rules for the Pattern Matcher could be subdivided into sure–fire rules and less–reliable rules (e.g. rules obtained statistically by some external component which can be easily converted into an appropriate format). In this case it would be convenient first to apply sure–fire rules, then to run the Gazetteer Matcher and finally to use the set of less–reliable rules as argued in [8]. For speeding up the adaptation to new scenarios the best system configuration can be automatically predicted by a diagnostic tool provided in our system.

Finally, in order to guarantee good run–time performance all components of the systems are implemented as optimized finite–state devices. We used the DFKI Finite–State Machine Toolkit [10] for constructing, combining and optimizing finite–state machines which are generalizations of weighted finite–state automata and weighted finite–state transducers.

3. Processing Resources

3.1 Tokenizer

The task of the tokenizer is to map character sequences of the input text documents into word–like units called tokens and to classify those tokens according to user–defined token classes. In the first step, the *Segmenter* splits a text document into tokens by using an abbreviation lexicon which allows a rough distinction between points being integral part of the token (e.g. abbreviations) and sentence delimiters. The segmented text is forwarded to the *Classifier*, which performs fine-grained categorization of tokens. In contrast to other tokenization tools our tokenizer allows multiple token classification, as illustrated in figure

2. First each token is classified according to a prespecified list of main token classes (currently the system provides about 50 default main token classes).

Example Tokens	Maintoken Classes	Subtoken Classes
1999	natural number	four digit number, year
Düsseldorf	first capital word	potential location
V3.5	number word compound	–
AT&T–CEO	complex compositum	may include company name
GmbH	mixed word first capital	corporate designator

Figure 2. Token classes

Secondly, tokens undergo additional domain and language specific sub-classification [15]. For instance, we could subclassify all first–capital tokens according to the type of suffix they end with (e.g. suffix exhibiting a potential location: "–dorf", "–hafen" in German). Such information could be used for defining of NE–recognition patterns (e.g. location prepositions followed by token subclassified as potential location). Each token may belong to several subtoken classes, but it is assigned to only one main token class. All token classes expressed as regular expressions are merged into a single optimized finite–state network which represents the token classifier. We claim that fine–grained tokenization as described here may be sufficient for solving some real–world NE tasks as we experienced in practice (e.g. keyword–spotting).

3.2   Pattern Matcher

The Pattern Matcher applies handcrafted regular patterns [8], [6] which rely on the tokenization information and information computed by the lexical processor (see section 3.4). These patterns are expressed as finite–state devices whose arcs are labeled with predicates on tokens. There are only five types of predicates (STRING, STEM, POS, SUBTOKEN AND TOKEN which allows for keeping the degree of non–determinicity of the corresponding finite–state grammar relatively low. An example pattern for recognition of company names is given in figure 3: The Pattern Matcher can be configured in several ways which can influence the coverage and runtime behavior of the system. First various matching techniques can be chosen (e.g. local vs. full backtracking). Another option allows for recognizing overlapping NEs. Consider the following example:

(3) Bei XtraMind Technologies GmbH, Stuhlsatzenhausweg 366121 Saarbrücken

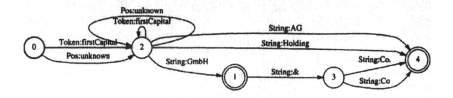

Figure 3.   A simple pattern for recognition of company names

In this text fragment two overlapping NEs could be identified: a location "Bei XtraMind" triggered by a location preposition, and "XtraMind Technologies GmbH" triggered by the company designator "GmbH". Such collision information could be used for semi–automatic fine–tuning of the rule–base (definition of new pattern covering the whole text fragment "Bei XtraMind ... GmbH"). Further, the above text fragment contains an error (e.g., originating from OCR), in so far as it misses a space between street number of "Stuhlsatzenhausweg" and city code of Saarbrücken (fusion of 3 and 66121). Using collision–matching option we can identify both street–number fragment and postcode–city phrase which would not be possible otherwise. Additionally, an option for determining the order and number of admissible predicates is provided which may be used for optimizing the Pattern Matcher in terms of efficiency. Pattern Matcher also allows for rule prioritization which prevents multiple assignment to same token sequences. Finally, on demand previously recognized NEs can be consumed by the Pattern Matcher, e.g. person names recognized by Gazetteer Checker. Note that an input text can be partially annotated.

3.3   Gazetteer Checker

The task of the Gazetteer Checker is the recognition of NEs stored in static NE–lexica. Such lexica contain usually location, organization and person names. Simple NE–Recognition systems only rely on performing a lexicon lookup. The advantage of using gazetteers may be verified by the fact that many NEs do neither exhibit internal nor external evidence of being a named entity. For instance, consider the German phrase "Dynamik in Handel" (*dynamic in trade*. It is a magazine title, but also a valid NP in German. Using Gazetteer seems to be the only alternative for recognizing such named entities. An interesting discussion of the importance of using gazetteer and their application at different stages of NE–recognition process can be found in [8]. In case of ambiguous entries in static lexica, we can switch between an option of returning the highest–priority interpretation or returning all possible interpretations. For converting the static lexica into their corresponding optimized finite–state representation we use the new method for efficient incremental construction of acyclic deterministic and minimal finite–state automata presented in [5] and provided by the FSM Toolkit.

3.4 Lexical Processor

The task of Lexical Processor is the retrieval of lexical information for each token identified as potential word form. This includes also recognition of compounds (e.g. "Produktionsumstellungen" – *production reorganization* which are usually not lexicalized [4]. They constitute a significant part of business texts [5]. Lexical Processor uses full-form lexicon (750 000 entries for German) and first tries to associate each processed token with a corresponding lexical information including part–of–speech and stem information. If no such information can be found, the token is either a compound or an unknown word. We apply fast and robust shallow compound recognition strategy outlined in [11] which computes only a single syntactically valid segmentation and determines the head while leaving internal bracketing underspecified. This information is sufficient for the purpose of NE recognition. The stand–alone status of the Lexical Processor may be verified by the fact that one aims at applying other components to text fragments consisting of tokens not recognized as valid word forms. Analogously to static lexica we encode full–form lexicon into an optimized finite-state network.

3.5 Context Explorer

The task of the Context Explorer is the identification of variants of already recognized NEs. Hence, this component fulfills partial coreference resolution. The text including annotations of previously recognized entities is scanned in order to identify candidates for NEs (which do not exhibit a strong evidence of being a named entity). Secondly, Context Explorer searches for associations between such candidates and already identified NEs within a parametrizable context frame. For instance, first occurence of a given company name usually includes a designator, whereas subsequent occurrences are frequently abbreviated variants which do not include such designators and are thus harder to find (e.g.

---

[4] Note that, for instance, in German compounds are in general orthographically single words.
[5] We found out that 7,19 percent of the words in our test corpus, consisting of business articles from the German business news magazine "Wirtschaftswoche", were compounds.

"Appollinaris & Schweppes" and "Appollinaris" could refer to the company name "Appollinaris & Schweppes GmbH & Co."). This is achieved by storing certain types of NEs (e.g. company name without corporate designator) in a dynamic lexicon. Any subsequent occurrence of a prefix or suffix of previously stored NEs can then be identified and an appropriate reference can be set correctly. It is known that such reference resolution heuristic achieves high accuracy.

Another advantage of using a dynamic lexicon is that it can be used for disambiguating NE types. Consider the text in example 4:

(4) "Ich könnte niemals auf irgend etwas schiessen", versichert der 57jährige Chef des US–Rüstungskonzerns Martin Marietta Corp. (MM). Doch die private Waffenabstinenz hat Augustine nicht daran gehindert, sein Unternehmen zur grössten Waffenschmiede der Welt aufzurüsten: Für drei Milliarden Dollar hat <u>*Martin Marietta*</u> *gerade erst die Luftfahrtabteilung des ehemaligen Konkurrenten* <u>*General Electric (GE)*</u> *übernommen und damit seinen Jahresumsatz von rund sechs auf über elf Milliarden Dollar fast verdoppelt."*

The first occurrence of the sequence "Martin Marietta Corp." can be easily identified as a company name, since it contains a reliable corporate designator. The subsequent occurrence of the substring "Martin Marietta" could first be recognized by the Pattern Matcher or the Gazetteer Checker as a person name. Nevertheless, this token sequence obviously refers to the company name introduced previously. A simple heuristic may be applied to solve this problem: whenever a person, company or location name is recognized by the Pattern Matcher or Gazetteer Checker, the Context Explorer performs an additional lookup in order to check whether such NE is a prefix or suffix of an already recognized named entity in the surrounding context frame, and modifies the type of this NE appropriately.

The Context Explorer's ability of varying the size of the context window (e.g. paragraph vs. the entire document) is crucial since the system has to cope with different types of documents (e.g. emails, web pages or newswire articles).

3.6   Acronym Finder

We noticed by looking over a lot of business documents that they include a huge number of acronyms which can be treated in most cases as NEs (e.g. "GE" in example 4 stands for "General Electric"). In order to recognize acronyms and their corresponding definitions we apply two strategies: (1) by the definition of lexico–syntactic patterns expressing introduction and definition of an acronym (e.g. X steht für Y - *X stands for Y*, (2) by applying rules for identifying acronym candidates and associating these candidates with their definitions in an parametrizable context frame using heuristics as described in [12]. The two strategies can be applied simultaneously or separately. With regard to (2) a more detailed description follows:

By taking advantage of the information computed by the Tokenizer it is possible to find short character sequences (e.g. the length of a sequence lies between 2 and 10 characters, tokens consisting solely of consonants) which constitute *acronym candidates*. For each acronym candidate an abbreviation pattern reflecting its structure is constructed. The pattern consists of a sequence of symbols which correspond to the subsequent characters in the acronym candidate ("n" stands for number and "c" stands for character). Some characters like "&" or "\" have no corresponding symbol in the pattern. Figure 4 shows some example acronyms and their corresponding patterns:

Acronym	Pattern
AT&T	ccc
2D	nc
T/C/F	ccc

Definition	Pattern
Anglo–Australien Observatory	www
ALGOrithmic Language	hw

Figure 4. Acronym Patterns 　　　　　*Figure 5.* Definition Patterns

Subsequently, Acronym Finder tries to identify *definition candidates* in the surrounding context of the acronym candidate using several heuristics. Consider again the example 4, where "GE" stands for "General Electric". An appropriate heuristic for recognizing the definition candidate would be as follows: the initial character of each word of the definition candidate must match the corresponding character in the acronym candidate. In the next step a *definition pattern* representing the structure of the definition candidate is built. Some examples of acronym definitions with their corresponding definition patterns are given in figure 5 ("w"- words initialized with a capital, "h"- words containing two or more capitals and "s"- stopwords). Equally to abbreviation patterns, some separator symbols are ignored.

After the identification of acronym and definition candidates and the generation of their corresponding patterns, the Acronym Finder compares the pattern pair with pattern pairs stored in the *Acronym Rulebase*, and returns one or more corresponding Formation Rules. *Formation Rules* express the way how an acronym is formed from its definition. Finally the returned set of formation rules is applied to the definition candidate in order to validate the acronym candidate. The formation rule $< wwsw, ccc, (1, f)(2, f)(4, f) >$ can be interpreted in the following way: take the initial letter of the first, second and fourth word in the definition and omit the stopword (third word). In this way the acronym "USA" is constructed from the phrase "United States of America". Currently, the Acronym Rulebase contains a collection of ca. 50 handcrafted formation rules, which can be extended by machine–learning techniques [12]. Note that already recognized NEs occurring in an immediate context of acronym candidates are used as preferred definition candidates.

4. Diagnostic Tools

In order to reduce the time for the adaptation of the system to new scenarios, a diagnostic tool for automatic prediction of best system configuration is provided. The optimal configuration respectively precision, recall or f–measure can be computed by means of an annotated text corpus provided by the user, and a set of candidate configurations (workflow schedules). A configuration candidate is an ordered list of instances of processing resources. The set of configurations can be automatically computed, which is done in the following way. First the user selects available linguistic resources, e.g. static NE–lexica, pattern sets, etc. Subsequently, the system generates a set of all corresponding instances of processing resources. Finally, for each element of the power set of this set, all possible permutations are computed. These permutations constitute configuration candidates.

Since the number of all permutations for a larger set of instances of processing resources is obviously too numerous to be computed efficiently, several options may be used for reducing the number of configuration candidates to be considered. First the user may restrict the number of potential candidates by defining partial linear precedence constraints (e.g. "component X cannot be used before component Y") or by using other filters such as: "consider only configuration candidates consisting of three components". Besides the option of computing all permutations, several efficient heuristics for predicting sub–optimal configurations may be applied. For instance, in the "bottom–up" heuristic, we first evaluate all configurations consisting of two components and use k top scoring pairs wrt. the chosen measure in order to generate configuration candidates consisting of three components. Further, we evaluate the three–component configurations and proceed in the same way (take k top scoring triples) until configurations consisting of maximal number of components have been evaluated. This can be done in $O(n^3)$ time for $k = 1$, where n denotes the number of instances of pro-

322

cessing resources (see figure 6, where C_{ij} is the i–th component in the (sub)optimal sequence consisting of j components). In order to avoid unnecessary recomputations we use cashing–techniques. Furthermore, the

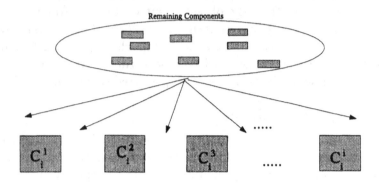

Figure 6. Computation of the suboptimal workflow schedule in the i–th step

user may also specify his preferred configurations and edit the automatically created list of candidate configurations in order to fine–tune the evaluation process. The best configurations are presented to the user in form of ranked lists according to the chosen evaluation measure, where the evaluation process can be done in two fashions: exact vs. partial matching (i.e. left or right boundary of the recognized entity matches with the entity annotated in the test corpus).

For the sake of clarity we summarize the configuration options of all components in the table of figure 7. The following example scenario illustrates the importance of the diagnostic feature of the system. Let us assume that we are interested in the recognition of company and person names. The set of linguistic resources contains of gazetteers for first and last names, and a set of patterns for recognition of person and company names. Let A denote the workflow schedule in which we first apply Gazetteer Checker and subsequently the Pattern Matcher; and let B denote the workflow in which the above processing resources are applied in reverted order. Assuming that we use the pattern [TOKEN:PERSON ∘ STRING:& ∘ TOKEN:PERSON] for the recognition of company names (which is obviously more reliable than the pattern [TOKEN:FIRST_CAPITAL ∘ STRING:& ∘ TOKEN:FIRST_CAPITAL], the workflow schedule A seems to be superior to B in order to identify "Alexander & Alexander" as a company name.

Now, let us consider the following phrase: "Der Müller Klaus Kinski" – *the miller Klaus Kinski*, where Müller is a valid last name in German.

Configuration Options		
Components	*Multiple Instances*	*Main Configuration Options*
Tokenizer	yes	Language and domain adaptive token subclassification
Lexical Processor	no	no
Context Explorer	yes	Size of context window NE–type disambiguation
Gazetteer Checker	yes	Filters for selecting text passages to be analyzed Lexicon Prioritization
Acronym Finder	yes	2 acronym recognition strategies
Pattern Matcher	yes	Rule Prioritization Various backtracking options Longest match vs. collision match Predicate order and number Consuming already identified NEs

Figure 7.   Overview of the Configuration Options

For recognizing person names we would expect to achieve good coverage by applying the following patterns:

(1) [(POS:UNKNOWN)$^+$o TOKEN:ENDS_WITH_SUFFIX_SKI],

(2) [TOKEN:LAST_NAMEoTOKEN:FIRST_NAME] and

(3) [TOKEN:FIRST_NAME oTOKEN:LAST_NAME].

B is superior to A in order to identify the text fragment "Klaus Kinski" as person name correctly (only pattern (1) matches). If the application of Gazetteer Checker precedes the application of Pattern Matcher (workflow schedule A) two colliding person names would be identified ("Müller Klaus Kinski" – pattern (1) vs. "Müller Klaus" – pattern(2) vs. "Klaus Kinski" – pattern(3)). Note that it would be only possible in the collision match modus of the Pattern Matcher. This example proves that both workflow schedules exhibit advantages and disadvantages for the recognition of different types of NEs, which validates the relevance of the diagnostic tool.

Further, the list of top–scoring configurations might give an insight into the contribution and usefulness of the particular processing and linguistic resources being used. In this way, time and space expensive resources which do not significantly contribute to achieve good precision and recall values, can be eliminated. In particular, the information concerning best configurations for different text fragments allows for merging different workflow schedules. The figure 8 shows precision/recall values for some workflow schedules for the following tasks: (a) company

Company name detection

Workflow Candidates	Precision	Recall
COMP–G	93,50%	10,82%
COMP–PM	**96,83%**	20,13%
COMP–G CE	92,81%	14,58%
COMP–G CE COMP–PM	96,06%	34,43%
COMP–G CE COMP–PM CE	85,30%	50,24%
COMP–G CE COMP–PM CE AF	82,22%	**75,26%**

Company name and person name detection

Workflow Candidates	Precision	Recall
Comp-G CE Comp-PM CE	85,30% (Comp)	**50,24%** (Comp)
PN-G CE PN-PM CE	77,17% (PN)	76,28% (PN)
PN-G CE PN-PM CE	**77,78%** (PN)	**77,53%** (PN)
Comp-G CE Comp-PM CE	89,66% (Comp)	48,92% (Comp)

Company name, person name and location name detection

Workflow Candidates	Precision	Recall
Comp-G CE Comp-PM CE	85,30% (Comp)	**50,24%** (Comp)
PN-G CE PN-PM CE	76,22% (PN)	75,12% (PN)
Loc-G CE Loc-PM CE	**88,69%** (Loc)	55,90% (Loc)
PN-G CE PN-PM CE	77,78% (PN)	**77,53%** (PN)
Loc-G CE Loc-PM CE	87,13% (Loc)	58,63% (Loc)
Comp-G CE Comp-PM CE	88,13% (Comp)	37,72% (Comp)
Loc-G CE Loc-PM CE	87,30% (Loc)	**63,22%** (Loc)
Comp-G CE Comp-PM CE	**88,18%** (Comp)	48,45% (Comp)
PN-G CE PN-PM CE	**82,83%** (PN)	73,96% (PN)

Figure 8. Evaluation of some Workflow Candidates for several tasks

name detection, (b) company name and person name detection, and (c) company name, person name and location name detection. In order to solve these tasks, we used a gazetteer for company names (COMP-G), containing 3271 entries, a gazetteer for male person names (PN-G), containing 2300 entries and a gazetteer for location names (Loc-G) containing over 5000 entries; we also used sets of ca. 70 recognition patterns for companies (COMP-PM), for person names (PN-PM) and for location names (Loc-PM). Further, we allowed to use Context Explorer (CE) and Acronym Finder (AF). For the evaluation we used a test corpus, consisting of business news articles from the German business news magazine "Wirtschaftswoche" (200 000 tokens).

5. Summary

Robust NE–recognition is prerequisite for successfully performing other more complex extraction and mining tasks in the context of business information systems. Most of the recent research in the area of extracting named entities from free texts centers around systems tailored to a specific domain. This paper describes a Domain and Task adaptive Named Entity recognition framework. It consists of several clear–cut subcomponents which can be flexibly and variably combined together in order to construct a task–specific NE–recognition engine. Further, it provides a diagnostic tool which aims at automatically predicting the optimal configuration of the system (e.g., which processing and linguistic resources to use) in a given scenario. In this way the one can speed up the time–consuming adaptation and optimization process. The system has been mainly implemented in JAVA, except the Finite–State Toolkit, which has been implemented in C++. To our knowledge no similar NE–Recognition tools have been described in the literature, and therefore it is difficult to compare the presented framework with other approaches.

Currently, we continue testing the system on texts drawn from the financial domain using a larger amount of instances of processing resources in order to evaluate the configurability features. Future work will focus on the integration of trainable agents based on machine learning techniques for discovering NE-recognition patterns [2], which could be applied when sufficient training data is provided. Further, we intend to investigate the usability of integrating an ontology component (e.g. for synonym recognition). Finally, additional work will be spent on improving the techniques for the approximation of the best system configuration.

References

[1] Abramowicz, W. and Zurada, J., editors. *Knowledge Discovery for Business Information Systems.* Kluwer Academic Publishers, 2001.

[2] Bikel, Miller, S. and Weischedel, N. A high-performance learning name-finder. In *Proceedings of ANLP, Washington, DC, 1997, pp. 195-201.*

[3] Borthwick, A. *A Maximum Entropy Approach to Named Entity Recognition.* PhD thesis, New York University, 1999.

[4] Coates-Stephens. *The Analysis and Acquisition of Proper Names for Robust Text-Understanding.* PhD thesis, Department of Computer Science, City University London, 1992.

[5] Daciuk, J. *Incremental Construction of Finite–State Automata and Transducers and their use in the Natural Language Processing.* PhD thesis, University of Gdansk, Poland, 1998.

[6] Gallippi, A. F. A synopsis of learning to recognize names across languages. In *Proceedings of ACL,* 1996.

[7] McDonald, D. . Internal and external evidence in the identification and semantic categorization of proper names. In *Proceedings of the SINGLEX workshop on "Acquisition of Lexical Knowledge from Text",* 1993.

[8] Mikheev, A., Moens, M., and Grover, C. Named entity recognition without gazetters. In *Proceedings of the ninth international Conference of the European Chapter of the Association for Computational Linguistics (EACL 99),* 1999.

[9] Mohri, M. On some applications of finite-state automata theory to natural language processing. *Natural Language Engineering Vol. 2 No. 1,* 1996, 2(1):61–80.

[10] Piskorski, J. Dfki finite state machine toolkit. Technical report, DFKI GmbH, Saarbrücken, Germany, 2002.

[11] Piskorski, J. and Neumann, G. An intelligent text extraction and navigation system. In *Proceedings of the 6th International Conference on Computer Assisted Information Retrieval (RIAO–2000),* Paris, 2000.

[12] Roy, Y. P. Hybrid text mining for finding abbreviations and their definitions. In *Proceedings of NACL,* 2001.

[13] SAIC, editor *Seventh Message Understanding Conference (MUC-7).* http://www.muc.saic.com, 1998.

[14] Srihari, R. K., Srikanth, M., Niu, C., and Li, W. Use of maximum entropy in back-off modeling for a named entity tagger. In *Proceedings of the HKK Conference,* Canada, 1999.

[15] Thielen, C. An approach to proper name tagging in german. In *Proceedings EACLSIGDAT 95,* 1995.

[16] Wakao, T., Gaizauskas, R., and Wilks, Y. Evaluation of an algorithm for the recognition and classification of proper names. In *Proceedings of the 16th International Conference on Computational Linguistics (Coling96), Copenhagen,* 1996.

Author Index

Subject Index